Modern Oracle Database Programming

Level Up Your Skill Set to Oracle's Latest and Most Powerful Features in SQL, PL/SQL, and JSON

Alex Nuijten
Patrick Barel

Foreword by Chris Saxon

Apress®

Modern Oracle Database Programming: Level Up Your Skill Set to Oracle's Latest and Most Powerful Features in SQL, PL/SQL, and JSON

Alex Nuijten
Oosterhout, Noord-Brabant, The Netherlands

Patrick Barel
Almere, Flevoland, The Netherlands

ISBN-13 (pbk): 978-1-4842-9165-8
https://doi.org/10.1007/978-1-4842-9166-5

ISBN-13 (electronic): 978-1-4842-9166-5

Managing Director, Apress Media LLC: Welmoed Spahr
Acquisitions Editor: Jonathan Gennick
Development Editor: Laura Berendson
Editorial Assistant: Shaul Elson
Copyeditor: Kim Burton

Cover designed by eStudioCalamar

Cover image by Omar Flores on Unsplash

Distributed to the book trade worldwide by Springer Science+Business Media New York, 1 New York Plaza, Suite 4600, New York, NY 10004-1562, USA. Phone 1-800-SPRINGER, fax (201) 348-4505, e-mail orders-ny@springer-sbm.com, or visit www.springeronline.com. Apress Media, LLC is a California LLC and the sole member (owner) is Springer Science + Business Media Finance Inc (SSBM Finance Inc). SSBM Finance Inc is a **Delaware** corporation.

For information on translations, please e-mail booktranslations@springernature.com; for reprint, paperback, or audio rights, please e-mail bookpermissions@springernature.com.

Apress titles may be purchased in bulk for academic, corporate, or promotional use. eBook versions and licenses are also available for most titles. For more information, reference our Print and eBook Bulk Sales web page at http://www.apress.com/bulk-sales.

Any source code or other supplementary material referenced by the author in this book is available to readers on GitHub via the book's product page, located at https://github.com/Apress/modern-oracle-database-programming. For more detailed information, please visit http://www.apress.com/source-code.

Printed on acid-free paper

Table of Contents

About the Authors

Alex Nuijten is an independent consultant specializing in Oracle Database development with PL/SQL and Oracle Application Express (APEX). Besides his consultancy work, he conducts training classes in APEX, SQL, and PL/SQL. He is a speaker at numerous international conferences, including ODTUG, Oracle Open World, HrOUG, UKOUG, IOUG, OUGF, BGOUG, NLOUG APEX World, OBUG, and many more. He has received several Best Speaker awards and writes regularly about APEX and Oracle Database development on his Notes on Oracle blog. He is a co-author of *Oracle APEX Best Practices* (Packt Publishing, 2012) and *Real World SQL and PL/SQL* (McGraw Hill, 2016). Because of his contributions to the Oracle community, Alex was awarded the Oracle ACE Director membership in August 2010.

Patrick Barel is a PL/SQL developer for Qualogy in The Netherlands. Besides working with SQL and PL/SQL, he has written different plug-ins for PL/SQL Developer. He publishes articles on his own blog and the Qualogy blog. He is a speaker at international conferences, such as ODTUG, UKOUG, AUSOUG, NZOUG, IOUG, OUGN, NLOUG, DOUG, HrOUG, and many more. In 2011, Patrick was awarded the Oracle ACE membership. In 2015, he received the Oracle Developer Choice Award in the PL/SQL Category. In 2019, he was promoted to Oracle ACE Director.

About the Technical Reviewer

 **Kim Berg Hansen** is a database developer from Middelfart, Denmark.

As a youngster originally wanting to work with electronics, he tried computer programming. He discovered that the programs he wrote worked well—unlike the electronics projects he soldered that often failed. This led to a VIC-20 with 5 KB RAM and many hours of programming in Commodore Basic.

Having discovered his talent, Kim financed computer science studies at Odense University with a summer job as sheriff of Legoredo while learning methodology and programming in Modula-2 and C. From there, he moved into consulting as a developer making customizations to ERP software. That gave him his first introduction to Oracle SQL and PL/SQL, with which he has worked extensively since 2000.

His professional passion is to work with data inside the database utilizing the SQL language to achieve the best application experience for users. With a background fitting programs into 5 KB RAM, Kim hates unnecessarily wasting computing resources.

Kim shares his experience and knowledge by blogging at www.kibeha.dk, presenting at various Oracle User Group conferences, and being the SQL quizmaster at the Oracle Dev Gym. His motivation comes from peers who say, "now I understand," after his explanations, and end users who "can't live without" his application coding. He is on the conference committee of ODTUG Kscope, a certified Oracle OCE in SQL, and an Oracle ACE Director.

Outside the coding world, Kim is married, loves to cook, and is a card-carrying member of the Danish Beer Enthusiasts Association.

Foreword

SQL is a powerful language. With a few lines, you can answer complex questions.

PL/SQL includes many extensions to make SQL even easier to work with. This tight integration makes these languages perfect for data management.

Yet it can be unclear *which* SQL or PL/SQL features you should use to solve a problem. The documentation for Oracle Database is huge. Browsing through it in the hopes of finding the syntax or feature to help you is an endless task.

Sadly, this means many applications have pages of code re-creating features Oracle Database offers. Often this is because the developers were unaware this functionality was available to them.

So, I'm thrilled to see Alex and Patrick write this book. They have a long history of sharing their knowledge to help others use Oracle Database. Their real-world experience and willingness to help others understand Oracle SQL and PL/SQL have led both to the deserved recognition of Oracle ACE Director. This makes them ideal candidates to make this guide.

Reading this book will teach you how to use the more powerful database options, many of which are unavailable on other platforms. It's filled with examples to show you how this SQL and PL/SQL language features work. But most importantly, the scripts help illustrate when and why you should use these options.

When working with any technology, I think you should know what features it offers. Using inbuilt functionality saves you time and simplifies your code. Alex and Patrick have done a great job showing you how to do this.

I've learned a lot from them both over the years. I hope this book helps you write better SQL and PL/SQL too.

—Chris Saxon, Oracle Developer Advocate

Acknowledgments

When I was first approached to write this book, my first reaction was, "No, not again, too much work, don't have the time." After a good night's sleep, it changed to "Yes, but not alone." Thankfully, my dear friend and colleague Patrick Barel was brave enough to join me on this quest. I enjoyed working with you and bouncing ideas off you. Thanks, Patrick.

Without a thorough technical review, this book would have looked totally different. Thank you, Kim Berg Hansen, for your insights, suggestions, and valuable feedback. Any outstanding errors in my chapters are, of course, my own.

The data we used to show examples throughout the book comes from `http://ergast.com`. Chris, the admin, was kind enough to allow us to use it.

Without the continuing support of my wife, Rian, and my children, Tim and Lara, I could never have worked on this. Spending countless hours locked up in my office would not have been possible if you weren't so understanding.

Finally, I thank Apress for having confidence in this project. Thanks, Jonathan Gennick, for the initial idea, and Sowmya Thodur for keeping us on the straight and narrow.

—Alex

I want to thank everyone who made this project possible, Jonathan Gennick for inviting us to write this book, Apress for having confidence in us for writing this book; Sowmya Thodur for keeping us focussed on getting the book done on time; and Kim Berg Hansen for reviewing all the chapters—thanks for extra insights and nit-picking.

I also thank Alex for inviting me to write this book with him. Writing a book was high on my bucket list, but I never came around to it. I really enjoyed working together with you on this project.

And, of course, I want to thank my loving wife, Dana, for giving me the space and time to spend writing, and my children—Quinty, Kayleigh, and Mitchell, for keeping up with me when my mind was distracted by the book, instead of paying attention to them. Love you much.

—Patrick

Introduction

When writing a book on database technology, you have to come up with a data set to write your examples with. We could have used the standard EMP and DEPT tables that have been available in the SCOTT schema forever. Still, since this is a book on modern Oracle Database programming, we wanted to use a different data set.

Because we are both fans of Formula 1 and Oracle is a big sponsor of the Red Bull Racing team, which happens to be the team where our countryman Max Verstappen is driving, we went looking for a Formula 1–related data set. Of course, not all examples in this book are related to Max; many other drivers and results also play an important role.

The Ergast Developer API (`https://ergast.com/mrd/`) lets you query all kinds of motor racing data and retrieve that in multiple formats. This site also offers all the tables in a CSV format, so we created an `F1DATA` schema where we could import the data. The original data set was a MySQL database, so we had to make some minor tweaks to the data model.

The source files for this book can be found on GitHub at `https://github.com/Apress/modern-oracle-database-programming`.

Part I: Advanced Basics

In the first part of the book, several topics are bundled together, which should be in the toolbox of every Oracle Database developer. Frequently we meet experienced developers unfamiliar with collections and bulk operations, which have been around forever. The same is true for ANSI joins, analytic functions, row pattern matching, or conditional compilation.

Part II: Multiple Techniques and Languages

The second part of the book highlights the integration between SQL and PL/SQL. Keeping context switches between the SQL and PL/SQL engine to a minimum is always better for performance.

After the introduction of JSON into Oracle Database, it has taken flight in functionality and performance. There is a lot to learn when dealing with JSON in the database, and there are several chapters to get a headstart.

Part III: Oracle-Provided Functionality

Out of the box, Oracle Database has a lot of functionality ready to use. In the third part of this book, some of these functionalities play a central role.

Even if APEX is not used for front-end development, it offers some very useful packages that can be used in everyday database development. Edition-based redefinition enables zero downtime upgrades of your bespoke application. Getting data that is currently based on a period where it is valid can be handled by the database without having to write complicated SQL statements.

The Schema in the Oracle Cloud

The data model used for most of the examples in this book was taken from the Ergast motor racing data website (`https://ergast.com/mrd/`) and imported into Oracle Database 19c and 21c.

A schematic display of the Ergast F1 data model is displayed in Figure I-1. We used Oracle Always Free Cloud Services for our database. We took the following steps to get the schemas up and running. Assuming you already have a database created and have access to the `admin` user.

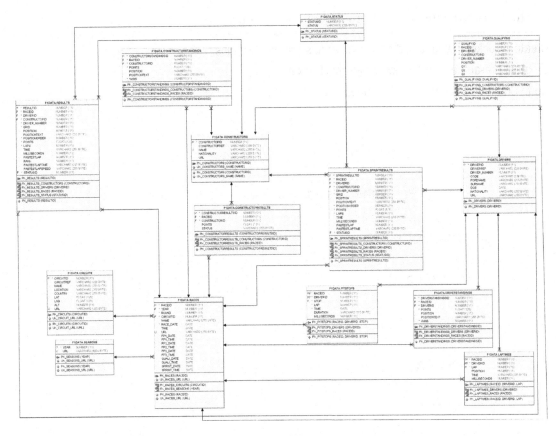

Figure I-1. *F1DATA schema*

Execute the following scripts using the schema listed.

Schema	Description	Script
ADMIN	Create a user F1DATA.	F1Data_Create_User
F1DATA	Create the tables.	F1Data_Tables
F1DATA	Apply the comments to the columns.	F1Data_Comments
F1DATA	Create public synonyms and grant access to the tables to the public.	F1Data_Grants_And_Synonyms
F1DATA	Create the polymorphic table function to split the CSV lines. The function is explained in Chapter 8.	F1Data_Separated_PTF

In the cloud console, perform the following steps.

Create a bucket in your cloud environment to store the CSV files.

Create a pre-authenticated request for this bucket.

Go to Create Pre-Authenticated Request.

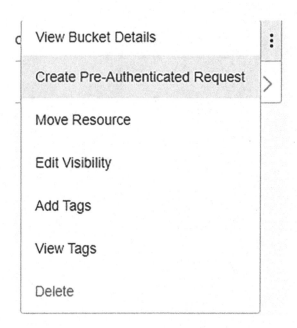

Figure I-2. *Create a Pre-Authenticated Request menu*

Fill in the details and click Create Pre-Authenticated Request.

Create Pre-Authenticated Request

Help

Name

par-F1Data

Pre-Authenticated Request Target

Bucket	Object	Objects with prefix
Create a pre-authenticated request that applies to all objects in the bucket. ✓	Create a pre-authenticated request that applies to a specific object.	Create a pre-authenticated request that applies to all objects with a specific prefix.

Access Type

⦿ Permit object reads
◯ Permit object writes
◯ Permit object reads and writes

☐ Enable Object Listing
   Let users list the objects in the bucket.

Expiration

Dec 29, 2022 03:56 UTC   📅

[Create Pre-Authenticated Request]   Cancel

Figure I-3. *Create Pre-Authenticated Request*

Copy the Pre-Authenticated Request URL and store it in a safe place. *It will not be shown again.*

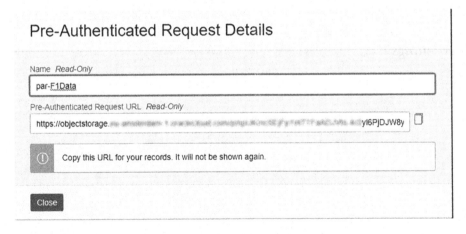

Pre-Authenticated Request Details

Name *Read-Only*

par-F1Data

Pre-Authenticated Request URL *Read-Only*

https://objectstorage. ⟨...⟩ yl6PJDJW8y   ⧉

ⓘ Copy this URL for your records. It will not be shown again.

[Close]

Figure I-4. *Pre-Authenticated Request Details*

Download the latest CSV files from the Ergast Developer API `http://ergast.com/downloads/` website. `f1db_csv.zip`

Unzip the CSV to your local machine.

Upload the files to your bucket.

Create an object store auth token.
Go to *User settings*.

Figure I-5. *User settings*

Click *Auth Tokens* under Resources.

Resources

Groups

API Keys

Auth Tokens

Customer Secret Keys

Database Passwords

OAuth 2.0 Client Credentials

SMTP Credentials

Figure I-6. *Auth Tokens*

Click *Generate Token*.

Auth Tokens

Generate Token

Figure I-7. *Generate Token*

Copy the generated token and store it in a safe place. *It will not be shown again.*

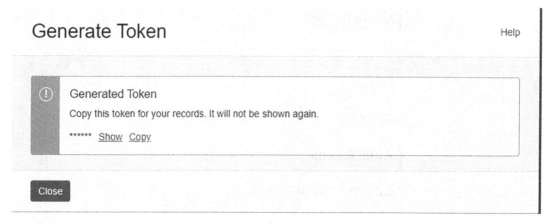

Figure I-8. *Generated token*

In the ADMIN schema, execute the following files.

Schema	Description	Script
ADMIN	Create a credential. Replace <<Authorization Token>> with the token you generated in the previous step.	F1Data_Create_Credential
ADMIN	Import the data into the tables. Replace <<URL Path (URI)>> with your Pre-Authenticated Request URL path.	F1Data_Import_Data

PART I

Advanced Basics

CHAPTER 1

Underutilized Functionality and Enhancements

With each Oracle Database release, more and more functionality is added to make database development easier, simpler, and/or more performant. Some of these enhancements are still relatively unknown to the average developer, and that's a shame. Oracle Database has a lot to offer, which should be exploited to its full potential before you roll your own solution. In this chapter, the focus is on these functions that deserve more attention, like bulk operations, compound triggers, and error logging, to name a few. This chapter gives a short introduction and example of how to use them to raise awareness and for you to explore further. See the introduction for the tables used to follow along with the examples.

Merge

Let's say you want to update the CONSTRUCTORRESULTS table based on the RESULTS table. You could create a PL/SQL block to determine which rows already exist and need updating and which ones need to be created. But you can do this in a single merge statement.

The MERGE statement (introduced in Oracle Database 9i) conditionally inserts or updates data in a table, depending on its presence. If the record doesn't exist, it is inserted; if the record already exists, it is updated. An optional delete where clause can be added to the matched clause. This deletes only those rows that match the on clause and the delete where clause. This technique is displayed in Listing 1-1.

Listing 1-1. Merge the RESULTS into the CONSTRUCTORRESULTS table

```
merge into constructorresults tgt
using (select rsl.raceid           as raceid
            , rsl.constructorid    as constructorid
            , sum( rsl.points )    as points
        from   f1data.results rsl
        where  rsl.raceid = g_raceids(indx).raceid
        and    rsl.constructorid = g_raceids(indx).constructorid
        group  by rsl.raceid
                 , rsl.constructorid) src
on (    tgt.raceid = src.raceid
    and tgt.constructorid = src.constructorid )
when matched
then
  update
  set    tgt.points = src.points
when not matched
then
  insert
    ( constructorresultsid
    , raceid
    , constructorid
    , points)
  values
    ( f1data.constructorresults_seq.nextval
    , src.raceid
    , src.constructorid
    , src.points)
/
```

Collections

Collections in PL/SQL have been available since PL/SQL was introduced in Oracle Database. Nowadays, there are three types of collections to choose from.

- associative array

- nested table

- varray

The *associative array* is available in PL/SQL only. The other two are also available in SQL, so they can be used as a column data type in a table or as a stand-alone SQL object.

The collections have a lot of similarities, but there are some important differences, as described in Table 1-1.

Table 1-1. *Collection Comparison*

	Associative Array	Nested Table	Varray
Used in Language	PL/SQL only	SQL and PL/SQL	SQL and PL/SQL
Index type	(Alpha)Numeric	Numeric	Numeric
Range	Unlimited $-2^{31}+1$ to $2^{31}-1$	Unlimited 1 to $2^{31}-1$	Limited
Sparse	Sparse	Initially Dense / Sparse after deletes	Dense
Ordered	Unordered	Unordered	Ordered
When stored in a database table	n/a	Out of line	Inline
Usage	Any set of data	Any set of data	Small sets of data

When selecting data from the database into PL/SQL variables or writing data from PL/SQL variables to the database, you can do this row-by-row (also called slow-by-slow). But, since Oracle Database 8i, you have the bulk operations available. To be able to do this, collections are essential.

Bulk Collect

You can use the bulk collect option to retrieve data from the database. Instead of selecting a single record from the database, you can select a whole set of records from the database and store them in a collection in a single trip to the database.

If you want to retrieve only the Dutch drivers from the database, you must create a collection type to hold the data. In this case, make a collection of records based on the structure of the cursor.

```
declare
  cursor c_dutch_drivers
  is
  select *
  from    f1data.drivers drv
  where   drv.nationality = 'Dutch'
  ;

  type dutch_drivers_tt is table of f1data.drivers%rowtype
    index by pls_integer;
```

And then create a variable based on this collection type.

```
l_dutch_drivers dutch_drivers_tt;
```

Then in the cursor, bulk collect into the collection variable instead of fetching into a single record.

```
begin
  open   c_dutch_drivers;
  fetch c_dutch_drivers
  bulk   collect
  into   l_dutch_drivers;
  close c_dutch_drivers;
```

This way, the entire result set is fetched into the local variable in a single pass to the database.

This statement does not generate an error if no data is found; instead, it returns an empty collection. So, before you start processing the collection, it is good practice to see if there is anything to process in the first place.

```
  if l_dutch_drivers.count > 0
  then
    for indx in l_dutch_drivers.first ..
l_dutch_drivers.last
    loop
dbms_output.put_line(  l_dutch_drivers( indx ).forename
|| ' '
|| l_dutch_drivers( indx ).surname);
    end loop;
  end if;
end;
```

Listing 1-2 is the complete anonymous block.

Listing 1-2. Display the names of the Dutch drivers

```
declare
  cursor c_dutch_drivers
  is
  select drv.*
  from    f1data.drivers drv
  where   drv.nationality = 'Dutch'
  ;

  type dutch_drivers_tt is table of f1data.drivers%rowtype
    index by pls_integer;

  l_dutch_drivers dutch_drivers_tt;
begin
  open  c_dutch_drivers;
  fetch c_dutch_drivers
  bulk  collect
  into  l_dutch_drivers;
  close c_dutch_drivers;
  if l_dutch_drivers.count > 0
  then
    for indx in l_dutch_drivers.first ..
l_dutch_drivers.last
```

```
    loop
  dbms_output.put_line(  l_dutch_drivers( indx ).forename
  || ' '
  || l_dutch_drivers( indx ).surname);
    end loop;
  end if;
end;
/
```

Limit

If you bulk collect the result set into a collection variable, be aware that all data is transferred into memory. This can take up a lot of memory and since chances are that multiple processes are running, performing similar queries, you can run out of available memory. Oracle Database provides the limit clause to limit the amount of memory used.

This takes a bit more coding because you must build a loop to fetch all the records in multiple passes. Listing 1-3 implements the same code but now uses the limit clause.

Listing 1-3. Display the names of the Dutch drivers using the limit clause

```
declare
  cursor c_dutch_drivers
  is
  select drv.*
  from   f1data.drivers drv
  where  drv.nationality = 'Dutch'
  ;

  type dutch_drivers_tt is table of f1data.drivers%rowtype
    index by pls_integer;

  l_dutch_drivers dutch_drivers_tt;
begin
  open  c_dutch_drivers;
  loop
    fetch c_dutch_drivers
```

```
      bulk   collect
      into   l_dutch_drivers
      limit 5;
      dbms_output.put_line(  '----- '
      || to_char( l_dutch_drivers.count )
      || ' -----');
      if l_dutch_drivers.count > 0
      then
  for indx in l_dutch_drivers.first ..
    l_dutch_drivers.last
  loop
    dbms_output.put_line(  l_dutch_drivers( indx ).forename
    || ' '
    || l_dutch_drivers( indx ).surname);
  end loop;
      else
  exit;
      end if;
    end loop;
    close c_dutch_drivers;
  end;
  /

  ----- 5 -----
  Michael Bleekemolen
  Boy Lunger
  Roelof Wunderink
  Gijs van Lennep
  Christijan Albers
  ----- 5 -----
  Robert Doornbos
  Jos Verstappen
  Jan Lammers
  Huub Rothengatter
  Dries van der Lof
```

```
----- 5 -----
Jan Flinterman
Giedo van der Garde
Max Verstappen
Carel Godin de Beaufort
Ernie de Vos
----- 2 -----
Ben Pon
Rob Slotemaker
----- 0 -----

PL/SQL procedure successfully completed
```

forall

Since you can get the data from the database in bulk, you can also write data back to the database in bulk using a `forall` statement.

The syntax for the `forall` statement looks a lot like a loop statement, but instead of sending the individual statements to the SQL engine, they are bundled and sent in one pass.

There are three ways you can use the `forall` statement. The easiest way to use it is to specify a range from a dense collection. If your collection is sparse, you can use the `indices of` clause. And if you want to use the values of your collection as pointers to another collection, you can use the `values of` clause. For these examples, create a table to hold the drivers who have a fixed driver number.

```
create table drivers_with_number
as
select drv.*
from   f1data.drivers drv
where  1=2
/
```

Note All these examples can be done using a single SQL statement, but it is to display the different possible usages.

Range

When you specify the start and end index of a collection you want to use in your statement, you use the (implicit) range option of the `forall` statement. This collection has to be a dense collection. An example using the range clause in a forall statement is displayed in Listing 1-4. An exception is raised if one element is missing in the range you specify.

```
ORA-22160: element at index [xxx] does not exist
```

Listing 1-4. Using forall with the range option

```
declare
  cursor c_drivers
  is
  select drv.*
  from   f1data.drivers drv
  where  drv.driver_number is not null
  order  by drv.dob
  ;

  type drivers_tt is table of f1data.drivers%rowtype
    index by pls_integer;

  l_drivers drivers_tt;
begin
  open  c_drivers;
  fetch c_drivers
  bulk  collect into l_drivers;
  close c_drivers;

  if l_drivers.count > 0
  then
    forall indx in l_drivers.first .. l_drivers.last
      insert into drivers_with_number
      values l_drivers( indx );
  end if;
end;
/
```

indices of

If you have a sparse collection (i.e., some elements are missing in the range), you can use the `indices of` option. Unlike the previous example, where you did not select the drivers with no fixed `driver_number` in the first place, you now select all the drivers from the database into our collection.

```
open c_drivers;
fetch c_drivers
bulk  collect into l_drivers;
close c_drivers;
```

Then remove the drivers with no fixed `driver_number` from the collection, creating a sparse collection.

```
for indx in l_drivers.first .. l_drivers.last
loop
  if l_drivers( indx ).driver_number is null
  then
    l_drivers.delete( indx );
  end if;
end loop;
```

Now that you have a sparse collection, use the `indices of` option of the `forall` statement to insert the rows from the sparse collection into the database.

```
forall indx in indices of l_drivers
  insert into drivers_with_number values l_drivers( indx );
```

Listing 1-5 is the complete script.

Listing 1-5. Using forall with the indices of option

```
declare
  cursor c_drivers
  is
  select drv.*
  from   f1data.drivers drv
  ;
```

```
  type drivers_tt is table of f1data.drivers%rowtype
    index by pls_integer;

  l_drivers drivers_tt;

begin
  open c_drivers;
  fetch c_drivers
  bulk  collect into l_drivers;
  close c_drivers;

  if l_drivers.count > 0
  then
    for indx in l_drivers.first .. l_drivers.last
    loop
      if l_drivers( indx ).driver_number is null
      then
        l_drivers.delete( indx );
      end if;
    end loop;
  end if;

  if l_drivers.count > 0
  then
    forall indx in indices of l_drivers
      insert into drivers_with_number values l_drivers( indx );
  end if;
end;
/

select dwn.driverid      as id
     , dwn.driverref      as ref
     , dwn.driver_number as num
from    drivers_with_number dwn
order  by dwn.driver_number
/
```

```
  ID REF                  NUM
----- -------------------- ---
 838 vandoorne              2
 817 ricciardo              3
 846 norris                 4
 820 chilton                4
  20 vettel                 5
   3 rosberg                6
 849 latifi                 6
   8 raikkonen              7
 154 grosjean               8
 853 mazepin                9
 828 ericsson               9
 155 kobayashi             10
 842 gasly                 10
 815 perez                 11
 831 nasr                  12
 813 maldonado             13
   4 alonso                14
 844 leclerc               16
 824 jules_bianchi         17
 840 stroll                18
  13 massa                 19
 825 kevin_magnussen       20
 821 gutierrez             21
  18 button                22
 852 tsunoda               22
 848 albon                 23
 855 zhou                  24
 818 vergne                25
 826 kvyat                 26
 807 hulkenberg            27
 843 brendon_hartley       28
 829 stevens               28
 835 jolyon_palmer         30
```

```
839 ocon                   31
830 max_verstappen         33
845 sirotkin               35
  1 hamilton               44
827 lotterer               45
854 mick_schumacher        47
850 pietro_fittipaldi      51
834 rossi                  53
832 sainz                  55
847 russell                63
822 bottas                 77
  9 kubica                 88
837 haryanto               88
851 aitken                 89
836 wehrlein               94
833 merhi                  98
841 giovinazzi             99
 16 sutil                  99
```

51 rows selected

values of

If you want to use your collection as a set of pointers in another collection, you can use the values of clause.

After fetching all the rows from the table into our collection, fill another collection (l_drivers_with_number) with the records that have a driver_number available. The index of this collection is the driver_number. Also, save the driver_number into a different collection (l_driver_numbers). These are our pointers into the l_drivers_with_number collection.

```
for indx in l_drivers.first .. l_drivers.last
loop
  if l_drivers( indx ).driver_number is not null
  then
    l_drivers_with_number(l_drivers( indx ).driver_number) :=
      l_drivers( indx );
```

```
    l_driver_numbers( l_driver_numbers.count + 1 ) :=
      l_drivers( indx ).driver_number;
  end if;
end loop;
```

Using these two collections, you can use the values of clause to insert the rows into the database. The values of the l_driver_numbers collection are the indices of the l_drivers_with_number collection.

```
forall indx in values of l_driver_numbers
  insert into drivers_with_number
  values l_drivers_with_number( indx );
```

Listing 1-6 is the complete script.

Listing 1-6. Using forall with the values of option

```
declare
  cursor c_drivers
  is
  select drv.*
  from    f1data.drivers drv
  ;

  type drivers_tt is table of f1data.drivers%rowtype
    index by pls_integer;
  type driver_numbers_tt is table of pls_integer
    index by pls_integer;

  l_drivers              drivers_tt;
  l_drivers_with_number drivers_tt;
  l_driver_numbers      driver_numbers_tt;

begin
  open c_drivers;
  fetch c_drivers
  bulk  collect into l_drivers;
  close c_drivers;
```

```
  if l_drivers.count > 0
  then
    for indx in l_drivers.first .. l_drivers.last
    loop
      if l_drivers( indx ).driver_number is not null
      then
        l_drivers_with_number(l_drivers( indx ).driver_number) :=
          l_drivers( indx );
        l_driver_numbers( l_driver_numbers.count + 1 ) :=
          l_drivers( indx ).driver_number;
      end if;
    end loop;
  end if;

  if l_driver_numbers.count > 0
  then
    forall indx in values of l_driver_numbers
      insert into drivers_with_number
      values l_drivers_with_number( indx );
  end if;
end;
/

select dwn.driverid      as id
     , dwn.driverref      as ref
     , dwn.driver_number as num
from    drivers_with_number dwn
order  by dwn.driver_number
/

  ID REF                    NUM
----- -------------------- ---
  838 vandoorne              2
  817 ricciardo              3
  846 norris                 4
  846 norris                 4
   20 vettel                 5
```

```
849 latifi               6
849 latifi               6
  8 raikkonen            7
154 grosjean             8
853 mazepin              9
853 mazepin              9
842 gasly               10
842 gasly               10
815 perez               11
831 nasr                12
813 maldonado           13
  4 alonso              14
844 leclerc             16
824 jules_bianchi       17
840 stroll              18
 13 massa               19
825 kevin_magnussen     20
821 gutierrez           21
852 tsunoda             22
852 tsunoda             22
848 albon               23
855 zhou                24
818 vergne              25
826 kvyat               26
807 hulkenberg          27
843 brendon_hartley     28
843 brendon_hartley     28
835 jolyon_palmer       30
839 ocon                31
830 max_verstappen      33
845 sirotkin            35
  1 hamilton            44
827 lotterer            45
854 mick_schumacher     47
850 pietro_fittipaldi   51
```

```
834 rossi              53
832 sainz              55
847 russell            63
822 bottas             77
837 haryanto           88
837 haryanto           88
851 aitken             89
836 wehrlein           94
833 merhi              98
841 giovinazzi         99
841 giovinazzi         99

51 rows selected
```

As you can see, this results in duplicate records since `driver_number` was used as an index in the l_drivers_with_number collection, thus possibly overwriting an existing record. For example, the entry at index 99 might first get the Sutil value but is later overwritten by Giovinazzo. This results in two entries in the l_driver_numbers collection, but they both point to the same record in the l_drivers_with_number collection, resulting in the `forall` statement inserting the same record twice.

Bulk Exceptions

The "DML Error Logging" section in this chapter discusses bulk exceptions.

Compound Triggers

When performing DML on tables (or views), Oracle Database can fire triggers at four different points during the execution of the statement.

- Before the firing statement
- Before each row that the firing statement affects
- After each row that the firing statement affects
- After the firing statement

Different triggers can be built for each DML action: `insert`, `update`, and `delete`.

The concept of compound triggers was introduced in Oracle Database 11g. All the actions can be built into a single trigger with a compound trigger. Not only does this limit the number of objects, and therefore source files, needed, but the compound trigger allows sharing of state between all the trigger points using variables. The compound trigger has a declaration section, similar to the declaration section of a package. The common state is created at the start of the triggering statement and is destroyed at the completion of the trigger.

Before the introduction of compound triggers, the same behavior could (and still can) be accomplished using packages to share the data, except that you had to take care of the creation and destruction of the data structures yourself. The following is the skeleton of a compound trigger with a short explanation of each section.

```
create or replace trigger compound_trigger_name
for [insert|delete]update] [of column] on table
compound trigger
  -- declarative section (optional)
  -- variables declared here have firing-statement duration.

  --executed before dml statement
  before statement is
  begin
    null;
  end before statement;

  --executed before each row change- :new, :old are available
  before each row is
  begin
    null;
  end before each row;

  --executed after each row change- :new, :old are available
  after each row is
  begin
    null;
  end after each row;
```

```
--executed after dml statement
after statement is
begin
  null;
end after statement;

end compound_trigger_name;
/
```

Two common use cases exist where a compound trigger outshines the traditional triggers and packages combination. The first is custom journaling on tables, and the second is a workaround for a mutating table problem. These two use cases are described in more detail in the next sections.

Journaling

When you must keep journaling tables for all the transactions you do on a certain table, using compound triggers can speed up this process by using bulk processing. Instead of inserting a row in the journal table after a row has been processed, you can accumulate all the data of the rows affected in collections in the compound trigger and then use bulk operations to push this data to the journaling table.

First, create a journaling table.

```
create table constructors_jn
as
select constructorid
, constructorref
, name
, nationality
, url
, CAST( null as varchar2( 1 ) ) jn_action
, systimestamp jn_date
from    f1data.constructors
where   1 = 2
/
```

You can create a single compound trigger for the insert, update and delete events.

```
create or replace trigger tr_constructors_cti
  for insert or update or delete on constructors
  compound trigger
```

In the compound trigger, declare a collection type for the journaling records.

```
-- declarative section (optional)
type constructors_tt is table of constructors_jn%rowtype
  index by pls_integer;
```

Next, declare a global variable to hold the collection.

```
-- variables declared here have firing-statement duration.
g_constructors_jn constructors_tt;
```

Then, record all the information needed for the journaling table in the after each row section.

```
--executed aftereach row change- :new, :old are available
after each row is
  l_constructor constructors_jn%rowtype;
begin
  if inserting
or updating
  then
    l_constructor.constructorid  := :new.constructorid;
    l_constructor.constructorref := :new.constructorref;
    l_constructor.name := :new.name;
    l_constructor.nationality    := :new.nationality;
    l_constructor.url  := :new.url;
  else
    l_constructor.constructorid  := :old.constructorid;
    l_constructor.constructorref := :old.constructorref;
    l_constructor.name := :old.name;
    l_constructor.nationality    := :old.nationality;
    l_constructor.url  := :old.url;
  end if;
```

```
if inserting
then
  l_constructor.jn_action := 'I';
elsif updating
then
  l_constructor.jn_action := 'U';
else
  l_constructor.jn_action := 'D';
end if;
l_constructor.jn_date := systimestamp;
g_constructors_jn(g_constructors_jn.count + 1) :=
                                      l_constructor;
end after each row;
```

And in the `after statement` section, perform the bulk operation to push the data to the database.

```
--executed after dml statement
after statement is
begin
  forall indx in g_constructors_jn.first ..
  g_constructors_jn.last
    insert
    into    constructors_jn
    values g_constructors_jn( indx );
end after statement;
```

Listing 1-7 is the complete compound trigger.

Tip If you expect the journaling collection to become very big, you can build a FORALL BULK INSERT in the AFTER EACH ROW part of the compound trigger when the size of the collections reaches a certain size and then empty the collection.

Listing 1-7. Compound Trigger tr_constructors_cti

```
create or replace trigger tr_constructors_cti
  for insert or update or delete on constructors
  compound trigger
  -- declarative section (optional)
  type constructors_tt is table of constructors_jn%rowtype
    index by pls_integer;
  -- variables declared here have firing-statement duration.
  g_constructors_jn constructors_tt;
  --executed after each row change- :new, :old are available
  after each row is
    l_constructor constructors_jn%rowtype;
  begin
    if inserting
  or updating
    then
      l_constructor.constructorid  := :new.constructorid;
      l_constructor.constructorref := :new.constructorref;
      l_constructor.name           := :new.name;
      l_constructor.nationality     := :new.nationality;
      l_constructor.url            := :new.url;
    else
      l_constructor.constructorid  := :old.constructorid;
      l_constructor.constructorref := :old.constructorref;
      l_constructor.name           := :old.name;
      l_constructor.nationality     := :old.nationality;
      l_constructor.url            := :old.url;
    end if;
    if inserting
    then
      l_constructor.jn_action := 'I';
    elsif updating
    then
      l_constructor.jn_action := 'U';
    else
```

```
      l_constructor.jn_action := 'D';
    end if;
    l_constructor.jn_date := systimestamp;
    g_constructors_jn(g_constructors_jn.count + 1) :=
      l_constructor;
  end after each row;

  --executed after dml statement
  after statement is
  begin
    forall indx in g_constructors_jn.first ..
    g_constructors_jn.last
      insert
      into    constructors_jn
      values g_constructors_jn( indx );
  end after statement;

end tr_constructors_cti;
/
```

Mutating Table

Suppose you want to update the CONSTRUCTORRESULTS table when you add the result of a race to the RESULTS table. If you try to do this in a trigger, as you see in Listing 1-8, you receive an error when you try to insert or update a row in the RESULTS table.

```
ORA-04091: table F1DATA.RESULTS is mutating, trigger/function may
not see it
```

Listing 1-8. After row trigger on RESULTS to update the CONSTRUCTORRESULTS

```
create or replace trigger tr_results_ariu
  after insert or update on f1data.results
  for each row
begin
  merge into f1data.constructorresults tgt
  using (select rsl.raceid       as raceid
               , rsl.constructorid as constructorid
```

```
                , sum( rsl.points ) as points
        from    f1data.results rsl
        where   rsl.raceid        = :new.raceid
        and     rsl.constructorid = :new.constructorid
        group   by rsl.raceid
                  , rsl.constructorid) src
  on (     tgt.raceid        = src.raceid
      and tgt.constructorid = src.constructorid)
  when matched then
    update
    set     tgr.points = src.points
  when not matched then
    insert
      ( constructorresultsid
      , raceid
      , constructorid
      , points)
    values
      ( f1data.constructorresults_seq.nextval
      , src.raceid
      , src.constructorid
      , src.points);
end tr_results_ariu;
/
```

You can work around this problem by creating a compound trigger that, in the after row, adds the different constructors to a collection, which is used in the after statement trigger to perform the actual merge statement.

Listing 1-9. Compound trigger on RESULTS to update the CONSTRUCTORRESULTS

```
create or replace trigger f1data.tr_results_cti
  for insert or update or delete on f1data.results
  compound trigger
-- declarative section (optional)
  type raceid_t is record
    ( raceid        number
```

```
, constructorid number);
type raceids_tt is table of raceid_t
  index by pls_integer;
-- variables declared here have firing-statement duration.
g_raceids raceids_tt;
--executed before dml statement
before statement is
begin
  null;
end before statement;

--executed aftereach row change- :new, :old are available
after each row is
begin
  g_raceids(:new.constructorid).raceid :=
                          :new.raceid;
  g_raceids(:new.constructorid).constructorid :=
                          :new.constructorid;
end after each row;

--executed after dml statement
after statement is
begin
  forall indx in indices of g_raceids
    merge into f1data.constructorresults tgt
    using (select rsl.raceid
                , rsl.constructorid
                , sum( rsl.points ) as points
          from   f1data.results rsl
          where  rsl.raceid =
                    g_raceids( indx ).raceid
          and    rsl.constructorid =
                    g_raceids(indx).constructorid
          group  by rsl.raceid
                  ,rsl.constructorid) src
    on (    tgt.raceid       = src.raceid
```

```
         and tgt.constructorid = src.constructorid)
     when matched then
       update
       set    tgt.points = src.points
     when not matched then
       insert
         ( constructorresultsid
         , raceid
         , constructorid
         , points)
       values
         ( f1data.constructorresults_seq.nextval
         , src.raceid
         , src.constructorid
         , src.points);
   end after statement;

end tr_results_cti;
/
```

DML Error Logging

When performing DML, things can go wrong. For example, when a constraint is violated, the action does not complete, and the transaction is rolled back. This is not a problem when you are working with a single record. Either fix the data and run the statement again, or log the error somewhere. But if you run a statement where you insert a million rows, and the millionth row fails, the entire transaction is rolled back. Oracle Database provides a mechanism to work around this problem.

Log Errors

Create a table of all the drivers who have a permanent number assigned to them.

```
create table drivers_with_number
as
select drv.*
```

```
from    f1data.drivers drv
where   1=2
/
```

To ensure the permanent number is unique, add a unique constraint to the table.

```
alter table drivers_with_number add constraint un_driver_number
unique (driver_number)
/
```

To use this feature, you must create a table to hold the problematic records. The dbms_errlog package has a procedure (create_error_log) to facilitate this.

```
procedure create_error_log
   ( dml_table_name varchar2
   , err_log_table_name  varchar2 default NULL
   , err_log_table_owner varchar2 default NULL
   , err_log_table_space varchar2 default NULL
   , skip_unsupported     boolean  default FALSE
   );
```

Use this procedure with all the default values, as follows.

```
begin
   dbms_errlog.create_error_log
    (dml_table_name => 'drivers_with_number');
end;
/
```

A ERR$_DRIVERS_WITH_NUMBER table is created in the current schema. This table has five columns describing the error.

```
desc err$_drivers_with_number
```

Name	Type	Nullable	Default	Comments
ORA_ERR_NUMBER$	NUMBER	Y		
ORA_ERR_MESG$	VARCHAR2(2000)	Y		
ORA_ERR_ROWID$	UROWID	Y		
ORA_ERR_OPTYP$	VARCHAR2(2)	Y		
ORA_ERR_TAG$	VARCHAR2(2000)	Y		

And for every column in the source table, it creates a VARCHAR2 column. If the original column is of type VARCHAR2, the new column is of type VARCHAR2 with the max string size. Every other column is of type VARCHAR2(4000). In a database with max_string_size=extended, you see columns like these with a VARCHAR2(32767) data type.

```
DRIVERID           VARCHAR2(4000)  Y
DRIVERREF          VARCHAR2(32767) Y
DRIVER_NUMBER      VARCHAR2(4000)  Y
CODE               VARCHAR2(32767) Y
FORENAME           VARCHAR2(32767) Y
SURNAME            VARCHAR2(32767) Y
DOB                VARCHAR2(4000)  Y
NATIONALITY        VARCHAR2(32767) Y
URL                VARCHAR2(32767) Y
```

To use this table as an error log, you must extend your DML statement with a log errors clause.

```
log errors
  [into [schema_name.]table_name]
  [('error_tag')]
  [reject limit integer|unlimited]
```

- The into clause allows you to specify the name of the error log table. The default is err$_<tablename> in the current schema.

- error_tag allows you to specify any string you can use to identify the records connected to this statement.

- reject limit allows you to specify the number of errors you want to accept before an exception is raised.

```
insert into drivers_with_number
select *
from   f1data.drivers drv
where  drv.driver_number is not null
log errors into err$_drivers_with_number ('with limit unlimited') reject
limit unlimited
/
```

All the errors are written in the error log table. Table 1-2 shows one of these errors.

Table 1-2. *An Error Record*

ORA_ERR_NUMBER$	1
ORA_ERR_MESG$	ORA-00001: unique constraint (BOOK.UN_DRIVER_ NUMBER) violated
ORA_ERR_ROWID$	
ORA_ERR_OPTYP$	I
ORA_ERR_TAG$	with limit unlimited
DRIVERID	846
DRIVERREF	Norris
DRIVER_NUMBER	4
CODE	NOR
FORENAME	Lando
SURNAME	Norris
DOB	13-NOV-99
NATIONALITY	British
URL	http://en.wikipedia.org/wiki/Lando_Norris

The target table contains the records that raise no errors. All the problematic records are logged in the error logging table. The data in the error logging table is persisted, regardless of whether you commit or rollback the transaction.

Note   ORA_ERR_ROWID$ points to the original record row ID; therefore, it is empty when performing an insert. It contains a value when an update is issued.

Save Exceptions

When performing bulk DML statements in PL/SQL using the `forall` statement, you have a similar option. In this case, the errors are not logged into a table but into a collection in memory.

Oracle Database raises a special exception that you can handle.

```
failure_in_forall exception;
pragma exception_init( failure_in_forall, -24381 );
```

All the exceptions are saved into a pseudo-collection: `sql%bulk_exceptions`. The following are the attributes available in this collection.

- `error_code`: Holds the corresponding error code

- `error_index`: Holds the iteration number of the current forall statement

- `count`: Holds the total number of exceptions

Listing 1-10. Using forall with save exceptions

```
declare
  cursor c_drivers is
    select drv.*
    from   f1data.drivers drv
    where  drv.driver_number is not null
    order  by drv.dob;

  type drivers_tt is table of f1data.drivers%rowtype
    index by pls_integer;

  l_drivers drivers_tt;

  failure_in_forall exception;
  pragma exception_init( failure_in_forall, -24381 );
begin
  open  c_drivers;
  fetch c_drivers
  bulk  collect into l_drivers;
  close c_drivers;
```

```
if l_drivers.count > 0
then
  begin
    forall indx in l_drivers.first .. l_drivers.last
      save exceptions
        insert
        into drivers_with_number values l_drivers(indx);
  exception
    when failure_in_forall then
      for indx in 1 .. sql%bulk_exceptions.count
      loop
        dbms_output.put_line(  'Error '
                            || indx
                            || ' occurred on index '
                            || sql%bulk_exceptions( indx ).
                                 error_index
                            || '.'
                            );
        dbms_output.put_line(  'Oracle error is '
                            || sqlerrm( -1 *
                                 sql%bulk_exceptions( indx ).
                                   error_code)
                            );          end loop;
  end;
  end if;
end;
/

Error 1 occurred on index 25.
Oracle error is ORA-00001: unique constraint (.) violated
Error 2 occurred on index 31.
Oracle error is ORA-00001: unique constraint (.) violated
Error 3 occurred on index 32.
Oracle error is ORA-00001: unique constraint (.) violated
Error 4 occurred on index 36.
Oracle error is ORA-00001: unique constraint (.) violated
```

```
Error 5 occurred on index 39.
Oracle error is ORA-00001: unique constraint (.) violated
Error 6 occurred on index 47.
Oracle error is ORA-00001: unique constraint (.) violated
Error 7 occurred on index 50.
Oracle error is ORA-00001: unique constraint (.) violated
Error 8 occurred on index 51.
Oracle error is ORA-00001: unique constraint (.) violated

PL/SQL procedure successfully completed
```

> **Note**   The error code is a positive number, but Oracle error codes are negative, so you must multiply the code by −1 to get the correct error message.

Summary

This chapter looked at how to take advantage of collections, with bulk operations, to retrieve data from the database and write it back into database tables. Collections are also very useful when combined with a compound trigger for journaling purposes or to circumvent a *mutating table* problem.

Handling errors for DML operations was also covered for straight DML (insert, update, delete) and bulk operations.

CHAPTER 2

Analytic Functions and (un)Pivoting

It happens all too often that end users of a database application ask for exports in Excel so that they can manipulate the data to get the information they need to make business decisions. Often the required information can be retrieved by using SQL in a format that the end users are looking for, thus eliminating the manual manipulation of data after export. The more extensive your knowledge of SQL, the more options you have to assist the end user in their needs. This chapter discusses two important techniques: analytic functions and pivoting.

Analytic functions are an important tool to master and are still relatively unknown, despite being over 23 years old.

Pivoting the result set is a common requirement to turn rows into columns, just like unpivoting to turn columns into rows.

Analytic Functions

Analytic functions were introduced in Oracle Database 8.1.6 Enterprise Edition, yet they are still relatively unknown. Analytic functions enable access to values from more than one row without the need for a self-join, creating aggregate values without a `group by`. Another example where analytic functions shine is determining ranking within a group of values.

The processing order of a query with analytic functions happens in three stages. In the first stage, the joins,where conditions, group by, and having clauses are resolved. Analytic functions are applied to the result set in the second stage. Finally, the `order by` is applied to the complete result set. The processing order is relevant because a standard aggregate might suffice. A tell-tale sign is a query that combines an analytic function and a distinct operator. This query can probably be written with a normal aggregate.

© Alex Nuijten, Patrick Barel 2023
A. Nuijten and P. Barel, *Modern Oracle Database Programming*, https://doi.org/10.1007/978-1-4842-9166-5_2

Where aggregate functions reduce the number of rows in the final result set, a count(*) only returns one row, analytic functions don't do that. Analytic functions return a value for each row in the final result set.

Building Blocks

The first step in working with analytic functions is to decide which function is needed, the *what*. Many aggregate functions have an analytic counterpart, like count, sum, or avg. The following example shows the skeleton of the analytic counterpart of the avg function.

```
avg (<..>) over ()
```

The keyword over signals that the function is indeed an analytic function.

After deciding which function to use, the next step is determining those parts of the result set to which the function should be applied. Rows in the result set are "grouped" together, called *partitions*, and the analytic function is applied to these sets.

Note   Partitions in the context of analytic functions are not related to table partitioning. Analytic partitions are a logical grouping of data.

A partition can be as small as a single row or as large as the whole result set. The criteria in the partition clause determine how many different groups there are—never more than one per record, never less than one per result set. The whole result set is considered a single partition when the partition clause is omitted. The result of the function of choice is applied to a single partition. It can't cross partitions. The following example shows the skeleton of the analytic function to include the partition clause.

```
avg (<..>) over (partition by <..>)
```

Within a partition, it is possible to specify a *window*. The window determines which range of rows in the current partition are available to perform the function upon. Analytic functions are always performed from the perspective of the current row. Window sizes can be based on either a physical number of rows or a logical interval, such as a numeric value or time.

Currently, there are three options to define the windowing clause. Oracle Database 21c introduced the groups window.

- **rows** specify the number of rows relative to the current row. This can be either forward or backward from the current row.

- **range** specifies the range of values relative to the current row. The number of rows depends on the value of the current row. The sort key must allow for addition or subtraction operations, like numeric, date, or interval data types.

- **groups** are where the data is divided based on the ordered values. Ties are part of the same group. The offset specified refers to the preceding or following group.

Because the windowing clause relies on an ordered result set, it is required to include an order by in the analytic clause. The windowing clause defaults to range unbounded preceding and current row when an order by is present. Listing 2-2 is an example of the differences between rows, range, and groups.

The DRIVERS, RACES, and LAPTIMES tables are used in the examples to demonstrate how analytic functions work unless otherwise noted.

Running Totals

Creating a running total, where the totals are accumulated as the rows progress, is trivial with analytic functions. The laptimes table records the time (in milliseconds) it takes to complete a lap around the circuit. The following example filters the data on the first 2022 season Bahrain Grand Prix race for Charles Leclerc using only the first ten laps.

The analytic counterpart of the sum function is used to create a running total. The over keyword signals that it is an analytic function. The partition clause is missing in the following example, indicating that the complete result set is the partition. There is, however, a window that expands with each row because of the order by clause in the analytic clause. In this case, the implicit window is the default window: range unbounded preceding and current row, all preceding lap times are added to the current row's value creating a running total, as well as the lap times that have the same value as the current row. Even though it *appears* to work in this case, it only works because the values of the lap times are unique. When there are duplicate values, all preceding lap times are added, as well as any following with the same value as the current row. A true running total would require the following explicit window: rows between unbounded preceding and current row.

In Listing 2-1, the running_total column in the result set shows the running total time for the first ten laps for Charles Leclerc. The third row (lap 3) shows the total time in milliseconds for the first three rows (99070 + 97853 + 98272 = 295195).

Listing 2-1. Running total for a single driver

```
select ltm.lap
     , ltm.milliseconds
     , sum (ltm.milliseconds) over (
          order by ltm.lap
          rows between unbounded preceding
                    and current row
       ) as running_total
from    f1data.laptimes ltm
join    f1data.races rcs
   on   rcs.raceid = ltm.raceid
where   rcs.race_date between trunc (sysdate, 'yy') and sysdate
and     ltm.driverid = 844 -- Charles Leclerc
and     rcs.raceid = 1074 -- Bahrain Grand Prix
and     ltm.lap between 1 and 10
order   by ltm.lap
/

       LAP MILLISECONDS RUNNING_TOTAL
---------- ------------ -------------
         1        99070         99070
         2        97853        196923
         3        98272        295195
         4        98414        393609
         5        98471        492080
         6        98712        590792
         7        98835        689627
         8        98951        788578
         9        98807        887385
        10        99123        986508
```

To create a running total per driver, add a partition clause, as is done in the following example. The results are filtered on just four drivers for the first three laps.

```
select ltm.lap
     , drv.forename||' '||drv.surname as driver
     , ltm.milliseconds
     , sum (ltm.milliseconds)
           over (partition by ltm.driverid
                     order by ltm.lap) as running_total
from    f1data.laptimes ltm
join    f1data.races rcs
  on    rcs.raceid = ltm.raceid
join    f1data.drivers drv
  on    drv.driverid = ltm.driverid
where   rcs.race_date between trunc (sysdate, 'yy') and sysdate
and     rcs.raceid = 1074 -- Bahrain Grand Prix
and     ltm.lap between 1 and 3
and     ltm.driverid in (1, 815, 830, 844)
order   by ltm.lap
          ,ltm.milliseconds
          ,ltm.driverid
/
```

LAP	DRIVER	MILLISECONDS	RUNNING_TOTAL
1	Charles Leclerc	99070	99070
1	Max Verstappen	100236	100236
1	Lewis Hamilton	101555	101555
1	Sergio Pérez	102993	102993
2	Charles Leclerc	97853	196923
2	Max Verstappen	97880	198116
2	Lewis Hamilton	99002	200557
2	Sergio Pérez	99092	202085
3	Charles Leclerc	98272	295195
3	Max Verstappen	98357	296473
3	Lewis Hamilton	99075	299632
3	Sergio Pérez	99473	301558

```
12 rows selected.
```

The final order by (last line in the preceding query) determines the order of the result set. The running total might not be immediately obvious, but when focusing on the running total for Charles Leclerc, the same results are shown as in the first query in Listing 2-1.

To help visualize the window the functions first_value and last_value can assist with that. In the following query the first_value and last_value have the same analytic clause as the sum function and show the lap number where the window starts (in the win_start column) and where the window ends (in the win_end column).

```
select lt.lap
     , lt.milliseconds
     , sum (lt.milliseconds)
          over (partition by lt.driverid
                    order by lap) as running_total
     , first_value (lt.lap)
          over (partition by lt.driverid
                    order by lt.lap) as win_start
     , last_value (lt.lap)
          over (partition by lt.driverid
                    order by lt.lap) as win_end
from   f1data.laptimes lt
join   f1data.races r
  on   r.raceid = lt.raceid
where  race_date between trunc (sysdate, 'yy') and sysdate
and    r.raceid = 1074 -- Bahrain Grand Prix
and    lt.lap between 1 and 3
and    lt.driverid = 844 -- Charles Leclerc
order  by lt.lap
        ,lt.milliseconds
/
```

LAP	MILLISECONDS	RUNNING_TOTAL	WIN_START	WIN_END
1	99070	99070	1	1
2	97853	196923	1	2
3	98272	295195	1	3

In the preceding result set, the `win_start` column keeps the value of 1 as the start of the window, while the `win_end` column shows it is increased with the rows.

Note   When you want to know the last value in the *partition*, instead of the current last row in the window, specify unbounded `following`. This expands the window from the current row to the last row.

Since Oracle Database 21c, it is possible to define a reusable windowing clause. The following query is a variation of the preceding query where the window can be visualized with `first_value` and `last_value` functions. The reusable window clause is named "win" and is used in all three analytic functions.

```
select  ltm.lap
     ,  ltm.milliseconds
     ,  sum (ltm.milliseconds) over win as running_total
     ,  first_value (ltm.lap) over win as win_start
     ,  last_value (ltm.lap) over win as win_end
from    f1data.laptimes ltm
join    f1data.races rcs
   on   rcs.raceid = ltm.raceid
where   rcs.race_date between trunc (sysdate, 'yy') and sysdate
and     rcs.raceid = 1074 -- Bahrain Grand Prix
and     ltm.lap between 1 and 3
and     ltm.driverid = 844 -- Charles Leclerc
window win as (partition by ltm.driverid
                    order by ltm.lap)
order   by ltm.lap
        , ltm.milliseconds
/
       LAP MILLISECONDS RUNNING_TOTAL  WIN_START   WIN_END
---------- ------------ -------------  ---------- ----------
         1        99070         99070          1          1
         2        97853        196923          1          2
         3        98272        295195          1          3
```

More on the reusable window clause in the section "Reusable windowing clause".

Accessing Values from Other Rows

Several functions allow accessing values from other rows in the result set without needing a self-join. In a previous example, `first_value` and `last_value` have already been shown to help visualize where a window starts and ends. A variation of these functions is `nth_value`.

Where `first_value` retrieves a value from the first row in the window, and `last_value` retrieves a value from the last row in the window, `nth_value` allows retrieving a value from any row in the window.

The first argument for the `nth_value` function specifies which value needs to be retrieved. The second argument specifies the offset of the row that needs to be returned. This can be a constant, bind variable, column, or expression involving each of them if it resolves to a positive integer.

In the following example, the difference between the current lap (current row) and the elapsed time of the second lap is examined per driver. The differences between the second lap are shown in the column labeled `diff`.

In this example, every row is compared to the second in the result set, even the first row. The window `rows between unbounded preceding and unbounded following` are not restricted to only "look behind." It can also "look ahead."

Lewis Hamilton and Sergio Pérez were faster in the fourth lap than in the second.

```
select ltm.lap
     , drv.forename||' '||drv.surname as driver
     , ltm.milliseconds
     , ltm.milliseconds
       - nth_value (ltm.milliseconds, 2)
           over (partition by ltm.driverid
                   order by ltm.lap
                   rows between unbounded preceding
                        and unbounded following)
       as diff
from    f1data.laptimes ltm
join    f1data.races rcs
  on    rcs.raceid = ltm.raceid
join    f1data.drivers drv
  on    drv.driverid = ltm.driverid
```

```
where  rcs.race_date between trunc (sysdate, 'yy') and sysdate
and    rcs.raceid = 1074 -- Bahrain Grand Prix
and    ltm.lap between 1 and 4
and    ltm.driverid in (1, 815, 830, 844)
order  by ltm.lap
       , ltm.milliseconds
/
```

```
       LAP DRIVER           MILLISECONDS       DIFF
---------- ---------------- ------------ ----------
         1 Charles Leclerc        99070       1217
         1 Max Verstappen        100236       2356
         1 Lewis Hamilton        101555       2553
         1 Sergio Pérez          102993       3901
         2 Charles Leclerc        97853          0
         2 Max Verstappen         97880          0
         2 Lewis Hamilton         99002          0
         2 Sergio Pérez           99092          0
         3 Charles Leclerc        98272        419
         3 Max Verstappen         98357        477
         3 Lewis Hamilton         99075         73
         3 Sergio Pérez           99473        381
         4 Charles Leclerc        98414        561
         4 Max Verstappen         98566        686
         4 Sergio Pérez           98741       -351
         4 Lewis Hamilton         98892       -110
```

16 rows selected.

Comparing lap times from one lap to the next can be done with the lag and lead functions. With lag, it is possible to retrieve values from previous rows, while lead retrieves values from the following rows in the result set.

The following example compares lap times for a single driver with the lap time of the previous lap. Because the filter only selects a single driver, the partitioning clause is omitted from the analytic function. As seen in the result set, the second lap was significantly faster than the first.

```
select ltm.lap
     , ltm.milliseconds
     , ltm.milliseconds
       - lag (ltm.milliseconds)
           over (partition by ltm.driverid
                     order by ltm.lap)
       as diff
from    f1data.laptimes ltm
join    f1data.races rcs
  on    rcs.raceid = ltm.raceid
join    f1data.drivers drv
  on    drv.driverid = ltm.driverid
where   rcs.race_date between trunc (sysdate, 'yy') and sysdate
and     rcs.raceid = 1074 -- Bahrain Grand Prix
and     ltm.lap between 1 and 4
and     ltm.driverid = 830 -- Max Verstappen
order   by ltm.lap
       , ltm.milliseconds
/

       LAP MILLISECONDS        DIFF
---------- ------------ ----------
         1       100236
         2        97880       -2356
         3        98357         477
         4        98566         209
```

By default, the lag function accesses the value from the previous row. The offset is one row. The same is true for the lead function, the offset is one row, but it retrieves the value from the row following the current row. Both functions can take a second argument to change the row offset. When it is needed to look back two rows, the following statement can be used.

```
lag (ltm.milliseconds, 2)
  over (partition by ltm.driverid
            order by ltm.lap)
```

The first row in the preceding result set has no value for the diff column, which is explainable because there is no previous row. The function goes beyond the scope of the window. By default, the returned value is NULL when this is the case. A third argument can overrule this; this way, it is possible to distinguish between NULL values (point to a previous row where the value is NULL) and when the analytic function points to a row outside the window. The previous example could be amended to show an appropriate value in the diff column with the following expression by setting the default value to the lap time of the first lap.

```
lag (ltm.milliseconds, 1, ltm.milliseconds)
  over (partition by ltm.driverid
           order by ltm.lap)
```

This would then give the following results.

LAP	MILLISECONDS	DIFF
1	100236	0
2	97880	-2356
3	98357	477
4	98566	209

The Fastest Lap and the Slowest Lap

Unlike aggregate functions, analytic functions do not reduce the number of rows. Showing all lap times and marking the fastest and slowest lap at the same time is trivial to do with analytic function without the need for a self-join. The fastest lap is the one where the lap time is the lowest, which calls for the min function, and the slowest lap calls for the max function.

The following example uses a case expression to compare the lap time of the current row with the overall fastest lap. When the lap times match, the word $FAST$ is shown. Something similar is done for the slowest lap.

Because the result set has a filter on the race (Bahrain Grand Prix) and the driver (Charles Leclerc), there is no need to use the partition clause in the analytic functions.

```
select ltm.lap
     , ltm.milliseconds
     , case
       when min (ltm.milliseconds) over ()
            = ltm.milliseconds
       then 'F A S T'
       end as fastest
     , case
       when max (ltm.milliseconds) over ()
            = ltm.milliseconds
       then 'S L O W'
       end as slowest
from   f1data.laptimes ltm
join   f1data.races rcs
  on   rcs.raceid = ltm.raceid
where  rcs.race_date between trunc (sysdate, 'yy') and sysdate
and    ltm.driverid = 844 -- Charles Leclerc
and    rcs.raceid = 1074 -- Bahrain Grand Prix
/

       LAP MILLISECONDS FASTEST SLOWEST
---------- ------------- ------- -------
         1         99070
         2         97853
         3         98272
         4         98414
         5         98471
         6         98712
         7         98835
< rows removed for brevity>
        46        125151
        47        163846           S L O W
        48        151364
        49        146221
        50        144429
```

```
   51        94570 F A S T
   52        95027
   53        95127
< rows removed for brevity>
```

Ranking: Top-N

You cannot examine race data without talking about ranking, as each race ends with a podium for the first three. Three different analytic functions deal with ranking, and the differences are subtle. Dealing with equal values is resolved differently.

There are three ranking functions.

- rank means equal values are assigned the same ranking. The next ranking skips the number of equal values, which causes a nonconsecutive ranking. This ranking is referred to as *Olympic ranking*.

- dense_rank means equal values are assigned the same ranking. The next ranking does not skip a value; it creates a consecutive ranking.

- row_number ignores duplicate values comparable to the workings of rownum creates a consecutive ranking.

In the example, the total points per driver, regardless of season or race, are ranked. The DRIVERSTANDINGS table contains all points that a driver has accumulated. The rows are partitioned by DRIVERID and sorted by the points in descending order. The results are only shown for Sergio Pérez, who scored 190 points.

The rank() analytic function (the rk column in the following result set) ranks the first three rows with 1, while the fourth row has a value of 4. The dense_rank() function (dr column) also assigns a value of 1 for the first three rows, while the fourth row has a value of 2. Lastly, the row_number() function (rn column) assigns arbitrary values to each row.

```
select drv.forename ||' '|| drv.surname as driver
     , drs.points
     , rank () over win rk
     , dense_rank () over win dr
     , row_number() over win rn
```

```
from    f1data.driverstandings drs
join    f1data.drivers drv
  on    drv.driverid = drs.driverid
where   drv.driverid  = 815
window win as (partition by drv.driverid
                  order by drs.points desc)
/
```

DRIVER	POINTS	RK	DR	RN
Sergio Pérez	190	1	1	1
Sergio Pérez	190	1	1	2
Sergio Pérez	190	1	1	3
Sergio Pérez	178	4	2	4
Sergio Pérez	165	5	3	5

Deduplication

The row_number() ranking function is very useful when data needs to be deduplicated. For the following example, a new table, DUP_DRIVERS, is created based on the DRIVERS table, and this data is duplicated.

```
create table dup_drivers
as
select *
  from f1data.drivers
/
insert into dup_drivers
select *
  from dup_drivers
/
commit
/
```

Currently, there are over 1700 drivers in this table.

```
select count(*)
  from dup_drivers
/
  COUNT(*)
----------
      1708
```

The idea behind deduplication with the row_number() ranking function is to create partitions based on duplicated values (like driverid), assign an arbitrary ranking to each row in that partition, and remove all records that have a ranking greater than one.

For the first step, the data set is partitioned by driverid and row_number() is used to assign a ranking to each row (only eight rows are shown). In this case, the order of the rows within the partition is not important. The sorting within the analytic functions reflects that (order by null).

```
select rowid as rid
     , forename ||' '|| surname as driver
     , row_number() over
          (partition by driverid
              order by null
          ) as rn
from    dup_drivers
fetch   first 8 rows only
/
RID                   DRIVER              RN
------------------    ----------------    ----------
AAAYwqAAAAABAB7AAA    Lewis Hamilton       1
AAAYwqAAAAABAEHAAA    Lewis Hamilton       2
AAAYwqAAAAABAB7AAB    Nick Heidfeld        1
AAAYwqAAAAABAEHAAB    Nick Heidfeld        2
AAAYwqAAAAABAB7AAC    Nico Rosberg         1
AAAYwqAAAAABAEHAAC    Nico Rosberg         2
AAAYwqAAAAABAB7AAD    Fernando Alonso      1
AAAYwqAAAAABAEHAAD    Fernando Alonso      2

8 rows selected.
```

The next step is to filter out all records with a ranking greater than 1. Because analytic functions can't be used in the final predicate (the where clause), it is needed to push the preceding query into an inline view.

```
select rid
     , driver
from   (select rowid as rid
              , forename ||' '|| surname as driver
              , row_number() over
                (partition by driverid
                    order by null
                ) as rn
        from   dup_drivers
        fetch  first 8 rows only)
where  rn > 1
/
 RID                DRIVER
------------------- ----------------
AAAYwqAAAAAABAEHAAA Lewis Hamilton
AAAYwqAAAAAABAEHAAB Nick Heidfeld
AAAYwqAAAAAABAEHAAC Nico Rosberg
AAAYwqAAAAAABAEHAAD Fernando Alonso
```

The last step is to remove the rows from the table. The restriction on the first eight rows is removed from the query.

```
delete
from   dup_drivers
where  rowid in (
   select rid
   from   (select rowid as rid
                , row_number() over
                  (partition by driverid
                      order by null
                  ) as rn
```

```
        from    dup_drivers)
   where   rn > 1)
/
854 rows deleted.
```

Reusable Windowing Clause

Since Oracle Database 21c, it is possible to define a reusable named windowing clause. A named windowing clause allows you to use the same definition for multiple analytic functions in a query instead of copying over the definition. The named windowing clause can also include other named windows.

In Listing 2-2, there are five named windows defined. The first window (w_part) defines a partition by driverid. The second window uses w_part and sorts the data by points in descending order. The third, fourth, and fifth use the sorted partition, and each specifies a different windowing clause using rows, range, and groups offset.

Listing 2-2. Reusable windowing clause

```
select points
     , whole_partition
     , rows_
     , groups_
     , range_
  from (
select drv.driverid
     , drs.points
     , max (drs.points) over w_part  as whole_partition
     , max (drs.points) over w_rows  as rows_
     , max (drs.points) over w_group as groups_
     , max (drs.points) over w_range as range_
from    f1data.driverstandings drs
join    f1data.drivers drv
  on    drv.driverid = drs.driverid
window w_part  as (partition by drv.driverid)
       ,w_sort  as (w_part order by drs.points desc)
```

```
      ,w_rows  as (w_sort rows    between 10 preceding
                                      and current row)
      ,w_group as (w_sort groups between 10 preceding
                                      and current row)
      ,w_range as (w_sort range  between 10 preceding
                                      and current row)
)
where  driverid = 815
and    rownum <= 20
order  by driverid, points desc
/
```

POINTS	WHOLE_PARTITION	ROWS_	GROUPS_	RANGE_
190	190	190	190	190
190	190	190	190	190
190	190	190	190	190
178	190	190	190	178
165	190	190	190	165
150	190	190	190	150
147	190	190	190	150
135	190	190	190	135
129	190	190	190	135
129	190	190	190	135
125	190	190	190	135
125	190	190	190	135
120	190	190	190	129
118	190	178	190	125
110	190	165	190	120
108	190	150	178	118
104	190	147	165	110
104	190	135	165	110
104	190	129	165	110
104	190	129	165	110

```
20 rows selected.
```

The rows windowing clause uses a physical offset. The preceding example shows up to ten rows before the current row is within the window. The range windowing clause uses a logical offset. Values of 10 less than the current row's value are in scope. The groups windowing clause divides the values into groups where ties are in the same group. In the preceding example, the offset is the number of groups before the current row.

Note In the preceding example, the syntax over `<window_name>` is used. Using parenthesis around the window name: over (`<window_name>`) is also possible. These are not equivalent. The latter implies copying and modifying the window specification and is rejected if the referenced window specification includes a windowing clause.

Pivot and Unpivot

End users don't always want to see data going down the page; instead, they prefer it go across the page. The pivot clause is an aggregate operator that turns rows into columns. Similarly, occasionally the opposite makes more sense, and the unpivot clause can assist with that.

Pivot

For the examples, the results table is used. This table is denormalized to contain information about drivers, constructors, points scored, and laps completed per race. The following is an excerpt from this table.

```
select rcs.year
     , drv.driverref
     , rsl.points
     , rsl.laps
from   f1data.results rsl
join   f1data.races rcs
  on   rcs.raceid = rsl.raceid
join   f1data.drivers drv
```

```
  on    drv.driverid = rsl.driverid
where   drv.driverref in ('norris', 'bottas')
/
```

YEAR	DRIVERREF	POINTS	LAPS
2013	bottas	0	57
2013	bottas	0	56
2013	bottas	0	56
2013	bottas	0	57
2013	bottas	0	52

`< rows omitted for brevity >`

YEAR	DRIVERREF	POINTS	LAPS
2022	norris	2	51
2022	bottas	0	50
2022	bottas	6	70
2022	norris	0	70
2022	norris	8	52
2022	bottas	0	20

The objective is to gather all points for each year for Norris and Bottas and show the results for both drivers next to each other.

For this initial requirement, only the year, driverref, and points are needed. The laps from the preceding data set can be ignored for now. The preceding query is the input for the pivot clause. The aggregate is sum (to collect all the points). The aggregate and pivot columns need to be specified in the pivot clause. The pivot columns are not dynamic.

In the following query, the input query has been factored out in a named subquery (called results), and the points are aggregated for drivers Norris and Bottas. Columns that are part of the input query but not used in the pivot clause (like year) can be considered the "group by" columns. All columns that are part of the input query but not used in the pivot clause are used implicitly as "group by" columns.

Tip   Use an inline view or subquery factoring (with clause) when pivoting a result set, even when only using a single table. This safeguards the pivot action if the underlying table or view gets a new column.

```sql
with results as (
select rcs.year
     , drv.driverref
     , rsl.points
from   f1data.results rsl
join   f1data.races rcs
  on   rcs.raceid = rsl.raceid
join   f1data.drivers drv
  on   drv.driverid = rsl.driverid
where  drv.driverref in ('norris', 'bottas')
)
select year
     , norris
     , bottas
from   results
pivot  (
         sum (points)
         for driverref in ( 'norris' as norris
                          , 'bottas' as bottas
                          )
       )
/
```

```
      YEAR     NORRIS     BOTTAS
---------- ---------- ----------
      2013                     4
      2014                   186
      2015                   136
      2016                    85
      2017                   305
      2018                   247
      2019         49        326
      2020         97        223
      2021        160        219
      2022         54         44
```

The pivot columns are aliased to prevent the column names from becoming case-sensitive i.e., the column name would be 'norris', including the quotes.

There can be multiple aggregate functions in the pivot clause. When the number of completed laps should also be summarized, the laps must be in the input query, and an aggregate for the completed laps must be in the pivot clause.

```
with results as (
select rcs.year
     , drv.driverref
     , rsl.points
     , rsl.laps --<----- Laps added to input
from   f1data.results rsl
join   f1data.races rcs
  on   rcs.raceid = rsl.raceid
join   f1data.drivers drv
  on   drv.driverid = rsl.driverid
where  drv.driverref in ('norris', 'bottas')
)
select year
     , norris_points
     , norris_laps
     , bottas_points
     , bottas_laps
from   results
pivot  ( sum (points) as points
     , sum (laps)    as laps
        for driverref in ( 'norris' as norris
                         , 'bottas' as bottas
                         )
        )
order  by year
/
```

YEAR	NORRIS_POINTS	NORRIS_LAPS	BOTTAS_POINTS	BOTTAS_LAPS
2013			4	1070
2014			186	1110
2015			136	1037
2016			85	1186
2017			305	1168
2018			247	1202
2019	49	1102	326	1233
2020	97	1015	223	994
2021	160	1223	219	1134
2022	54	570	44	541

10 rows selected.

The aggregate functions are also aliased to distinguish the values and what they represent. The column names are derived from the pivot column, and the alias from the aggregate.

Unpivot

Where pivoting is the action of turning rows into columns, unpivot does the opposite. The QUALIFYING table has three columns, one for each qualification. Qualifications are used the day before the race to determine the starting grid and who starts in the pole position. Each qualification round is an elimination. Only the fastest go on to the next round. The following is an excerpt from the qualifications table for Robert Doornbos; he only managed to get to the second round twice and once to the final round.

```
select drv.forename ||' '||drv.surname as driver
     , rcs.name
     , qlf.q1
     , qlf.q2
     , qlf.q3
from   f1data.qualifying qlf
join   f1data.drivers drv
  on   drv.driverid = qlf.driverid
join   f1data.races rcs
```

```
 on    rcs.raceid = qlf.raceid
where  drv.driverref = 'doornbos'
and    qlf.q1 is not null
/
DRIVER           NAME                     Q1       Q2       Q3
--------------- -------------------- -------- -------- --------
Robert Doornbos Chinese Grand Prix   1:46.387 1:45.747 1:48.021
Robert Doornbos Japanese Grand Prix  1:32.402
Robert Doornbos Brazilian Grand Prix 1:12.530 1:12.591
Robert Doornbos German Grand Prix    1:18.313
Robert Doornbos Hungarian Grand Prix 1:25.484
Robert Doornbos Italian Grand Prix   1:24.904
Robert Doornbos Belgian Grand Prix   1:49.779
Robert Doornbos Japanese Grand Prix  1:52.894
Robert Doornbos Chinese Grand Prix   1:39.460

9 rows selected.
```

The objective is to turn the three qualifying times columns (Q1, Q2, and Q3) into rows.

The input query is the same as the preceding query, only now as a named query block. The columns that need to be unpivoted must be in the input query, in this case, the three qualifying columns. In the unpivot clause, the new column is labeled qtime, which contains the unpivoted value of the three qualifying columns, and quali_round labels what it represents.

```
with qualies as (
select drv.forename ||' '||drv.surname as driver
     , rcs.name
     , qlf.q1
     , qlf.q2
     , qlf.q3
from   f1data.qualifying qlf
join   f1data.drivers drv
  on   drv.driverid = qlf.driverid
join   f1data.races rcs
  on   rcs.raceid = qlf.raceid
```

```
where   drv.driverref = 'doornbos'
and     qlf.q1 is not null
)
select driver
     , name
     , quali_round
     , qtime
from   qualies
unpivot (
        qtime for quali_round in (q1, q2, q3)
        )
/
DRIVER          NAME                    QU QTIME
--------------- ----------------------- -- --------
Robert Doornbos Chinese Grand Prix      Q1 1:46.387
Robert Doornbos Chinese Grand Prix      Q2 1:45.747
Robert Doornbos Chinese Grand Prix      Q3 1:48.021
Robert Doornbos Japanese Grand Prix     Q1 1:32.402
Robert Doornbos Brazilian Grand Prix    Q1 1:12.530
Robert Doornbos Brazilian Grand Prix    Q2 1:12.591
Robert Doornbos German Grand Prix       Q1 1:18.313
Robert Doornbos Hungarian Grand Prix    Q1 1:25.484
Robert Doornbos Italian Grand Prix      Q1 1:24.904
Robert Doornbos Belgian Grand Prix      Q1 1:49.779
Robert Doornbos Japanese Grand Prix     Q1 1:52.894
Robert Doornbos Chinese Grand Prix      Q1 1:39.460

12 rows selected.
```

By default, NULL columns are excluded from the result set. There are no rows in the output where Q2 or Q3 is NULL. This behavior can be overridden by stating include nulls after the unpivot clause.

```
with qualies as (
select drv.forename ||' '||drv.surname as driver
     , rcs.name
     , qlf.q1
```

```
       , qlf.q2
       , qlf.q3
from    f1data.qualifying qlf
join    f1data.drivers drv
  on    drv.driverid = qlf.driverid
join    f1data.races rcs
  on    rcs.raceid = qlf.raceid
where   drv.driverref = 'doornbos'
and     qlf.q1 is not null
)
select driver
     , name
     , quali_round
     , qtime
from    qualies
unpivot include nulls (
                    qtime for quali_round in (q1, q2, q3)
                    )
/
DRIVER          NAME                    QU QTIME
--------------- --------------------    -- --------
Robert Doornbos Chinese Grand Prix      Q1 1:46.387
Robert Doornbos Chinese Grand Prix      Q2 1:45.747
Robert Doornbos Chinese Grand Prix      Q3 1:48.021
Robert Doornbos Japanese Grand Prix     Q1 1:32.402
Robert Doornbos Japanese Grand Prix     Q2
Robert Doornbos Japanese Grand Prix     Q3
Robert Doornbos Brazilian Grand Prix Q1 1:12.530
Robert Doornbos Brazilian Grand Prix Q2 1:12.591
Robert Doornbos Brazilian Grand Prix Q3
< rows omitted for brevity >
```

Summary

This chapter discussed analytic functions and the most common use cases. Once you start using analytic functions, the more possibilities you recognize. There also lies a warning: analytic functions are applied after the result set is determined (join, where, group by, having) and before the final sort (order by). When you use an analytic function with a distinct operator, maybe you need an aggregate instead of an analytic function.

At the end of the chapter, pivoting and unpivoting a result set are discussed. To pivot results, the measures are aggregated in the pivot clause. With pivot, rows are turned into columns, and with unpivot, columns are turned into rows.

CHAPTER 3

Joins

Discussing join syntax with other database developers almost always leads to discussing the preferred style of joining data sources. Some are fanatic supporters of ANSI-style joins, while others prefer to stick to the traditional way. Our preferred method is the former—ANSI style.

This chapter discusses the advantages of using ANSI-style joins and describes the most common joins: outer, inner, and full. It also covers some lesser-known joins, like the partition outer and the lateral join. Where tables are mentioned, all types of data sources that can be used in a query are meant, such as views or materialized views.

Why Choose ANSI Joins?

The main advantage of using ANSI-style join syntax is the separation of join and filter criteria. Where the traditional syntax mixes the join and filter criteria, this is simply *not* possible with ANSI-style. The join criteria specifies *how* the tables are joined, while the filter criteria is located in the where clause.

The traditional style of joining tables is listing the table in the from clause and specifying the join criteria in the where clause. When the data needs extra filters, they also go into the where clause. This could potentially lead to confusion as to whether a condition in the where clause is a join or filter criteria.

ANSI-style syntax forces to specify the join criteria in either an on clause or a using clause. The filter criteria *always* go in the where clause.

Forgetting a join criteria with the traditional style leads to a cartesian product.

You cannot create an accidental cartesian product with ANSI-style syntax. When the intention is to create a cartesian product traditionally, the code needs to be properly commented to signal the next developer that this cartesian product is, in fact, intentional. An ANSI-style cartesian product is clear as day: cross join. This signals to

© Alex Nuijten, Patrick Barel 2023
A. Nuijten and P. Barel, *Modern Oracle Database Programming*, https://doi.org/10.1007/978-1-4842-9166-5_3

the next developer that this cartesian product is intentional without needing additional comments.

Outer joining tables together is not as intuitive as the traditional style. Should the outer join notation (+) go on the outer joined table, or should it be on the other? The use of (+) must be applied to all outer joined columns for the join to remain an outer join. Database developers from other database vendors will not be familiar with this Oracle-style syntax of outer joining.

ANSI-style outer joins are easier to understand. To write a query that performs an outer join of tables A and B and should return all rows from A (the table located to the *left* of the join keyword), specify the left outer join in the from clause. With the traditional style of writing an outer join, the outer join operator (+) must be applied to all columns of table B, which can be counterintuitive.

Under the hood, it doesn't matter which style of join is used. They are rewritten by the optimizer and executed in the same way.

Regardless of your join style preference, a common agreement can be that both styles shouldn't be mixed within the same query. Although this is possible, it is considered a bad practice. Most commonly, the query style is agreed upon by all database developers at the start of a project.

Natural Joins

A natural join is where the join criteria are derived from the name of the columns in both tables. This abomination is in the ANSI standard but shouldn't be used.

The DRIVERS, RESULTS, and CONSTRUCTORS tables are used to demonstrate the absurdity of the natural join. Using natural joins, these tables are combined, and the following query is executed.

```
select ctr.name
       ,drv.forename
       ,drv.surname
   from f1data.drivers drv
natural
   join f1data.results rst
natural
   join f1data.constructors ctr
```

```
/

no rows selected
```

There are no results for this query, and the reason for this becomes clear when the explain plan is inspected.

```
explain plan for
select ctr.name
     , drv.forename
     , drv.surname
from   f1data.drivers drv
natural
join   f1data.results rst
natural
join   f1data.constructors ctr
/

select *
from   table (dbms_xplan.display (format => 'BASIC +PREDICATE' ))
/
```

```
-----------------------------------------------------------
| Id  | Operation                    | Name         |
-----------------------------------------------------------
|   0 | SELECT STATEMENT             |              |
|*  1 |  HASH JOIN                    |              |
|   2 |   JOIN FILTER CREATE          | :BF0000      |
|*  3 |    HASH JOIN                  |              |
|   4 |     TABLE ACCESS STORAGE FULL| CONSTRUCTORS |
|   5 |     TABLE ACCESS STORAGE FULL| DRIVERS      |
|   6 |   JOIN FILTER USE             | :BF0000      |
|*  7 |    TABLE ACCESS STORAGE FULL  | RESULTS      |
-----------------------------------------------------------

Predicate Information (identified by operation id):
-----------------------------------------------------

   1 - access("RST"."CONSTRUCTORID"="CTR"."CONSTRUCTORID" AND
            "DRV"."DRIVERID"="RST"."DRIVERID")
```

```
3 - access("DRV"."URL"="CTR"."URL" AND
            "DRV"."NATIONALITY"="CTR"."NATIONALITY")
7 - storage(SYS_OP_BLOOM_FILTER(:BF0000,"RST"."DRIVERID"))
    filter(SYS_OP_BLOOM_FILTER(:BF0000,"RST"."DRIVERID"))
```

As seen in the access predicate information, the join criteria performed by the natural joins are based on the similarity between column names. Some are correct, like constructorid and driverid, but others don't make sense, like nationality or url. Again, this abomination in the ANSI standard shouldn't be used.

Inner Joins

The most common method of tying two tables together is done with an inner join. Tables are joined together on certain columns specified in the join criteria. The following example shows an inner join between the drivers and the results table.

```
select crt.raceid
     , crt.points
     , csr.name
     , csr.nationality
from   f1data.constructors csr
inner
join   f1data.constructorresults crt
  on   csr.constructorid = crt.constructorid
/
```

RACEID	POINTS	NAME	NATIONALITY
18	14	McLaren	British
18	8	BMW Sauber	German
18	9	Williams	British
18	5	Renault	French
18	2	Toro Rosso	Italian
18	1	Ferrari	Italian
18	0	Toyota	Japanese
18	0	Super Aguri	Japanese
18	0	Red Bull	Austrian
18	0	Force India	Indian

In this query, it is explicitly stated that this concerns an inner join by use of the optional keyword: `inner`. The join criteria are specified in the `on` clause. It is also possible to use the `using` clause, which implies a common column between the two tables. The `using` clause makes an equality comparison between the two columns. The `on` clause allows other types of comparison between the joining columns. The following example is equivalent to the previous example, but now uses the `using` clause in the join criteria.

```
select crt.raceid
     , crt.points
     , csr.name
     , csr.nationality
from   f1data.constructors csr
join   f1data.constructorresults crt
using  (constructorid)
/
```

RACEID	POINTS	NAME	NATIONALITY
18	14	McLaren	British
18	8	BMW Sauber	German
18	9	Williams	British
18	5	Renault	French
18	2	Toro Rosso	Italian
18	1	Ferrari	Italian
18	0	Toyota	Japanese
18	0	Super Aguri	Japanese
18	0	Red Bull	Austrian
18	0	Force India	Indian

```
< rows removed for brevity >
```

The `using` clause cannot specify the columns used in the join condition with an alias anywhere in the query. To be clear, the columns can be used; however, they can't be prefixed by the table alias. After all, the columns that join the tables are common columns to join the tables together.

Outer Joins

An outer join shows rows from one table, regardless of having a match in the other table. There can be constructors that don't have any results yet.

With ANSI-style outer join, the order of the tables as they appear in the query is important. A left outer join directs that *all rows* from the table located on the left of the join keyword are shown, even if there is no match with the table on the right of the join keyword. A right outer join does the same, but now regarding the rows on the right side of the join keyword.

Note   The most common way of writing outer joins that can be found in forums and examples around the internet is to use a left outer join. Maybe the reason for this is that the leading table is often written down first. Even though common, it is not a requirement, but still a best practice. In this chapter and throughout the book, a left outer join is used.

In the following example, all constructors are shown even when they don't have any points in the constructor results table.

```
select crt.raceid
     , crt.points
     , csr.name
     , csr.nationality
from   f1data.constructors csr
left outer
join   f1data.constructorresults crt
  on   csr.constructorid = crt.constructorid
/
    RACEID     POINTS NAME              NATIONALITY
---------- ---------- ---------------- -----------
        18         14 McLaren           British
        19         10 McLaren           British
        20          4 McLaren           British
< results omitted for brevity >
                      Pawl              American
```

```
Rae           American
Adams         American
```

Note   The outer and inner keywords are optional, but it is highly recommended to use them for syntactic clarity.

Almost Outer Joins

An "almost outer join" is where an outer join is written in the query, but it has been negated by extra conditions in the where clause.

In the following example, the objective is to see all constructors and their constructor results; however, if the team is Red Bull, you want to also see their points. For other teams, this information is irrelevant and doesn't need to be shown. The first attempt for this query is the following.

```
select crt.raceid
     , crt.points
     , csr.name
     , csr.nationality
from   f1data.constructors csr
left outer
join   f1data.constructorresults crt
  on   csr.constructorid = crt.constructorid
where  csr.constructorref = 'red_bull'
/
   RACEID      POINTS NAME            NATIONALITY
---------- ---------- --------------- ----------------
      1062          2 Red Bull        Austrian
      1063       12.5 Red Bull        Austrian
< results omitted for brevity >
      1072         18 Red Bull        Austrian
      1073         26 Red Bull        Austrian
      1074          0 Red Bull        Austrian
      1075         37 Red Bull        Austrian
```

```
     1076              18 Red Bull        Austrian
     1077              58 Red Bull        Austrian
```

336 rows selected.

As seen in the example, there is an outer join in the query, but the results only show Red Bull data. The constructor results for all other constructors are missing. This query doesn't show the results that were the objective stated earlier. To get the requested result set, the filter criteria must be a join criteria.

```
select crt.raceid
     , crt.points
     , csr.name
     , csr.nationality
from   f1data.constructors csr
left outer
join   f1data.constructorresults crt
  on       csr.constructorid  = crt.constructorid
     and csr.constructorref = 'red_bull'
/
     RACEID     POINTS NAME             NATIONALITY
---------- ---------- ---------------- ----------------
     1062          2 Red Bull         Austrian
     1063       12.5 Red Bull         Austrian
< results omitted for brevity >
                      Alpine F1 Team  French
                      McLaren         British
                      Martini         French
                      Pawl            American
                      Cooper-BRM      British
```

546 rows selected.

Now the query shows the results the way specified, only points for team Red Bull.

Full Outer Joins

The data model doesn't have a good example where a full outer join can be applied, but for demonstration purposes, the foreign key between RACES and CIRCUITS is changed from mandatory to optional. The idea is that it should be possible to schedule a race in the future where the circuit is unknown. It is also possible to have a circuit, but there are no races for it yet.

In each table, an extra record is added with fictitious data.

```
Insert into f1data.races
( raceid
, year
, round
, circuitid
, name
, race_date
)
values
( 0
, 2023
, 42
, null
, 'Hitchhiker Race'
, date '2023-10-07'
)
/
insert into f1data.circuits
( circuitid
, circuitref
, name
, location
, country
)
values
( 0
, 'brabantbaan'
```

```
, 'Brabant Baan'
, 'Oosterhout'
, 'Netherlands')
/
```

In the following example, a full outer join is performed, and the results are filtered to only show the rows that were just added in the preceding code.

```
select rce.name as race
     , rce.race_date
     , cct.name as circuit
     , cct.location
from   f1data.races rce
full outer
join   f1data.circuits cct
  on   rce.circuitid = cct.circuitid
where     rce.rowid is null
       or cct.rowid is null
/
RACE            RACE_DATE CIRCUIT          LOCATION
--------------- --------- ---------------- -----------
Hitchhiker Race 07-OCT-23 Brabant Baan     Oosterhout
```

A record from the RACES table is shown, even when there is no circuit to host the event, and a circuit is shown where no race is planned.

Cross Joins

In a cartesian product, all records from the first table are joined with the records from the second table. Using the ANSI join syntax, it is very clear that this is on purpose and not because a join condition is missing by accident. In ANSI join syntax, this is called a cross join. The following example creates a cartesian product of drivers; the drivers table is joined with itself. To show the effect of the cross join, a count is used.

```
select count(*)
from   f1data.drivers drv
```

```
/
   COUNT(*)
----------
       854
```

There are 854 drivers in the table. When this table is joined to itself as a cartesian product, all possible combinations of drivers are made, resulting in 854 × 854 records: 729316 records.

```
select count(*)
from    f1data.drivers drv
cross
join    f1data.drivers drv2
/
   COUNT(*)
----------
    729316
```

Because of the explicit `cross join` syntax, it is clear to the next developer reading this code that the cartesian product is on purpose.

Partitioned Outer Joins

A regular outer join remedies the situation where there is a missing matched row in the join condition by adding a null record to the result set. However, there are situations when a single row added to the result set is insufficient.

Earlier in the chapter, an extra race was added to the calendar. There are no race results for this race. The objective is to show a result for each driver for this race, even if there is no result (which there isn't).

The tables involved are RACES, RESULTS, and DRIVERS (to show each driver's name). A first attempt would be to outer join the results to the races and the drivers.

```
select rce.name
     , drv.forename||' '||drv.surname as driver
     , rst.result_number
from    f1data.races rce
left outer
```

```
join   f1data.results rst
  on   rce.raceid = rst.raceid
left outer
join   f1data.drivers drv
  on   drv.driverid = rst.driverid
where  rce.raceid = 0
/
NAME              DRIVER            RESULT_NUMBER
---------------   ---------------   -------------
Hitchhiker Race
```

The result is not what is requested. There is only one row for the race. There are no drivers listed, which is requested. The outer join to RESULTS only adds a single row as there is no match, but it should add a row for each driver. The RESULTS table should be subdivided by driverid and outer joined to the RACES table; that way, there is a record for each driver. By adding the partition by clause to the table, the outer join is *per partition* instead of the whole table. As the partition is per driverid, each driver has a RESULTS record. Because there is a record of the result for each driver, it is no longer necessary to have an outer join to the drivers table. The following query shows the partition outer join only for the drivers in the current season (2022).

```
select rce.name
     , drv.forename||' '||drv.surname as driver
     , rst.result_number
from   f1data.races rce
left outer
join   f1data.results rst partition by (rst.driverid)
  on   rce.raceid = rst.raceid
join   f1data.drivers drv
  on   drv.driverid = rst.driverid
where  rce.raceid = 0
and    drv.driverid in ( 1, 4, 830, 815, 847
                       , 844, 832, 846, 839
                       , 20, 822, 817, 842
                       , 855, 854, 825, 840
                       , 852, 848, 849)
```

```
/
NAME            DRIVER              RESULT_NUMBER
--------------- ------------------- -------------
Hitchhiker Race Lewis Hamilton
Hitchhiker Race Fernando Alonso
Hitchhiker Race Sebastian Vettel
Hitchhiker Race Sergio Pérez
Hitchhiker Race Daniel Ricciardo
Hitchhiker Race Valtteri Bottas
Hitchhiker Race Kevin Magnussen
Hitchhiker Race Max Verstappen
Hitchhiker Race Carlos Sainz
Hitchhiker Race Esteban Ocon
Hitchhiker Race Lance Stroll
Hitchhiker Race Pierre Gasly
Hitchhiker Race Charles Leclerc
Hitchhiker Race Lando Norris
Hitchhiker Race George Russell
Hitchhiker Race Alexander Albon
Hitchhiker Race Nicholas Latifi
Hitchhiker Race Yuki Tsunoda
Hitchhiker Race Mick Schumacher
Hitchhiker Race Guanyu Zhou
```

When the records are not filtered to only show data for certain drivers, there is a record for each driver listed in the RESULTS table. Since the results table has records for all races since the 1950s, there would be more data.

Lateral Joins

You cannot join a table to a correlated subquery unless a lateral join is used. With a lateral inline view, you can specify tables that appear to the left of the lateral inline view in the from clause of a query.

The most common use case for a lateral join is to convert JSON documents to a relational format using the JSON_TABLE operator or similarly converted XML documents with the XML_TABLE operator.

The following query shows a select group of drivers and their points in the driverstandings table, but only the first two (ordered by the highest points) and if points are scored. There is a correlation from the lateral inline view to the drivers table in the driverid column.

```
select drv.driverid
     , drv.forename ||' '||drv.surname as driver
     , dsg.points
     , dsg.position
from    f1data.drivers drv
cross
join lateral
        (select dsg.points
              , dsg.position
         from    f1data.driverstandings dsg
         where   dsg.driverid = drv.driverid
         and     dsg.points > 0
         order   by dsg.points desc
         fetch   first 2 rows only) dsg
where   drv.driverid in ( 855, 854, 840, 852, 848, 849)
order   by driverid desc
/
```

DRIVERID	DRIVER	POINTS	POSITION
855	Guanyu Zhou	6	17
855	Guanyu Zhou	6	18
854	Mick Schumacher	12	15
854	Mick Schumacher	12	15
852	Yuki Tsunoda	32	14
852	Yuki Tsunoda	20	14
849	Nicholas Latifi	7	17
849	Nicholas Latifi	7	16
848	Alexander Albon	105	7

```
848 Alexander Albon        93          8
840 Lance Stroll           75         11
840 Lance Stroll           74         10
```

In the results, two columns were selected from the correlated subquery. With a scalar subquery, this would not be possible. A scalar subquery can only return a single value.

Note   In addition to `cross join lateral`, you can also use `inner join lateral`; however, an inner join also requires a join condition (on clause or `using` clause). Because there is already a correlation between the table and the inline view, having a join condition is superfluous and doesn't contribute to readability or maintainability. It is not recommended to use `inner join lateral`.

The `cross apply` join is a variation of the `cross join` and can use a correlated subquery, unlike the latter. The same results from the preceding example can be achieved using a `cross apply` instead of `cross join lateral`. In the following example, the `cross apply` join is applied.

```
select drv.driverid
     , drv.forename ||' '||drv.surname as driver
     , dsg.points
from    f1data.drivers drv
cross
apply  (select dsg.points
             , dsg.driverid
        from    f1data.driverstandings dsg
        where   dsg.driverid = drv.driverid
        and     dsg.points > 0
        order   by dsg.points desc
        fetch   first 2 rows only
        ) dsg
where   drv.driverid in ( 855, 854, 840, 852, 848, 849)
order   by driverid desc
/
```

```
    DRIVERID DRIVER                      POINTS
    ---------- -------------------- ----------
         855 Guanyu  Zhou                   5
         855 Guanyu  Zhou                   5
         854 Mick  Schumacher               4
         852 Yuki  Tsunoda                 32
         852 Yuki  Tsunoda                 20
         849 Nicholas  Latifi               7
         849 Nicholas  Latifi               7
         848 Alexander  Albon             105
         848 Alexander  Albon              93
         840 Lance  Stroll                 75
         840 Lance  Stroll                 74
```

To demonstrate the outer apply join, an extra driver is added to the drivers table.

```
insert into f1data.drivers
( driverid
, driverref
, driver_number
, code
, forename
, surname
)
values
( 0
, 'alxntn'
, 53
, 'ALX'
, 'Alex'
, 'Nuijten'
)
/
```

The `outer apply` join is a variation of the left outer join and can use a correlated inline view. The following example shows the same results as earlier but includes the extra driver that was just created and has no driver standings record (he's not that good).

```
select drv.driverid
     , drv.forename ||' '||drv.surname as driver
     , dsg.points
from   f1data.drivers drv
outer
apply  (select dsg.points
             , dsg.driverid
        from   f1data.driverstandings dsg
        where  dsg.driverid = drv.driverid
        and    dsg.points > 0
        order  by dsg.points desc
        fetch  first 2 rows only
       ) dsg
where  drv.driverid in (0, 855, 854, 840, 852, 848, 849)
order  by driverid desc
/
 DRIVERID DRIVER              POINTS
---------- ------------------ ----------
       855 Guanyu Zhou              5
       855 Guanyu Zhou              5
       854 Mick Schumacher          4
       852 Yuki Tsunoda            32
       852 Yuki Tsunoda            20
       849 Nicholas Latifi          7
       849 Nicholas Latifi          7
       848 Alexander Albon        105
       848 Alexander Albon         93
       840 Lance Stroll            75
       840 Lance Stroll            74
         0 Alex Nuijten

12 rows selected.
```

Because of the `outer apply` join, the newly added driver is also listed even though he has no points.

Summary

This chapter covered ANSI joins. The separation of join and filter criteria makes these types of joins significantly more elegant than the traditional method of joining tables. There will always be a discussion between developers on the benefits of one over the other, and it will always be a matter of preference. Choose what you're most comfortable with but know the possibilities of ANSI joins and know how to interpret and apply them when needed. Once you embrace ANSI joins, you will never go back.

There is one thing that both sides of the discussion can hopefully agree upon: don't mix the traditional syntax with ANSI joins in a single query.

CHAPTER 4

Finding Patterns

Oracle Database 12c introduced row pattern matching, where it is possible to analyze patterns in sets of data. The `match_recognize` clause implements this. To a certain extent, analytic functions can also be used to do some rudimentary pattern matching, but it has its limitations. Other workarounds to find patterns in a sequence of rows were difficult to write, often hard to understand, and inefficient to execute. The `match_recognize` clause solves these problems using native SQL to allow pattern detection in data sets.

Looking for Contracts

The data model has no information about the contracts between teams and drivers. Maybe the contracts can be deduced by looking at the races. When a driver races for a particular team, you can assume there is a contract between them.

There is information about races, drivers, and teams (constructors). The assumption is made that during a race, the driver was under contract by the constructor and that the contract starts at the first race of the season and ends with the last race of the season. The following query retrieves information about Kimi Räikkönen over the years.

```
select rcs.year
     , ctr.name            as constructor
     , min (rcs.race_date) as startrace
     , max (rcs.race_date) as endrace
  from f1data.results rsl
  join f1data.races rcs
    on rsl.raceid = rcs.raceid
  join f1data.constructors ctr
    on ctr.constructorid = rsl.constructorid
 where rsl.driverid = 8 -- Kimi Räikkönen
```

© Alex Nuijten, Patrick Barel 2023
A. Nuijten and P. Barel, *Modern Oracle Database Programming*, https://doi.org/10.1007/978-1-4842-9166-5_4

```
group by rcs.year
        ,ctr.name
order by rcs.year
/
```

```
    YEAR CONSTRUCTO STARTRACE ENDRACE
---------- ---------- --------- ---------
    2001 Sauber     04-MAR-01 14-OCT-01
    2002 McLaren    03-MAR-02 13-OCT-02
    2003 McLaren    09-MAR-03 12-OCT-03
    2004 McLaren    07-MAR-04 24-OCT-04
    2005 McLaren    06-MAR-05 16-OCT-05
    2006 McLaren    12-MAR-06 22-OCT-06
    2007 Ferrari    18-MAR-07 21-OCT-07
    2008 Ferrari    16-MAR-08 02-NOV-08
    2009 Ferrari    29-MAR-09 01-NOV-09
    2012 Lotus F1   18-MAR-12 25-NOV-12
    2013 Lotus F1   17-MAR-13 03-NOV-13
    2014 Ferrari    16-MAR-14 23-NOV-14
    2015 Ferrari    15-MAR-15 29-NOV-15
    2016 Ferrari    20-MAR-16 27-NOV-16
    2017 Ferrari    26-MAR-17 26-NOV-17
    2018 Ferrari    25-MAR-18 25-NOV-18
    2019 Alfa Romeo 17-MAR-19 01-DEC-19
    2020 Alfa Romeo 05-JUL-20 13-DEC-20
    2021 Alfa Romeo 28-MAR-21 12-DEC-21
```

This result set is based on the results of the races over the years by Kimi Räikkönen for different constructors. His career started with Sauber, followed by McLaren, Ferrari, Lotus, Ferrari again, and ended with Alfa Romeo.

The objective is to group consecutive values, meaning that when the constructor remains the same season after season, they collapse into a single group. The years when Kimi raced with McLaren would be collapsed into a single group: 2002 to 2006.

The preceding query is the *input* to the pattern-matching `match_recognize` clause. In the following example, it is named `races` and used in the subquery factoring clause (`with` clause).

The pattern we want groups the records based on the same constructors with respect to *consecutive* years. That would mean that there are two separate periods in which Kimi was under contract by Ferrari.

In looking for consecutive patterns in a data set, sorting order is important. In this case, the sorting is done on year, which makes the most sense. This is implemented with `order` by in the `match_recognize` clause:

```
order by year
```

Classifying the Records

Before you can look for a pattern, each row must be classified. How rows are classified depends on the requirement. The following definition compares the current row's constructor to the *first* one in the group.

```
define eq as constructor = first (constructor)
```

For the first row in the result set, the start of the group is the current row (Sauber). The second row in the result set is the start of the next group (McLaren). The third row still belongs to the McLaren group, and so on. With this definition in place, the pattern can be determined. The pattern is defined as follows.

```
pattern (eq+)
```

This means that one or more of the records classified as "eq" belong in the same group. In the pattern clause, regular expressions can be used, which specify the pattern that needs to be matched in the data set. Table 4-1 overviews the most common regular expression quantifiers.

Table 4-1. *Regular Expressions Quantifiers*

Type	Description
*	Zero or more
+	One or more
?	Zero or one
{n}	Exactly n
{n,}	At least n
{,m}	At most m
{n, m}	Between n and m
|	Alteration; try this, else try that

The following query uses the built-in match_number() function to show the different groups in this data set.

```
with race_years as (
select rcs.year
     , ctr.name as constructor
     , min (rcs.race_date) as startrace
     , max (rcs.race_date) as endrace
from   f1data.results rsl
join   f1data.races rcs
  on   rsl.raceid = rcs.raceid
join   f1data.constructors ctr
  on   ctr.constructorid = rsl.constructorid
where  rsl.driverid = 8 -- Kimi Räikkönen
group  by rcs.year
       , ctr.name
)
select rce.mnr
     , rce.constructor
     , rce.startrace
     , rce.endrace
```

```
from    race_years
match_recognize (
        order by year
        measures
          match_number() as mnr
        all rows per match
        pattern (eq+)
        define eq as constructor = first (constructor)
      ) rce
order  by year
/
```

MNR CONSTRUCTOR	STARTRACE ENDRACE
---------- ------------------------------	--------- ---------
1 Sauber	04-MAR-01 14-OCT-01
2 McLaren	03-MAR-02 13-OCT-02
2 McLaren	09-MAR-03 12-OCT-03
2 McLaren	07-MAR-04 24-OCT-04
2 McLaren	06-MAR-05 16-OCT-05
2 McLaren	12-MAR-06 22-OCT-06
3 Ferrari	18-MAR-07 21-OCT-07
3 Ferrari	16-MAR-08 02-NOV-08
3 Ferrari	29-MAR-09 01-NOV-09
4 Lotus F1	18-MAR-12 25-NOV-12
4 Lotus F1	17-MAR-13 03-NOV-13
5 Ferrari	16-MAR-14 23-NOV-14
5 Ferrari	15-MAR-15 29-NOV-15
5 Ferrari	20-MAR-16 27-NOV-16
5 Ferrari	26-MAR-17 26-NOV-17
5 Ferrari	25-MAR-18 25-NOV-18
6 Alfa Romeo	17-MAR-19 01-DEC-19
6 Alfa Romeo	05-JUL-20 13-DEC-20
6 Alfa Romeo	28-MAR-21 12-DEC-21

As seen in the results, the column MNR shows the `match_number()` to identify the different groups. It is a consecutive numbering of the matches found. In the preceding query, all rows are shown. The `all rows per match` clause returns all rows, so it is easy to identify which records are grouped. The `all rows per match` clause also ensures that all columns of the input data set are returned, as well as everything listed in the `measures` clause.

Note   The table alias goes after the final parenthesis of the `match_recognize` clause.

Now that it is clear which records should be bundled together, the query can be modified to only show `one row per match`. The measures are expressions that are usable in other parts of the query. The following are the measures of interest.

- The constructor of the group: For this, the `first (constructor)` expression is used. In this case, it could also be `last (constructor)` as the constructor remains the same in the group.

- The first year under contract for this constructor: The expression for this measure is `first (startrace)`.

- The last year under contract for this constructor: The expression for this measure is `last (endrace)`.

```
with race_years as (
select rcs.year
     , ctr.name as constructor
     , min (rcs.race_date) as startrace
     , max (rcs.race_date) as endrace
from   f1data.results rsl
join   f1data.races rcs
  on   rsl.raceid = rcs.raceid
join   f1data.constructors ctr
  on   ctr.constructorid = rsl.constructorid
where  rsl.driverid = 8
group  by rcs.year
```

```
      , ctr.name
)
select rce.constructor
     , rce.strt
     , rce.stp
from   race_years
match_recognize (
        order by year
        measures
          first (constructor) as constructor
        , extract (year from first (startrace)) as strt
        , extract (year from last (endrace)) as stp
        one row per match
        pattern (eq+)
        define eq as constructor = first (constructor)
        ) rce
 order by rce.strt
/
CONSTRUCTOR                     STRT       STP
------------------------ ---------- ----------
Sauber                          2001       2001
McLaren                         2002       2006
Ferrari                         2007       2009
Lotus F1                        2012       2013
Ferrari                         2014       2018
Alfa Romeo                      2019       2021

6 rows selected.
```

The extract function is used to get the year. It shows only the year rather than a specific date.

Note   The expressions in the measures clause must *always* be aliased, even when the expression is a column of the input table.

Logical Groups

Just like with analytic functions, it is in the match_recognize clause also possible to partition the input data set. That way, the pattern is applied to each logical data set group. The next example determines the contracts, in the same way as before, for the years after 2021 and this time for all drivers. The subquery factoring clause is amended to include the driver's name. The following partition clause is added to the match_ recognize clause.

```
partition by driver
```

This creates logical groups, one for each driver, and applies the same pattern detection. The following is the complete query to determine the contracts for each driver since 2021.

```
with race_years as (
select drv.forename || ' ' || drv.surname as driver
      , rcs.year
      , ctr.name as constructor
      ,min (rcs.race_date) as startrace
      ,max (rcs.race_date) as endrace
from    f1data.results rsl
join    f1data.races rcs
   on   rsl.raceid = rcs.raceid
join    f1data.constructors ctr
   on   ctr.constructorid = rsl.constructorid
join    f1data.drivers drv
   on   drv.driverid = rsl.driverid
where   rcs.year >= 2021
group   by rcs.year
          ,ctr.name
          ,drv.forename
          ,drv.surname
)
select rce.driver
      , rce.constructor
      , rce.strt
```

```
        , rce.stp
from    race_years
match_recognize (
        partition by driver
        order by year
        measures
          first (constructor) as constructor
        , extract (year from first (startrace)) as strt
        , extract (year from last (endrace)) as stp
        , match_number() as mnr
        one row per match
        pattern (eq+)
        define eq as constructor = first (constructor)
        ) rce
order  by rce.constructor
        , rce.strt
/
```

DRIVER	CONSTRUCTOR	STRT	STP
Robert Kubica	Alfa Romeo	2021	2021
Antonio Giovinazzi	Alfa Romeo	2021	2021
Kimi Räikkönen	Alfa Romeo	2021	2021
Valtteri Bottas	Alfa Romeo	2022	2022
Guanyu Zhou	Alfa Romeo	2022	2022
Yuki Tsunoda	AlphaTauri	2021	2022
Pierre Gasly	AlphaTauri	2021	2022
Fernando Alonso	Alpine F1 Team	2021	2022
Esteban Ocon	Alpine F1 Team	2021	2022
Sebastian Vettel	Aston Martin	2021	2022
Lance Stroll	Aston Martin	2021	2022
Nico Hülkenberg	Aston Martin	2022	2022
Charles Leclerc	Ferrari	2021	2022
Carlos Sainz	Ferrari	2021	2022
Mick Schumacher	Haas F1 Team	2021	2022
Nikita Mazepin	Haas F1 Team	2021	2021

Kevin Magnussen	Haas F1 Team	2022	2022
Lando Norris	McLaren	2021	2022
Daniel Ricciardo	McLaren	2021	2022
Valtteri Bottas	Mercedes	2021	2021
Lewis Hamilton	Mercedes	2021	2022
George Russell	Mercedes	2022	2022
Sergio Pérez	Red Bull	2021	2022
Max Verstappen	Red Bull	2021	2022
George Russell	Williams	2021	2021
Nicholas Latifi	Williams	2021	2022
Alexander Albon	Williams	2022	2022
Nyck de Vries	Williams	2022	2022

Faster at the End

The elapsed time of each race is recorded in the LAPTIMES table. Often you hear that the lap times are shorter towards the end of a race because there is less fuel in the car, making the car lighter. However, tire degradation would cause laps to take longer. Let's put this theory to the test and examine what is really going on.

First, you must determine if a lap was slower or faster than the previous lap. The following are the definitions of faster and slower.

```
faster as laptime < prev (laptime)
slower as laptime > prev (laptime)
```

The definition compares the current lap time to the previous lap time with the prev () function.

In this case, all records need to be classified with either a FASTER or SLOWER tag, so all rows per match is used. The following pattern is used.

```
pattern ( faster* slower* )
```

The pattern reads zero or more records identified by FASTER followed by zero or more records identified as SLOWER. Putting everything together results in the following query.

```
with cota as (
select ltm.lap
     , numtodsinterval( ltm.milliseconds / 1000
                      , 'second') as laptime
from   f1data.laptimes ltm
where  ltm.raceid = 1093  -- Circuit of the Americas
and    ltm.driverid = 830 -- Max Verstappen
)
select *
from   cota
match_recognize (
         order by lap
         measures
           match_number() as mnr
          ,classifier() as cls
         all rows per match
         pattern (faster* slower* )
         define
           faster as laptime < prev (laptime)
         , slower as laptime > prev (laptime)
  )
order  by lap
/
       LAP        MNR CLS     LAPTIME
---------- ---------- ------- -------------------
         1          1         +00 00:01:41.343000
         2          2 SLOWER  +00 00:01:41.696000
         3          2 SLOWER  +00 00:01:41.893000
         4          2 SLOWER  +00 00:01:42.581000
         5          2 SLOWER  +00 00:01:42.870000
         6          3 FASTER  +00 00:01:42.826000
         7          3 FASTER  +00 00:01:42.314000
         8          3 SLOWER  +00 00:01:42.830000
         9          4 FASTER  +00 00:01:42.412000
        10          4 SLOWER  +00 00:01:42.492000
```

```
<< rows removed for brevity >>
            37         13 FASTER   +00 00:01:39.541000
            38         13 SLOWER   +00 00:01:40.211000
            39         13 SLOWER   +00 00:01:40.337000
            40         14 FASTER   +00 00:01:40.108000
            41         14 FASTER   +00 00:01:40.077000
            42         14 FASTER   +00 00:01:40.010000
            43         14 FASTER   +00 00:01:39.776000
            44         14 SLOWER   +00 00:01:40.410000
            45         15 FASTER   +00 00:01:39.986000
            46         15 FASTER   +00 00:01:39.945000
            47         15 SLOWER   +00 00:01:40.058000
            48         15 SLOWER   +00 00:01:40.271000
            49         16 FASTER   +00 00:01:40.230000
            50         16 SLOWER   +00 00:01:40.830000
            51         17 FASTER   +00 00:01:40.152000
            52         17 SLOWER   +00 00:01:40.431000
            53         18 FASTER   +00 00:01:40.297000
            54         18 FASTER   +00 00:01:40.168000
            55         18 SLOWER   +00 00:01:40.674000
            56         19 FASTER   +00 00:01:40.654000
```

The first lap doesn't have a classification, as there is no lap to compare it to. The second through fifth lap is classified as slower, which can be deducted from the data in the laptime column. Finally, lap 6 is the first time a lap was faster than the previous one.

Note   In the preceding result set, there is also a column MNR which shows the match number. The records with the same match_number belong to the same matching pattern. Lap 5 is the last lap to match the pattern. Lap 6 is classified as a faster record, which restarts the pattern again.

Now it is also possible to analyze if there are *consecutive* laps that were faster than the previous ones. When more than two consecutive laps are faster, these should go in the output. The following is the pattern.

```
faster{2,}
```

The pattern reads at least two records classified as faster.

```
with cota as (
select ltm.lap
     , numtodsinterval( ltm.milliseconds / 1000
                      , 'second') as laptime
from    f1data.laptimes ltm
where   ltm.raceid = 1093  -- Circuit of the Americas
and     ltm.driverid = 830 -- Max Verstappen
)
select first_lap
     , last_lap
     , lap_count
from    cota
match_recognize (
          order by lap
          measures
            first (lap) as first_lap
          , last (lap)  as last_lap
          , count(*)    as lap_count
          one row per match
          pattern ( faster{2,} )
          define
            faster as laptime < prev (laptime)
   )
/

FIRST_LAP   LAST_LAP  LAP_COUNT
----------  ----------  ----------
         6          7           2
        15         16           2
        25         26           2
        40         43           4
        45         46           2
        53         54           2

6 rows selected.
```

Starting in lap 40, each lap was faster than the previous one and lasted four laps. The count of faster laps is also included in the output.

When relaxing the pattern a little bit, let's say it's all right to have one slower lap in a fast streak. The pattern looks like the following.

```
faster{2,} slower {1} faster{1,}
```

The pattern reads two (or more) faster laps, followed by one (and only one) slower lap, followed by one (or more) faster laps.

With this pattern in place and with the definition of what defines a slower lap, the results are as follows.

```
FIRST_LAP    LAST_LAP   LAP_COUNT
---------- ---------- ----------
         6          9          4
        40         46          7
        53         56          4
```

Based on these results, it is very plausible that the laps get faster—despite tire degradation—toward the end of the race.

Winning?

The CONSTRUCTORSTANDINGS table contains each race, constructor, and recorded cumulative wins. The following is the output for the first five rounds of the 2022 season for Ferrari and Red Bull only.

```
select ctr.name
     , cts.wins
     , rcs.name as race_name
     , rcs.round
     , rcs.year
from   f1data.constructorstandings cts
join   f1data.constructors ctr
  on   ctr.constructorid = cts.constructorid
join   f1data.races rcs
  on   rcs.raceid = cts.raceid
```

```
where  rcs.year = 2022
and    ctr.constructorid in (6,9)
and    rcs.round <= 5
order  by ctr.name
       , rcs.round
/
```

NAME	WINS	RACE_NAME	ROU	YEAR
Ferrari	1	Bahrain Grand Prix	1	2022
Ferrari	1	Saudi Arabian Grand Prix	2	2022
Ferrari	2	Australian Grand Prix	3	2022
Ferrari	2	Emilia Romagna Grand Prix	4	2022
Ferrari	2	Miami Grand Prix	5	2022
Red Bull	0	Bahrain Grand Prix	1	2022
Red Bull	1	Saudi Arabian Grand Prix	2	2022
Red Bull	1	Australian Grand Prix	3	2022
Red Bull	2	Emilia Romagna Grand Prix	4	2022
Red Bull	3	Miami Grand Prix	5	2022

The wins column has the cumulative number of wins. Ferrari won the first round but lost the second round leaving the number of wins at one. They did win the third round, so the wins increased to two, and so on.

Based on this data, the following definition of *winning* can be made.

```
winning as (wins > prev (wins))
```

The round is won when the current win count is larger than the previous win count. Similarly, the definition of not winning can be as follows.

```
not_winning as (wins = prev (wins))
```

When the current record's win count stays the same compared to the previous win count, some other teams must have won (i.e., the current record's team didn't win).

The following is the pattern to classify each record in the data set.

```
( winning | not_winning )
```

Meaning that a record is either classified as winning *or* not winning. Let's put this to the test.

```
with ctrs as (
select ctr.name
     , cts.wins
     , rcs.name as race_name
     , rcs.round
     , rcs.year
from    f1data.constructorstandings cts
join    f1data.constructors ctr
  on    ctr.constructorid = cts.constructorid
join    f1data.races rcs
  on    rcs.raceid = cts.raceid
where   rcs.year = 2022
and     ctr.constructorid in (6,9)
and     rcs.round <= 5
)
select round
     , race_name
     , name
     , cls
     , wins
from    ctrs
match_recognize (
        partition by name
                   , year
        order by round
        measures
          classifier () as cls
        , year as yr
        all rows per match
        pattern ( winning | not_winning )
        define
          winning as (wins > prev (wins))
        , not_winning as (wins = prev (wins))
```

```
    )
order  by year, round, name
/
ROU RACE_NAME                   NAME      CLS           WINS
--- ------------------------    --------  ------------  ----
  2 Saudi Arabian Grand Prix    Ferrari   NOT_WINNING      1
  2 Saudi Arabian Grand Prix    Red Bull  WINNING          1
  3 Australian Grand Prix       Ferrari   WINNING          2
  3 Australian Grand Prix       Red Bull  NOT_WINNING      1
  4 Emilia Romagna Grand Prix   Ferrari   NOT_WINNING      2
  4 Emilia Romagna Grand Prix   Red Bull  WINNING          2
  5 Miami Grand Prix            Ferrari   NOT_WINNING      2
  5 Miami Grand Prix            Red Bull  WINNING          3
```

Now there are only eight records in the result set. Round one is missing from the results. This record can't be compared to the previous one, and there is no classification yet.

Undefined Classification

One way to solve the problem of the missing first round is by adding an extra classification to the pattern.

```
pattern ( winning | not_winning | unknown )
```

An extra definition is expected to be added to the define clause, but that is not needed. The pattern is assumed to be true when it encounters an undefined definition. Since the first round does not match any of the other defined classifications, it is matched with the "always true" definition, which was named unknown. The first records in the result set would become the following.

```
ROU RACE_NAME                   NAME      CLS           WINS
--- ------------------------    --------  ------------  ----
  1 Bahrain Grand Prix          Ferrari   UNKNOWN          1
  1 Bahrain Grand Prix          Red Bull  UNKNOWN          0
  2 Saudi Arabian Grand Prix    Ferrari   NOT_WINNING      1
  2 Saudi Arabian Grand Prix    Red Bull  WINNING          1
```

This would solve the problem of missing records, but it is incorrect. Ferrari won the season's first race, but it is labeled as UNKNOWN. The same is true for Red Bull; it is known that they didn't win the first race. It might be tempting to change the definition of winning to the following.

```
winning as (wins > prev (wins) or wins = 1)
```

But this is not correct either; it would label the first race correctly for Ferrari, but the second race would also be labeled as WINNING for Ferrari (because the win count remains 1). Applying this changed definition would lead to these results.

```
ROU RACE_NAME                    NAME     CLS            WINS
--- ------------------------     -------- ------------   ----
  1 Bahrain Grand Prix           Ferrari  WINNING           1
  1 Bahrain Grand Prix           Red Bull UNKNOWN           0
  2 Saudi Arabian Grand Prix     Ferrari  WINNING           1
  2 Saudi Arabian Grand Prix     Red Bull WINNING           1
```

The solution would be to expand the definition of WINNING as follows.

```
winning as (wins > prev (wins)
        or (wins = 1 and round = 1))
```

This specifically checks for a win in the first round of the year. The match_recognize clause becomes the following.

```
match_recognize (
    partition by name
                ,year
    order by round
    measures
        classifier () as cls
    all rows per match
    pattern ( winning | not_winning )
    define
        winning as (wins > prev (wins)
                or (wins = 1 and round = 1))
```

```
, not_winning as (wins = prev (wins)
            or  wins = 0)
)
```

The following are the results.

```
ROU RACE_NAME                   NAME     CLS          WINS
--- ------------------------    -------- ------------ ----
  1 Bahrain Grand Prix          Ferrari  WINNING         1
  1 Bahrain Grand Prix          Red Bull NOT_WINNING     0
  2 Saudi Arabian Grand Prix    Ferrari  NOT_WINNING     1
  2 Saudi Arabian Grand Prix    Red Bull WINNING         1
  3 Australian Grand Prix       Ferrari  WINNING         2
  3 Australian Grand Prix       Red Bull NOT_WINNING     1
  4 Emilia Romagna Grand Prix   Ferrari  NOT_WINNING     2
  4 Emilia Romagna Grand Prix   Red Bull WINNING         2
  5 Miami Grand Prix            Ferrari  NOT_WINNING     2
  5 Miami Grand Prix            Red Bull WINNING         3
```

Each record now has the correct classification: WINNING or NOT_WINNING.

Longest Winning Streak

When this book was written, the 2022 season was still underway, and only the Ferrari and Red Bull teams had won a race. But which team had the most consecutive wins? Let's find out.

The last section identified a race as won using the following `define` clause.

```
winning as (wins > prev (wins)
      or (wins = 1 and round = 1))
```

With this definition in place, the following pattern can be applied to find at least one record with this classification.

```
( winning+ )
```

The following is the complete query to find the longest winning streak by a team.

```
with ctr as (
select ctr.name
     , cts.wins
     , rcs.name as race_name
     , rcs.round
     , rcs.year
from    f1data.constructorstandings cts
join    f1data.constructors ctr
  on    ctr.constructorid = cts.constructorid
join    f1data.races rcs
  on    rcs.raceid = cts.raceid
where   rcs.year = 2022
)
select *
from    ctr
match_recognize (
          partition by name
          order by round
          measures
            classifier () as cls
          , first (round) as first_win
          , last (round)  as last_win
          , count(*)       as race_count
          one row per match
          pattern ( winning+ )
          define
            winning as (wins > prev (wins)
                    or (wins = 1 and round = 1))
)
order  by race_count desc
/
```

```
NAME      CLS          FIRST_WIN   LAST_WIN RACE_COUNT
--------  ------------ ----------  ---------- ----------
Red Bull  WINNING             12          19          8
Red Bull  WINNING              4           9          6
Ferrari   WINNING             10          11          2
Red Bull  WINNING              2           2          1
Ferrari   WINNING              1           1          1
Ferrari   WINNING              3           3          1

6 rows selected.
```

Red Bull won eight consecutive races: rounds 12 through 19.

Pit Stops and Hazards

Analyzing the lap times can also give insights into when a pit stop occurs during the race. When a driver makes a pit stop, the next lap (the out lap) takes longer than the average time during the race. Similarly, hazardous situations can be detected. When there is a yellow flag situation, the speed of the cars needs to be reduced, which increases the lap times. When a driver makes a pit stop during a hazardous situation, always a good strategy, these are not detected.

Before the pattern matching can be used, the input data must be prepped. Besides the driver, laps, and lap times, the average lap time (per driver) is also needed. For this, the avg analytic function is used, like in the following example.

```
select drv.driverid
     , drv.forename||' '||drv.surname as driver
     , ltm.lap
     , ltm.milliseconds
     , avg (ltm.milliseconds)
           over (partition by drv.driverid
           ) as avg_laptime
from   f1data.laptimes ltm
join   f1data.drivers drv
  on   drv.driverid = ltm.driverid
where  ltm.raceid = 1093 -- Circuit of the Americas
```

```
order  by drv.driverid
          , ltm.lap
/
```

```
   DRIVERID DRIVER                    LAP MILLISECONDS AVG_LAPTIME
---------- ---------------- ---------- ------------ -----------
         1 Lewis Hamilton            1       102630  109584.107
         1 Lewis Hamilton            2       102325  109584.107
         1 Lewis Hamilton            3       102175  109584.107
         1 Lewis Hamilton            4       102798  109584.107
         1 Lewis Hamilton            5       103196  109584.107
         1 Lewis Hamilton            6       102576  109584.107
         1 Lewis Hamilton            7       102702  109584.107
         1 Lewis Hamilton            8       103212  109584.107
<< 977 rows omitted for brevity >>
       855 Guanyu Zhou             52       103373  110854.482
       855 Guanyu Zhou             53       105200  110854.482
       855 Guanyu Zhou             54       104102  110854.482
       855 Guanyu Zhou             55       103812  110854.482
       855 Guanyu Zhou             56       103881  110854.482
```

With the following definitions, the faster_than_avg and slow_lap can be defined as follows.

```
faster_than_avg as milliseconds < avg_laptime
```

```
slow_lap as milliseconds > avg_laptime
```

With the definitions in place, it's easiest to start by showing all records and classifying them using the following pattern.

```
faster_than_avg* slow_lap*
```

This leads to the following match_recognize clause.

```
match_recognize (
 partition by driverid
 order by lap
 measures
  classifier() as what
```

```
all rows per match
pattern (
  faster_than_avg* slow_lap*
)
define
    faster_than_avg as milliseconds < avg_laptime
  , slow_lap as milliseconds > avg_laptime
)
```

A closer look at Guanyu Zhou's first 26 laps and classifying each lap accordingly reveals the following.

DRIVER	LAP	MILLISECONDS	WHAT
Guanyu Zhou	1	112824	SLOW_LAP
Guanyu Zhou	2	105535	FASTER_THAN_AVG
Guanyu Zhou	3	104538	FASTER_THAN_AVG
Guanyu Zhou	4	104511	FASTER_THAN_AVG
Guanyu Zhou	5	104904	FASTER_THAN_AVG
Guanyu Zhou	6	104476	FASTER_THAN_AVG
Guanyu Zhou	7	104454	FASTER_THAN_AVG
Guanyu Zhou	8	105360	FASTER_THAN_AVG
Guanyu Zhou	9	105956	FASTER_THAN_AVG
Guanyu Zhou	10	127583	SLOW_LAP
Guanyu Zhou	11	103895	FASTER_THAN_AVG
Guanyu Zhou	12	104152	FASTER_THAN_AVG
Guanyu Zhou	13	104739	FASTER_THAN_AVG
Guanyu Zhou	14	103824	FASTER_THAN_AVG
Guanyu Zhou	15	103741	FASTER_THAN_AVG
Guanyu Zhou	16	104030	FASTER_THAN_AVG
Guanyu Zhou	17	104266	FASTER_THAN_AVG
Guanyu Zhou	18	134425	SLOW_LAP
Guanyu Zhou	19	138587	SLOW_LAP
Guanyu Zhou	20	144384	SLOW_LAP
Guanyu Zhou	21	142312	SLOW_LAP
Guanyu Zhou	22	133593	SLOW_LAP

Guanyu Zhou	23	169446 SLOW_LAP
Guanyu Zhou	24	184224 SLOW_LAP
Guanyu Zhou	25	139116 SLOW_LAP
Guanyu Zhou	26	105555 FASTER_THAN_AVG

As seen in the output, the first lap was slower than his average lap time. It is not likely that this is due to a pit stop or a hazardous situation. Lap 10 was a slow lap, so this could be due to a pit stop. It is also clear to see that something happened during laps 18 through 25, as the lap times are significantly slower than the others.

As stated, the lap following a pit stop takes longer. To determine which lap the pitlane was entered, one lap must be subtracted to get the correct lap number. This can be corrected in the final query.

Based on these assumptions, lap times increase after a pit stop for one lap and multiple laps when there is a hazardous situation. The following pattern can be deducted.

```
faster_than_avg{1} slow_lap{1,} faster_than_avg{1}
```

The pattern reads only one lap, which is faster than average, followed by one or more slow laps, followed by one (and only one) faster than an average lap. This eliminates the first lap when that one is a slow lap, like with Guanyu Zhou.

The following is the complete query to detect (possible) pit stops and hazardous situations.

```
with laps
as (
select drv.driverid
    , drv.forename||' '||drv.surname as driver
    , ltm.lap
    , ltm.milliseconds
    , avg (ltm.milliseconds)
        over (partition by drv.driverid) as avg_laptime
from   f1data.laptimes ltm
join   f1data.drivers drv
  on   drv.driverid = ltm.driverid
where  ltm.raceid = 1093 -- Circuit of the Americas
)
```

```
select driver
     , case lap_count
       when 1
       then 'Probably a pit stop in lap '||to_char (firstlap -1)
       else
          '** Hazard starting starting in lap '
          ||to_char (firstlap - 1)
          ||' for '||to_char (lap_count)
          ||' laps'
          ||', ending in '||to_char (lastlap)
       end as what_happened
from   laps
match_recognize (
         partition by driverid
         order by lap
         measures
           first (slow_lap.lap) as firstlap
         , last  (slow_lap.lap) as lastlap
         , count (slow_lap.lap) as lap_count
         , driver               as driver
         one row per match
         pattern (
           faster_than_avg{1} slow_lap{1,} faster_than_avg{1}
         )
         define
           faster_than_avg as milliseconds < avg_laptime
         , slow_lap as milliseconds > avg_laptime
)
/
DRIVER           WHAT_HAPPENED
---------------- ----------------------------------------
Lewis Hamilton   Probably a pit stop in lap 12
Lewis Hamilton   ** Hazard starting starting in lap 17
                 for 8 laps, ending in 25
```

```
Lewis Hamilton    Probably a pit stop in lap 34
Fernando Alonso   ** Hazard starting starting in lap 17
                  for 8 laps, ending in 25

Sebastian Vettel ** Hazard starting starting in lap 17
                  for 8 laps, ending in 25

Sebastian Vettel Probably a pit stop in lap 41
Sergio Pérez      Probably a pit stop in lap 14
Sergio Pérez      ** Hazard starting starting in lap 17
                  for 8 laps, ending in 25
Sergio Pérez      Probably a pit stop in lap 38
<< rows omitted for brevity >>
Yuki Tsunoda      Probably a pit stop in lap 10
Yuki Tsunoda      ** Hazard starting starting in lap 17
                  for 8 laps, ending in 25

Yuki Tsunoda      Probably a pit stop in lap 33
Mick Schumacher   ** Hazard starting starting in lap 17
                  for 8 laps, ending in 25

Mick Schumacher  Probably a pit stop in lap 33
Guanyu Zhou      Probably a pit stop in lap 9
Guanyu Zhou      ** Hazard starting starting in lap 17
                  for 8 laps, ending in 25

43 rows selected.
```

Summary

Searching for a particular pattern in a data set can be very useful to the business. Prior to the introduction of the match_recognize clause, finding patterns in a set of data was a difficult task. Bringing row pattern matching close to the data makes executing it very efficient.

This chapter barely scratched the surface of what is possible with match_recognize. There are many more use cases for row pattern matching, like solving a bin-fitting problem.

CHAPTER 5

Pagination and Set Operators

Working with large sets of data is quite common when an Oracle Database is involved. But not always should all the data be shown to the user of a database application. Often, only the first 50 records are enough for users to interact with. A typical top-N query is examined in this chapter, retrieving the first 50 records. Showing the following 50 records, or any offset is an example of a pagination-type query that also takes center stage.

Also, in this chapter, the different set operators, getting the difference between multiple sets of data and the common denominators, are being looked at. In this area, Oracle Database 21c added more functionality to be more compliant with the ANSI standard.

Top-N and Pagination

Getting the first few records of a larger set, like the top 5, has always been possible in Oracle, but it was always a bit "clunky" and not always as straightforward as it could be.

For the following examples, a view is created with the following definition.

```
create view all_driverstandings
as
select rcs.year
     , rcs.round
     , cct.name
     , drs.position
     , drv.driverid
```

© Alex Nuijten, Patrick Barel 2023
A. Nuijten and P. Barel, *Modern Oracle Database Programming*, https://doi.org/10.1007/978-1-4842-9166-5_5

```
       , drv.forename ||' '||drv.surname as driver
       , drs.points
       , drs.wins
from    f1data.driverstandings drs
join    f1data.drivers drv
  on    drv.driverid = drs.driverid
join    f1data.races rcs
  on    rcs.raceid = drs.raceid
join    f1data.circuits cct
  on    cct.circuitid = rcs.circuitid
/
```

The ALL_DRIVERSTANDINGS view shows the drivers' standing by year and round. The view exposes more than 33,000 records because the data goes back to the 1950s.

The following is a first attempt at getting the first five rows in this view for the 2021 season and only for two drivers.

```
select round
       , position
       , driver
       , points
       , wins
from    all_driverstandings
where   year = 2021
and     driverid in (830, 844) -- Leclerc, Verstappen
and     rownum <= 5
order   by round
/
```

ROU	POSITION	DRIVER	POINTS	WINS
1	2	Max Verstappen	18	0
1	6	Charles Leclerc	8	0
2	4	Charles Leclerc	20	0
20	1	Max Verstappen	351.5	9
20	6	Charles Leclerc	152	0

As you can see in the output, the result set is not correct. In the first five rows, there shouldn't be data for round 20. The problem with this query is that the rownum pseudo-column is determined *before* the final sorting operation. When a row is considered for output as it matches the filter criteria, rownum assigns a value, starting with one. The next row that matches the filter criteria is assigned the value 2, and so on. No more records are selected when rownum reaches five (in the preceding query). After this step, the result set is sorted by round, as specified in the order by clause. This behavior can be observed in the explain plan (only the relevant parts are shown).

```
select *
  from dbms_xplan.display_cursor(null, null, 'BASIC PREDICATE')
/

PLAN_TABLE_OUTPUT
-----------------------------------------------------------------
| Id  | Operation                        | Name             |
-----------------------------------------------------------------
|   0 | SELECT STATEMENT                 |                  |
|   1 |   SORT ORDER BY                  |                  |
|*  2 |    COUNT STOPKEY                 |                  |
<< irrelevant output removed >>

Predicate Information (identified by operation id):
----------------------------------------------------
   2 - filter(ROWNUM<=5)
<< irrelevant output removed >>
```

The filter is applied (rownum <= 5) in operation ID 2. The resulting data set is sorted in step 1.

To correctly get the intended output, the sorted data set needs to be pushed into an inline view (or in the subquery factoring clause).

```
select *
from   (select round
             , position
             , driver
             , points
             , wins
```

```
  from    all_driverstandings
  where   year = 2021
  and     driverid in (830, 844) -- Leclerc, Verstappen
  order   by round
  )
where   rownum <= 5
/
ROU   POSITION DRIVER                POINTS     WINS
---   --------- ------------------    --------   --------
 1           2 Max Verstappen           18        0
 1           6 Charles Leclerc           8        0
 2           4 Charles Leclerc          20        0
 2           2 Max Verstappen           43        1
 3           2 Max Verstappen           61        1
```

Now the optimizer understands the intention, which is reflected in the explain plan (only the relevant parts are shown).

```
|   0 | SELECT STATEMENT            |
|*  1 |   COUNT STOPKEY             |
|   2 |    VIEW                     |
|*  3 |     SORT ORDER BY STOPKEY   |
<< irrelevant output removed >>
Predicate Information (identified by operation id):
------------------------------------------------------
   1 - filter(ROWNUM<=5)
   3 - filter(ROWNUM<=5)
<< irrelevant output removed >>
```

Row-Limiting Clause

Since Oracle Database 12c, this top-N query is greatly simplified and offers extra functionality like pagination with the row-limiting clause.

Getting the first five rows for the current season for two drivers would be queried as follows.

```
select round
     , position
     , driver
     , points
     , wins
from    all_driverstandings
where   year = 2022
and     driverid in (830, 844) -- Leclerc, Verstappen
order   by round
fetch   first 5 rows only
/
ROU    POSITION DRIVER                    POINTS         WINS
---    ---------- ------------------- ---------- ----------
  1         19 Max Verstappen              0            0
  1          1 Charles Leclerc            26            1
  2          1 Charles Leclerc            45            1
  2          3 Max Verstappen             25            1
  3          1 Charles Leclerc            71            2
```

The intention of the query is immediately clear; get the first five records. What determines the "first records" is determined by the sorting clause in the query.

The row-limiting clause accommodates a static, fixed number of rows that need to be queried, and it can also be a bind variable. The following example has been executed using SQLcl to declare a bind variable named "b".

```
var b number
begin
  :b := 5;
end;
/
select round
     , position
     , driver
     , points
     , wins
```

```
from    all_driverstandings
where   year = 2022
and     driverid in (830, 844) -- Leclerc, Verstappen
order   by round
fetch   first :b rows only
/
```

```
ROU   POSITION DRIVER                    POINTS        WINS
---   ---------- ------------------   ----------  ----------
  1         19 Max Verstappen              0           0
  1          1 Charles Leclerc            26           1
  2          1 Charles Leclerc            45           1
  2          3 Max Verstappen             25           1
  3          1 Charles Leclerc            71           2
```

As requested, the preceding query returns five rows, but what if there are tied values? In this case, you might argue that the query should return six records because both drivers participated in the first three rounds. When the value sorted by is not deterministic (round in this case), the last record is arbitrary. The row-limiting clause can also provide for tied values, using the rows with ties clause instead of rows only.

```
select round
     , position
     , driver
     , points
     , wins
from    all_driverstandings
where   year = 2022
and     driverid in (830, 844) -- Leclerc, Verstappen
order   by round
fetch   first 5 rows with ties
/
```

ROU	POSITION	DRIVER	POINTS	WINS
1	19	Max Verstappen	0	0
1	1	Charles Leclerc	26	1
2	1	Charles Leclerc	45	1
2	3	Max Verstappen	25	1
3	1	Charles Leclerc	71	2
3	6	Max Verstappen	25	1

Besides a fixed number of rows, static or with a bind variable, that is to be returned by the row-limiting clause, it is also possible to return a percentage of the total row count to be returned. The following example returns six percent of the records. In this case, the total result set is 38 records, and six percent is 2.28 records.

```
select round
     , position
     , driver
     , points
     , wins
from   all_driverstandings
where  year = 2022
and    driverid in (830, 844)
order  by round
fetch  first 6 percent rows only
/
```

ROU	POSITION	DRIVER	POINTS	WINS
1	19	Max Verstappen	0	0
1	1	Charles Leclerc	26	1
2	1	Charles Leclerc	45	1

The percentage is rounded up (using the ceil function in the background), resulting in three records to be shown in the preceding results. Of course, using percentages in combination with rows with ties is also possible.

```
select round
     , position
     , driver
     , points
     , wins
from   all_driverstandings
where  year = 2022
and    driverid in (830, 844)
order  by round
fetch  first 6 percent rows with ties
/
```

ROU	POSITION	DRIVER	POINTS	WINS
1	19	Max Verstappen	0	0
1	1	Charles Leclerc	26	1
2	1	Charles Leclerc	45	1
2	3	Max Verstappen	25	1

Pagination

The row-limiting clause also provides functionality for pagination-type queries. Instead of showing the first x number of rows, it is possible to skip the first x number of rows and show the next set of records. The following example shows an offset clause, skipping the first ten rows from the first round in 2022.

```
select round
     , position
     , driver
     , points
     , wins
from   all_driverstandings
where  year = 2022
and    round = 1
order  by points desc
offset 10 rows
/
```

ROU	POSITION	DRIVER	POINTS	WINS
1	11	Mick Schumacher	0	0
1	12	Lance Stroll	0	0
1	13	Alexander Albon	0	0
1	14	Daniel Ricciardo	0	0
1	15	Lando Norris	0	0
1	16	Nicholas Latifi	0	0
1	17	Nico Hülkenberg	0	0
1	18	Sergio Pérez	0	0
1	20	Pierre Gasly	0	0
1	19	Max Verstappen	0	0

The offset clause is limited to x number of rows; you cannot specify a percentage of rows. It is possible to specify an expression if it evaluates to a numeric value.

The most common way to paginate through a set of data is to show first a set of rows (let's say five records) and, when navigating to the next page, show the next five records skipping the first five that have already been seen. This can be implemented using the offset clause and the fetch clause. The following example skips the first five rows and returns the next five rows.

```
select position
     , driver
     , points
     , wins
from   all_driverstandings
where  year = 2022
and    round = 1
order  by position
offset 5 rows
fetch  next 5 rows only
/
```

```
   POSITION DRIVER                POINTS      WINS
---------- ------------------- ---------- ----------
         6 Valtteri Bottas             8         0
         7 Esteban Ocon                6         0
         8 Yuki Tsunoda                4         0
         9 Fernando Alonso             2         0
        10 Guanyu Zhou                 1         0
```

Instead of using fetch first, fetch next is used for pagination. Having the number of rows hard coded in a pagination query doesn't make sense, most likely the application that uses this query wants to dictate the offset and how many rows are shown to the user. The following query shows the pagination query for the next five records using bind variables in SQLcl.

```
var offset number
var next   number
begin
  :offset := 10;
  :next := 5;
end;
/

select position
     , driver
     , points
     , wins
from   all_driverstandings
where  year = 2022
and    round = 1
order  by position
offset :offset rows
fetch  next :next rows only
/
```

```
POSITION DRIVER                    POINTS        WINS
---------- -------------------- ---------- ----------
        11 Mick Schumacher           0           0
        12 Lance Stroll              0           0
        13 Alexander Albon           0           0
        14 Daniel Ricciardo          0           0
        15 Lando Norris              0           0
```

Using this query, it is also possible to show the first five records from the result set when using a value of 0 as the offset.

```
begin
    :offset := 0;
End;
/
```

<< execute the SQL statement from above >>

```
POSITION DRIVER                    POINTS        WINS
---------- -------------------- ---------- ----------
         1 Charles Leclerc          26           1
         2 Carlos Sainz             18           0
         3 Lewis Hamilton           15           0
         4 George Russell           12           0
         5 Kevin Magnussen          10           0
```

Depending on the query that is used, it could be that retrieving the tenth page is more time-consuming than the first one.

Under the Hood

Under the hood, the row-limiting clause utilizes analytic functions, like row_number or rank, which can be observed when the predicate information of the explain plan is examined from the first query in the row-limiting section (only the relevant information is shown).

```
select *
  from dbms_xplan.display_cursor (null, null, 'BASIC PREDICATE')
/

PLAN_TABLE_OUTPUT
-----------------------------------------------------------------
| Id  | Operation                      | Name            |       |
-----------------------------------------------------------------
|   0 | SELECT STATEMENT               |                 |       |
|*  1 |   VIEW                         |                 |       |
|*  2 |     WINDOW SORT PUSHED RANK    |                 |       |

Predicate Information (identified by operation id):
-----------------------------------------------------

   1 - filter("from$_subquery$_002"."rowlimit_$$_rownumber"<=5)
   2 - filter(ROW_NUMBER() OVER ( ORDER BY "RCS"."ROUND")<=5)
```

As can be seen in the predicate information, the analytic function row_number is used in combination with the sorting that was in the original query.

Caution   Omitting the order by clause from the query doesn't raise an error or give a warning. Leaving order by out of the query results in an "order by null" in the analytic function might not give the expected results.

Set Operators

Let's use two subsets of data from the drivers table to demonstrate the workings of the set operators. First, there is a set of drivers whose first name is Graham.

```
create view grahams
as
select drv.driverid
     , drv.driverref
     , drv.forename
     , drv.surname
```

```
     , drv.nationality
from    f1data.drivers drv
where   drv.forename = 'Graham'
/
```

The view exposes the following result set.

```
DRIVERID DRIVERREF          FORENAME   SURNAME    NATIONALITY
-------- ------------------ ---------- ---------- ---------------
     336 mcrae              Graham     McRae      New Zealander
     289 hill               Graham     Hill       British
     745 graham_whitehead   Graham     Whitehead  British
```

Second, there is a set of drivers whose surname is Hill.

```
create view hills
as
select drv.driverid
     , drv.driverref
     , drv.forename
     , drv.surname
     , drv.nationality
from    f1data.drivers drv
where   drv.surname = 'Hill'
/
```

The view exposes the following result set.

```
DRIVERID DRIVERREF          FORENAME   SURNAME    NATIONALITY
-------- ------------------ ---------- ---------- ---------------
      71 damon_hill         Damon      Hill       British
     289 hill               Graham     Hill       British
     403 phil_hill          Phil       Hill       American
```

These views are based off the same table, with a subset of the data each.

Union

Combining the two views created earlier can be achieved with the union operator. For this operator, both sets must have the same shape and form; that is, the data types of each column must match or at least be in the same family. Integers and floats can be mixed and matched, but you cannot mix VARCHAR2 with numbers.

Joining the two result sets gives the following result.

```
select g.driverid
     , g.driverref
     , g.forename
     , g.surname
     , g.nationality
from   grahams g
union
select h.driverid
     , h.driverref
     , h.forename
     , h.surname
     , h.nationality
from   hills h
/
```

```
  DRIVERID DRIVERREF         FORENA SURNAME    NATIONALITY
---------- ----------------- ------ ---------- -------------
        71 damon_hill        Damon  Hill       British
       289 hill              Graham Hill       British
       336 mcrae             Graham McRae      New Zealander
       403 phil_hill         Phil   Hill       American
       745 graham_whitehead  Graham Whitehead  British
```

The union operator does more than just join the two result sets. It also sorts them and removes the duplicate rows from the final result. This behavior can be observed in the explain plan for the preceding query.

```
select *
  from dbms_xplan.display_cursor(null, null, 'BASIC')
/
```

PLAN_TABLE_OUTPUT

```
--------------------------------------------------
| Id  | Operation                  | Name    |
--------------------------------------------------
|   0 | SELECT STATEMENT           |         |
|   1 |  SORT UNIQUE               |         |
|   2 |   UNION-ALL                |         |
|*  3 |    TABLE ACCESS STORAGE FULL| DRIVERS |
|*  4 |    TABLE ACCESS STORAGE FULL| DRIVERS |
--------------------------------------------------
```

The sort unique step is seen in step 1 of the explain plan, resulting in five records in the output. Graham Hill only occurs once, although he appears in both views.

This union operator can, starting in Oracle Database 21c, be written more explicitly by adding distinct to it.

union distinct

The workings remain the same; it adds syntactic clarity.

When all the data is needed, regardless of whether there are duplicates, use the union all operator. This eliminates the need for the sort unique step in the explain plan.

```
select g.driverid
     , g.driverref
     , g.forename
     , g.surname
     , g.nationality
from   grahams g
union all
select h.driverid
     , h.driverref
     , h.forename
     , h.surname
     , h.nationality
from   hills h
/
```

```
DRIVERID DRIVERREF        FORENA SURNAME    NATIONALITY
---------- ----------------- ------ --------- -------------
       336 mcrae           Graham McRae      New Zealander
       289 hill            Graham Hill       British
       745 graham_whitehead Graham Whitehead British
        71 damon_hill      Damon  Hill       British
       289 hill            Graham Hill       British
       403 phil_hill       Phil   Hill       American
```

As you can see in the final result, driver 289 (Graham Hill) appears twice. In the explain plan, sort unique is no longer present.

```
-------------------------------------------------
| Id  | Operation                   | Name      |
-------------------------------------------------
|   0 | SELECT STATEMENT            |           |
|   1 |   UNION-ALL                 |           |
|   2 |     TABLE ACCESS STORAGE FULL| DRIVERS  |
|   3 |     TABLE ACCESS STORAGE FULL| DRIVERS  |
-------------------------------------------------
```

Minus and Except

The following view is added to demonstrate the workings of the minus and minus all operators.

```
create or replace view grahams_and_hills
as
select g.driverid
     , g.driverref
     , g.forename
     , g.surname
     , g.nationality
from   grahams g
union all
select h.driverid
     , h.driverref
```

```
        , h.forename
        , h.surname
        , h.nationality
from    hills h
/
```

This view exposes the following data.

```
DRIVERID DRIVERREF         FORENA SURNAME   NATIONALITY
---------- ----------------- ------ --------- -------------
       336 mcrae             Graham McRae     New Zealander
       289 hill              Graham Hill      British
       745 graham_whitehead Graham Whitehead British
        71 damon_hill        Damon  Hill      British
       289 hill              Graham Hill      British
       403 phil_hill         Phil   Hill      American
```

Note that *Graham Hill* appears twice in the result set.

The minus operator filters out only the rows that exist in the first input set but doesn't exist in the second. To demonstrate this operation, let's take the grahams_and_hills view and use the minus operator with a query that selects all the *British* drivers.

```
select gh.driverid
       , gh.driverref
       , gh.forename
       , gh.surname
       , gh.nationality
    from grahams_and_hills gh
minus
select drv.driverid
       , drv.driverref
       , drv.forename
       , drv.surname
       , drv.nationality
from    f1data.drivers drv
where   drv.nationality = 'British'
/
```

123

```
DRIVERID DRIVERREF            FORENAME   SURNAME    NATIONALITY
-------- -------------------- ---------- ---------- ----------------
     336 mcrae                Graham     McRae      New Zealander
     403 phil_hill            Phil       Hill       American
```

As you can see, even though *Graham Hill* (a British driver) appears twice in the first set (the grahams_and_hills view), he doesn't appear in the final result set anymore. Both occurrences of Graham Hill are removed from the first result set.

This minus operator can, starting in Oracle Database 21c, be written more explicitly by adding distinct to it.

```
minus distinct
```

The workings remain the same; it adds syntactic clarity.

Since Oracle Database 21c, the minus operator also has an all version. You get a different result if the script is altered to use the minus all operator.

```
select gh.driverid
     , gh.driverref
     , gh.forename
     , gh.surname
     , gh.nationality
from   grahams_and_hills gh
minus all
select drv.driverid
     , drv.driverref
     , drv.forename
     , drv.surname
     , drv.nationality
from   f1data.drivers drv
where  drv.nationality = 'British'
/
```

```
DRIVERID DRIVERREF            FORENAME   SURNAME    NATIONALITY
-------- -------------------- ---------- ---------- ----------------
     336 mcrae                Graham     McRae      New Zealander
     289 hill                 Graham     Hill       British
     403 phil_hill            Phil       Hill       American
```

In this case, *Graham Hill* does appear in the final result set. That is because he appears twice in the first set (the `grahams_and_hills` view) but only once in the second set. The record is removed only once instead of all appearances.

The `except` operator is also implemented to comply with the ANSI standard. The workings of `except` are like `minus`, including all variations.

```
except
except distinct
except all
```

Intersect

The `intersect` operator filters out only the rows that exist in both input sets. The `grahams_and_hills` view from the previous section is used to demonstrate this operation.

The first set, before the `intersect` operator, are all the rows in the views (six records in total). The second set, after the `intersect` operator, is filtered to only include Graham Hill (two records).

```
select gh.driverid
     , gh.driverref
     , gh.forename
     , gh.surname
     , gh.nationality
from   grahams_and_hills gh
intersect
select gh.driverid
     , gh.driverref
     , gh.forename
     , gh.surname
     , gh.nationality
from   grahams_and_hills gh
where  gh.driverref = 'hill'
/
```

```
   DRIVERID DRIVERREF        FORENA SURNAME    NATIONALITY
---------- ----------------- ------ --------- --------------
       289 hill              Graham Hill       British
```

Like, with the union operator, this performs a distinct on the result set. So, even though *Graham Hill* appears twice is both sets, he only appears once in the final result set.

This `intersect` operator can, starting in Oracle Database 21c, be written more explicit by adding distinct to it.

```
intersect distinct
```

The workings remain the same; it adds syntactic clarity.

The `intersect` operator has had an `all` version since Oracle Database 21c. You get a different result if the script is altered to use the `intersect all` operator.

```
select gh.driverid
     , gh.driverref
     , gh.forename
     , gh.surname
     , gh.nationality
from   grahams_and_hills gh
intersect all
select gh.driverid
     , gh.driverref
     , gh.forename
     , gh.surname
     , gh.nationality
from   grahams_and_hills gh
where  gh.driverref = 'hill'
/
```

```
   DRIVERID DRIVERREF        FORENA SURNAME    NATIONALITY
---------- ----------------- ------ --------- --------------
       289 hill              Graham Hill       British
       289 hill              Graham Hill       British
```

As you can see in the result set, Graham Hill occurs twice in each result set and twice in the final result set.

Summary

This chapter examined top-N and pagination queries. Inline views, analytic functions, and the `offset` and `fetch` clauses make queries more readable and easier to maintain.

Enhancements to the set operations add syntactic clarity and increase adherence to the ANSI standard.

CHAPTER 6

Conditional Compilation

Conditional compilation has been available since Oracle 10g. There are countless scenarios in which this can be useful. For example, you can use conditional compilation to check the database (develop, test, production), check the compiler optimization level, include or exclude code depending on the environment, and prepare your code for release on future versions of the database.

Directives

The conditional compilation syntax consists of three directives. The selection directive, the inquiry directive, and the error directive. The directives are prefixed by the dollar sign ($) to distinguish them from the normal PL/SQL syntax.

Selection Directive

The selection directive uses these building blocks.

```
$if $then [ $elsif ] [ $else ] $end
```

A block could look something like the following.

```
$if some_condition = true $then
  select 'Patrick' into l_name from dual;
$else
  select 'Alex' into l_name from dual;
$end
```

This looks a lot like normal PL/SQL conditions, but the dollar sign tells the compiler it is entering a conditional compilation block. If the condition (inquiry directive) evaluates to true, the code block following $then is included in the compiled program.

129

© Alex Nuijten, Patrick Barel 2023
A. Nuijten and P. Barel, *Modern Oracle Database Programming*, https://doi.org/10.1007/978-1-4842-9166-5_6

If the inquiry directive is false, then the compiler evaluates the $elsif condition if available. If none of the conditions are true, then the block in the $else branch, if available, is included.

Inquiry Directive

After the selection directive, you specify an inquiry directive to determine which branch of the selection directive should be included in the compiled program. The inquiry directive can be a flag, defined using the plsql_ccflags setting. You can set these flags using an alter session statement.

```
alter session set plsql_ccflags = 'myflag:true'
```

But you can also specify the flags when compiling the program.

```
alter package mypackage compile plsql_ccflags='myflag:true'
```

If a flag is non-existent, it is evaluated as false. Flags can only hold static boolean values. To use numeric values, you must create a package to hold these values as constants. Prior to Oracle Database 19c, you could only use integers or pls_integers; all numeric data types have been available since then. Inquiry directives must be static boolean expressions.

Note   You cannot use a VARCHAR2 constant in an inquiry directive.

The DBMS_DB_VERSION Package

Oracle ships a package that holds a constant for the current RDBMS version and one for the current release number. The name of this package is DBMS_DB_VERSION. It also contains a set of boolean values you can use to determine the current version. Listing 6-1 shows the current DBMS_DB_VERSION package shipped with Oracle Database 21c.

Listing 6-1. 21c version of the DBMS_DB_VERSION package

```
package sys.dbms_db_version is
  version constant pls_integer :=
          21; -- RDBMS version number
```

```
release constant pls_integer := 0;   -- RDBMS release number
```

```
/* The following boolean constants follow a naming convention.
   Each constant gives a name for a boolean expression.
   For example,
   ver_le_9_1  represents version <=  9 and release <= 1
   ver_le_10_2 represents version <= 10 and release <= 2
   ver_le_10   represents version <= 10
```

Code that references these boolean constants (rather than directly referencing version and release) will benefit from fine grain invalidation as the version and release values change.

A typical usage of these boolean constants is

```
    $if dbms_db_version.ver_le_10 $then
      version 10 and ealier code
    $elsif dbms_db_version.ver_le_11 $then
      version 11 code
    $else
      version 12 and later code
    $end
```

This code structure will protect any reference to the code for version 12. It also prevents the controlling package constant dbms_db_version.ver_le_11 from being referenced when the program is compiled under version 10. A similar observation applies to version 11. This scheme works even though the static constant ver_le_11 is not defined in version 10 database because conditional compilation protects the $elsif from evaluation if the dbms_db_version.ver_le_10 is TRUE.
```
*/
```

```
/* Deprecate boolean constants for unsupported releases */
```

```
ver_le_9_1    constant boolean := FALSE;
PRAGMA DEPRECATE(ver_le_9_1);
```

```
ver_le_9_2    constant boolean := FALSE;
PRAGMA DEPRECATE(ver_le_9_2);
ver_le_9      constant boolean := FALSE;
PRAGMA DEPRECATE(ver_le_9);
ver_le_10_1   constant boolean := FALSE;
PRAGMA DEPRECATE(ver_le_10_1);
ver_le_10_2   constant boolean := FALSE;
PRAGMA DEPRECATE(ver_le_10_2);
ver_le_10     constant boolean := FALSE;
PRAGMA DEPRECATE(ver_le_10);
ver_le_11_1   constant boolean := FALSE;
PRAGMA DEPRECATE(ver_le_11_1);
ver_le_11_2   constant boolean := FALSE;
ver_le_11     constant boolean := FALSE;
ver_le_12_1   constant boolean := FALSE;
ver_le_12_2   constant boolean := FALSE;
ver_le_12     constant boolean := FALSE;
ver_le_18     constant boolean := FALSE;
ver_le_19     constant boolean := FALSE;
ver_le_20     constant boolean := FALSE;
ver_le_21     constant boolean := TRUE;

end dbms_db_version;
```

The flags are FALSE in all lower versions of the database. Only the current version is set to TRUE.

If you use the DBMS_DB_VERSION constants, inquire them from the lowest version number available. If an inquiry directive evaluates to true, the code in the $then block is included, and the rest of the code is ignored and, therefore, not included. Since this code is not evaluated anymore, it doesn't matter if this block references objects; for example, a constant in the package that doesn't exist.

If your application is currently running on an Oracle 12c instance, your conditional compilation block should start inquiring if the version is 12 (or less).

```
$if dbms_db_version.ver_le_12 $then
dbms_output.put_line( 'This will run 12c code.' );
```

If you want your program to include code for multiple versions to use the best features available in every version of the database, use the $elsif directive for multiple inquiry directives comparable to a case statement.

```
$elsif dbms_db_version.ver_le_18 $then
dbms_output.put_line( 'This will run 18c code.' );
$elsif dbms_db_version.ver_le_19 $then
dbms_output.put_line( 'This will run 19c code.' );
$elsif dbms_db_version.ver_le_20 $then
dbms_output.put_line( 'This will run 20c code.' );
$elsif dbms_db_version.ver_le_21 $then
dbms_output.put_line( 'This will run 21c code.' );
```

If neither of the inquiry directives is true, include a catch-all $else directive.

```
$else
dbms_output.put_line( 'This version is not supported' );
```

Listing 6-2 shows the complete script.

Listing 6-2. Which version is running?

```
begin
  $if dbms_db_version.ver_le_12 $then
  dbms_output.put_line( 'This will run 12c code.' );
  $elsif dbms_db_version.ver_le_18 $then
  dbms_output.put_line( 'This will run 18c code.' );
  $elsif dbms_db_version.ver_le_19 $then
  dbms_output.put_line( 'This will run 19c code.' );
  $elsif dbms_db_version.ver_le_20 $then
  dbms_output.put_line( 'This will run 20c code.' );
  $elsif dbms_db_version.ver_le_21 $then
  dbms_output.put_line( 'This will run 21c code.' );
  $else
  dbms_output.put_line( 'This version is not supported' );
  $end
end;
```

If you build a block with multiple conditions, the case-like statement, be sure to include all the possible flags so your code compiles on every version of the database.

The following code cannot compile on an Oracle 20c instance because although ver_le_21 means "version less than or equal to 21," this variable isn't declared in the DBMS_DB_VERSION package on an Oracle 20c database. Therefore, the compile throws an error.

```
begin
  $if dbms_db_version.ver_le_12 $then
  dbms_output.put_line( 'This will run 12c code.' );
  $elsif dbms_db_version.ver_le_18 $then
  dbms_output.put_line( 'This will run 18c code.' );
  $elsif dbms_db_version.ver_le_19 $then
  dbms_output.put_line( 'This will run 19c code.' );
  $elsif dbms_db_version.ver_le_21 $then
  dbms_output.put_line( 'This will run 21c code.' );
  $else
  dbms_output.put_line( 'This version is not supported' );
  $end
end;
```

Also, conditional compilation does not do short-circuit evaluation, so make sure you don't mix multiple, possibly illegal, conditions in one statement.

```
 begin
  $if dbms_db_version.ver_le_12
   or dbms_db_version.ver_le_18
   or dbms_db_version.ver_le_19 $then
  dbms_output.put_line( 'This will run pre 20c code.' );
  $elsif dbms_db_version.ver_le_20 $then
  dbms_output.put_line( 'This will run 20c code.' );
  $elsif dbms_db_version.ver_le_21 $then
  dbms_output.put_line( 'This will run 21c code.' );
  $else
  dbms_output.put_line( 'This version is not supported' );
  $end
end;
```

This code cannot compile on an Oracle 12c instance, for example. Again, the DBMS_DB_VERSION.VER_LE_18 and DBMS_DB_VERSION.VER_LE_19 constants simply don't exist yet.

Predefined CCFLAGS

There are some CCFLAGS defined automatically for any program unit. These may not be very useful as an inquiry directive in a selection directive, but they can give you helpful information about your program. For instance, when instrumenting your code, it can be helpful to know the line number where something is done. Table 6-1 shows a list of the predefined CCFLAGS.

Table 6-1. *Predefined CCFLAGS*

Flag	Description
$$PLSQL_LINE	A PLS_INTEGER literal whose value is the number of the source line on which the directive appears in the current PL/SQL unit.
$$PLSQL_UNIT	A VARCHAR2 literal that contains the name of the current PL/SQL unit. If the current PL/SQL unit is an anonymous block, then $$PLSQL_UNIT contains a NULL value. Only the top-level object, not the subprograms.
$$PLSQL_UNIT_OWNER	A VARCHAR2 literal that contains the name of the owner of the current PL/SQL unit. If the current PL/SQL unit is an anonymous block, then $$PLSQL_UNIT_OWNER contains a NULL value.
$$PLSQL_UNIT_TYPE	A VARCHAR2 literal that contains the type of the current PL/SQL unit—ANONYMOUS BLOCK, FUNCTION, PACKAGE, PACKAGE BODY, PROCEDURE, TRIGGER, TYPE, or TYPE BODY. Inside an anonymous block or non-DML trigger, $$PLSQL_UNIT_TYPE has the value ANONYMOUS BLOCK.

Error Directive

To stop compilation completely, for instance, because certain conditions aren't met, you use the error directive. The error directive consists of this building block.

```
$error 'error message' $end
```

As soon as this code is included in the compiled program, it remains in an invalid state. Listing 6-3 shows a package that cannot compile.

Listing 6-3. This code will not compile successfully

```
create or replace package willnotcompile as
  the_answer constant number := 42;
  $error 'This package should not be compiled' $end
  wear_towel constant boolean := true;
end willnotcompile;
```

The code in Listing 6-3 results in a compilation failure.

```
Warning: Package created with compilation errors

Errors for PACKAGE BOOK.CCWILLNOTCOMPILE:
LINE/COL ERROR
-------- --------------------------------------------------------
3/3     PLS-00179: $ERROR: This package should not be compiled
```

Compilation is terminated right after this directive. The rest of the code is not even parsed. Since the program is in an invalid state, you cannot reference anything from it, not even the constants that were defined before the error directive.

DEPRECATE Pragma Directive

If the error directive is too harsh since it prevents your code from being compiled completely, it might be a good idea to use the DEPRECATE pragma directive. This way, the code still compiles, but there is a warning that this part of the code is deprecated and removed in a future version. The DEPRECATE pragma should follow directly after the declaration. If you add a pragma at any other position in your code, it raises a plw-06021 warning. You can deprecate a procedure, a function, or a package. If you try to deprecate the package in the package body, the plw-06022 warning is raised.

Listing 6-4 shows some of the warnings that can be issued.

Listing 6-4. Deprecated warnings

```
create or replace package deprecatedwarnings is
  procedure deprecate_this_later;
  procedure deprecate_this_now;
  pragma deprecate( deprecate_this_now,
  'This will raise PLW-6019, when this program is compiled' );
  pragma deprecate( deprecate_this_later,
  'This will raise PLW-6021, because this pragma is misplaced' );
  procedure call_the_deprecated_procedure;
end deprecatedwarnings;
```

The plw-06020 exception is raised in the calling program. Warnings are raised at compile time if enabled using the following statement.

```
alter session set plsql_warnings='enable:(6019,6020,6021,6022)';
```

The warnings that can be issued are shown in Table 6-2.

Table 6-2. *Deprecated warnings*

Warning	Meaning
6019	The entity was deprecated and could be removed in a future release. Do not use the deprecated entity.
6020	The referenced entity was deprecated and could be removed in a future release. Do not use the deprecated entity. Follow the specific instructions in the warning if any are given.
6021	Misplaced pragma. The DEPRECATE pragma should follow immediately after the declaration of the entity that is being deprecated. Place the pragma immediately after the declaration of the entity that is being deprecated.
6022	This entity cannot be deprecated. Deprecation only applies to entities that may be declared in a package or type specification and to top-level procedure and function definitions. Remove the pragma.

To see the warnings issued, the compiler warnings must be enabled while compiling.

```
alter session set plsql_warnings='enable:(6019,6020,6021,6022)'
```

Or you may want to enable all warnings.

```
alter session set plsql_warnings='enable:all'
```

This can also be set when compiling a specific object.

```
alter package deprecatedwarnings compile
  plsql_warnings = 'enable:(6019,6020,6021,6022)'
```

Using Directives

A conditional compilation block generally starts with a $if selection directive.

```
$if dbms_db_version.version <= 19 $then
```

If this evaluates to true, the code following the $then directive is included. All the code until the next directive is found.

```
dbms_output.put_line( 'pre Oracle 19c code' );
```

If you want to include a different part of the code, include a $else directive with a different block of code.

```
$else
dbms_output.put_line( 'post Oracle 19c code' );
```

A conditional compilation block ends with a $end directive.

Listing 6-5 shows the complete script.

Listing 6-5. Include code depending on the database version

```
begin
  $if dbms_db_version.version <= 19 $then
  dbms_output.put_line( 'pre Oracle 19c code' );
  $else
  dbms_output.put_line( 'post Oracle 19c code' );
  $end
end;
```

You get the following output if you run this anonymous block on an Oracle 19c instance.

```
pre Oracle 19c code
```

You get the following output if you run the same anonymous block on an Oracle 21c instance.

```
post Oracle 19c code
```

Use Cases

There are countless situations in which conditional compilation can be useful. For example, you can use conditional compilation to prepare your application for new database versions, test private programs, check whether the database is for development, test, or production, check the compiler optimization level, and include or exclude code depending on the environment. And there are probably many more use cases you can think of.

Checking for the Presence of New Features

If you have access to a sandbox database, for instance, a free tier, you probably know about new features you want to use in your application. However, you can't implement them because your production environment is still running an older version of the database. In this case, you have (at least) two options.

- You note the feature, where you want to use it, and where you can find the documentation, so you can start developing your new solution when your production environment is upgraded to the newer version. Now, you must remember that you want to use this feature when the database is upgraded.

- You can implement the new solution in your current codebase and 'hide' this code from the older database using conditional compilation.

Let's look at a simple example. Oracle 21c comes with a simpler implementation of a stepped iterator. First, check the version of the instance you are compiling the program for.

```
$if dbms_db_version.version >= 21 $then
```

You can use the new iterator construct if running at least version 21 of the database.

```
-- code using the iterators available from 21c
  for n in 2 .. 10 by 2 loop
    dbms_output.put_line(n);
  end loop;
```

If you are running an older version, you must revert to the construction that has been available since Oracle 7.

```
-- code using the iterators as available before 21c
  for n in 2 .. 10 loop
    if mod(n, 2) = 0 then
      dbms_output.put_line(n);
    end if;
  end loop;
```

The complete script can be found in Listing 6-6.

Listing 6-6. Use the new iterator if available

```
begin
  $if dbms_db_version.version >= 21 $then
  -- code using the iterators available from 21c
  for n in 2 .. 10 by 2 loop
    dbms_output.put_line(n);
  end loop;
  $else
  -- code using the iterators as available before 21c
  for n in 2 .. 10 loop
    if mod(n, 2) = 0 then
      dbms_output.put_line(n);
    end if;
```

```
  end loop;
  $end
end;
```

Showing Output of Debug and Test Code

Conditional compilation can also expose and hide procedures and functions in your package. If you want to test a private procedure or function on a package, you must change the package specification to expose this program. Then, when you release your code, you must hide the program again.

Using conditional compilation, you can make these programs visible or hidden depending on the value of a flag in the CCFLAGS setting. If this flag is not defined, its inquiry evaluates to false, so you don't have to define it before compiling your source.

A selection directive using your own flag defines if the program is visible or not.

```
$if $$expose_for_test $then
procedure private_procedure;
$end
```

You can put this anywhere in your package specification. The code is not included in the compiled program if you compile the package source without the flag defined or set to false.

The complete package specification is shown in Listing 6-7.

Listing 6-7. Package specification with conditionally exposed programs

```
create or replace package cctestdemo as
  $if $$expose_for_test $then
  procedure private_procedure;
  $end
  procedure public_procedure;
end cctestdemo;
```

Listing 6-8 shows the implementation of this package.

Listing 6-8. Package body with all the programs implemented

```
create or replace package body cctestdemo as
  procedure private_procedure
  is
  begin
    dbms_output.put_line('=> This is the private_procedure <=');
  end private_procedure;

  procedure public_procedure
  is
  begin
    dbms_output.put_line('=> This is the public_procedure <=');
  end public_procedure;
end cctestdemo;
```

If you describe the current package, you only see the public procedure defined.

```
SQL> desc cctestdemo
PROCEDURE PUBLIC_PROCEDURE
```

If you want to execute the private procedure, you get an error that this procedure must be declared.

```
SQL> exec cctestdemo.private_procedure
BEGIN ccdemo.private_procedure; END;

              *

ERROR at line 1:
ORA-06550: line 1, column 14:
PLS-00302: component 'PRIVATE_PROCEDURE' must be declared
ORA-06550: line 1, column 7:
PL/SQL: Statement ignored
```

You can expose the code for testing without changing the source code but by defining the value of the inquiry directive using an alter session statement.

```
SQL> alter session set PLSQL_CCFLAGS = 'expose_for_test:true'
```

Then recompile the existing package in the database.

```
SQL> alter package cctestdemo compile
```

By doing this, you can expose this procedure, making it available for testing. Alternatively, you can specify the CCFLAGS directly when compiling.

```
alter package cctestdemo compile plsql_ccflags='expose_for_test:true'
```

If you describe the package now, you see that the private procedure has been exposed.

```
SQL> desc cctestdemo
PROCEDURE PRIVATE_PROCEDURE
PROCEDURE PUBLIC_PROCEDURE
```

You can now access the private procedure to test its contents.

```
SQL> exec cctestdemo.private_procedure
=> This is the private_procedure <=
```

To recompile a program using the last settings of the conditional compilation flags use reuse settings in your compile statement.

```
alter package cctestdemo compile reuse settings
```

This is especially useful if your program depends on different settings in different environments.

Use this statement to find out what settings were used when the program was compiled.

```
select plsql_ccflags
from   all_plsql_object_settings
where  name  = :object_name
and    owner = :object_owner
and    type  = :object_type
```

You can test private programs and check if your program handles all your exceptions gracefully, even the ones that are very unlikely to happen.

If, for example, you rely on your unique constraints being in place, you are unlikely to encounter the too_many_rows exception. If the constraint is absent or disabled, you want your code to handle this exception gracefully and not throw an error.

First, you have to implement your code and include the exception handlers.

```
function getdobfordriver( driverid_in in number )
  return date
is
  l_dob date;
begin
  begin
    select drv.dob
    into   l_dob
    from   f1data.drivers drv
    where  drv.driverid = driverid_in;
  exception
    when no_data_found
    then
      l_dob := null;
    when too_many_rows
    then
      l_dob := to_date('19721229', 'YYYYMMDD');
  end;
  return l_dob;
end getdobfordriver;
```

Then, using an inquiry directive, you include all the code necessary to test the exceptions.

```
begin
  $if $$testexceptions $then
  case
    when mod( driverid_in, 2 ) = 0
    then raise no_data_found;
    else raise too_many_rows;
  end case;
```

```
$else
select drv,dob
into   l_dob
from   f1data.drivers drv
where  drv.driverid = driverid_in;
$end
```

If you want to see which exception is raised and handled, it may be a nice idea to extend the exception handlers to also show which exception they handled.

```
exception
  when no_data_found
  then
    $if $$testexceptions $then
    dbms_output.put_line( 'no_data_found' );
    $end
    l_dob := null;
  when too_many_rows
  then
    $if $$testexceptions $then
    dbms_output.put_line( 'too_many_rows' );
    $end
    l_dob := to_date('19721229', 'YYYYMMDD');
end;
```

Listing 6-9 shows the package specification, and Listing 6-10 shows the package body.

Listing 6-9. Testing exceptions package specification

```
create or replace package ccexception as
  function getdobfordriver( driverid_in in number )
    return date;
end ccexception;
/
```

Listing 6-10. Testing exception package body

```
create or replace package body ccexception as
  function getdobfordriver( driverid_in in number )
    return date
  is
    l_dob date;
  begin
    begin
      $if $$testexceptions $then
      case
        when mod( driverid_in, 2 ) = 0
        then raise no_data_found;
        else raise too_many_rows;
      end case;
      $else
      select drv.dob
      into   l_dob
      from   f1data.drivers drv
      where  drv.driverid = driverid_in;
      $end
    exception
      when no_data_found
      then
        $if $$testexceptions $then
        dbms_output.put_line( 'no_data_found' );
        $end
        l_dob := null;
      when too_many_rows
      then
        $if $$testexceptions $then
        dbms_output.put_line( 'too_many_rows' );
        $end
        l_dob := to_date('19721229', 'YYYYMMDD');
    end;
    return l_dob;
```

```
  end getdobfordriver;
end ccexception;
/
```

You get the expected output if you run the getdobfordriver function without the inquiry directive set.

```
begin
  dbms_output.put_line( 'Date or birth for unknown: '
                        || ccexception.getdobfordriver ( -1 )
                      );
  dbms_output.put_line( 'Date or birth for Hamilton: '
                        || ccexception.getdobfordriver ( 1 )
                      );
  dbms_output.put_line( 'Date or birth for Verstappen: '
                        || ccexception.getdobfordriver ( 830 )
                      );
end;
/
Date or birth for unknown:
Date or birth for Hamilton: 07-JAN-85
Date or birth for Verstappen: 30-SEP-97
```

For a different result, set the inquiry directive while recompiling the package body.

```
alter package ccexception compile
plsql_ccflags = 'testexceptions:true'
```

Now when you run the code, you also see the different exceptions that can be raised.

```
begin
  dbms_output.put_line( 'Date or birth for unknown: '
                        || ccexception.getdobfordriver ( -1 )
                      );
  dbms_output.put_line( 'Date or birth for Hamilton: '
                        || ccexception.getdobfordriver ( 1 )
                      );
```

```
     dbms_output.put_line( 'Date or birth for Verstappen: '
                          || ccexception.getdobfordriver ( 830 )
                          );
end;
/
too_many_rows
Date or birth for unknown: 29-DEC-72
too_many_rows
Date or birth for Hamilton: 29-DEC-72
no_data_found
Date or birth for Verstappen:
```

Checking for the Correct Database Environment

Using the error directive, you can prevent code from being compiled on different environments, for instance, your production environment. You can create code that should not be compiled in a production environment because it holds utilities that might be considered unsafe but very helpful in a development environment.

You can check your environment using a selection directive with an inquiry directive.

```
$if environment_pkg.development $then
```

If your environment is correct, you include the code.

```
  procedure still_in_development;
```

If it is not the correct environment, you use the $error directive to prevent the code from compiling.

```
$else
  $error 'This package is for the development environment only'
  $end
$end
```

Listing 6-11 shows the complete implementation.

Listing 6-11. Code for development environment only

```
create or replace package only_for_dev is
  $if environment_pkg.development $then
    procedure still_in_development;
  $else
    $error 'This package is for the development environment only'
    $end
  $end
end only_for_dev;
```

Using an environment package that holds the different flags, you compile the code depending on the environment. Listing 6-12 creates the environment package with the correct flags' values.

Listing 6-12. Create the environment package

```
declare
  l_pack_spec varchar2( 32767 );
  l_env       varchar2( 128 );
  function tochar(
    p_val in boolean)
    return varchar2
  as
  begin
    return case p_val
            when true then 'TRUE'
            when false then 'FALSE'
            else null
          end;
  end tochar;
begin
  l_env       := sys_context( 'userenv', 'db_name' );
  l_pack_spec := 'create or replace package environment_pkg'
                  || chr( 10 );
  l_pack_spec := l_pack_spec || 'is' || chr( 10 );
  l_pack_spec := l_pack_spec || '    --==' || chr( 10 );
```

```
    l_pack_spec := l_pack_spec
                     || '    -- Environment Information'
                     || chr( 10 );
    l_pack_spec := l_pack_spec
                     || '   development constant boolean := '
                     || lower( tochar( l_env like '%DEV%' ) )
                     || ';' || chr( 10 );
    l_pack_spec := l_pack_spec
                     || '   test          constant boolean := '
                     || lower( tochar( l_env like '%TST%' ) )
                     || ';' || chr( 10 );
    l_pack_spec := l_pack_spec
                     || '   acceptance  constant boolean := '
                     || lower( tochar( l_env like '%ACC%' ) )
                     || ';' || chr( 10 );
    l_pack_spec := l_pack_spec
                     || '   production  constant boolean := '
                     || lower( tochar( l_env like '%PRD%' ) )
                     || ';' || chr( 10 );
    l_pack_spec := l_pack_spec || '   --==' || chr( 10 );
    l_pack_spec := l_pack_spec || 'end environment_pkg;'
                     || chr( 10 );
    execute immediate l_pack_spec;
end;
/
```

If you include this anonymous block in your deployment scripts, you can be sure the flags contain the correct values, and your code with be compiled according to the settings of these flags. You must create a package to hold the values because the inquiry directive must contain static constants, and SYS_CONTEXT is not considered a static boolean expression.

Using the check for the environment can also prevent code from being executed in different environments. A good example is preventing the program from sending emails while not running in the production environment.

Showing What's Compiled

You can issue the following command to view the code compiled based on your CCFLAGS settings, database version, or environment settings.

```
dbms_preprocessor.print_post_processed_source
```

Seeing your code as it is compiled can be very useful when analyzing what the code is doing.

Listing 6-13 shows the actual source code.

Listing 6-13. Post-processed demo

```
create or replace package postprocesseddemo as
  $if $$exposeprocedure $then
  procedure private_procedure;
  $end
  procedure public_procedure;
end postprocesseddemo;
```

When you call the procedure with the correct parameters.

```
begin
  dbms_preprocessor.print_post_processed_source
  (object_type => 'PACKAGE'
  ,schema_name => 'BOOK'
  ,object_name => 'POSTPROCESSEDDEMO');
end;
```

You get a result like the following.

```
package ccdemo as

  procedure public_procedure;
end ccdemo;
```

Notice the empty lines in the output. These empty lines are inserted for all the lines that didn't make it to the compiled source, including the lines with the directives. This is done to preserve the line number when reporting an error.

If you recompile the package and set the flag to TRUE.

```
alter package postprocesseddemo compile plsql_ccflags =
'exposeprocedure:true'
```

You get a different result.

```
package postprocesseddemo as

  procedure private_procedure;

  procedure public_procedure;
end postprocesseddemo;
```

Tip   when using this utility, make sure you have set format wrapped when setting server output on; otherwise, the empty lines are deleted. `set serveroutput on size unlimited format wrapped`

Summary

This chapter covered selection, inquiry, and error directives, the building blocks of conditional compilation. With conditional compilation, you can create a single codebase for different Oracle Database versions, make sure that code is deployed to the correct environment (code that should only be deployed to a development environment and certainly not to production), and expose private procedures for testing purposes. Several use cases and some tips on working with conditional compilation were discussed.

CHAPTER 7

Iterations and Qualified Expressions

Oracle Database has had loop statements since it first introduced PL/SQL into the database. All kinds of loops were possible with a little coding and creating special logic. Many of these "home brew" loop types, like stepped loops and loops with conditional exit points, are now available in standard code.

Iterations

The `for` loop specifies an iterator and the iteration controls. If necessary, the iteration controls can be stacked, resulting in multiple loops condensed into one loop. The iterator only has scope inside the loop. Statements outside the loop cannot reference the iterator, which is undefined after the loop.

Iteration Controls

In versions released prior to Oracle Database 21c, the `for` loop had a static signature `for <iterator> in [reverse] <iteration_start> .. <iteration_end>`, which was the only iteration control. Loops were always an integer, run from start to end or from end to start if the reverse, visiting all values between start and end. When you wanted to skip values or wanted to do something special, it had to be built by you.

153

© Alex Nuijten, Patrick Barel 2023
A. Nuijten and P. Barel, *Modern Oracle Database Programming*, https://doi.org/10.1007/978-1-4842-9166-5_7

Multiple Iteration Controls

There used to be only a single iteration control for an iterator, so if you wanted to do the same thing for multiple sets, you would have to come up with multiple loops and copy the logic here. Of course, you would create a (local) procedure for this, but still, you would create code, as seen in Listing 7-1.

Listing 7-1. Multiple iterations pre-21c

```
begin
  for i in 1 .. 3
  loop
    dbms_output.put_line(i);
  end loop;
  for i in 100 .. 104
  loop
    dbms_output.put_line(i);
  end loop;
  for i in 200 .. 202
  loop
    dbms_output.put_line(i);
  end loop;
end;
/

1
2
3
100
101
102
103
104
200
201
202
```

Since Oracle Database 21c, you can stack up multiple iteration controls within one loop. To achieve the same logic, you can create code as written in Listing 7-2.

Listing 7-2. Multiple iterations 21c and up

```
begin
  for i in 1 .. 3, 100 .. 104, 200 .. 202
  loop
    dbms_output.put_line(i);
  end loop;
end;
/

1
2
3
100
101
102
103
104
200
201
202
```

Stepped Iteration Controls

If you have an iteration where you want a stepped control, you must build it yourself. You can either build a short for loop and then do some arithmetic with the iterator value or build a long loop and then skip over the iterator values you don't want to use. The latter solution is displayed in Listing 7-3.

Listing 7-3. Stepped iteration pre-21c

```
begin
  for i in 1 .. 20
  loop
    if mod(i, 3) = 1
```

```
    then
      dbms_output.put_line(i);
    end if;
  end loop;
end;
/
```

```
1
4
7
10
13
16
19
```

Since Oracle Database 21c, you can write the step directly into the iteration, as shown in Listing 7-4.

Listing 7-4. Stepped iteration 21c and up

```
begin
  for i in 1 .. 20 by 3
  loop
    dbms_output.put_line(i);
  end loop;
end;
/
```

```
1
4
7
10
13
16
19
```

You can even take fractional steps if you declare the iterator as a non-integer variable instead of an integer. Listing 7-5 is an example.

Listing 7-5. Fractional stepped iteration 21c and up

```
begin
  for i number(3, 1) in 1 .. 10 by 0.5
  loop
    dbms_output.put_line(i);
  end loop;
end;
/

1
1.5
2
2.5
3
3.5
4
4.5
5
5.5
6
6.5
7
7.5
8
8.5
9
9.5
10
```

The while Loop in Iteration Controls

You could build while loops in previous Oracle Database versions, but that would mean declaring a variable, initializing it, and building the loop. The problem was always, how do you initialize the variable, and where do you alter its value? Listing 7-6 shows a while loop in a pre-21c database.

Listing 7-6. while loop

```
declare
  power2 number;
begin
  power2 := 1;
  while power2 <= 1024 loop
    dbms_output.put_line( power2 );
    power2 := power2 * 2;
  end loop;
end;
/

1
2
4
8
16
32
64
128
256
512
1024
```

In Oracle Database 21c, you can include a while loop in a for loop, as seen in Listing 7-7.

Listing 7-7. A while loop in iteration control

```
begin
  for power2 in 1, repeat power2 * 2 while power2 <= 1024
  loop
    dbms_output.put_line(power2);
  end loop;
end;
/
```

```
1
2
4
8
16
32
64
128
256
512
1024
```

when in Iteration Controls

Where you would normally run all the iterations in your loop and, within each iteration, check for a specified condition to be satisfied before executing some logic, these conditions can now be handled in the iteration control itself.

If you create a function returning a BOOLEAN value, as shown in Listing 7-8, you can use this as part of a condition inside your iteration control used in Listing 7-9.

Listing 7-8. The is_prime function

```
create or replace function is_prime(number_in in number)
  return boolean is
  l_returnvalue boolean := true;
begin
  for indx in 2 .. number_in / 2
  loop
    if mod(number_in, indx) = 0
    then
      l_returnvalue := false;
      exit;
    end if;
  end loop;
  return l_returnvalue;
end;
/
```

Using this function, you can ensure the loop is only executed when our condition is satisfied. The example in Listing 7-9 shows the use of this function to determine the condition to execute the code block inside the block.

Listing 7-9. when in iteration control

```
begin
  for i in 1 .. 100 when is_prime(i) and i not in (19, 37)
  loop
    dbms_output.put_line(i);
  end loop;
end;
/

1
2
3
5
7
11
13
17
23
29
31
41
43
47
53
59
61
67
71
73
79
```

83
89
97

The loop is only executed for the values that satisfy the condition specified in the when clause.

Cursor in Iteration Controls

The cursor for loop statement has been available since the first implementation of PL/SQL in Oracle Database. You could use the iterator record to process the cursor's data. Listing 7-10 shows an implementation of such a cursor for loop.

Listing 7-10. Cursor for loop displaying information

```
begin
  dbms_output.put_line( 'Drivers:');
  for rec in (select d.driverid
                   , d.driverref
                   , d.forename || ' ' || d.surname as name
                   , d.nationality
              from   f1data.drivers d
          ) loop
    dbms_output.put_line( rec.driverid
                        ||'('
                        ||rec.driverref
                        ||')'
                        ||rec.name
                        ||'-'
                        ||rec.nationality
                        );
  end loop;
  dbms_output.put_line( 'Constructors:');
  for rec in (select c.constructorid
                   , c.constructorref
                   , c.name
                   , c.nationality
```

```
                from    f1data.constructors c
            ) loop
    dbms_output.put_line( rec.constructorid
                        ||'('
                        ||rec.constructorref
                        ||')'
                        ||rec.name
                        ||'-'
                        ||rec.nationality
                        );
    end loop;
end;
/
```

```
Drivers:
1(hamilton)Lewis Hamilton-British
2(heidfeld)Nick Heidfeld-German
3(rosberg)Nico Rosberg-German
4(alonso)Fernando Alonso-Spanish
5(kovalainen)Heikki Kovalainen-Finnish
6(nakajima)Kazuki Nakajima-Japanese
7(bourdais)Sébastien Bourdais-French
8(raikkonen)Kimi Räikkönen-Finnish
9(kubica)Robert Kubica-Polish
10(glock)Timo Glock-German
<<results removed for brevity>>
Constructors:
1(mclaren)McLaren-British
2(bmw_sauber)BMW Sauber-German
3(williams)Williams-British
4(renault)Renault-French
5(toro_rosso)Toro Rosso-Italian
6(ferrari)Ferrari-Italian
7(toyota)Toyota-Japanese
8(super_aguri)Super Aguri-Japanese
9(red_bull)Red Bull-Austrian
```

```
10(force_india)Force India-Indian
<<results removed for brevity>>
```

As you can see, to display the information, you must copy the logic between the two cursor for loop statements. In Oracle Database 21c, it is possible to define the iterator as a predefined record type, which you can use as a parameter in a display procedure. Listing 7-11 is an example of this usage; it declares a record type info_t and uses this type as the iterator instead of a standard scalar value.

Listing 7-11. Cursor for loop with predefined record type

```
declare
  type info_t is record
    ( id           number(11)
    , ref          varchar2(255)
    , name         varchar2(255)
    , nationality varchar2(255)
    );
  procedure printit(rec_in in info_t)
  is
  begin
    dbms_output.put_line
    ( rec_in.id
    ||'('
    ||rec_in.ref
    ||')'
    ||rec_in.name
    ||'-'
    ||rec_in.nationality
    );
  end;
begin
  dbms_output.put_line( 'Drivers:');
  for rec info_t in (select d.driverid
                          , d.driverref
                          , d.forename || ' ' || d.surname
                          , d.nationality
```

```
                   from    f1data.drivers d
                   where   rownum < 11) loop
   printit(rec_in => rec);
  end loop;
  dbms_output.put_line( 'Constructors:');
  for rec info_t in (select c.constructorid
                          , c.constructorref
                          , c.name
                          , c.nationality
                   from    f1data.constructors c
                   where   rownum < 11) loop
   printit(rec_in => rec);
  end loop;
end;
/

Drivers:
1(hamilton)Lewis Hamilton-British
2(heidfeld)Nick Heidfeld-German
3(rosberg)Nico Rosberg-German
4(alonso)Fernando Alonso-Spanish
5(kovalainen)Heikki Kovalainen-Finnish
6(nakajima)Kazuki Nakajima-Japanese
7(bourdais)Sébastien Bourdais-French
8(raikkonen)Kimi Räikkönen-Finnish
9(kubica)Robert Kubica-Polish
10(glock)Timo Glock-German
<<results removed for brevity>>
Constructors:
1(mclaren)McLaren-British
2(bmw_sauber)BMW Sauber-German
3(williams)Williams-British
4(renault)Renault-French
5(toro_rosso)Toro Rosso-Italian
6(ferrari)Ferrari-Italian
7(toyota)Toyota-Japanese
```

```
8(super_aguri)Super Aguri-Japanese
9(red_bull)Red Bull-Austrian
10(force_india)Force India-Indian
<<results removed for brevity>>
```

This technique can also create procedures or functions that accept a ref cursor as one of the parameters. Listing 7-12 implements this in a package. Instead of creating a cursor for loop, you create a loop over the values of a cursor variable.

Listing 7-12. Display information package

```
create or replace package information is
  procedure display(refcursor_in in sys_refcursor);
end information;
/

create or replace package body information is
  type rec_t is record
    ( id           number(11)
    , ref          varchar2(255)
    , name         varchar2(255)
    , nationality varchar2(255)
    );
  procedure printit(rec_in in rec_t)
  is
  begin
    dbms_output.put_line
    ( rec_in.id
    ||'('
    ||rec_in.ref
    ||')'
    ||rec_in.name
    ||'-'
    ||rec_in.nationality
    );
  end;
  procedure display(refcursor_in in sys_refcursor)
```

```
  is
  begin
    for rec rec_t in values of refcursor_in loop
      printit(rec_in => rec);
    end loop;
  end display;
end information;
/
```

You can call this procedure with any ref cursor if the returning record type adheres to the defined record definition.

```
declare
  rc sys_refcursor;
begin
  open rc for select d.driverid
                   , d.driverref
                   , d.forename || ' ' || d.surname
                   , d.nationality
              from   f1data.drivers d
  information.display(rc);
end;
/

1(hamilton)Lewis Hamilton-British
2(heidfeld)Nick Heidfeld-German
3(rosberg)Nico Rosberg-German
4(alonso)Fernando Alonso-Spanish
5(kovalainen)Heikki Kovalainen-Finnish
6(nakajima)Kazuki Nakajima-Japanese
7(bourdais)Sébastien Bourdais-French
8(raikkonen)Kimi Räikkönen-Finnish
9(kubica)Robert Kubica-Polish
10(glock)Timo Glock-German
<<results removed for brevity>>

declare
  rc sys_refcursor;
```

```
begin
  open rc for select c.constructorid
                   , c.constructorref
                   , c.name
                   , c.nationality
              from   f1data.constructors c
  information.display(rc);
end;
/
```

```
1(mclaren)McLaren-British
2(bmw_sauber)BMW Sauber-German
3(williams)Williams-British
4(renault)Renault-French
5(toro_rosso)Toro Rosso-Italian
6(ferrari)Ferrari-Italian
7(toyota)Toyota-Japanese
8(super_aguri)Super Aguri-Japanese
9(red_bull)Red Bull-Austrian
10(force_india)Force India-Indian
<<results removed for brevity>>
```

Mutable Iterator

How many times have you tried to assign a value to your iterator? For example, you wanted to skip an arbitrary number of steps in the iterations. Consider the script shown in Listing 7-13.

Listing 7-13. Try to assign a value to the iterator

```
begin
  for i in 1 .. 10
  loop
    dbms_output.put_line(i);
    i := i + 3;
  end loop;
end;
/
```

```
ORA-06550: line 7, column 7:
PLS-00363: expression 'I' cannot be used as an assignment target
ORA-06550: line 7, column 7:
PL/SQL: Statement ignored
```

Oracle Database 21c comes with a new option: the *mutable iterator*. Using the keyword mutable after the name of the iterator makes it modifiable during the execution of the loop so that the code in Listing 7-14 runs.

Listing 7-14. Make the iterator mutable

```
begin
  for i mutable in 1 .. 10
  loop
    dbms_output.put_line(i);
    i := i + 3;
  end loop;
end;
/

1
5
9
```

The default behavior is to have an immutable iterator, which can be specified in a more verbose way, like in Listing 7-15.

Listing 7-15. Make the iterator immutable

```
begin
  for i immutable in 1 .. 10
  loop
    dbms_output.put_line(i);
    i := i + 3;
  end loop;
end;
/
```

```
ORA-06550: line 7, column 7:
PLS-00363: expression 'I' cannot be used as an assignment target
ORA-06550: line 7, column 7:
PL/SQL: Statement ignored
```

Augmenting the Iterator

When a numeric iterator is not mutable unless you specify a mutable keyword, the record in a cursor for loop is mutable; that is, the values of the individual attributes are mutable, even though the iterator itself is not declared mutable. Let's say you have a procedure to reverse a string, as shown in Listing 7-16.

Listing 7-16. Reverse string procedure

```
create or replace procedure
  reversestring(string_inout in out varchar2)
is
  l_reversed varchar2( 32767 );
  l_strlen number;
begin
  l_strlen := length( string_inout );
  for i in reverse 1..l_strlen
  loop
    l_reversed := l_reversed || substr( string_inout, i, 1 );
  end loop;
  string_inout := l_reversed;
end;
/
```

If you create a cursor for loop, where the iterator is a record from the cursor, even though the iterator is not defined as mutable, you can still assign values to the different elements of the record. This has been possible since Oracle Database version 7.

```
begin
  for driver in (select *
                 from   f1data.drivers d
                 where  d.nationality = 'Dutch')
```

```
  loop
    dbms_output.put_line( driver.forename
                          || ' '
                          || driver.surname );
    reversestring( driver.forename );
    reversestring( driver.surname );
    dbms_output.put_line( driver.surname
                          || ' '
                          || driver.forename );
  end loop;
end;
/
```

The for loop in an Array

Instead of creating a for loop and then assigning values to an associative array inside the loop, as you can see in Listing 7-17, you can define the loop inside the assignment statement, as you can see in Listing 7-18.

Listing 7-17. Use loops to assign values pre-21c

```
declare
  type num_list is table of int index by pls_integer;
  s1 num_list;
  s2 num_list;
begin
  for i in 1 .. 10
  loop
    s1(i) := i * 10;
  end loop;

  for i in 1 .. 10
  loop
    if mod(i, 2) = 0
    then
      s2(i) := s1(i);
```

```
    end if;
  end loop;
end;
/
```

Listing 7-18. Use loop inside array in 21c

```
declare
  type num_list is table of int index by pls_integer;
  s1 num_list;
  s2 num_list;
begin
  s1 := num_list( for i in 1 .. 10 => i );
  s2 := num_list( for i in 2 .. 10 by 2 => s1( i ) );
end;
/
```

The Indices of an Array

The complementary statement to the bulk collect construction to retrieve the data
from the database in a single pass is the forall statement to write changes back to the
database in a single pass. The forall statement has, besides using the <collection>.
first .. <collection>.last construction for dense collections, the possibility to
use the indices of and values of constructions. Starting in Oracle Database 21c, it
is possible to use these constructions in a for loop. Instead of writing a while loop as
is displayed in Listing 7-19, you can use the indices of construction as you can see in
Listing 7-20.

Listing 7-19. Displaying a sparse collection pre 21c

```
declare
  type num_list is table of int index by pls_integer;

  s2 num_list;
  idx int;
begin
```

```
  s2 := num_list(2  => 20
                ,4  => 40
                ,6  => 60
                ,8  => 80
                ,10 => 100);

  idx := s2.first;
  while idx is not null
  loop
    dbms_output.put_line(idx || '=' || s2(idx));
    idx := s2.next(idx);
  end loop;
end;
/

2=20
4=40
6=60
8=80
10=100
```

Listing 7-20. Displaying a sparse collection since 21c

```
declare
  type num_list is table of int index by pls_integer;

  s2 num_list;
begin

  s2 := num_list(for i in 2 .. 10 by 2 => i * 10);

  for idx in indices of s2
  loop
    dbms_output.put_line(idx || '=' || s2(idx));
  end loop;
end;
/
```

```
2=20
4=40
6=60
8=80
10=100
```

Tip   The s2 variable is initialized using a qualified expression in the iteration control. Read more in the qualified expressions section later in this chapter.

The Values of an Array

If you are only interested in an array's values, you can call a for loop using the values of operator, as seen in Listing 7-21.

Listing 7-21. Displaying the values of a collection since 21c

```
declare
  type num_list is table of int index by pls_integer;

  s2 num_list;
begin

  s2 := num_list(for i in 2 .. 10 by 2 => i * 10);

  for idx in values of s2
  loop
    dbms_output.put_line(idx);
  end loop;
end;
/

20
40
60
80
100
```

The iterator doesn't have to be a scalar; it can also be a record, as shown in Listing 7-22.

Listing 7-22. Using values of with records

```
declare
  type driver_aa is table of f1data.drivers%rowtype
    index by pls_integer;
  l_drivers driver_aa;
  cursor drivers is
    select d.driverid
         , d.driverref
         , d.driver_number
         , d.code
         , d.forename
         , d.surname
         , d.dob
         , d.nationality
         , d.url
      from   f1data.drivers d
      where  d.nationality = 'Dutch';
begin
  l_drivers := driver_aa( for i in drivers
                            index i.driverid => i );
  for driver in values of l_drivers
  loop
    dbms_output.put_line( 'l_drivers['
                        || driver.driverid
                        || ']='
                        || driver.driverref
                        );
  end loop;
end;
/

l_drivers[27]=albers
l_drivers[38]=doornbos
```

```
l_drivers[50]=verstappen
l_drivers[136]=lammers
l_drivers[179]=rothengatter
l_drivers[247]=bleekemolen
l_drivers[257]=hayje
l_drivers[295]=wunderink
l_drivers[298]=lennep
l_drivers[430]=beaufort
l_drivers[450]=vos
l_drivers[457]=pon
l_drivers[458]=slotemaker
l_drivers[758]=lof
l_drivers[759]=flinterman
l_drivers[823]=garde
l_drivers[830]=max_verstappen
```

Note   The initialization of the collection is explained in the qualified expressions section later in this chapter.

The pairs of Array

In Oracle Database 21c, you can use pairs of construction. Instead of creating an index iterator and using that to get the value from the collection (see Listing 7-23), you can get both the index and the value as iterators in the loop (see Listing 7-24). This also works with sparse collections.

Listing 7-23. Use index iterator to get value

```
declare
  type num_list is table of int index by pls_integer;
  s1 num_list;
  s2 num_list;
begin
  s1 := num_list(10, 20, 30, 40, 50, 60, 70, 80, 90, 1000);
  s2 := num_list(for i in 2 .. 10 by 2 => s1(i));
```

```
  for idx in values of s2
  loop
    dbms_output.put_line(idx);
  end loop;
end;
/

20
40
60
80
1000
```

Listing 7-24. Use pairs of to get index and value

```
declare
  type num_list is table of int index by pls_integer;
  s1 num_list;
  s2 num_list;
begin
  s1 := num_list(10, 20, 30, 40, 50, 60, 70, 80, 90, 1000);
  s2 := num_list(for i in 2 .. 10 by 2 => s1(i));

  for x, y in pairs of s2
  loop
    dbms_output.put_line(x || ',' || y);
  end loop;
end;
/

2,20
4,40
6,60
8,80
10,1000
```

The value doesn't have to be a scalar value; it can also be a record, as seen in Listing 7-25.

Listing 7-25. Using pairs of with records

```
declare
  type driver_aa is table of f1data.drivers%rowtype
    index by pls_integer;
  l_drivers driver_aa;
  cursor drivers is
    select d.driverid
         , d.driverref
         , d.driver_number
         , d.code
         , d.forename
         , d.surname
         , d.dob
         , d.nationality
         , d.url
    from    f1data.drivers d
    where   d.nationality = 'Dutch';
begin
  l_drivers := driver_aa( for i in drivers
                              index i.driverid => i );
  for driverid, driver in pairs of l_drivers
  loop
    dbms_output.put_line( 'l_drivers[' || driverid || ']=' ||
                      driver.driverref );
  end loop;
end;
/

l_drivers[27]=albers
l_drivers[38]=doornbos
l_drivers[50]=verstappen
l_drivers[136]=lammers
l_drivers[179]=rothengatter
l_drivers[247]=bleekemolen
l_drivers[257]=hayje
```

```
l_drivers[295]=wunderink
l_drivers[298]=lennep
l_drivers[430]=beaufort
l_drivers[450]=vos
l_drivers[457]=pon
l_drivers[458]=slotemaker
l_drivers[758]=lof
l_drivers[759]=flinterman
l_drivers[823]=garde
l_drivers[830]=max_verstappen
```

PL/SQL Qualified Expressions

Since Oracle Database 18c, it is possible to use qualified expressions. Qualified expressions look a lot like calling a procedure or function with named parameters.

Records

In previous Oracle Database versions, you could initialize records by initializing the variable and then providing values for all the attributes of the record (see Listing 7-26).

Listing 7-26. Initializing variable pre-18c

```
declare
  type circuit_t is record
  ( circuitid  number(11)
  , circuitref varchar2(255)
  , name       varchar2(255)
  , location   varchar2(255)
  , country    varchar2(255)
  , lat        float
  , lng        float
  , alt        number(11)
  , url        varchar2(255));
  l_circuit circuit_t;
begin
```

```
  l_circuit := circuit_t();
  l_circuit.circuitid  := 2912;
  l_circuit.circuitref := 'tt_circuit';
  l_circuit.name        := 'TT Circuit Assen';
  l_circuit.location    := 'Assen';
  l_circuit.country     := 'Netherlands';
  l_circuit.lat         := 52.961667;
  l_circuit.lng         := 6.523333;
  l_circuit.url         :=
          'https://en.wikipedia.org/wiki/TT_Circuit_Assen';
  dbms_output.put_line( 'Name      : ' || l_circuit.name );
  dbms_output.put_line( 'Location : ' || l_circuit.location );
  dbms_output.put_line( 'Latitude : ' || l_circuit.lat );
  dbms_output.put_line( 'Lngitude : ' || l_circuit.lng );
  dbms_output.put_line( 'Altitude : ' || l_circuit.alt );
end;
/
```

```
Name      : TT Circuit Assen
Location : Assen
Latitude : 52.961667
Lngitude : 6.523333
Altitude :
```

Providing the values could also be done in the initialization by providing these values as parameters. If they were unknown, you could supply NULL (see Listing 7-27).

Listing 7-27. Initializing variable in initialization pre-18c

```
declare
  type circuit_t is record
  ( circuitid  number(11)
  , circuitref varchar2(255)
  , name       varchar2(255)
  , location   varchar2(255)
  , country    varchar2(255)
  , lat        float
```

```
  , lng          float
  , alt          number(11)
  , url          varchar2(255));
  l_circuit circuit_t;
begin
  l_circuit := circuit_t
    ( 2912
    , 'tt_circuit'
    , 'TT Circuit Assen'
    , 'Assen'
    , 'Netherlands'
    , 52.961667
    , 6.523333
    , null
    , 'https://en.wikipedia.org/wiki/TT_Circuit_Assen'
    );
  dbms_output.put_line( 'Name      : ' || l_circuit.name );
  dbms_output.put_line( 'Location : ' || l_circuit.location );
  dbms_output.put_line( 'Latitude : ' || l_circuit.lat );
  dbms_output.put_line( 'Lngitude : ' || l_circuit.lng );
  dbms_output.put_line( 'Altitude : ' || l_circuit.alt );
end;
/

Name      : TT Circuit Assen
Location : Assen
Latitude : 52.961667
Lngitude : 6.523333
Altitude :
```

Since Oracle Database 18c, you can use qualified expressions to initialize a record (see Listing 7-28).

Listing 7-28. Initializing variable in 18c

```
declare
  type circuit_t is record
  ( circuitid  number(11)
  , circuitref varchar2(255)
  , name       varchar2(255)
  , location   varchar2(255)
  , country    varchar2(255)
  , lat        float
  , lng        float
  , alt        number(11)
  , url        varchar2(255));
  l_circuit circuit_t;
begin
  l_circuit := circuit_t
    ( circuitid  => 2912
    , circuitref => 'tt_circuit'
    , name       => 'TT Circuit Assen'
    , location   => 'Assen'
    , country    => 'Netherlands'
    , lat        => 52.961667
    , lng        => 6.523333
    , url        => 'https://en.wikipedia.org/wiki/TT_Circuit_Assen'
    );
  dbms_output.put_line( 'Name     : ' || l_circuit.name );
  dbms_output.put_line( 'Location : ' || l_circuit.location );
  dbms_output.put_line( 'Latitude : ' || l_circuit.lat );
  dbms_output.put_line( 'Lngitude : ' || l_circuit.lng );
  dbms_output.put_line( 'Altitude : ' || l_circuit.alt );
end;
/
```

```
Name     : TT Circuit Assen
Location : Assen
Latitude : 52.961667
Lngitude : 6.523333
Altitude :
```

Collections

Similar to records, you can also initialize collections using *qualified expressions*. In previous Oracle Database versions, you had to initialize the collection on an item-per-item basis (see Listing 7-29).

Listing 7-29. Initializing collections pre-18c

```
declare
  type numbers_tt is table of number index by pls_integer;
  l_numbers numbers_tt;
begin
  l_numbers(72) := 29;
  l_numbers(76) := 6;
  l_numbers(98) := 18;
  l_numbers(69) := 5;

  for indx in indices of l_numbers loop
    dbms_output.put_line( '('
                      ||indx
                      ||') '
                      ||l_numbers(indx)
                      );
  end loop;
end;
/

(69) 5
(72) 29
(76) 6
(98) 18
```

The same script becomes clearer and more concise using a qualified expression (see Listing 7-30).

Listing 7-30. Initializing collections in 18c

```
declare
  type numbers_tt is table of number index by pls_integer;
  l_numbers numbers_tt;
begin
  l_numbers := numbers_tt( 72 => 29
                         , 76 => 6
                         , 98 => 18
                         , 69 => 5
                         );

  for indx in indices of l_numbers loop
    dbms_output.put_line( '('
                        ||indx
                        ||') '
                        ||l_numbers(indx)
                        );
  end loop;
end;
/

(69) 5
(72) 29
(76) 6
(98) 18
```

If you want to initialize a dense collection with indices starting at number 1, Oracle Database 21c does not require using qualified expressions (see Listing 7-31).

Listing 7-31. Initializing dense collections in 21c

```
declare
  type numbers_tt is table of number index by pls_integer;
  l_numbers numbers_tt;
```

```
begin
  l_numbers := numbers_tt( 29, 6, 18, 5 );

  for indx in indices of l_numbers loop
    dbms_output.put_line( '('
                          ||indx
                          ||') '
                          ||l_numbers(indx)
                          );
  end loop;
end;
/

(1) 29
(2) 6
(3) 18
(4) 5
```

You can also use a cursor directly in the constructor of the collection. There are two ways to populate the collection using a cursor. You can populate it as a dense collection in the same way your collection would be populated using a bulk collect. In this case, you use the sequence keyword for the index in your collection (see Listing 7-32).

Listing 7-32. Initializing dense collections using cursor in 21c

```
declare
  type circuit_tt is table of f1data.circuits%rowtype
    index by pls_integer;
  l_circuits circuit_tt;
begin
  l_circuits := circuit_tt
                (for rec in
                  (select c.circuitid
                        , c.circuitref
                        , c.name
                        , c.location
                        , c.country
                        , c.lat
```

```
                            , c.lng
                            , c.alt
                            , c.url
                      from   f1data.circuits c
                      order  by c.circuitref
                  ) sequence => rec);

   dbms_output.put_line( l_circuits(1).name
                        ||' ('
                        ||l_circuits(1).location
                        ||' ['
                        ||l_circuits(1).lat
                        ||','
                        ||l_circuits(1).lng
                        ||'])'
   );
end;
/
```

```
Circuit Park Zandvoort (Zandvoort [52.3888,4.54092])
```

Sometimes it makes more sense to use the table's primary key as an index, or even a unique key, like in this case, the circuitref field. Here you use the index keyword to assign a field from the cursor as an index (see Listing 7-33).

Listing 7-33. Initializing sparse collections using cursor in 21c

```
declare
  type circuit_tt is table of f1data.circuits%rowtype
    index by varchar2(256);
  l_circuits circuit_tt;
begin
  l_circuits := circuit_tt
                    (for rec in
                      (select c.circuitid
                            , c.circuitref
                            , c.name
                            , c.location
```

```
                             , c.country
                             , c.lat
                             , c.lng
                             , c.alt
                             , c.url
                     from    f1data.circuits c
                   ) index rec.circuitref => rec);

  dbms_output.put_line( l_circuits('zandvoort').name
                    ||' ('
                    ||l_circuits('zandvoort').location
                    ||' ['
                    ||l_circuits('zandvoort').lat
                    ||','
                    ||l_circuits('zandvoort').lng
                    ||'])'
  );
end;
/

Circuit Park Zandvoort (Zandvoort [52.3888,4.54092])
```

Summary

Since Oracle Database 21c, you have access to an extensive range of possibilities in loops. The iterator doesn't have to be an integer. It can also be a non-integer or a string value. The iterator can now be declared mutable, so you can alter the value inside the loop. Iteration controls can be stepped and stacked.

Using qualified expressions makes your code clear and more self-documenting.

PART II

Multiple Techniques and Languages

CHAPTER 8

Polymorphic Table Functions and SQL Macros

A lot of functionality is provided by Oracle Database out of the box. Most common functions and procedures are at your fingertips. But what do they offer when you need something not provided by Oracle? Suppose you have to figure out the total work hours when you only have a check-in and check-out time. An aggregate to sum up the interval differences between the start and end times would be very helpful. Unfortunately, Oracle Database does not provide an aggregate that sums up intervals yet. (You never know when they will implement a function like that.) You could create a "normal" PL/SQL function, but then you would always take a performance hit.

What if you're migrating from a different database, like SQL Server, where there is a function to determine the current date and time (SYSDATE), and you don't want to change all the code the application uses?

In previous Oracle Database releases, you could take advantage of the Oracle Data Cartridge Interface (ODCI), but that was not trivial to implement correctly. One of the hardest things to implement was to make your ODCI function work correctly with parallel query processing.

With the introduction of the *polymorphic table function* (PTF), implementing your own SQL functions is a lot simpler, not trivial. Oracle takes care of the underlying plumbing to ensure that the PTF plays nicely with parallel queries.

SQL Macros can also be used in this area, making some implementations of PTFs a little easier. With SQL Macros, you can create reusable SQL snippets. Implement once, use in your SQL statements, and don't have the performance impact that a regular PL/SQL function call has.

189

© Alex Nuijten, Patrick Barel 2023
A. Nuijten and P. Barel, *Modern Oracle Database Programming*, https://doi.org/10.1007/978-1-4842-9166-5_8

Polymorphic Table Functions

The SQL:2016 standard describes *polymorphic table functions* as follows.

> *… user-defined functions that can be invoked in the FROM clause. They can process tables whose row type is not declared at definition time and produce a result table whose row type may or may not be declared at definition time. Polymorphic Table Functions allow application developers to leverage the long-defined dynamic SQL capabilities to create powerful and complex custom functions.*

Oracle Database18c introduces this concept. Depending on the input parameters, the return type is defined at runtime. This differs from the conventional table functions, where the return type is fixed at compile time.

A polymorphic table function consists of two parts.

- A PL/SQL package that holds all the code for the PTF implementation.

- A stand-alone or packaged function that acts as an interface naming the PTF and its associated implementation package.

The PL/SQL package contains the programs to implement the PTF. The programs accept the PL/SQL version of the arguments supplied in the interface function.

Function

The wrapper function performs the interface from the SQL statement to the PTF. The table pseudo-operator is used to translate the table object to the `dbms_tf.table_t` PL/SQL type. A new pseudo-operator, `columns,` is introduced to facilitate the translation of the columns to the `dbms_tf.columns_t` type. The other parameters, if any, use their SQL counterpart. The wrapper function does not have a function body. It is just the interface to the PTF package.

The function specifies the following things.

- The PTF name

- Exactly one argument of type `table` and any number of `non-table` arguments

- The return type is `table`

- The type of PTF, either `row` or `table semantics`

- The package name where the PTF is implemented

```
create [ or replace ] [ editionable | noneditionable ]
  function [ schema. ] function_name
  [ ( parameter_declaration [, parameter_declaration]... ) ]
return table
  pipelined ( row | table ) polymorphic
  using [ schema. ] implementation_package
```

If the PTF is defined as *row semantics*, the input is a single row. All the information the PTF needs is available in this single row. The PTF doesn't know or need to know anything about other rows. The input is a set of rows if the PTF is defined as table semantics. The PTF can use the information from multiple rows, for example, to build your own aggregate function. When you have a table semantics PTF, you can optionally extend the table argument with a `partition` by clause and/or an `order` by clause.

Package

The package contains all the code necessary to implement the PTF. It must contain a `describe` function but can also contain `open`, `fetch_rows`, and `close` procedures. The `describe` function is mandatory; all other procedures are optional.

describe

The arguments passed to the `describe` function can be the standard scalar arguments that can be passed to a regular table function. But a PTF also accepts a table argument. A table argument must be a basic table name, which can be a `with` clause query or any schema-level object allowed in a `from` clause (table, view, or table function). The `describe` function can also accept a `columns` parameter.

In the `describe` function, you can tell which input table columns should be read (`for_read`) and which columns should be passed through (`pass_through`) to the result. If a column has its `for_read` property set to true, then its *values* are available in the other procedures of the PTF. If it is set to FALSE, they are not.

If you want the column to appear in the resulting columns, you must set the pass_ through property to true. If this property is set to FALSE, the column is not visible in the resulting columns.

Not only can you choose to show or hide existing columns, but you can also create completely new columns that only exist in the result set.

open

The open procedure, if present, is invoked once before the fetch_rows procedure. It can be used to initialize and allocate specific states. It is mostly useful when implementing a table semantics PTF. Since the execution state is session and the cursor private, like a normal package, a table semantics PTF can use package globals for storing the execution state. The PTF uses the database-provided unique execution ID to identify that state. You can use the get_xid function to get a unique id for this execution state. This ID remains the same for all the execution functions of the PTF.

fetch_rows

The fetch_rows procedure is where the real work is done. It produces an output rowset that gets sent back to the requesting process. This procedure can be invocated multiple times, depending on the data. How often it is invoked is determined during query execution. It looks like this procedure is called for every batch of 1024 rows, but this does not seem to be documented anywhere.

close

The close procedure is called once at the end of the PTF execution. Use this procedure to release resources associated with the PTF execution state. You can also reset global settings back to their original values.

Usage

While developing your PTF, you probably want to use tracing to see what your program is doing. You could use dbms_output.put_line for this, but the DBMS_TF package provides an overloaded trace procedure. Not only can you write messages similar to dbms_output.put_line, but it also has overloading to print out the entire row set, table information, the complete environment, and more.

```
procedure trace(msg                    varchar2,
                with_id                boolean  default false,
                separator              varchar2 default null,
                prefix                 varchar2 default null);
procedure trace(rowset              in row_set_t);
procedure trace(env                 in env_t);
procedure trace(columns_new         in columns_new_t);
procedure trace(cols                in columns_t);
procedure trace(columns_with_type   in columns_with_type_t);
procedure trace(tab                 in table_t);
procedure trace(col                 in column_metadata_t);
```

This can give a lot of information when developing. You may want to include calls to the trace functions using conditional compilation (see Chapter 6), so you can turn this on and off at compile time without changing the source code.

Use Cases

A common requirement is to split strings into smaller bits, depending on a delimiter. Since there is no built-in functionality in SQL to do this, it is where a PTF can fill the hiatus.

Split

Suppose you have many CSV files that need to be loaded into a database. There are a lot of different layouts possible, so you would have to create different code for each of them. Not only is this a tedious job, but it is also error-prone. You probably copy the code from an earlier program and adjust it to your needs. Chances are that you miss one or two.

If you use a PTF, you not only make your usage a lot easier, but chances are also that there are fewer errors.

For this PTF, assume the lines to be split are in the first column of the result set (table, view, etc.) and that a semicolon (;) is used as the separator. You need a package (split_ptf) with the mandatory describe function and a fetch_rows procedure, because you want to process every row individually. This PTF has row semantics, so you do not need the open and close procedures.

The describe function needs to accept the PL/SQL version of the table parameter (called tab in the following code) and a parameter (cols) to tell the PTF which columns to create in the output.

```
function describe
(
  tab  in out dbms_tf.table_t
, cols in     dbms_tf.columns_t default null
) return dbms_tf.describe_t;
```

The fetch_rows procedure doesn't need any parameters.

Listing 8-1 is the complete package header.

Listing 8-1. split_ptf package header

```
create or replace package split_ptf is
  function describe
  (
    tab  in out dbms_tf.table_t
  , cols in     dbms_tf.columns_t default null
  ) return dbms_tf.describe_t;

  procedure fetch_rows;
end split_ptf;
/
```

The setup for the function is done in the describe function. Since the first column of the table must hold the data to be split, mark this column to be read by the engine that transforms the semicolon-separated string into individual parts.

```
tab.column( 1 ).for_read    := true;
```

After the string is split into individual parts, you do not want to display it in the result set anymore. To remove it from the result set, set the pass_through argument to FALSE.

```
tab.column( 1 ).pass_through := false;
```

After this is done, create the new columns as specified in the cols argument. This argument is of type dbms_tf.columns but only holds the names of the columns. You define all these columns as type VARCHAR2 with a maximum length of 4000. You could rely on the defaults for these values, but we like to make our code more explicit. This way, the code works the same, even if the defaults change.

```
l_new_col := dbms_tf.column_metadata_t
             ( type    => dbms_tf.type_varchar2
             , max_len => 4000
             , name    => cols( indx )
             );
-- add the new column to the list of columns new columns
l_new_cols( l_new_cols.count + 1 ) := l_new_col;
```

When you build a new set of columns, the following is returned.

```
return dbms_tf.describe_t( new_columns => l_new_cols );
```

Now it is time for the fetch_rows procedure. This procedure is called for 1024 rows at a time, so it is not row-by-row processing. Therefore, you must create collections to hold the incoming and resulting data.

```
type colset is table of dbms_tf.tab_varchar2_t
  index by pls_integer;

-- variable to hold the rowset as retrieved
l_rowset dbms_tf.row_set_t;

-- variable to hold the number of rows as retrieved
l_rowcount pls_integer;

-- variable to hold the number of (out)put columns
l_putcolcount pls_integer :=
  dbms_tf.get_env().put_columns.count;

-- variable to hold the new values
l_newcolset colset;
```

Now that all the variables and settings are in place, let's start the actual code. First, fetch the rows in a local row set. This result in a collection of a maximum of 1024 rows. The second argument gives you the row count of the current set, you could also have the column count returned, but you can ignore that for this function.

```
dbms_tf.get_row_set( rowset      => l_rowset
                   , row_count =>  l_rowcount );
```

Now that you have the rows in the collection, it is time to start processing the data. Therefore, start with two loops. The first is a loop for every row.

```
for rowindx in 1 .. l_rowcount
loop
```

And within that loop, start a loop for every column defined in the output set.

```
for colindx in 1 .. l_putcolcount
loop
```

Using the dbms_tf.col_to_char function, retrieve the column to split with regular expressions to extract the right part for the right output column.

```
l_columnvalue := trim(both '"' from
                    dbms_tf.col_to_char( l_rowset( 1 )
                                       , rowindx ) );
l_newcolset(colindx)(rowindx) := trim( ';' from
                            regexp_substr( l_columnvalue
                                         , '[^;]*;{0,1}'
                                         , 1
                                         , colindx
                                         )
                                 );
```

After processing every row in the current set, add the resulting collections to the output row set.

```
for indx in 1 .. l_putcolcount
loop
  dbms_tf.put_col( columnid    => indx
```

```
              , collection => l_newcolset( indx )
              );
    end loop;
```

Listing 8-2 shows the complete implementation of the split_ptf package body.

Listing 8-2. split_ptf package body

```
create or replace package body split_ptf as
  subtype maxvarchar2 is varchar2( 32767 );
  function describe
  (
    tab  in out dbms_tf.table_t
  , cols in       dbms_tf.columns_t default null
  ) return dbms_tf.describe_t as
    -- metadata for column to add
    l_new_col dbms_tf.column_metadata_t;

    -- table of columns to add
    l_new_cols dbms_tf.columns_new_t;
  begin
-- Mark the first column to be read and don't display it anymore
    tab.column( 1 ).for_read      := true;
    tab.column( 1 ).pass_through := false;
    -- Add the new columns, as specified in the cols parameter
    for indx in 1 .. cols.count
    loop
      -- define metadata for column named cols(indx)
      l_new_col := dbms_tf.column_metadata_t
                  ( type     => dbms_tf.type_varchar2
                  , max_len => 4000
                  , name     => cols( indx )
                  );
      -- add the new column to the list of columns new columns
      l_new_cols( l_new_cols.count + 1 ) := l_new_col;
    end loop;
    -- Now we return a specific DESCRIBE_T that adds new columns
```

```
    return dbms_tf.describe_t( new_columns => l_new_cols );
  end;

  procedure fetch_rows is
    -- define a table type of varchar2 tables
    type colset is table of dbms_tf.tab_varchar2_t
      index by pls_integer;

    -- variable to hold the rowset as retrieved
    l_rowset dbms_tf.row_set_t;

    -- variable to hold the number of rows as retrieved
    l_rowcount pls_integer;

    -- variable to hold the number of (out)put columns
    l_putcolcount pls_integer :=
      dbms_tf.get_env().put_columns.count;

    -- variable to hold the new values
    l_newcolset colset;
    -- the value of the column
    l_columnvalue maxvarchar2;
  begin
    -- fetch rows into a local rowset
    -- at this point the rows will have columns
    -- from the the table/view/query passed in
    dbms_tf.get_row_set( rowset     => l_rowset
                       , row_count => l_rowcount
                       );
    -- for every row in the rowset...
    for rowindx in 1 .. l_rowcount
    loop
      -- for every column
      for colindx in 1 .. l_putcolcount
      loop
        l_columnvalue := trim(both '"' from
                              dbms_tf.col_to_char( l_rowset( 1 )
                                                  , rowindx ) );
```

```
        l_newcolset(colindx)(rowindx) := trim( ';' from
                                    regexp_substr( l_columnvalue
                                                , '[^;]*;{0,1}'
                                                , 1
                                                , colindx
                                                )
                                   );
      end loop; -- every column
    end loop; -- every row in the rowset
    -- add the newly populated columns to the rowset
    for indx in 1 .. l_putcolcount
    loop
      dbms_tf.put_col( columnid   => indx
                     , collection => l_newcolset( indx )
                     );
    end loop;
  end;
end split_ptf;
/
```

Now that the package is complete, let's write the wrapper function for this PTF. The wrapper function has the same parameters as the describe function in the package, only this time, the SQL equivalent of the PL/SQL types is used. Also, the semantics type of a PTF is declared. In this case, it is a row semantics function as the PTF works per row.

Listing 8-3 features the wrapper function.

Listing 8-3. Split wrapper function

```
create or replace function split
(
  tab  in table
, cols in columns default null
) return table
pipelined row polymorphic using split_ptf;
/
```

Calling the Polymorphic Function

Table 8-1 lists Formula 1 drivers.

Table 8-1. *Formula 1 Drivers in Semicolon-Separated Format*

DRIVER
44;HAM;Lewis;Hamilton;1985-01-07;British
16;LEC;Charles;Leclerc;1997-10-16;Monegasque
4;NOR;Lando;Norris;1999-11-13;British
11;PER;Sergio;Pérez;1990-01-26;Mexican
3;RIC;Daniel;Ricciardo;1989-07-01;Australian
63;RUS;George;Russell;1998-02-15;British
55;SAI;Carlos;Sainz;1994-09-01;Spanish
33;VER;Max;Verstappen;1997-09-30;Dutch

The PTF makes transforming these separated values into individual columns trivial.

```
select  permanentNumber
     ,  code
     ,  givenName
     ,  familyName
     ,  dateOfBirth
     ,  nationality
from    split( tab  => f1drivers
            ,  cols => columns( permanentNumber
                             ,  code
                             ,  givenName
                             ,  familyName
                             ,  dateOfBirth
                             ,  nationality
                             )
            )
/
```

Note   Make sure you use the same names for the arguments in the wrapper function as you do in the package; otherwise, using named notation fails.

Table 8-2. *Output of Split Polymorphic Table Function*

PERMANENTNUMBER	CODE	GIVENNAME	FAMILYNAME	DATEOFBIRTH	NATIONALITY
44	HAM	Lewis	Hamilton	1985-01-07	British
16	LEC	Charles	Leclerc	1997-10-16	Monegasque
4	NOR	Lando	Norris	1999-11-13	British
11	PER	Sergio	Pérez	1990-01-26	Mexican
3	RIC	Daniel	Ricciardo	1989-07-01	Australian
63	RUS	George	Russell	1998-02-15	British
55	SAI	Carlos	Sainz	1994-09-01	Spanish
33	VER	Max	Verstappen	1997-09-30	Dutch

Sum Intervals

If you have a set of interval values you want to add up, Oracle Database doesn't provide you with a sum aggregation function to do this (yet). Using a PTF lets you build this functionality yourself.

Let's start by building the package specification. The describe function needs a parameter for the table (mandatory) and one for the columns you want to calculate the sum of.

```
function describe
(
  tab  in out dbms_tf.table_t
, cols in      dbms_tf.columns_t default null
) return dbms_tf.describe_t;
/
```

The fetch_rows procedure doesn't need any specific parameters.

Listing 8-4 shows the full package specification for the sum interval PTF.

Listing 8-4. suminterval_ptf package specification

```
create or replace package suminterval_ptf is
  function describe
  (
    tab  in out dbms_tf.table_t
  , cols in     dbms_tf.columns_t default null
  ) return dbms_tf.describe_t;

  procedure fetch_rows;
end suminterval_ptf;
/
```

In the describe function, mark every column not to be passed through to the result set because you are not interested in these column values, only in the aggregate they produce.

```
for indx in tab.column.first .. tab.column.last
loop
  tab.column(indx).pass_through := false;
```

Only the columns that you are interested in should be marked to be read. All others can be ignored (i.e., set for_read to FALSE). The columns marked to be read sum up the intervals.

```
tab.column(indx).for_read := false;
for colindx in cols.first .. cols.last
loop
  if tab.column(indx).description.name = cols(colindx)
  then
    tab.column(indx).for_read := true;
```

Since this is a column of interest, create a new column, to distinguish it from the actual column, with a specific name (SUM_<columnname>_), but with the same type as the original column.

```
      -- and add a new column of the same type but with the
      -- name SUM_colname_
      sum_cols(colindx) :=
```

```
dbms_tf.column_metadata_t
( name => 'SUM_' ||
          replace( tab.column(indx).description.name
                 , '"'
                 ) ||
      '_'
, type => tab.column( indx ).description.type );
```

The following is returned after you have built the new set of columns.

```
-- Now we return a specific DESCRIBE_T that adds new columns
return dbms_tf.describe_t( new_columns => sum_cols );
```

In the fetch_rows procedure, initialize a variable to hold the environment of this function.

```
env dbms_tf.env_t := dbms_tf.get_env();
```

This record contains metadata about execution time properties for the PTF. One of the attributes of this record is a collection of get_columns. These are the columns whose data is available in the PTF (for_read = true).

Looping over this collection, check the column's data type since both supported data types need different processing.

```
for colindx in 1 .. env.get_columns.count
loop
  case env.get_columns( colindx ).type
```

For every supported type, fetch the complete column into a local collection.

```
-- when the column type is INTERVAL YEAR TO MONTH
  when dbms_tf.type_interval_ym then
    -- Get the contents of the column
    dbms_tf.get_col( columnid   => colindx
                   , collection => l_intervalym
                   );
```

Then loop through all the values in this collection and simply add them together.

```
-- Loop through all the values and add them together
for indx in 1 .. l_intervalym.count
loop
  l_sum_recs( colindx ).sumym :=
    l_sum_recs( colindx ).sumym + l_intervalym( indx );
end loop;
```

For the other interval type, INTERVAL DAY TO SECOND, add similar code.

When you are done with all the columns, it is time to build the returning row set. This holds only a single row but with summed values.

```
-- completely ignore the current rowset from now on, just
-- start a new set, with just the totals
-- loop through the put_columns to fill the resulting row
for colindx in 1 .. env.put_columns.count
loop
  case env.put_columns( colindx ).type
  -- when the column type is INTERVAL YEAR TO MONTH
    when dbms_tf.type_interval_ym then
      -- add this value to the resulting row
      l_rowset( colindx ).tab_interval_ym( 1 ) :=
        l_sum_recs( colindx ).sumym;
      -- when the column type is INTERVAL DAY TO SECOND
    when dbms_tf.type_interval_ds then
      -- add this value to the resulting row
      l_rowset(colindx ).tab_interval_ds( 1 ) :=
        l_sum_recs( colindx ).sumds;
  end case;
end loop;
```

Then return this row set, instead of everything that has been sent in.

```
dbms_tf.put_row_set( l_rowset );
```

Listing 8-5 shows the complete implementation of the package body for the sum interval PTF.

Listing 8-5. suminterval_ptf package body

```
create or replace package body suminterval_ptf as
  -- Record type to hold the different INTERVAL sums
  type sum_rec is record(
    sumym interval year to month
  , sumds interval day to second
  );
  -- Collection type for every column
  type sum_recs is table of sum_rec index by pls_integer;
  --
  function describe
  (
    tab  in out dbms_tf.table_t
  , cols in     dbms_tf.columns_t default null
  ) return dbms_tf.describe_t as

    sum_cols dbms_tf.columns_new_t;
  begin
    -- check every column from the source table
    for indx in tab.column.first .. tab.column.last
    loop
      -- mark every columns pass_through as false so it won't
      -- show up in the result anymore
      tab.column( indx ).pass_through := false;
      -- first mark the column not to be read, unless...
      tab.column( indx ).for_read     := false;
      for colindx in cols.first .. cols.last
      loop
        if tab.column( indx ).description.name = cols( colindx )
        then
          -- ...the result of the sum is requested
          -- the read this column
          tab.column( indx ).for_read := true;
          -- and add a new column of the same type but with the
          -- name SUM_colname_
```

```
        sum_cols( colindx ) :=
          dbms_tf.column_metadata_t
          ( name => 'SUM_' ||
                    replace( tab.column(indx).description.name
                           , '"' ) ||
                    '_'
          , type => tab.column( indx ).description.type
          );
      end if;
    end loop;
  end loop;
  -- Instead of returning NULL we will RETURN a specific
  -- DESCRIBE_T that adds new columns
  return dbms_tf.describe_t( new_columns => sum_cols );
end;

procedure fetch_rows is
  -- variable to hold the rowset as retrieved
  l_rowset dbms_tf.row_set_t;
  -- variable to hold the sum of each column

  l_sum_recs sum_recs;
  -- variable to hold the enviroment value

  env dbms_tf.env_t := dbms_tf.get_env();
  -- variable to hold all the YEAR TO MONTH INTERVALs

  l_intervalym dbms_tf.tab_interval_ym_t;
  -- variable to hold all the DAY TO SECOND INTERVALs

  l_intervalds dbms_tf.tab_interval_ds_t;
begin
  for colindx in 1 .. env.get_columns.count
  loop
    case env.get_columns( colindx ).type
    -- when the column type is INTERVAL YEAR TO MONTH
      when dbms_tf.type_interval_ym then
        -- Get the contents of the column
```

```
          dbms_tf.get_col( columnid   => colindx
                         , collection => l_intervalym
                         );
          -- Initialize the record value, otherwise you'll add
          -- something to NULL which results in NULL
          l_sum_recs( colindx ).sumym := interval '0-0' year
                                         to month;
          -- Loop through all the values and add them together
          for indx in 1 .. l_intervalym.count
          loop
            l_sum_recs( colindx ).sumym :=
              l_sum_recs( colindx ).sumym + l_intervalym( indx );
          end loop;
          -- when the column type is INTERVAL DAY TO SECOND
    when dbms_tf.type_interval_ds then
          -- Get the contents of the column
          dbms_tf.get_col( columnid   => colindx
                         , collection => l_intervalds
                         );
          -- Initialize the record value, otherwise you'll add
          -- something to NULL which results in NULL
          l_sum_recs( colindx ).sumds := interval '0 0:0:0' day
                                         to second;
          -- Loop through all the values and add them together
          for indx in 1 .. l_intervalds.count
          loop
            l_sum_recs( colindx ).sumds :=
              l_sum_recs( colindx ).sumds + l_intervalds( indx );
          end loop;
      else
          -- Catch all others
          dbms_output.put_line( q'[Columns of this type (]' ||
                                env.get_columns(colindx).type ||
                                q'[) are not supported (yet).]'
                              );
  end case;
```

```
    end loop;
    -- completely ignore the current rowset from now on, just
    -- start a new set, with just the totals
    -- loop through the put_columns to fill the resulting row
    for colindx in 1 .. env.put_columns.count
    loop
      case env.put_columns( colindx ).type
      -- when the column type is INTERVAL YEAR TO MONTH
        when dbms_tf.type_interval_ym then
          -- add this value to the resulting row
          l_rowset( colindx ).tab_interval_ym( 1 ) :=
            l_sum_recs( colindx ).sumym;
          -- when the column type is INTERVAL DAY TO SECOND
        when dbms_tf.type_interval_ds then
          -- add this value to the resulting row
          l_rowset( colindx ).tab_interval_ds( 1 ) :=
            l_sum_recs( colindx ).sumds;
      end case;
    end loop;
    dbms_tf.put_row_set( l_rowset );
  end;
end suminterval_ptf;
/
```

Now that the package is complete, let's write the wrapper function for this PTF. The wrapper function has the same parameters as the describe function in the package, only this time, the SQL equivalent of the PL/SQL types is used. Also, the type of PTF is declared. In this case, it is a table semantics function because you need multiple rows to calculate the final result.

Listing 8-6 features the wrapper function.

Listing 8-6. suminterval wrapper function

```
create or replace function suminterval_fnc
(
  tab  in table
 ,cols in columns default null
```

```
) return table
pipelined table polymorphic using suminterval_ptf;
/
```

Aggregating Intervals

Suppose you have a table of lap times of Formula 1 races. Note that the lap times are recorded in intervals: INTERVAL_DAY_TO_SECOND. A sample of the lap times is listed in Table 8-3.

Table 8-3. *table of laptimes*

RACENUMBER	LAPNUMBER	DRIVERID	POSITION	LAPTIME
15	1	max_verstappen	1	+000000000 00:01:17.665000000
15	2	max_verstappen	1	+000000000 00:01:14.978000000
15	3	max_verstappen	1	+000000000 00:01:14.813000000
15	4	max_verstappen	1	+000000000 00:01:14.917000000
...				
15	21	max_verstappen	1	+000000000 00:01:18.594000000
15	22	max_verstappen	2	+000000000 00:01:32.574000000
15	23	max_verstappen	2	+000000000 00:01:14.223000000
15	24	max_verstappen	2	+000000000 00:01:14.257000000
15	25	max_verstappen	2	+000000000 00:01:14.607000000
15	26	max_verstappen	2	+000000000 00:01:15.352000000
15	27	max_verstappen	2	+000000000 00:01:14.393000000
15	28	max_verstappen	2	+000000000 00:01:14.683000000
15	29	max_verstappen	2	+000000000 00:01:15.222000000
15	30	max_verstappen	1	+000000000 00:01:16.362000000
15	31	max_verstappen	1	+000000000 00:01:15.134000000
15	32	max_verstappen	1	+000000000 00:01:14.886000000

...

Using the PTF calculating the total race time for Max Verstappen is easy.

```
with verstappen_zandvoort as
( select l.laptime
  from    laps l
  where   l.racenumber = 15
  and     l.driverid = 'max_verstappen'
)
select *
from    suminterval_fnc( tab  => verstappen_zandvoort
                       , cols => columns( laptime ) )
where   rownum = 1
/

SUM_LAPTIME_
---------------
+0 01:30:05
```

Note   The rows are not aggregated; add where rownum = 1 to get only one row.

SQL Macros

Oracle Database 21c (21.1) introduced SQL Macros. It was backported to 19c (19.10) but only for table-type SQL Macros. With SQL Macros, you can use all the power of PL/SQL—including everything introduced in PTF—to create a SQL snippet at runtime, which is included in the SQL statement executed by the SQL engine.

You can utilize a lot of what you learned in the PTFs in SQL Macros. Where the PTFs gave you access to the actual data running through the process, SQL Macros only offer access to manipulate the SQL statement before it gets executed. You call a PL/SQL function only once, before the SQL statement gets executed, and return a SQL fragment that gets placed in the text that gets executed. You can use SQL Macros to centralize functionality that you might previously have captured in a PL/SQL function, but without the cost of all the context switching.

There should be no PL/SQL logic in the function; incoming string arguments are null. All the logic should go into the SQL expression.

There are two types of SQL Macros: scalar and table. What is the difference?

A table-type SQL Macro can be used in a `from` clause of a SQL statement. A scalar-type SQL Macro can be used everywhere else in the SQL statement, the `select` list, `where`, `having`, `group by,` and `order` by clauses.

When you have a formula encapsulated in a PL/SQL function to centralize its implementation, and this formula could be written in pure SQL, then you have a use case for SQL Macros.

Table-Type SQL Macros

A table-type SQL Macro returns a piece of SQL text that results in a set of rows. A parametrized view is one of the use cases for a table-type SQL Macro. A view gives you access to a limited set of data. A parametrized view in a SQL Macro can give you access to a subset of that data set, depending on the parameters you provide.

Of course, you can implement a pseudo-parameterized view by utilizing an application context and using SYS_CONTEXT in the `where` clause of the view, but this requires many more components and might not always be obvious how to utilize the view. Using a SQL Macro, it is immediately obvious that you can pass an argument limiting the output of the result set.

```
select *
from   drivers( nationality => 'Dutch' )
/
```

Note   See "parametrized view" in the column splitter use case for implementing this SQL Macro.

But you can also manipulate the data returned for each row. As long as you can build it in pure SQL, you can build a SQL Macro for it.

Scalar-Type SQL Macro

A scalar-type SQL Macro returns a piece of SQL text that results in a scalar value. A scalar-type SQL Macro cannot have table arguments, only scalar arguments.

Use Cases

There are endless use cases for SQL Macros. You can build a column splitter, like the one done as a PTF—only a lot simpler. You can build parametrized views. You can build scalar macros to capture formulas that you would normally implement in PL/SQL functions. You can also implement support for functionality available in other databases, like MySQL.

Parametrized View

If you want to show the total time, the lap count, and the average lap times per driver for a specific race, create a view that returns these values for all races (see Listing 8-7).

Listing 8-7. v_averagelaptime view

```
create or replace view v_averagelaptime as
select ltm.raceid          as raceid
     , ltm.driverid        as driverid
     , sum( ltm.milliseconds ) as totalmilliseconds
     , count( ltm.lap )    as lapcount
     , avg( ltm.milliseconds ) as averagemilliseconds
from   f1data.laptimes ltm
group  by ltm.raceid
        , ltm.driverid
/
```

In your query, you must limit the result returned by adding a predicate.

```
select *
from   v_averagelaptime alp
where  alp.raceid = 1093 -- United States Grand Prix 2022
  and  alp.driverid = 830 -- Max Verstappen
```

/

```
RACEID DRIVERID TOTALMILLISECONDS LAPCOUNT AVERAGEMILLISECONDS
------ -------- ---------------- -------- -------------------
  1093      830          6131687       56  109494,410714286
```

```
select *
from   v_averagelaptime alp
where  alp.raceid = 1093 -- United States Grand Prix 2022
  and  alp.driverid = 1   -- Lewis Hamilton
/
```

```
RACEID DRIVERID TOTALMILLISECONDS LAPCOUNT AVERAGEMILLISECONDS
------ -------- ---------------- -------- -------------------
  1093        1          6136710       56  109584,107142857
```

If you encapsulate this view in a SQL Macro, you make it a parametrized view.

Listing 8-8. averagelaptime SQL Macro

```
create or replace
function averagelaptime( raceid_in    in number
                       , driverid_in in number )
  return varchar2 sql_macro( table ) is
begin
  return q'[
select ltm.raceid              as raceid
     , ltm.driverid            as driverid
     , sum( ltm.milliseconds ) as totalmilliseconds
     , count( ltm.lap )        as lapcount
     , avg( ltm.milliseconds ) as averagemilliseconds
from   f1data.laptimes ltm
where  ltm.raceid   = raceid_in
and    ltm.driverid = driverid_in
group  by ltm.raceid
        , ltm.driverid
]';
end;
/
```

Then your queries become simpler.

```
select *
from    averagelaptime( raceid_in   => 1093
                      , driverid_in => 830 )
/
```

```
RACEID DRIVERID TOTALMILLISECONDS LAPCOUNT AVERAGEMILLISECONDS
------ -------- ----------------- -------- -------------------
  1093      830           6131687       56   109494,410714286
```

```
select *
from    averagelaptime( raceid_in   => 1093
                      , driverid_in => 1 )
/
```

```
RACEID DRIVERID TOTALMILLISECONDS LAPCOUNT AVERAGEMILLISECONDS
------ -------- ----------------- -------- -------------------
  1093        1           6136710       56   109584,107142857
```

Column Splitter (Table)

You already saw an example of splitting a column into separate columns using PTFs.
Let's revisit that functionality, but now using SQL Macros.

For this function, you need a table parameter for the table (or view or result set) to be
processed and a parameter to tell the macro which columns to create in the output.

```
create or replace function split
(
  table_in    in dbms_tf.table_t
, columns_in in dbms_tf.columns_t default null
)
```

The function returns a VARCHAR2, which is a sql_macro of type table.

```
  return varchar2 sql_macro( table ) is
```

In the macro, build up the SQL text to split the column into the new columns.

```
  for cols in columns_in.first .. columns_in.last
  loop
    l_split := l_split || q'[, trim( ';]' ||
              q'[' from regexp_substr( ]' ||
              table_in.column( 1 ).description.name ||
              q'[, '{0,1}', 1, ]' ||
              cols || q'[ ) ) ]' ||
              columns_in( cols );
  end loop;
```

This is roughly the same code used in the PTF example.

Because every new column has a leading space, you end up with a list of columns where you must strip the leading comma (,) to make it a valid piece of SQL text.

```
  l_split := trim( leading ',' from l_split );
```

Now let's build the complete SQL statement that results in the table you can select from.

```
  l_sql   := q'[select t.*, ]' ||
            l_split ||
            q'[ from table_in t]';
```

In the preceding statement, table_in is replaced with the value of the table_in parameter.

Listing 8-9 is the complete script.

Listing 8-9. Split SQL Macro

```
create or replace function split
(
  table_in    in dbms_tf.table_t
, columns_in in dbms_tf.columns_t default null
)
  return varchar2 sql_macro( table ) is
  l_sql         varchar2( 32767 );
  l_split       varchar2( 32767 );
```

```
begin
  for cols in columns_in.first .. columns_in.last
  loop
    l_split := l_split ||
              q'[, trim( ';' from regexp_substr( ]'||
              table_in.column( 1 ).description.name ||
              q'[, '[^;]*;{0,1}', 1, ]' ||
              cols || q'[ ) ) ]' ||
              columns_in( cols );
  end loop;
  l_split := trim( leading ',' from l_split );
  l_sql   := q'[select t.*, ]' ||
             l_split ||
             q'[ from table_in t]';

  dbms_tf.trace( l_sql );
  return l_sql;
end;
/
```

Splitting Columns with a SQL Macro

With the same table in the PTF example of a split function, you can use a similar SQL
statement to transform these separated values into individual columns.

```
select permanentNumber
     , code
     , givenName
     , familyName
     , dateOfBirth
     , nationality
  from split( f1drivers
            , columns( permanentNumber
                     , code
                     , givenName
                     , familyName
                     , dateOfBirth
```

```
         , nationality
         )
      )
/
```

You get the same result as with the PTF. As you can see, there is a lot less code involved in this approach.

Parametrized View

You cannot nest SQL Macros within SQL Macros, but you can build a view based on this query, as seen in Listing 8-10.

Listing 8-10. view v_f1drivers

```
create or replace view v_f1drivers as
select permanentNumber
     , code
     , givenName
     , familyName
     , dateOfBirth
     , nationality
  from split( table_in   => f1drivers
            , columns_in => columns( permanentNumber
                                   , code
                                   , givenName
                                   , familyName
                                   , dateOfBirth
                                   , nationality
                                   )
          )
/
```

You must limit the result returned in your query by adding a predicate.

```
select d.givenname
     , d.familyname
     , d.nationality
```

```
from    v_f1drivers d
where   d.nationality like 'British'
/
```

```
GIVENNAME         FAMILYNAME        NATIONALITY
---------------   ---------------   ---------------
Lewis             Hamilton          British
Lando             Norris            British
George            Russell           British
```

```
select d.givenname
     , d.familyname
     , d.nationality
from    v_f1drivers d
where   d.givenname like 'M%'
/
```

```
GIVENNAME         FAMILYNAME        NATIONALITY
---------------   ---------------   ---------------
Max               Verstappen        Dutch
```

If you encapsulate this view in a SQL Macro, you can make it parametrized. You can use multiple, optional arguments, as seen in Listing 8-11.

Listing 8-11. drivers SQL Macro

```
create or replace
function drivers( code          in varchar2 default null
                , givenName     in varchar2 default null
                , familyName    in varchar2 default null
                , nationality   in varchar2 default null
                ) return varchar2 sql_macro( table )
is
begin
  return q'[
select f1d.permanentnumber
     , f1d.code
     , f1d.givenname
     , f1d.familyname
```

218

```
    , f1d.dateofbirth
    , f1d.nationality
from    v_f1drivers              f1d
where  (   drivers.code          is null
        or f1d.code              like drivers.code)
and    (   drivers.givenname     is null
        or f1d.givenname         like drivers.givenname)
and    (   drivers.familyname    is null
        or f1d.familyname        like drivers.familyname)
and    (   drivers.nationality   is null
        or f1d.nationality       like drivers.nationality)
]';
end;
/
```

You can now query the view using parameters.

```
select d.givenname
    , d.familyname
    , d.nationality
from   drivers( nationality => 'British' ) d
/
```

```
GIVENNAME         FAMILYNAME        NATIONALITY
---------------   ---------------   ---------------
Lewis             Hamilton          British
Lando             Norris            British
George            Russell           British
```

```
select d.givenname
    , d.familyname
    , d.nationality
from   drivers( givenname => 'M%' ) d
/
```

```
GIVENNAME         FAMILYNAME        NATIONALITY
---------------   ---------------   ---------------
Max               Verstappen        Dutch
```

Mimic Other Databases (Scalar)

If your code worked in a different database (e.g., MySQL), and you are migrating to an Oracle database, you may run into issues with functions that have been used in the SQL statements that are not available in Oracle Database. You can build a set of SQL Macros to ensure your statement works and that the correct Oracle SQL is executed.

Date Functions

Table 8-4 describes SQL Macros for several MySQL date functions.

Table 8-4. *MySQL Date Functions*

Function	Description
CURDATE()	Gives the current date.
NOW()	Returns the date and time of statement execution.
DAY()	Returns the day of the specified date.
DAYNAME()	Returns the day name for the specified date.
DAYOFWEEK()	Returns the day of the week index for a specified date.
MONTH()	Returns the month number of the specified date.
WEEK()	It returns the week number of a specified date.
WEEKDAY()	Returns the index of the weekday of a specified date.
YEAR()	Returns the year from a specified date.

The curdate() function returns the current date without the time component. Oracle dates always include a time component, so let's return a string representation of the sysdate without the time component.

Listing 8-12. curdate SQL Macro

```
create or replace function curdate
  ( format_in in varchar2 default 'DD/MM/YYYY' )
  return varchar2 sql_macro( scalar ) is
begin
  return 'to_char( sysdate, format_in )';
end;
/
```

The now() function returns the current date, including the time component. That is the same as sysdate.

Listing 8-13. now SQL Macro

```
create or replace function now
  return varchar2 sql_macro( scalar ) is
begin
  return 'sysdate';
end;
/
```

The day() function returns the day of the month of the specified date. That can be implemented as extract(day from date_in).

Listing 8-14. day sql macro

```
create or replace function day( date_in in date )
  return varchar2 sql_macro( scalar ) is
begin
  return q'[extract( day from date_in )]';
end;
/
```

The dayname() function returns the day name of the specified date. That can be implemented as to_char(date_in, 'DAY').

Listing 8-15. dayname SQL Macro

```
create or replace function dayname( date_in in date )
  return varchar2 sql_macro( scalar ) is
begin
  return q'[to_char( date_in, 'DAY' )]';
end;
/
```

The dayofweek() function returns the day of the week (1–7) of the specified date. That can be implemented as to_char(date_in, 'D').

Listing 8-16. dayofweek sql macro

```
create or replace function dayofweek( date_in in date )
  return varchar2 sql_macro( scalar ) is
begin
  return q'[to_char( date_in, 'D' )]';
end;
/
```

The month() function returns the month number of the specified date. That can be implemented as extract(month from date_in).

Listing 8-17. month SQL Macro

```
create or replace function month( date_in in date )
  return varchar2 sql_macro( scalar ) is
begin
  return q'[extract( month from date_in )]';
end;
/
```

The week() function returns the week number of the specified date. That can be implemented as to_char(date_in, 'IW').

Listing 8-18. week sql macro

```
create or replace function week( date_in in date )
  return varchar2 sql_macro( scalar ) is
begin
  return q'[to_char( date_in, 'IW' )]';
end;
/
```

The weekday() function returns the day of the week (1–7) of the specified date. This is the same as the dayofweek() function. Instead of returning another string, you can also call another SQL Macro. Since it returns a string, you can just call the different function

Listing 8-19. weekday SQL Macro

```
create or replace function weekday( date_in in date )
  return varchar2 sql_macro( scalar ) is
begin
  return dayofweek( date_in );
end;
/
```

The year() function returns the year of the specified date. That can be implemented as extract(year from date_in).

Listing 8-20. year SQL Macro

```
create or replace function year( date_in in date )
  return varchar2 sql_macro( scalar ) is
begin
  return q'[extract( year from date_in )]';
end;
/
```

String Functions

The MySQL database has a `left` and a `right` string manipulation function. These are not available in Oracle SQL. But you can implement them using the `substr` functionality and wrap these in SQL Macros so you can port your MySQL queries directly to the Oracle database (see Table 8-5).

Table 8-5. *MySQL String Functions*

function	result
left ('Oracle Database', 6)	'Oracle'
left ('Oracle Database', 0)	''
left ('Oracle Database', -6)	''
right ('Oracle Database', 8)	'Database'
right ('Oracle Database', 0)	''
right ('Oracle Database', -8)	''

The `left` function is easy to implement. It is a substring, starting at position 1 and then getting the desired number of characters.

Listing 8-21. left sql macro

```
create or replace function left
(
  string_in in varchar2
, left_in    in number
) return varchar2 sql_macro( scalar ) is
  l_sql varchar2( 64 );
begin
  l_sql := 'substr( string_in, 1, left_in )';
  return l_sql;
end left;
/
```

The right function is a little more complex. You must make sure you handle the edge cases yourself. The function should return a NULL value if the number of characters requested is 0 or a negative number. If the number of characters requested is larger than the number available, then return the entire string. Otherwise, return the number of characters by starting from the right.

Listing 8-22. Right SQL Macro

```
create or replace function right
(
  string_in in varchar2
, right_in  in number
) return varchar2 sql_macro( scalar ) is
  l_sql varchar2( 32767 );
begin
  l_sql := '
case
  when right_in <= 0 then null
  when right_in > length( string_in ) then  string_in
  else substr( string_in, -right_in )
end
';
  return l_sql;
end right;
/
```

expand_sql_text

`dbms_utility.expand_sql_text` lets you check which statement executed. Let's say you have a simple SQL Macro.

Listing 8-23. total_laptime SQL Macro

```
create or replace
function total_laptime( raceid_in   in number
                      , driverid_in in number )
  return varchar2 sql_macro( table ) is
```

225

```
begin
  return q'[
select ltm.raceid              as raceid
     , ltm.driverid            as driverid
     , sum( ltm.milliseconds ) as totalmilliseconds
from   f1data.laptimes ltm
where  ltm.raceid   = raceid_in
and    ltm.driverid = driverid_in
group  by ltm.raceid
        , ltm.driverid
order  by ltm.raceid
        , ltm.driverid
  ]';
end;
/
```

The following is the statement you execute.

```
select * from total_laptime(1093, 830)
```

If you enter this statement as a parameter for the dbms_utility.expand_sql_text procedure as follows.

```
declare
  output_text clob;
begin
  dbms_utility.expand_sql_text(
    input_sql_text  => q'[select * from total_laptime(1093, 830)
]'
  , output_sql_text => output_text
  );
  dbms_output.put_line( output_text );
end;
/
```

You get the actual statement that has been executed (formatted for readability).

```
select "A1"."RACEID"              "RACEID"
     , "A1"."DRIVERID"            "DRIVERID"
     , "A1"."TOTALMILLISECONDS" "TOTALMILLISECONDS"
from   (select "A2"."RACEID"            "RACEID"
             , "A2"."DRIVERID"          "DRIVERID"
             , "A2"."TOTALMILLISECONDS" "TOTALMILLISECONDS"
        from   (select "A3"."RACEID" "RACEID"
                     , "A3"."DRIVERID" "DRIVERID"
                     , sum("A3"."MILLISECONDS")
                                             "TOTALMILLISECONDS"
                from   "F1DATA"."LAPTIMES" "A3"
                where  "A3"."RACEID"   = 1093
                and    "A3"."DRIVERID" = 830
                group  by "A3"."RACEID"
                        , "A3"."DRIVERID"
                order  by "A3"."RACEID"
                        , "A3"."DRIVERID") "A2") "A1"
```

Summary

This chapter discussed polymorphic table functions and how to build and use them. You also learned about SQL Macros, which can lead to simpler solutions than PTFs. So why should you learn about polymorphic table functions? Well, there are things you cannot solve in pure SQL which can be solved using PL/SQL. SQL Macros always return a SQL snippet. PL/SQL is being used to build this snippet, but the usage is pure SQL. PTFs let you access the actual values in the query, so you can manipulate what is coming out of your query. You can manipulate the statement using SQL Macros before executing it, but you are still creating pure SQL.

Subquery Factoring, the WITH Clause, Explained

Subquery factoring is also known as a *common table expression* (CTE). Commonly referred to as the with clause. A CTE is a named temporary result set that exists within the scope of a single statement, and that can be referred to later within that statement, possibly multiple times.

You can specify a subquery in the from clause of a query, which is called an *inline view*; but if you want to join the same query multiple times, you must repeat that query multiple times. And if that inline view changed, you had to make the same changes multiple times. No more with subquery factoring. You define the subquery once and reference it by name, complying with the "define once, reuse often" paradigm.

Monaco Podium

In the database are the results for all races driven in Monaco dating back to 1950. The objective is to retrieve the top three for the Monaco circuit and have them nicely laid out in a different column for each podium place. The example is contrived and can be simplified, but it is used to demonstrate the subquery factoring clause. Subquery factoring almost gives a procedural feel to writing SQL queries.

The first step is to get the top three drivers for Monaco. This can be accomplished by joining the CIRCUITS, RACES, and RESULTS tables. The following query shows a subquery named monaco. This named subquery is used in the main query after the with clause.

© Alex Nuijten, Patrick Barel 2023
A. Nuijten and P. Barel, *Modern Oracle Database Programming*, https://doi.org/10.1007/978-1-4842-9166-5_9

```
with monaco as (
select rsl.driverid
     , rsl.position
     , rcs.year
from   f1data.circuits cct
join   f1data.races rcs
  on   cct.circuitid = rcs.circuitid
join   f1data.results rsl
  on   rcs.raceid = rsl.raceid
where  cct.circuitref = 'monaco'
and    rsl.position <= 3
)
select driverid
     , position
     , year
from   monaco
/
  DRIVERID   POSITION   YEAR
---------- ---------- ------
       579          1   1950
       647          2   1950
       589          3   1950
       427          1   1955
       608          2   1955
       554          3   1955
       607          3   1955
       475          1   1956
       581          2   1956
       554          3   1956
       579          2   1956
       579          1   1957
       479          2   1957
       418          3   1957
<< results omitted for brevity >>
```

This gives a list of driver IDs, their position, and the year they were on the podium. Since driverid is meaningless, adding the driver's name would be more helpful. After the last bracket of the monaco subquery, the following named subquery is added to provide a nicely formatted driver's name.

```
, motorists as (
select drv.driverid
     , drv.forename
       || ' ' ||
       drv.surname as driver
from   f1data.drivers drv
)
```

Now the main query can be changed to include the driver's name.

```
select year
     , position
     , driver
from   monaco mon
join   motorists mtt
  on   mon.driverid = mtt.driverid
/
  YEAR   POSITION DRIVER
------ ---------- -------------------------
  1950          3 Louis Chiron
  1950          2 Alberto Ascari
  1950          1 Juan Fangio
  1955          1 Maurice Trintignant
  1955          3 Cesare Perdisa
  1955          3 Jean Behra
  1955          2 Eugenio Castellotti
  1956          2 Juan Fangio
  1956          3 Jean Behra
  1956          2 Peter Collins
  1956          1 Stirling Moss
  1957          2 Tony Brooks
  1957          1 Juan Fangio
```

```
 1957               3 Masten Gregory
<< results omitted for brevity >>
```

The result set includes the year, the podium position, and the driver's full name. This query is added to the subquery factoring clause and named monaco_podiums.

```
monaco_podiums as (
select mon.year
      , mon.position
      , mtt.driver
from   monaco mon
join   motorists mtt
  on   mon.driverid = mtt.driverid
)
```

The pivot clause can display the first, second, and third podium places in separate columns. This completes the task.

```
select year
     , first
     , second
     , third
  from monaco_podiums
 pivot (
        min(driver)
        for position in ( 1 as first
                        , 2 as second
                        , 3 as third
                        )
       )
/
```

The following is the complete query with all the subquery factoring in place.

Listing 9-1. Retrieve Monaco top 3

```
with monaco as (
select rsl.driverid
     , rsl.position
```

```
          , rcs.year
from      f1data.circuits cct
join      f1data.races rcs
   on     cct.circuitid = rcs.circuitid
join      f1data.results rsl
   on     rcs.raceid = rsl.raceid
where     cct.circuitref = 'monaco'
and       rsl.position <= 3
)
, motorists as (
select drv.driverid
          , drv.forename
          || ' ' ||
          drv.surname as driver
from      f1data.drivers drv
)
,monaco_podiums as (
select mon.year
          , mon.position
          , mtt.driver
from      monaco mon
join      motorists mtt
   on     mon.driverid = mtt.driverid
)
select year
          , first
          , second
          , third
from      monaco_podiums
pivot (
          min(driver)
          for position in ( 1 as first
                          , 2 as second
                          , 3 as third
                          )
```

```
      )
order by year
/
  YEAR FIRST                 SECOND               THIRD
 ------ -------------------- -------------------- ----------------
  1950 Juan Fangio          Alberto Ascari       Louis Chiron
  1955 Maurice Trintignant  Eugenio Castellotti  Cesare Perdisa
  1956 Stirling Moss        Juan Fangio          Jean Behra
  1957 Juan Fangio          Tony Brooks          Masten Gregory
<< results omitted for brevity >>
```

Note   These results don't reflect reality. In 1955, there were two third-place winners: Jean Behra and Cesare Perdisa. Since the position is not unique in a year, the MIN function resolves this alphabetically by first name. The same is true for 1956 when there were two second-place winners: Peter Collins and Juan Fangio.

Functions in the WITH clause

Starting with Oracle Database 12c, it is possible to build PL/SQL functions in the with clause. Calling a PL/SQL function from a SQL statement is expensive due to context switches and should be avoided when possible. When a function is added to the subquery factoring clause, the function is compiled in the SQL engine. This is not completely true, but it can be considered like that, eliminating the expensive context switch.

For the following example, there are two functions built in the with clause. One function is to format the name of the driver and the constructor into a single string, and one is to format the top three drivers into a single column.

The first function, called fullname, takes three arguments.

```
function fullname( forename_in    in varchar2
                 , surname_in     in varchar2
                 , constructor_in in varchar2 )
return varchar2
```

```
is
begin
  return forename_in
         || ' ' || surname_in
         || ' (' || constructor_in || ')';
end fullname;
```

The second function, called formattop3, also takes three arguments.

```
function formattop3( pos1 in varchar2
                   , pos2 in varchar2
                   , pos3 in varchar2 )
return varchar2
is
begin
  return '1) ' || pos1 || chr(10)
      || '2) ' || pos2 || chr(10)
      || '3) ' || pos3 || chr(10);
end formattop3;
```

The functions *must* be declared at the beginning of the with clause, that is, before any factored subquery. Unlike subqueries, functions are *not* separated by commas. There is also no comma before the first named query. Another peculiarity is that functions used in the SQL statements *can't* use the named notation to specify which argument is populated with which value.

Because there is a desire to also list the constructor, the named subquery from Listing 9-1 should be replaced with the following.

```
, motorists as (
select drv.driverid
     , fullname ( drv.forename
                , drv.surname
                , ctr.name
                ) as driver
from   f1data.drivers    drv
join   f1data.results    rsl
  on   drv.driverid = rsl.driverid
```

```
join    f1data.constructors ctr
  on    rsl.constructorid = ctr.constructorid
)
```

This formats the driver's name and constructor as requested by calling the `fullname` function.

The pivot query that ended Listing 9-1 is wrapped into the subquery named `monaco_pivot`. This query is used in the final query, shown in Listing 9-2. (Only the results through 1957 are shown.)

Listing 9-2. Retrieve formatted Monaco top 3

```
with
function fullname( forename_in    in varchar2
                , surname_in      in varchar2
                , constructor_in in varchar2 )
return varchar2
is
begin
  return forename_in
         || ' ' || surname_in
         || ' (' || constructor_in || ')';
end fullname;
function formattop3( pos1 in varchar2
                   , pos2 in varchar2
                   , pos3 in varchar2 )
return varchar2
is
begin
  return '1) ' || pos1 || chr(10)
     || '2) ' || pos2 || chr(10)
     || '3) ' || pos3 || chr(10);
end formattop3;
monaco as (
select rsl.driverid
     , rsl.position
     , rcs.year
```

```
from   f1data.circuits cct
join   f1data.races rcs
  on   cct.circuitid = rcs.circuitid
join   f1data.results rsl
  on   rcs.raceid = rsl.raceid
where  cct.circuitref = 'monaco'
and    rsl.position <= 3
)
, motorists as (
select drv.driverid
     , fullname ( drv.forename
                , drv.surname
                , ctr.name
                ) as driver
from   f1data.drivers      drv
join   f1data.results      rsl
  on   drv.driverid = rsl.driverid
join   f1data.constructors ctr
  on   rsl.constructorid = ctr.constructorid
)
, monaco_podiums as (
select mon.year
     , mon.position
     , mtt.driver
from   monaco mon
join   motorists mtt
  on   mon.driverid = mtt.driverid
)
, monaco_pivot as (
select year
     , first
     , second
     , third
from   monaco_podiums
pivot  (
```

```
        min(driver)
        for position in ( 1 as first
                         , 2 as second
                         , 3 as third
                         )
        )
)
select year
     , formattop3 ( first
                  , second
                  , third
                  ) as formatted
from    monaco_pivot
where   year < 1958
order by year
/

  YEAR FORMATTED
------ ----------------------------------------
  1950 1) Juan Fangio (Alfa Romeo)
       2) Alberto Ascari (Ferrari)
       3) Louis Chiron (Lancia)

  1955 1) Maurice Trintignant (Aston Martin)
       2) Eugenio Castellotti (Ferrari)
       3) Cesare Perdisa (Ferrari)

  1956 1) Stirling Moss (BRM)
       2) Juan Fangio (Alfa Romeo)
       3) Jean Behra (BRM)

  1957 1) Juan Fangio (Alfa Romeo)
       2) Tony Brooks (BRM)
       3) Masten Gregory (BRM)
```

It is also possible to create procedures in the with clause, but you cannot call them from SQL because a procedure has no return value. The advantage of using PL/SQL in your factored query is that the context switch's overhead is much lower than when calling a PL/SQL function. The disadvantage of using PL/SQL in your query is that the code is not reusable. Chapter 10 provides more information on calling PL/SQL from SQL. If you want to use the same code in a different query, you must duplicate the code there. An alternative is to use SQL Macros (see Chapter 8).

Recursive Subquery Factoring

Traditionally a recursive relationship in the data model is when there is a foreign key relation to the primary key of the same table. The typical example is in the SCOTT schema, specifically the EMP table. In that table are employees, as well as managers, stored. The `mgr` column (as a foreign key) refers to the primary key `empno` of the same table, creating a hierarchical relation between the two.

There is no such relationship in the data model used in this book. The following example explores the hierarchical relationship between CONSTRUCTORS and DRIVERS.

The first step is to create a list of constructors and drivers, where there are only three columns involved.

- A fake "primary key" consisting of the letter `'c'` and the real `constructorid` (when a driver record, it is `'d'` and the `driverid`)

- The name of the constructor or the driver

- "foreign key" to the "primary key"

This is done in a named subquery.

```
with constructor_drivers as (
select 'c'||to_char (ctr.constructorid) as pk
     , ctr.name
     , null as fk
from   f1data.constructors ctr
where  ctr.constructorref in ('ferrari', 'mercedes')
union all
select distinct
       'd'||to_char (drv.driverid)
     , drv.surname as driver
     , 'c'||to_char (rst.constructorid) ctr_id
from   f1data.results rst
```

```
join    f1data.drivers drv
  on    drv.driverid = rst.driverid)
select *
  from constructor_drivers
/
PK          NAME                            FK
---------- ----------------------------- -----------
c6          Ferrari
c131        Mercedes
d17         Webber                          c9
d14         Coulthard                       c9
d13         Massa                           c6
d8          Räikkönen                       c6
d847        Russell                         c131
d1          Hamilton                        c131
d844        Leclerc                         c6
d832        Sainz                           c6
d20         Vettel                          c6
d608        Castellotti                     c6
d802        Serafini                        c6
d791        Biondetti                       c6
<< records omitted for brevity >>
```

As seen in the output, the first column (PK) is a contraction of either a "c" (for constructor) or "d" (for driver) and the real primary key of the underlying table. The name column shows either a constructor *or* a driver name. The last column (FK) shows in case of a driver for which constructor he has driven or still drives. When the record is a constructor, the FK column is empty.

The reason for the contraction of the primary key of the underlying table and a letter is to prevent ambiguous relations between the parent and child. The FK column with a value of 6 could point to the constructor Ferrari or driver Kazuki Nakajima.

The recursive relation can easily be spotted with the data in this format: the FK column refers to the PK column in the result set.

The recursive subquery factoring clause *must* contain two query blocks combined with a union all set operator. The first block of the query defines the anchor record, which signifies the start of the recursion. The anchor for this result set can be queried as follows.

```
select pk
     , name
     , fk
from    constructor_drivers
where   fk is null
```

This anchor query *only* selects those records that contain constructors. The FK column is always null for them.

The next block, the recursive member, selects child records related to the anchor just selected and must reference the query name once.

```
select cdv.pk
     , cdv.name
     , cdv.fk
from    constructor_drivers cdv
join    hierarchy hier
  on    hier.pk = cdv.fk
```

The table "hierarchy" in the preceding query is the named query, referring to itself. This self-reference in the query block makes it a recursive subquery. Notice that the query named constructor_drivers also has a union all, but it has no self-reference and is not recursive.

The column aliases, listed between parentheses, following the query name (hierarchy in the following example), are required. The following is the complete recursive subquery.

```
hierarchy (pk, name, fk)
as (
select pk
     , name
     , fk
from    constructor_drivers
where   fk is null
union   all
select cdv.pk
     , cdv.name
     , cdv.fk
```

```
from    constructor_drivers cdv
join    hierarchy hier
  on    hier.pk = cdv.fk
)
```

In the main query, "hierarchy" shows the hierarchy between CONSTRUCTORS and DRIVERS. Putting everything together leads to the following query.

Listing 9-3. Hierarchical list of constructors and drivers

```
with constructor_drivers as
(
select 'c'||to_char (ctr.constructorid) as pk
     , ctr.name
     , null as fk
from    f1data.constructors ctr
where   ctr.constructorref in ('ferrari', 'mercedes')
union   all
select distinct
        'd'||to_char (drv.driverid)
     , drv.surname as driver
     , 'c'||to_char (rst.constructorid) ctr_id
from    f1data.results rst
join    f1data.drivers drv
  on    drv.driverid = rst.driverid
)
, hierarchy (pk, name, fk)
as (
select pk
     , name
     , fk
from    constructor_drivers
where   fk is null
union   all
select cdv.pk
     , cdv.name
     , cdv.fk
```

```
from   constructor_drivers cdv
join   hierarchy hier
  on   hier.pk = cdv.fk
)
select pk
     , name
     , fk
from   hierarchy
/
```

PK	NAME	FK
c6	Ferrari	
c131	Mercedes	
d3	Rosberg	c131
d579	Fangio	c131
d475	Moss	c131
d609	Simon	c131
d691	Lang	c131
d478	Herrmann	c131
d30	Schumacher	c131
d641	Taruffi	c131
d1	Hamilton	c131
d648	Kling	c131
d822	Bottas	c131
d847	Russell	c131
d386	Ginther	c6
d435	Mairesse	c6
d577	Musso	c6
d607	Perdisa	c6
d387	Parkes	c6
d483	Scarlatti	c6

The results look remarkably similar to what was shown earlier. The biggest difference is that not all drivers are listed, only Ferrari or Mercedes drivers, and a tree walk is performed.

243

Simulate Built-in Recursive Functions

With traditional recursive queries (start with ... connect by), some built-in functions are not available with recursive subquery factoring, but these can be easily simulated. For this section, only the query named hierarchy is shown. The named query constructor_drivers is defined as follows.

```
with constructor_drivers as
(
select 'c'||to_char (ctr.constructorid) as pk
    , ctr.name
    , null as fk
from    f1data.constructors ctr
where   ctr.constructorref in ('ferrari', 'mercedes')
union   all
select distinct
        'd'||to_char (drv.driverid)
    , drv.surname as driver
    , 'c'||to_char (rst.constructorid) ctr_id
from    f1data.results rst
join    f1data.drivers drv
  on    drv.driverid = rst.driverid
union   all
select 'champ'||to_char (min (dsg.driverstandingsid))
    , to_char (rce.year)
      ||' (' || to_char (max (dsg.points) )
      || ' points)' as points
    , 'd'||to_char (
              max (dsg.driverid)
              keep (dense_rank first
                        order by dsg.points desc
      )) as driver
  from f1data.races rce
  join f1data.driverstandings dsg
    on rce.raceid = dsg.raceid
 group by rce.year
)
```

The preceding named query adds a third level that lists the champions over the years, where the PK column is a contraction of "champ" and an ID, and the FK column is a contraction of "d" and the driverid that was champion in that year. The NAME column shows the year and the points scored. Some results include the following.

```
PK         NAME                 FK
---------- -------------------- ----------
champ43201 1950 (30 points)     d642
champ43620 1951 (31 points)     d579
champ44133 1952 (36 points)     d647
champ44723 1953 (34.5 points)   d647
champ51463 1954 (42 points)     d579
champ46077 1955 (40 points)     d579
champ46506 1956 (30 points)     d579
champ46985 1957 (40 points)     d579
champ48974 1958 (42 points)     d578
champ61951 1959 (31 points)     d356
```

Level Pseudocolumn

The level pseudocolumn returns an integer indicating the level of the hierarchy. The root level is 1, the level below is 2, the next level is 3, and so on.

To simulate the level pseudocolumn, the anchor member of the recursive subquery factoring gets an integer with a value of 1. In each iteration, this value is increased by one. In the following query, the LVL column is added.

```
, hierarchy (pk, name, fk, lvl)
as (
select pk
     , name
     , fk
     , 1 as lvl
from   constructor_drivers
where  fk is null
union  all
select cdv.pk
     , lpad ('.', hier.lvl * 2, '.')||cdv.name
```

```
        , cdv.fk
        , hier.lvl + 1
from    constructor_drivers cdv
join    hierarchy hier
  on    hier.pk = cdv.fk
)
select *
from    hierarchy
/
```

PK	NAME	FK	LVL
c6	Ferrari		1
c131	Mercedes		1
d63	..Salo	c6	2
d203	..Villeneuve	c6	2
d832	..Sainz	c6	2
d477	..Allison	c6	2
d278	..Amon	c6	2
d581	..Collins	c6	2

```
< rows omitted for brevity >
```

PK	NAME	FK	LVL
champ43201	....1950 (30 points)	d642	3
champ20433	....1985 (73 points)	d117	3
champ19944	....1986 (72 points)	d117	3
champ18159	....1989 (76 points)	d117	3
champ9351	....1993 (99 points)	d117	3
champ63737	....2010 (256 points)	d20	3

```
< rows omitted for brevity >
```

The LVL column is also used to format the name in the output. The Ferrari and Mercedes records are at level 1, the drivers are at level 2, and the champion information is at level 3.

sys_connect_by_path, connect_by_root, connect_by_isleaf

The sys_connect_by_path function returns the path of the root of the hierarchy to the current node.

To simulate this functionality in recursive subquery factoring, a column is added and designated as the root in the anchor member, aliased as SCBP in the following query. In each iteration, this value is extended by concatenating a value from the recursive member, as seen in Listing 9-4.

The connect_by_root unary operator returns the column that the current row uses as its root. Listing 9-4 simulates this in the CBR column. The root value is set in the anchor member and repeated in the recursive member.

The connect_by_isleaf pseudocolumn returns one when the current row is a leaf row in the hierarchy; otherwise, it returns a zero. This function can be implemented using a CASE expression and an analytic function in the final query. There is a catch, however. The shown CASE expression and analytic function only work when the search condition is set to search depth first.

This is shown in Listing 9-4.

Listing 9-4. sys_connect_by_path simulation

```
with constructor_drivers as
(
select 'c'||to_char (ctr.constructorid) as pk
     , ctr.name
     , null as fk
from   f1data.constructors ctr
where  ctr.constructorref in ('ferrari', 'mercedes')
union  all
select distinct
       'd'||to_char (drv.driverid)
     , drv.surname as driver
     , 'c'||to_char (rst.constructorid) ctr_id
from   f1data.results rst
join   f1data.drivers drv
  on   drv.driverid = rst.driverid
union  all
select 'champ'||to_char (min (dsg.driverstandingsid)),
     to_char (rce.year)||' ('
     || to_char (max (dsg.points)|| ' points)') as points,
```

```
      'd'||to_char (max (dsg.driverid) keep (dense_rank first order  by dsg.
      points desc)) as driver
from    f1data.races rce
join    f1data.driverstandings dsg
  on    rce.raceid = dsg.raceid
group  by rce.year
)
, hierarchy (pk, name, fk, lvl, scbp, cbr)
as (
select pk
     , name
     , fk
     , 1     as lvl
     , name as scbp
     , name as cbr
from    constructor_drivers
where  fk is null
union  all
select cdv.pk
     , lpad ('.', hier.lvl * 2, '.')||cdv.name
     , cdv.fk
     , hier.lvl + 1
     , hier.scbp ||', '||cdv.name
     , hier.cbr
from    constructor_drivers cdv
join    hierarchy hier
  on    hier.pk = cdv.fk
) search depth first by name set seq
select lvl
     , scbp
     , cbr
     , case
     when lvl >= lead ( lvl, 1, 1 )
               over ( order by seq )
     then 'Y'
```

```
      else 'N'
      end as leaf
from  hierarchy
order by seq
/
```

```
LV SCBP                                          CBR          L
-- --------------------------------------------- ---------- -
 1 Ferrari                                        Ferrari      N
 2 Ferrari, Adolff                                Ferrari      Y
 2 Ferrari, Alboreto                              Ferrari      Y
 2 Ferrari, Alesi                                 Ferrari      Y
 2 Ferrari, Allison                               Ferrari      Y
 2 Ferrari, Alonso                                Ferrari      N
 3 Ferrari, Alonso, 2005 (133 points)            Ferrari      Y
 3 Ferrari, Alonso, 2006 (134 points)            Ferrari      Y
 2 Ferrari, Amon                                  Ferrari      Y
 2 Ferrari, Andretti                              Ferrari      N
 3 Ferrari, Andretti, 1978 (64 points)           Ferrari      Y
 2 Ferrari, Arnoux                                Ferrari      Y
<rows omitted for brevity>
```

Sorting the Results

Recursive subquery factoring offers two options to sort the result set. The hierarchy can go from the root level to its nodes before going to the next root and its nodes. This method is the only way with the traditional method of writing hierarchical queries.

The hierarchy can navigate through all root nodes before descending one level down. It outputs all records at that level, goes down a level, outputs these records, and so on.

The search clause is added to the recursive subquery factoring query by specifying either

```
search depth first by <column name> set <ordering column>
```

or

```
search breadth first by <column name> set <ordering column>
```

search depth navigates from root to leaf nodes before going to the next root node. search breadth outputs everything at the same level before navigating to the next level.

Note   As with all queries not specifying an order by clause, return the result set in no particular order. This is also true with recursive subqueries. Add an order by clause to the query when sorting is needed. It seems that the default sorting of a recursive subquery is to do a breadth first search with an undetermined ordering at each level.

It can be any column to order the results by. After the set keyword, an ordering column is specified, like an alias for the search condition.

```
, hierarchy (pk, name, fk, lvl)
as (
select pk
     , name
     , fk
     , 1     as lvl
from   constructor_drivers
where  fk is null
union  all
select cdv.pk
     , lpad ('.', hier.lvl * 2, '.')||cdv.name
     , cdv.fk
     , hier.lvl + 1
from   constructor_drivers cdv
join   hierarchy hier
  on   hier.pk = cdv.fk
) search depth first by name set seq
select lvl
      ,name
from   hierarchy
order  by seq
/
```

```
LV NAME
-- ------------------------
 1 Ferrari
 2 ..Adolff
 2 ..Alboreto
 2 ..Alesi
 2 ..Allison
 2 ..Alonso
 3 ....2005 (133 points)
 3 ....2006 (134 points)
 2 ..Amon
 2 ..Andretti
 3 ....1978 (64 points)
 2 ..Arnoux
 2 ..Ascari
 3 ....1952 (36 points)
 3 ....1953 (34.5 points)
< rows omitted for brevity >
 1 Mercedes
 2 ..Bottas
 2 ..Fangio
 3 ....1951 (31 points)
 3 ....1954 (42 points)
 3 ....1955 (40 points)
 3 ....1956 (30 points)
 3 ....1957 (40 points)
< rows omitted for brevity >
```

The preceding result set shows the constructor Ferrari, followed by its drivers (in alphabetical order), and when this driver was champion. After all the drivers have been listed, the constructor Mercedes is shown with its drivers.

Change the search condition as follows.

```
search breadth first by name set seq
```

It yields the following results.

```
LV NAME
-- ------------------------
 1 Ferrari
 1 Mercedes
 2 ..Adolff
 2 ..Alboreto
 2 ..Alesi
 2 ..Allison
 2 ..Alonso
 2 ..Amon
<rows omitted for brevity>
 2 ..de Tomaso
 2 ..de Tornaco
 2 ..von Stuck
 2 ..von Trips
 3 ....1950 (30 points)
 3 ....1951 (31 points)
 3 ....1951 (31 points)
 3 ....1952 (36 points)
 3 ....1953 (34.5 points)
 3 ....1954 (42 points)
<rows omitted for brevity>
```

First, all records in level 1 are shown (in alphabetical order), followed by all records in level 2, and finally, all records in level 3.

Cycle Detection

For the following examples, the subquery named constructor_drivers is defined as follows.

```
with constructor_drivers as
(
select ctr.constructorid as pk
     , ctr.name
     , null as fk
from   f1data.constructors ctr
```

```
where  ctr.constructorid in ( 1    -- McLaren
                             , 131 -- Mercedes
                             )
union all
select distinct
       drv.driverid
     , drv.surname as driver
     , rst.constructorid
from   f1data.results rst
join   f1data.drivers drv
  on   drv.driverid = rst.driverid
where  drv.driverid in ( 1    -- Hamilton
                       , 131 -- Modena
                       )
)
/
```

```
      PK NAME                          FK
---------- ------------------------- ----------
         1 McLaren
       131 Mercedes
         1 Hamilton                            1
       131 Modena                             17
       131 Modena                             25
       131 Modena                             34
       131 Modena                             44
         1 Hamilton                          131
```

Only two constructors and two drivers are selected. The main difference with previous examples is that the prefixes of the columns PK and FK are removed, leading to false positive relations, and causing a cycle in the data.

With the traditional `start with ... connect by` syntax, it is also possible to do cycle detection. The following error is raised when there is a cycle in the data.

```
ORA-01436: CONNECT BY loop in user data
```

The connect_by_iscycle pseudocolumn returns a one when the current row has a child record which is also one of its parents (direct parent, grandparent, etc.). This pseudocolumn can only be used when nocycle is specified in the connect by clause.

With recursive subquery factoring, a cyclic relation is when the current row is also one of its ancestors. A cycle clause can be added to recursive subquery factoring to detect cyclic relations. When there is a cyclic relation in recursive subquery factoring, the following exception is raised.

ORA-32044: cycle detected while executing recursive WITH query

The following example shows the use of the cycle clause.

```
, hierarchy (pk, name, fk)
as (
select pk
     , name
     , fk
from   constructor_drivers
where  fk is null
union  all
select cdv.pk
     , cdv.name
     , cdv.fk
from   constructor_drivers cdv
join   hierarchy hier
  on   hier.pk = cdv.fk
) search depth first by name set seq
  cycle name set is_cycle to 'Y' default 'N'
select pk
     , name
     , fk
     , is_cycle
from   hierarchy
/
```

```
   PK NAME                   FK I
---------- ---------------- ---------- -
        1 McLaren                     N
        1 Hamilton               1 N
        1 Hamilton               1 Y
      131 Mercedes                    N
        1 Hamilton             131 N
        1 Hamilton               1 Y
```

As seen in the last column, the cyclic relation is detected. The column used for cycle detection can be set to any column, not necessarily the columns directly involved in the hierarchy, which isn't possible with a connect by hierarchical query.

Summary

Subquery factoring is a very useful technique for writing SQL statements. Because it is possible to break down the result set into smaller bite-size pieces, it has an almost procedural feel. Instead of writing a massive query, subquery factoring can help keep your SQL statement clean.

Recursive subquery factoring offers nearly the same functionality as the traditional start with .. connect by syntax but has more advanced cycle detection. Because the recursive member is a separate subquery, it can be much more flexible and include multiple tables, more complex column expressions, and results from previous iterations. It allows more flexibility and complexity when the need arises.

CHAPTER 10

Calling PL/SQL from SQL

Calling a reusable piece of code stored in a PL/SQL function—packaged or stand-alone—results in a context switch. The SQL engine stops whatever it is doing and gives control to the PL/SQL engine, which then does its work and returns control to the SQL engine after it's done. These context switches are relatively expensive. They involve a lot of work by both engines to transfer all the relative information before the real work can be done. Oracle Database offers a multitude of possible solutions to minimize the overhead.

UDF Pragma

The UDF pragma tells the compiler that this function is used primarily in SQL, so the code is optimized for this, which *might* improve performance. UDF stands for *user-defined function*. The only insurance you get is that it is not slower than a function not using this pragma when called from SQL. If this function is called from PL/SQL, you may see a decrease in performance. Listing 10-1 is an example of a function with the UDF pragma.

Listing 10-1. A function with UDF pragma

```
create or replace function fullname_udf
( forename_in in varchar2
, surname_in  in varchar2 )
return varchar2
is
  pragma udf;
  l_returnvalue varchar2( 32767 );
begin
  l_returnvalue := initcap( forename_in )
```

© Alex Nuijten, Patrick Barel 2023
A. Nuijten and P. Barel, *Modern Oracle Database Programming*, https://doi.org/10.1007/978-1-4842-9166-5_10

```
    || ' '
    || initcap( surname_in );
  return l_returnvalue;
end;
/
```

You may see a substantial performance increase or none at all. Your mileage may vary. If you are sure the function is only called from SQL, then it can be a good idea to include this pragma, otherwise, be sure you test the different scenarios and then determine whether you want to use this or not.

Deterministic

A function that is declared deterministic caches the parameters during the execution of a SQL statement. If the input parameters are the same as they were on a previous execution, then the body of the function is not executed again. The result is taken from the cache and returned directly. When you make a function deterministic, you tell the database that this function *always* returns the same output for the same input. That means you can never have the output of a deterministic function depend on table values, SYSDATE, or the like—the output must *only* depend on the input.

This can lead to a major performance increase since the body of the function doesn't have to be executed anymore. And no matter how fast your code is, not executing it is always faster.

To demonstrate the performance increase, create a simple table with a single column.

```
create table t ( c number )
/
```

Then add ten rows to this table with three distinct values.

```
begin
  insert into t( c ) values ( 1 );
  insert into t( c ) values ( 2 );
  insert into t( c ) values ( 3 );
  insert into t( c ) values ( 1 );
  insert into t( c ) values ( 2 );
```

```
  insert into t( c ) values ( 3 );
  insert into t( c ) values ( 1 );
  insert into t( c ) values ( 2 );
  insert into t( c ) values ( 3 );
  insert into t( c ) values ( 1 );
  commit;
end;
/
```

For demonstration purposes, create a function that does nothing but sleep for a second before returning the value provided in the in parameter (see Listing 10-2).

Listing 10-2. A very slow function

```
create or replace function myslowfunction( p_in in number )
  return number
is
begin
  dbms_session.sleep( 1 );
  return p_in;
end;
/
```

Then call the function for every row in the table.

```
set timing on
select myslowfunction( t.c ) from t
/
set timing off

MYSLOWFUNCTION(T.C)
-------------------
              1
              2
              3
              1
              2
```

```
      3
      1
      2
      3
      1
```

```
10 rows selected
```

```
Executed in 10,384 seconds
```

As you can see, the execution takes a little over 10 seconds, which makes sense because the function is called ten times and didn't do much more than sleep for a second.

If you alter the function and add the keyword deterministic, you can run the same query again (see Listing 10-3).

Listing 10-3. A very slow deterministic function

```
create or replace function myslowfunction( p_in in number )
return number
deterministic
is
begin
  dbms_session.sleep( 1 );
  return p_in;
end;
/

set timing on
select myslowfunction( t.c ) from t
/
set timing off

MYSLOWFUNCTION(T.C)
-------------------
      1
      2
```

```
                3
                1
                2
                3
                1
                2
                3
                1
```

10 rows selected

Executed in 3,234 seconds

As you can see, the statement now takes a little over 3 seconds. The function had to be executed three times because of the three distinct values. Every time the function was called with a parameter it had already seen, the body of the function was not executed, and the result was directly returned from the cache.

Result Cache

When a function is declared with the result_cache keyword, the effect is pretty much the same as when the function is declared as deterministic; but in this case, the function can rely on table data. Oracle Database automatically invalidates the cache when the table data changes.

Another advantage of declaring it as a result cached is that the cache is shared between sessions in the database. That means that the first one to call the function with a certain set of parameters takes the hit of executing the entire function. Also, a bit of time is used to fill up the cache. The second time this function gets called, by any session, just return the result from the cache without executing the function body (see Listing 10-4).

Listing 10-4. A very slow result_cache function

```
create or replace function myslowfunction( p_in in number )
return number
result_cache
is
```

```
begin
  dbms_session.sleep( 1 );
  return p_in;
end;
/

set timing on
select myslowfunction( t.c ) from t
/
set timing off

MYSLOWFUNCTION(T.C)
-------------------
        1
        2
        3
        1
        2
        3
        1
        2
        3
        1

10 rows selected

Executed in 3,237 seconds

disconnect

connect book/<<the_password>>

set timing on
select myslowfunction( t.c ) from t
/
set timing off
MYSLOWFUNCTION(T.C)
```

```
-------------------
        1
        2
        3
        1
        2
        3
        1
        2
        3
        1

10 rows selected

Executed in 0,097 seconds
```

Hierarchical Profiler

To determine where you should focus your attention to improve performance, it is a good idea to have insight into where your program is spending its time. You can do this by profiling your code. Start a profiling session and execute your program. A hierarchical profiler can help in this process.

There are a few steps to take if you have a block of code to analyze. First, compile the program you want to trace. Let's create a package to display info about the constructors and their drivers for a given year.

Note   This is not the best and/or fastest way to build a procedure that shows information about constructors and their drivers, but it is done to demonstrate hierarchical profiler usage.

The package specification consists of only one procedure, as shown in Listing 10-5.

Listing 10-5. f1info package

```
create or replace package f1info is
  procedure show_season(year_in in number);
end f1info;
/
```

In the body of the package, build a private procedure to display a driver's information.

```
procedure show_driver(driverid_in in number)
is
  l_forename    f1data.drivers.forename%type;
  l_surname     f1data.drivers.surname%type;
  l_nationality f1data.drivers.nationality%type;
begin
  select d.forename
       , d.surname
       , d.nationality
  into   l_forename
       , l_surname
       , l_nationality
  from   f1data.drivers d
  where  d.driverid = driverid_in;

  dbms_output.put_line( '   '
          ||l_forename
          ||' '
          ||l_surname
          ||'('
          ||l_nationality
          ||')'
          );
end show_driver;
```

Also, create a procedure to display the information of a constructor. This procedure calls the show_driver procedure for all the drivers that drive for this constructor in the requested year.

```
procedure show_constructor( year_in              in number
  , constructorid_in in number
  )
is
  l_name          f1data.constructors.name%type;
  l_nationality f1data.constructors.nationality%type;

begin
  select c.name
       , c.nationality
    into   l_name
       , l_nationality
    from   f1data.constructors c
    where  c.constructorid = constructorid_in;

  dbms_output.put_line( l_name
          ||'('
          ||l_nationality
          ||')'
          );
  for driver in
    (select distinct res.driverid
     from    f1data.results res
     join    f1data.races    r
       on    (res.raceid = r.raceid)
     where   1=1
     and     r.year = year_in
     and     res.constructorid = constructorid_in
    ) loop
    show_driver( driverid_in => driver.driverid );
  end loop;
end show_constructor;
```

265

Finally, implement the show_season procedure.

```
procedure show_season(year_in in number)
is
begin
  for constructor in
    (select distinct res.constructorid
     from    f1data.results res
     join    f1data.races   r
       on    (res.raceid = r.raceid)
     where   1=1
     and     r.year = year_in
    ) loop
    show_constructor
      ( year_in           => year_in
      , constructorid_in => constructor.constructorid
      );
  end loop;
end show_season;
```

Listing 10-6 is the complete package body, which can be downloaded from this book's GitHub page.

DBMS_HPROF

To help with profiling your code, you can use the DBMS_HPROF package. This package consists of a procedure to create the necessary tables, procedures, and functions to start and stop profiling and to analyze the acquired data.

create_tables

The create_tables procedure creates the tables needed to store all the profiling data.

```
begin
  dbms_hprof.create_tables;
end;
/
```

If you run this procedure a second time, you get an error telling you that the tables already exist. If you want to drop and re-create the tables, you can call the procedure with the force_it parameter set to TRUE.

```
begin
  dbms_hprof.create_tables( force_it => true );
end;
/
```

This procedure also re-creates two sequences.

start_profiling

To begin your profiling session, you call the start_profiling function.

```
function start_profiling( max_depth   PLS_INTEGER DEFAULT NULL
, profile_uga BOOLEAN    DEFAULT NULL
, profile_pga BOOLEAN    DEFAULT NULL
, sqlmonitor  BOOLEAN    DEFAULT TRUE
, run_comment VARCHAR2   DEFAULT NULL
) return number;
```

Table 10-1 explains the meaning of the parameters.

Table 10-1. dbms_hprof.start_profiling Function Parameters

Parameter	Description
max_depth	When NULL, profile information is gathered for all functions in all call level depths. When a non-NULL value is provided, profile information is gathered for all functions up to the specified call level depth. The time spent in functions with a call level depth greater than the supplied level is charged to the ancestor function.
profile_uga	This means profile session memory usage (undocumented, for internal use only).
profile_pga	This means profile process memory usage (undocumented, for internal use only).
sqlmonitor	When TRUE, a Real-Time monitoring report is generated at the end of the profiler run.
run_comment	This means an arbitrary comment for this profiler data collection run.

The data collected is stored in the DBMSHP_TRACE_DATA table (see Table 10-2).

Table 10-2. *DBMSHP_TRACE_DATA*

Name	Type	Nullable
trace_id	NUMBER	
Rawdata	CLOB	y
Sqlmonitor	CLOB	y
trace_timestamp	TIMESTAMP(6)	y
run_comment	VARCHAR2(2047)	y

When the data gets generated and stored in this table a unique `trace_id` is generated using the `dbmshp_tracenumber` sequence that is also created. This `trace_id` is returned by the function.

Now tell the Oracle database to start profiling. Retrieve `trace_id` in a local variable for later use. It is a good idea to give the profile a comment, so you can later easily find it.

```
l_trace_id := dbms_hprof.start_profiling( run_comment => 'HProf Demo' );
```

Next is the call to the program you want to trace.

```
f1info.show_season(2022);
```

stop_profiling

And as soon as the program is done, you tell the Oracle database to end your profiling session.

```
dbms_hprof.stop_profiling;
```

All data collected is flushed in the `dbmshp_trace_data` table. You can also call the `stop_profiling` function, which returns the profile in a CLOB variable.

```
function stop_profiling return clob;
```

The CLOB contains a text document that looks like the following.

```
P#V PLSHPROF Internal Version 1.0
P#! PL/SQL Timer Started
```

```
P#C SQL."SYS"."DBMS_HPROF"::11."__static_sql_exec_line700"
#700."8ggw94h7mvxd7"
P#! COMMIT
P#X 100
P#R
P#C PLSQL."BOOK"."F1INFO"::11."SHOW_SEASON"#e17d780a3c3eae3d #58
P#X 22
P#C SQL."BOOK"."F1INFO"::11."__sql_fetch_line62" #62."dajrzh30ttucf"
P#! SELECT DISTINCT RES.CONSTRUCTORID FROM F1DATA.RESU
P#X 84115
P#R
<<Rest removed for brevity>>
```

Table 10-3 shows the explanation of the prefixes.

Table 10-3. *Prefixes in the Document*

Prefix	Meaning
P#V	PLSHPROF banner with version number
P#C	Call to subprogram (call event)
P#R	Return from subprogram
P#X	The elapsed time between the preceding and following events
P#!	Comment

Instead of reviewing and analyzing the document yourself, you can call the analyze procedure or function.

analyze

The analyze procedure, there is also an overloaded function with the same name, analyzes profiler data in the profiler data table and produces either an HTML document with the profiler report or a set of rows in the tables, so you can build your reports.

```
procedure analyze
(
  trace_id     number
```

```
, report_clob out clob
, trace       varchar2 default null
, skip        pls_integer default 0
, collect     pls_integer default null
, profile_uga boolean default null
, profile_pga boolean default null
);
```

The analyze procedure takes the parameters described in Table 10-4 and returns a CLOB in its out parameter.

Table 10-4. *Analyze Procedure Parameters*

Parameter	Mandatory	Description
trace_id	Y	The traceid entry in profiler data table (dbmshp_data)
report_clob	Y	The analyzed HTML report in a CLOB (output)
Trace		When NULL (default), analysis/reporting generated for the entire run
		Analysis only for the subtrees rooted at the specified "trace" entry
		Must be specified in the qualified format; e.g.,
		"BOOK"."F1INFO"."SHOW_DRIVER"
		(If the procedure or function is overloaded, all of them is analyzed.)
Skip		Used only when "trace" is specified
		Skips first "skip" invocations to "trace"
		Default value is 0
Collect		Used only when "trace"is specified
		Analyzes "collect" number of invocations of "trace" (starting from "skip"+1'th invocation)
		Default is only 1 invocation collected
profile_uga		Report UGA usage
profile_pga		Report PGA usage

```
function analyze
(
  trace_id      number
```

```
, summary_mode boolean default false
, trace        varchar2 default null
, skip         pls_integer default 0
, collect      pls_integer default null
, run_comment  varchar2 default null
, profile_uga  boolean default null
, profile_pga  boolean default null
) return number;
```

The analyze function returns runnumber, which is the key to the rows it generates in different tables. The function takes arguments as described in Table 10-5.

Table 10-5. *Analyze Procedure Parameters*

Parameter	Mandatory	Description
trace_id	Y	The traceid entry in profiler data table (dbmshp_data)
summary_mode		When FALSE (default), does a full analysis When TRUE, only generates a top-level summary
Trace		When NULL (default), analysis/reporting generated for entire run Analysis only for the subtrees rooted at the specified "trace" entry Must be specified in the qualified format; e.g., "BOOK"."F1INFO"."SHOW_DRIVER" (If the procedure or function is overloaded, all are analyzed.)
Skip		Used only when "trace" is specified. Skips the first "skip" invocations to "trace" Default value is 0
collect		Used only when "trace" is specified Analyzes "collect" number of invocations of "trace" (starting from "skip"+1'th invocation) Default is 1 invocation collected
run_comment		Arbitrary comment analyzes run
profile_uga		Report UGA usage
profile_pga		Report PGA usage

The analyze function uses the following three tables (all created using the dbms_
hprof.create_tables procedure).

- dbmshp_runs

- dbmshp_function_info

- dbmshp_parent_child_info

For each trace record that has been analyzed, one record is added to the dbmshp_
runs table (see Table 10-6).

Table 10-6. *dbmshp_runs*

Name	Type	Nullable
Runid	NUMBER	
run_timestamp	TIMESTAMP(6)	y
total_elapsed_time	INTEGER	y
run_comment	VARCHAR2(2047)	y
trace_id	NUMBER	y

Every procedure, function, and SQL statement gets a row in the dbmshp_function_
info table using the same run ID as the one in the record in the dbmshp_runs table (see
Table 10-7).

Table 10-7. *dbmshp_function_info*

Name	Type	Nullable
Runid	NUMBER	
Symbolid	NUMBER	
Owner	VARCHAR2(128)	y
Module	VARCHAR2(128)	y
Type	VARCHAR2(32)	y
Function	VARCHAR2(4000)	y
line#	NUMBER	y
Hash	RAW(32)	y
Namespace	VARCHAR2(32)	y
subtree_elapsed_time	INTEGER	y
function_elapsed_time	INTEGER	y
Calls	INTEGER	y
sql_id	VARCHAR2(13)	y
sql_text	VARCHAR2(4000)	y

The `dbmshp_parent_child_info` table contains parent-child level profiler information. It also contains timing information for this procedure/function and the accumulated time spent in child procedures or functions (see Table 10-8).

Table 10-8. *dbmshp_parent_child_info*

Name	Type	Nullable
Runid	NUMBER	y
Parentsymid	NUMBER	y
Childsymid	NUMBER	y
subtree_elapsed_time	INTEGER	y
function_elapsed_time	INTEGER	y
Calls	INTEGER	y

The unique run number is generated using the dbmshp_runnumber sequence.

The profile data is stored in the dbmshp_trace_data table. You can call the analyze *procedure* to retrieve a CLOB with the trace report.

```
dbms_hprof.analyze( trace_id => l_trace_id
    , report_clob => l_clob
    );
```

You can also call the analyze *function* to write all the information into the tables.

```
l_analyze_id := dbms_hprof.analyze( trace_id => l_trace_id
        , run_comment => 'HProf Demo'
        );
```

Report

You can choose either of two options when analyzing the collected trace information. The script in Listing 10-7 analyzes the gathered data into an HTML report.

Listing 10-7. Script to generate an HTML document

```
create table profiler
( reports clob )
/

declare
  l_trace_id number;
  l_clob clob;
begin
  dbms_hprof.create_tables( force_it => true );
  l_trace_id := dbms_hprof.start_profiling
      ( run_comment => 'HProf Demo' );

  f1info.show_season(2022);

  dbms_hprof.stop_profiling;
```

```
  dbms_hprof.analyze( trace_id => l_trace_id
      , report_clob => l_clob
      );
  insert into profiler(reports) values (l_clob);
end;
/
```

Part of the report generated in the table is shown in Figure 10-1.

PL/SQL Elapsed Time (microsecs) Analysis

17386 microsecs (elapsed time) & 174 function calls

The PL/SQL Hierarchical Profiler produces a collection of reports that present information derived from the profiler's output log in a variety of formats. The following reports have been found to be the most generally useful as starting points for browsing:

- Function Elapsed Time (microsecs) Data sorted by Total Subtree Elapsed Time (microsecs)
- Function Elapsed Time (microsecs) Data sorted by Total Function Elapsed Time (microsecs)
- SQL ID Elapsed Time (microsecs) Data sorted by SQL ID

In addition, the following reports are also available:

- Function Elapsed Time (microsecs) Data sorted by Function Name
- Function Elapsed Time (microsecs) Data sorted by Total Descendants Elapsed Time (microsecs)
- Function Elapsed Time (microsecs) Data sorted by Total Function Call Count
- Function Elapsed Time (microsecs) Data sorted by Mean Subtree Elapsed Time (microsecs)
- Function Elapsed Time (microsecs) Data sorted by Mean Function Elapsed Time (microsecs)
- Function Elapsed Time (microsecs) Data sorted by Mean Descendants Elapsed Time (microsecs)
- Module Elapsed Time (microsecs) Data sorted by Total Function Elapsed Time (microsecs)
- Module Elapsed Time (microsecs) Data sorted by Module Name
- Module Elapsed Time (microsecs) Data sorted by Total Function Call Count
- Namespace Elapsed Time (microsecs) Data sorted by Total Function Elapsed Time (microsecs)
- Namespace Elapsed Time (microsecs) Data sorted by Namespace
- Namespace Elapsed Time (microsecs) Data sorted by Total Function Call Count
- Parents and Children Elapsed Time (microsecs) Data

Function Elapsed Time (microsecs) Data sorted by Total Subtree Elapsed Time (microsecs)

17386 microsecs (elapsed time) & 174 function calls

Subtree	Ind%	Function	Ind%	Descendants	Ind%	Calls	Ind%	Function Name	SQL ID	SQL TEXT
17282	99.4%	38	0.2%	17244	99.2%	1	0.6%	BOOK.F1INFO.SHOW_SEASON (Line 60)		
		157	0.9%	14636	84.2%	10	5.7%	BOOK.F1INFO.SHOW_CONSTRUCTOR (Line 27)		

Figure 10-1. *Hierarchical profiler output*

The script in Listing 10-8 re-creates the profiling tables, starts the profiler, runs the program, ends the profiler, and analyzes the gathered data into records in the tables.

Listing 10-8. Script to generate profile data in the tables

```
declare
  l_trace_id number;
  l_analyze_id number;
begin
  dbms_hprof.create_tables( force_it => true );
  l_trace_id := dbms_hprof.start_profiling
      ( run_comment => 'HProf Demo' );

  f1info.show_season(2022);

  dbms_hprof.stop_profiling;

  l_analyze_id := dbms_hprof.analyze
        ( trace_id => l_trace_id
        , run_comment => 'HProf Demo'
        );
  dbms_output.put_line( l_analyze_id );
end;
/

Ferrari(Italian)
  Carlos Sainz(Spanish)
  Charles Leclerc(Monegasque)
Haas F1 Team(American)
  Mick Schumacher(German)
  Kevin Magnussen(Danish)
Alfa Romeo(Swiss)
  Guanyu Zhou(Chinese)
  Valtteri Bottas(Finnish)
Mercedes(German)
  Lewis Hamilton(British)
  George Russell(British)
McLaren(British)
  Lando Norris(British)
  Daniel Ricciardo(Australian)
```

```
Red Bull(Austrian)
  Sergio Pérez(Mexican)
  Max Verstappen(Dutch)
Alpine F1 Team(French)
  Fernando Alonso(Spanish)
  Esteban Ocon(French)
Williams(British)
  Nyck de Vries(Dutch)
  Alexander Albon(Thai)
  Nicholas Latifi(Canadian)
AlphaTauri(Italian)
  Yuki Tsunoda(Japanese)
  Pierre Gasly(French)
Aston Martin(British)
  Lance Stroll(Canadian)
  Nico Hülkenberg(German)
  Sebastian Vettel(German)
1
```

You can query the tables with the run number returned by the function.

```
select runid, total_elapsed_time, run_comment
from dbmshp_runs
where runid = 1
/
RUNID TOTAL RUN_COMMENT
----- ----- -----------------
    1 17722 HProf Demo
```

```
select
  owner, module, type, function, line#, namespace, calls,
  function_elapsed_time, subtree_elapsed_time
from dbmshp_function_info
where runid = 1
/
```

```
<<Output formatted manually for readability>>
OWNER MODULE      TYPE          FUNCTION
LINE# NAMESPAC CALLS FUNCT SUBTR
----- ----------- ------------ ---------------------------------
----- --------- ----- ----- -----
BOOK  F1INFO      PACKAGE BODY SHOW_CONSTRUCTOR
                                27 PLSQL      10   173 15463
BOOK  F1INFO      PACKAGE BODY SHOW_DRIVER
                                 2 PLSQL      22   106   755
BOOK  F1INFO      PACKAGE BODY SHOW_SEASON
                                60 PLSQL       1    42 17865
SYS   DBMS_HPROF  PACKAGE BODY STOP_PROFILING
                               747 PLSQL       1     0     0
SYS   DBMS_OUTPUT PACKAGE BODY NEW_LINE
                               117 PLSQL      32    11    11
SYS   DBMS_OUTPUT PACKAGE BODY PUT
                                77 PLSQL      32    80    80
SYS   DBMS_OUTPUT PACKAGE BODY PUT_LINE
                               109 PLSQL      32    54   145
BOOK  F1INFO      PACKAGE BODY __sql_fetch_line48
                                48 SQL        10 14288 14288
BOOK  F1INFO      PACKAGE BODY __sql_fetch_line64
                                64 SQL         1  2360  2360
BOOK  F1INFO      PACKAGE BODY __static_sql_exec_line35
                                35 SQL        10   211   211
BOOK  F1INFO      PACKAGE BODY __static_sql_exec_line8
                                 8 SQL        22   540   540
SYS   DBMS_HPROF  PACKAGE BODY __static_sql_exec_line700
                               700 SQL         1    95    95
```

A script to show the analyzed data in a readable form is shown in Listing 10-9.

Listing 10-9. Show analyzed data

```
select
  lpad(' ', level, ' ')||pf.function||' -> '||cf.function call,
  pc.subtree_elapsed_time,
  pc.function_elapsed_time,
  pc.calls,
  cf.line#
from
  (select * from dbmshp_parent_child_info where runid=1) pc,
  dbmshp_function_info pf,
  dbmshp_function_info cf
where pc.runid=pf.runid
  and pc.parentsymid=pf.symbolid
  and pc.runid=cf.runid
  and pc.childsymid=cf.symbolid
connect by prior pc.childsymid=pc.parentsymid
start with pc.parentsymid = 3
/

<<Output formatted manually for readability>>
CALL
        SUBTREE_ELAPSED_ FUNCTION_ELAPSED CALLS LINE#
----------------------------------------------------------------
    ---------------- ---------------- ----- -----
 SHOW_SEASON -> SHOW_CONSTRUCTOR
                        14107              145    10    27
  SHOW_CONSTRUCTOR -> SHOW_DRIVER
                          673              120    22     2
   SHOW_DRIVER -> PUT_LINE
                           73               33    22   109
    PUT_LINE -> NEW_LINE
                            7                7    32   117
    PUT_LINE -> PUT
                           56               56    32    77
```

```
    SHOW_DRIVER ->  __static_sql_exec_line8
                                480             480     22       8
   SHOW_CONSTRUCTOR -> PUT_LINE
                                 28               5     10     109
    PUT_LINE -> NEW_LINE
                                  7               7     32     117
    PUT_LINE -> PUT
                                 56              56     32      77
   SHOW_CONSTRUCTOR -> __sql_fetch_line48
                              13059           13059     10      48
   SHOW_CONSTRUCTOR -> __static_sql_exec_line35
                                202             202     10      35
  SHOW_SEASON -> __sql_fetch_line64
                               2020            2020      1      64

12 rows selected
```

As you can see, most of the time is spent on line 48 in a SQL fetch. This line is called ten times, so the average time spent is 1306 milliseconds. The SQL fetch on line 64 is only performed once but costs 2020 milliseconds. If you can improve performance on the SQL fetch in line 48, that improvement impacts the overall performance ten times the individual improvement, so that might be a good candidate for optimizing. But maybe you can improve the SQL fetch in line 64 even more than the improvement on line 48 multiplied by ten. The profiler report doesn't tell you where to focus your optimization effort, but it can help you make your choice.

Note   The way the profiler works sometimes changes from version to version. The example was done using Oracle Database 19c.

Summary

To speed up your PL/SQL code, you have multiple possibilities in Oracle Database. The UDF pragma tells the compiler that this function is primarily for SQL, so it can be optimized for this. The deterministic and result_cache functions minimize the times the code is executed. If the parameters are the same, the outcome is expected to be the same, so it can be retrieved from a previous run.

All options come with a cost, such as to memory, performance, the cache not filled, or values flushed from the cache. To get an insight into where you should try to optimize, you can use the procedures and functions in the DBMS_HPROF package.

CHAPTER 11

Storing JSON in the Database

When you work with JSON documents, you must decide *if* and *how* you will store JSON in the database. The first decision, *if*, needs to be made early on. Do you need the JSON document in its original format? You can make the case to do this when you are not storing all the data in relational tables, and the JSON document might contain data that could prove valuable later.

When storing all JSON data in a relational format, do you need to keep the JSON document?

When you have decided to store the JSON document as-is, what would be the best way to store it? This chapter explores the possibilities.

Stage Data Before Processing

When you import data into the database, let's say by calling a web service that should return a JSON document, it could be beneficial to store the returned value in a table without restrictions.

A common problem is that a call to a web service that should respond with a JSON document might return an HTML document when the web service is not reachable. If either the web service is down or a firewall restricts access to the web service, an HTML document is returned.

Trying to parse an HTML document as if it was a JSON document does not work without throwing an exception. Before processing the JSON document, it is recommended to store the response and decide after loading how to process the document. Dumping the results into a staging table first also has the benefit that the call

© Alex Nuijten, Patrick Barel 2023
A. Nuijten and P. Barel, *Modern Oracle Database Programming*, https://doi.org/10.1007/978-1-4842-9166-5_11

to the web service doesn't have to take longer than it needs to. The processing of the document can be postponed to a later time. This is especially useful when the parsing of the JSON document takes a considerable amount of time.

Which Data Type to Choose?

Because a JSON document is just text but in a special format, most developers tend to store the JSON document in something "readable," like a VARCHAR2 or a CLOB column, but this might not always be the best choice.

Storing it in a text column is very convenient when inspecting the JSON document. You don't need any special queries to extract the relevant information. You can simply select the column and inspect the JSON document.

When you are only dealing with very small JSON documents, less than 4000 bytes, a VARCHAR2 column would suffice. Slightly larger documents can also be stored in a VARCHAR2 column if you enable extended data types, up to 32,767 bytes.

If you need to go larger that 32K, then choose a BLOB column. This recommendation is especially true when you have an Oracle Database release 19 or lower. The recommendation from Oracle Database 21 (or higher) is to use the native JSON data type.

Why would you choose a BLOB over a CLOB column? The main reason for this is storage. A CLOB column encodes characters as UCS2 (similar to UTF16), which means that every character takes up two bytes. This could mean that your JSON document, which is originally 100 bytes, stored in a CLOB column, takes up 200 bytes.

Textual JSON is encoded using Unicode encoding, either UTF-8 or UTF-16, but when loaded into the database, it is automatically converted to UTF-8. A BLOB column stores the JSON document as-is. It avoids character set conversion. This takes up less space than a CLOB column and takes less IO to load it.

There is a downside to using a BLOB column, mainly for the developer that needs to inspect the whole JSON document, as binary data is not easily readable. You need a query like the following to make the JSON document readable.

```
select json_query
        (stg.json_payload
        ,'$' returning clob pretty)
  from staging stg
/
```

This query returns the JSON document as a CLOB, which is also nicely formatted, complete with line breaks and indentations.

JSON Constraint

Regardless of which data type you use to store the JSON document, you want to make sure that the values contained within are properly formed JSON documents. With the native JSON data type, this constraint is implicit as long as the keys used in the JSON document are unique.

Let's look at an example of implementing a JSON check constraint, beginning with a table with a VARCHAR2 column.

```
create table json_test
   (json_document varchar2(500))
/
```

Implement the following check constraint to ensure that only JSON documents are stored in the `json_document` column.

```
alter table json_test
  add constraint jt_chk check (json_document is json)
/
```

The `is json` condition ensures that the entered data adhere to a well-formed JSON format. Consider the following insert statement.

```
insert into json_test
values ('{
       driverId: "max_verstappen",
       "permanentNumber": "33",
       "code": "VER",
       "url": "http://en.wikipedia.org/wiki/Max_Verstappen",
       "givenName": "Max",
       "familyName": "Verstappen",
       "dateOfBirth": "1997-09-30",
       "nationality": "Dutch"
     }')
```

```
/
```

```
1 row inserted.
```

The first key in this JSON document (driverId) is not in quotes, while all other keys are. This is not correct because all the keys *should* be in quotes. Unfortunately, not everybody adheres to this standard, so you might receive data where the keys are not in quotes. By default, is json checks work in a *tolerant mode* and allows the keys not to be in quotes.

This behavior is not always desirable, and you might want to prevent this. In that case, you want to create the constraint as follows.

```
alter table json_test
add constraint jt_chk check (json_document is json strict)
/
```

Adding the strict keyword in the check constraint definition prevents keys from being unquoted.

An exception is raised when attempting to execute the same insert statement as earlier.

```
insert into json_test
values ('{
        driverId: "max_verstappen",
        "permanentNumber": "33",
        "code": "VER",
        "url": "http://en.wikipedia.org/wiki/Max_Verstappen",
        "givenName": "Max",
        "familyName": "Verstappen",
        "dateOfBirth": "1997-09-30",
        "nationality": "Dutch"
    }')
/
```

```
Error starting at line : 1 in command -
insert into json_test
values ('{
        driverId: "max_verstappen",
```

```
        "permanentNumber": "33",
        "code": "VER",
        "url": "http://en.wikipedia.org/wiki/Max_Verstappen",
        "givenName": "Max",
        "familyName": "Verstappen",
        "dateOfBirth": "1997-09-30",
        "nationality": "Dutch"
    }')
Error report -
ORA-02290: check constraint (BOOK.JT_CHK) violated
```

With the strict addition to the check constraint, it is no longer allowed to leave the keys unquoted.

Unfortunately, the JSON specification does not mention anything about duplicate keys. The following insert statement creates a technically correct JSON document.

```
insert into json_test
values ('{
        "driverId": "max_verstappen",
        "driverId": "lewis_hamilton",
        "permanentNumber": "33",
        "code": "VER",
        "url": "http://en.wikipedia.org/wiki/Max_Verstappen",
        "givenName": "Max",
        "familyName": "Verstappen",
        "dateOfBirth": "1997-09-30",
        "nationality": "Dutch"
    }')
/

1 row inserted.
```

In the JSON document in the preceding insert statement, the key "driverId" occurs twice, and as you can see, this *is* allowed. Even though it is allowed, it is highly undesirable, as you can imagine. Luckily having a duplicate key in a JSON document seldom occurs.

Changing the check constraint prevents duplicate keys.

```
alter table json_test
add constraint jt_chk check
    (json_document is json with unique keys)
```

Adding a with unique keys check constraint ensures that keys only appear once in the JSON document.

```
insert into json_test
values ('{
        "driverId": "max_verstappen",
        "driverId": "lewis_hamilton",
        "permanentNumber": "33",
        "code": "VER",
        "url": "http://en.wikipedia.org/wiki/Max_Verstappen",
        "givenName": "Max",
        "familyName": "Verstappen",
        "dateOfBirth": "1997-09-30",
        "nationality": "Dutch"
    }')
/

Error starting at line : 1 in command -
insert into json_test
values ('{
        "driverId": "max_verstappen",
        "driverId": "lewis_hamilton",
        "permanentNumber": "33",
        "code": "VER",
        "url": "http://en.wikipedia.org/wiki/Max_Verstappen",
        "givenName": "Max",
        "familyName": "Verstappen",
        "dateOfBirth": "1997-09-30",
        "nationality": "Dutch"
    }')
Error report -
ORA-02290: check constraint (BOOK.JT_CHK) violated
```

The uniqueness of the key is only applicable at the same level where ambiguity might occur. So even though the "driverId", "givenName," and "familyName" keys occur multiple times in the JSON document in the following insert statement, they are at different levels and thus allowed.

```
insert into json_test
values ('{
         "driverId": "max_verstappen",
         "permanentNumber": "33",
         "code": "VER",
         "url": "http://en.wikipedia.org/wiki/Max_Verstappen",
         "givenName": "Max",
         "familyName": "Verstappen",
         "dateOfBirth": "1997-09-30",
         "nationality": "Dutch",
         "teammate": {"driverId": "sergio_perez",
                     "givenName": "Sergio",
                     "familyName": "Pérez"
                    }
        }')
/
```

1 row inserted.

You can specify strict and with unique keys in the check constraint. This make sure that all keys are in quotes and that they appear only once in the JSON document.

The native JSON data type, added in Oracle Database 21, is a constrained data type. Besides the obvious is json constraint, only with unique keys is implied. It is not possible to enforce the strict condition nor disable the with unique keys condition when using the JSON data type. The JSON document keys that are stored in the JSON column are in quotes, even if the original text does not have quotes around the keys.

Under the Hood

After you add the proper JSON check constraint to the column, these columns are visible as JSON columns in the data dictionary. There are three data dictionary tables where you can inspect the JSON columns.

- USER_JSON_COLUMNS

- ALL_JSON_COLUMNS

- DBA_JSON_COLUMNS

Let's see what the data dictionary says when you create all the different data types to store the JSON document and add the proper is json check constraint on them. First, the native JSON data type.

```
create table native_json
(json_document json)
```

This column doesn't need a check constraint to ensure that the data that is entered is well-formed JSON. When querying the data dictionary, you see the following results.

```
select object_type
     ,column_name
     ,format
     ,data_type
  from user_json_columns
 where table_name = 'NATIVE_JSON'
/
```

```
OBJECT_TYPE  COLUMN_NAME                  FORMAT     DATA_TYPE
-----------  ------------------------     ---------  -------------
TABLE        JSON_DOCUMENT                OSON       JSON
```

What stands out in the result set is the FORMAT column. The format for the native JSON data type is OSON. Oracle uses this internal binary format to load and scan JSON documents. This OSON format is unique to Oracle.

As OSON is a binary representation of the JSON document, does this mean that when you use a BLOB column to hold data, it also stores it in the OSON format? Let's examine this next.

```
create table blob_json
(json_document blob)
/

alter table blob_json
add constraint blob_chk check (json_document is json)
/
```

The BLOB_JSON table has a check constraint on the JSON_DOCUMENT column to ensure it is JSON. The data dictionary reveals the following information.

```
select object_type
      ,column_name
      ,format
      ,data_type
  from user_json_columns
 where table_name = 'BLOB_JSON'
/
```

```
OBJECT_TYPE  COLUMN_NAME               FORMAT     DATA_TYPE
-----------  ------------------------  ---------  -------------

TABLE        JSON_DOCUMENT             TEXT       BLOB
```

Short answer: no, the BLOB column uses the text format to store the JSON document. As mentioned, it stores the JSON document as-is without character set conversion.

The same is true for the other data types, VARCHAR2 and CLOB. The TEXT format is used for these columns.

```
create table clob_json
(json_document clob)
/

alter table clob_json
add constraint clob_chk check (json_document is json)
/

create table varchar2_json
(json_document varchar2(4000))
/
```

```
alter table varchar2_json
add constraint varchar2_chk check (json_document is json)
/

select object_type
      ,column_name
      ,format
      ,data_type
  from user_json_columns
 where table_name in ('CLOB_JSON', 'VARCHAR_JSON')
/

OBJECT_TYPE  COLUMN_NAME              FORMAT     DATA_TYPE
-----------  -----------------------  ---------  -------------

TABLE        JSON_DOCUMENT            TEXT       CLOB
TABLE        JSON_DOCUMENT            TEXT       VARCHAR2
```

In the data dictionary, objects also appear when a column is projecting JSON documents. Suppose you have a staging table containing JSON and non-JSON data. Two views cover this table: one exposing only the JSON data, and the other only exposing the non-JSON data. The following table definition is used for this example.

```
create table no_constraint_json
(document clob)
/
```

The document column holds either JSON or non-JSON data. The covering views are defined as follows.

```
create view json_view
as
select treat (document as json) as json_document
  from no_constraint_json
 where document is json
/

create view non_json_view
as
select document
```

```
 from no_constraint_json
 where document is not json
/
```

The where condition in the views determines which data is exposed through the view. Note that the view that exposes the JSON document uses the treat function to project the DOCUMENT column as JSON.

The JSON_VIEW shows up in the USER_JSON_COLUMNS data dictionary view with similar characteristics as when using a CLOB as the data type to store the JSON documents.

```
select object_type
      ,column_name
      ,format
      ,data_type
  from user_json_columns
 where table_name = 'JSON_VIEW'
/
```

```
OBJECT_TYPE COLUMN_NAME                     FORMAT    DATA_TYPE
----------- ------------------------------- --------- -------------
VIEW        JSON_DOCUMENT                   TEXT      CLOB
```

Using treat in the view definition, this technique can be used in releases prior to Oracle Database 21. From release 21 onward, you can also use the JSON constructor to project the column to a native JSON format.

```
create view native_json_view
as
select json (document) as json_document
  from no_constraint_json
 where document is json
/
```

View NATIVE_JSON_VIEW created.

```
select object_type
      ,column_name
      ,format
```

```
    ,data_type
  from user_json_columns
 where table_name = 'NATIVE_JSON_VIEW'
/

OBJECT_TYPE COLUMN_NAME              FORMAT    DATA_TYPE
----------- ------------------------ --------- -------------
VIEW        JSON_DOCUMENT            OSON      JSON
```

As you can see in the results from the data dictionary view, now the view exposes the JSON column in the OSON format.

Tip   When you choose the name for your JSON document columns, add something to identify them easily. For example, always name them JSON_ DOCUMENT or a suffix that identifies it as JSON. This way, you can use the data dictionary views: *_JSON_COLUMNS and *_TAB_COLUMNS to identify those columns that should have the `is json` check constraint on them but are missing.

Major Differences Between TREAT and JSON Constructor

Using the JSON constructor (in Oracle Database 21) to project a column (VARCHAR2, CLOB, BLOB) to a JSON data type sounds like a no-brainer. It uses the OSON internal binary format, so this must be the best way to convert any string to a JSON. The `treat` function casts it to a JSON but still uses the TEXT format to produce the JSON document.

There is a major difference in the behavior between the two options. Let's re-examine the table containing JSON and non-JSON data and the views covering this table. This time let's use two views to project the column to a JSON data type, one with the `treat` function and one with the JSON constructor.

```
create table staging_table
(document varchar2(500))
/
```

Also, add some data in this table, one row which is properly formatted JSON data and one row which is not.

```
insert into staging_table
values ('{"this":"that"}')
/

insert into staging_table
values ('this is surely no json data')
/
```

For the views covering this table, use the following definitions.

```
create or replace
view treat_json_view
as
select treat (document as json) as document
  from staging_table
/

create or replace
view native_json_view
as
select json (document) as document
  from staging_table
/
```

Note that both view definitions don't have a predicate to filter out valid JSON data. All data, JSON or not, is exposed via the views.

Querying the view that uses the treat function, all the data is returned from the underlying table, even the data that is clearly not JSON.

```
select *
  from treat_json_view
/
```

```
DOCUMENT
---------------------------
{"this":"that"}
this is surely no json data
```

The other view that projects the columns to native JSON behaves differently. In the following SELECT statement, you can see that an exception is raised.

```
select *
  from native_json_view
/

Error starting at line : 1 in command -
select *
  from native_json_view
Error report -
ORA-40441: JSON syntax error
```

Adding a predicate to filter out the JSON documents results in the same exception.

```
select *
  from native_json_view
 where document is json
/

Error starting at line : 1 in command -
select *
  from native_json_view
 where document is json
Error report -
ORA-40441: JSON syntax error
```

Effectively this view is unusable unless it is modified to only expose JSON documents using a where clause with the is json predicate. The lesson to learn here is to be careful when covering a table that contains JSON and non-JSON data and applying functions to convert it to JSON.

Determining the Structure

Once you have loaded the JSON document into the database, its structure might be unknown. To get information about the structure, you can use the `json_dataguide` aggregate to help you understand.

We took JSON documents returned by the Ergast Developer API (`http://ergast.com/mrd/`) web service for the examples. The web services return Formula 1 data. How to call this web service is outlined in Chapter 15.

In the table `native_json`, I have loaded all driver standings for all completed seasons (1950 – 2021). Refer to the `load_json_docs.sql` code file, which can be downloaded from this book's GitHub page.

With the aggregate `json_dataguide`, information about the structure of the JSON is returned. `json_dataguide` analyzes all the JSON documents in the table and identifies each attribute, its type, its length, and what path to follow to retrieve it. The result is another JSON document called a JSON schema. There is currently no built-in functionality to validate this JSON schema, nor to validate incoming JSON documents against this JSON schema.

The following query shows the first part of the JSON schema (the rest omitted for brevity).

```
select json_dataguide (json_document) as guide
  from native_json
/

GUIDE
---------------------------
[{"o:path":"$","type":"object","o:length":1},{"o:path":"$.
MRData","type":"object
```

Because the result is another JSON document, it is easy to get the results in a relational format (not all results are listed).

```
with dataguide
as
(select json_dataguide (json_document) as guide
   from native_json)
select jt.*
  from dataguide dg
 cross
```

```
join json_table (dg.guide, '$[*]'
        columns (
             json_path path '$."o:path"'
             ,json_type path '$."type"'
             ,len       path '$."o:length"'
        )
    ) jt
/
```

JSON_PATH	JSON_TYPE	LEN
$	object	1
$.MRData	object	1
$.MRData.url	string	64
$.MRData.limit	string	4
$.MRData.total	string	4
$.MRData.xmlns	string	32
$.MRData.offset	string	1
$.MRData.series	string	2
$.MRData.StandingsTable	object	1
$.MRData.StandingsTable.season	string	4
$.MRData.StandingsTable.StandingsLists	array	1
$.MRData.StandingsTable.StandingsLists.round	string	2
$.MRData.StandingsTable.StandingsLists.season	string	4

The analysis of the JSON document shows that the top level ($) is a JSON object, while the limit attribute is a string and StandingsLists is an array. The JSON path expressions can extract values from the JSON document.

Because json_dataguide analyses all JSON documents, it can take quite some time to get this done. It is also possible to store the data guide permanently using a JSON search index.

To create the data guide–enabled search index, issue the following statement.

```
create search index standing_idx on
  native_json (json_document)
  for json parameters ('dataguide on')
/
```

With the data guide, you have all the information to project the JSON document into a relational format. There are two procedures in the DBMS_JSON package which can generate a view for you.

- **CREATE_VIEW.** This procedure creates a view with relational columns based on the data guide you pass in as an argument. The data guide argument can be created with json_dataguide. This procedure can also be used when there is a data guide-enabled search index. In that case, you would use the dbms_json.get_index_dataguide function to pass in as an argument. The data guide argument must be in a hierarchical format.

- **CREATE_VIEW_ON_PATH.** This procedure creates a view with relational columns based on a data guide-enabled search index. This method is more flexible as you can pass in a JSON path expression to use for creating the view and a minimum frequency threshold. The frequency threshold is guided by the gathering of statistics on the JSON document.

You can run the following statement to generate a view of the JSON documents in the table with a data guide-enabled search index.

```
begin
  dbms_json.create_view
   (viewname  => 'standingsview'
   ,tablename => 'native_json'
   ,jcolname  => 'json_document'
   ,dataguide => dbms_json.get_index_dataguide
                  (tablename => 'native_json'
                  ,jcolname  => 'json_document'
                  ,format    => dbms_json.format_hierarchical
                  )
   );
end;
/
```

The view that is created has the following structure.

Name	Null?	Type
ID	NOT NULL	NUMBER
JSON_DOCUMENT$url		VARCHAR2(64)
JSON_DOCUMENT$limit		VARCHAR2(4)
JSON_DOCUMENT$total		VARCHAR2(4)
JSON_DOCUMENT$xmlns		VARCHAR2(32)
JSON_DOCUMENT$offset		VARCHAR2(1)
JSON_DOCUMENT$series		VARCHAR2(2)
JSON_DOCUMENT$season		VARCHAR2(4)
JSON_DOCUMENT$round		VARCHAR2(2)
JSON_DOCUMENT$season_1		VARCHAR2(4)
JSON_DOCUMENT$wins		VARCHAR2(2)
JSON_DOCUMENT$url_2		VARCHAR2(128)
JSON_DOCUMENT$code		VARCHAR2(4)
JSON_DOCUMENT$driverId		VARCHAR2(32)
JSON_DOCUMENT$givenName		VARCHAR2(32)
JSON_DOCUMENT$familyName		VARCHAR2(32)
JSON_DOCUMENT$dateOfBirth		VARCHAR2(16)
JSON_DOCUMENT$nationality		VARCHAR2(32)
JSON_DOCUMENT$permanentNumber		VARCHAR2(2)
JSON_DOCUMENT$points		VARCHAR2(8)
JSON_DOCUMENT$position		VARCHAR2(4)
JSON_DOCUMENT$positionText		VARCHAR2(4)
JSON_DOCUMENT$url_3		VARCHAR2(128)
JSON_DOCUMENT$name		VARCHAR2(32)
JSON_DOCUMENT$nationality_4		VARCHAR2(16)
JSON_DOCUMENT$constructorId		VARCHAR2(32)

All the column names are based on the data guide and are case-sensitive. To query the view, you would have to use quotes in the column names.

```
select "JSON_DOCUMENT$url"
  from standingsview
/
```

As you can imagine, this is far from ideal. There is a way to rename the columns using the procedure `dbms_json.rename_column`. However, there is a catch. This needs to be done before the view is (re)created and can only be done when there is a data guide-enabled search index, which was already created.

Tip   You can run `dbms_json.create_view` multiple times without first dropping the view. This is handled automatically for you.

You can rename the column with the following statement.

```
begin
  dbms_json.rename_column
    (tablename.      => 'native_json'
    ,jcolname        => 'json_document'
    ,path            => '$.MRData.url'
    ,type            => dbms_json.type_string
    ,preferred_name  => 'URL'
    );
end;
/
```

Note that the `preferred_name` argument in the preceding code is case-sensitive. When you specify a lowercase name for the column, it is created as such, making the column once again case-sensitive.

When the view is created for you, all the arrays in the JSON document are unnested. This means that the original 71 JSON documents are now over 3000 rows. This can be observed when you inspect the view definition, JSON_TABLE, in combination with several NESTED PATH expressions used to explode the JSON document. This is an excerpt of the FROM clause. Most columns were removed for brevity.

```
from
  "BOOK"."NATIVE_JSON" rt,
  json_table ( "JSON_DOCUMENT", '$[*]'
  columns
    "URL" varchar2 ( 64 ) path '$.MRData.url',
  ...
```

```
      nested path '$.MRData.StandingsTable.StandingsLists[*]'
      columns (
        "JSON_DOCUMENT$season_1" varchar2 ( 4 ) path '$.season',
         nested path '$.DriverStandings[*]'
         columns (
           "JSON_DOCUMENT$wins" varchar2 ( 2 ) path '$.wins',
...

           nested path '$.Constructors[*]'
           columns (
             "JSON_DOCUMENT$url_3" varchar2 ( 128 ) path '$.url',
...

          ),
...

               )))  jt
```

Indexing JSON Documents

As JSON documents can be quite large, it makes sense to index them to quickly find what you're looking for.

There are several ways to index JSON documents, and your chosen method strongly depends on your needs. This section explores several of these techniques.

To generate the explain plan for the different queries in the following sections, each statement is run as follows.

```
explain plan for
<the actual query>
```

To examine the explain plan, the following query is used.

```
select *
  from dbms_xplan.display (format => 'BASIC')
/
```

The basic format displays the minimum information, such as operation and name, which is sufficient to demonstrate the use of a specific index.

Searching for a Specific Key

Suppose you have a query to search for a specific season.

```
select *
  from native_json
 where json_value (
          json_document
          ,'$.MRData.StandingsTable.StandingsLists.season'
       ) = :season
/
```

The explain plan for this query shows that a full table scan is needed. There is simply no other way to get the information.

```
-------------------------------------------
| Id  | Operation          | Name         |
-------------------------------------------
|   0 | SELECT STATEMENT   |              |
|   1 |   TABLE ACCESS FULL| NATIVE_JSON  |
-------------------------------------------
```

To create an index for this query, you can create a function-based index with the same expression that you have in the query.

```
create index race_season_idx on
  native_json (
    json_value ( json_document
                ,'$.MRData.StandingsTable.StandingsLists.season' )
  )
/
```

This technique can only index one value per JSON document. Arrays can't be indexed in this way. Because there is no way to guarantee that the JSON document always stays the same (the creator of the web service can change their mind), it could lead to unexpected results. The following is a better and cleaner way to define this index.

```
create index race_season_idx on
  native_json (
```

```
    json_value (
      json_document
     ,'$.MRData.StandingsTable.StandingsLists.season'
        error on error
        null on empty
    )
  )
/
```

With this index in place, the explain plan changes, and you can see an *index range scan.*

```
---------------------------------------------------------------------
| Id  | Operation                          | Name             |
---------------------------------------------------------------------
|  0  | SELECT STATEMENT                   |                  |
|  1  |   TABLE ACCESS BY INDEX ROWID BATCHED| NATIVE_JSON    |
|  2  |    INDEX RANGE SCAN                | RACE_SEASON_IDX  |
---------------------------------------------------------------------
```

The same rules apply when an index can be used or not. One of them is the data type that is indexed vs. the data type used in the predicate as a bind variable.

In the preceding example, the season attribute is indexed, and the data type is VARCHAR2(4000). This means that when the query predicate compares the indexed column with a number, the index can't be used.

```
where json_value (
        json_document
       ,'$.MRData.StandingsTable.StandingsLists.season'
      ) = 1969 --<-- number
/
```

```
---------------------------------------------
| Id  | Operation          | Name          |
---------------------------------------------
|  0  | SELECT STATEMENT   |               |
|  1  |   TABLE ACCESS FULL| NATIVE_JSON   |
---------------------------------------------
```

The predicate needs to compare the indexed value with a string.

```
where json_value (
        json_document
        ,'$.MRData.StandingsTable.StandingsLists.season'
    ) = '1969' --<-- string
/
```

```
---------------------------------------------------------------
| Id  | Operation                          | Name            |
---------------------------------------------------------------
|   0 | SELECT STATEMENT                   |                 |
|   1 |  TABLE ACCESS BY INDEX ROWID BATCHED| NATIVE_JSON    |
|   2 |   INDEX RANGE SCAN                 | RACE_SEASON_IDX |
---------------------------------------------------------------
```

When you change the index definition to use the number() item method, you explicitly define that the indexed value is numeric. For the writer of the query, as they need to use the same expression as is defined in the function-based index, it is also clear that a numeric value should be used in the comparison.

```
create index race_season_idx on
  native_json (
    json_value (
      json_document
      ,'$.MRData.StandingsTable.StandingsLists.season.number()'
        error on error
        null on empty
    )
  )
/
```

Testing with this index revealed that the index is still used even if you use a string in the predicate. As long as the JSON path expression is the same as the expression in the function-based index, this is true.

This type of index, a function-based index, is fine as long as you know what you are looking for. It sounds like a downside, but realistically quite often, you know exactly what you are looking for when processing JSON documents.

Ad Hoc Searching with the JSON Search Index

Since Oracle Database 12.2, it is possible to index JSON documents with JSON search indexes. The behavior is similar to Oracle Text indexes, so they might seem familiar. In the background, an Oracle Text index is created for the JSON documents.

The syntax for a JSON search index is very simple, but the result is fantastic.

```
create search index standing_idx on
  native_json (
    json_document
  )
for json
/
```

Creating a JSON search index might take some time, and it creates all kinds of DR$-tables in your schema, similar to Oracle Text.

Tip   To create persistent data guide information as part of a JSON search index, you can specify this in the parameter clause.

```
create search index standing_idx on
native_json (json_document)
for json parameters ('dataguide on');
```

Or, later you can do this by rebuilding the JSON search index.

```
alter index standing_idx
rebuild parameters ('dataguide on');
```

Once the index is created, you can query any attribute that appears anywhere in the JSON document. For example, let's search for any JSON document that mentions "verstappen" anywhere.

```
select *
  from native_json
 where json_textcontains (
         json_document
         ,'$'
```

```
        ,'verstappen'
        )
/
```

As you can see in the preceding query, just like with Oracle Text, you can use a special predicate to use the JSON search index, although this is not strictly necessary.

```
-----------------------------------------------------
| Id | Operation                  | Name         |
-----------------------------------------------------
|  0 | SELECT STATEMENT           |              |
|  1 |  TABLE ACCESS BY INDEX ROWID| NATIVE_JSON  |
|  2 |   DOMAIN INDEX             | STANDING_IDX |
-----------------------------------------------------
```

It is important to know that the word that you are searching for needs to be an exact match. Passing "stap" as the search term does not yield any results. Searching for "VER" or "ver" yield results simply because that is the static driver code, just like "HAM" is for Hamilton, and "LEC" is for Leclerc (although there was also a constructor (1973, 1977) with the same identification: LEC Refrigeration).

Even if you are querying the JSON documents by using a JSON_VALUE in the predicate, the JSON search index can be used (for this example, the earlier created function-based index has been dropped).

```
select *
  from native_json
 where json_value (
         json_document
       , '$.MRData.StandingsTable.StandingsLists.season'
       ) = :season
/
```

This shows the following explain plan.

```
--------------------------------------------------------
| Id  | Operation                 | Name          |
--------------------------------------------------------
|   0 | SELECT STATEMENT          |               |
|   1 |   TABLE ACCESS BY INDEX ROWID| NATIVE_JSON   |
|   2 |     DOMAIN INDEX          | STANDING_IDX  |
--------------------------------------------------------
```

Multivalue Indexes

When you are using a JSON data type to store the JSON document, there is also a possibility to create a multivalue index to optimize queries that use the json_exists condition, either as scalar values individually or in an array.

For the following example, a table is created for all champions of F1.

```
create table f1_champions
(driver varchar2(50)
,season json
)
/
```

In the season JSON column, there is a JSON document listing all the seasons that this driver has been a world champion, such as the following.

```
{"winner":[1994, 1995, 2000, 2001, 2002, 2003, 2004]}
```

To query all drivers that have been world champions since 2010, you can write a query with the json_exists condition.

```
select driver
  from f1_champions f
 where json_exists (f.season
                   ,'$.winner?(@.number() >= 2010)')
/

DRIVER
-----------------
```

Sebastian Vettel
Lewis Hamilton
Nico Rosberg
Max Verstappen

A multivalue index can be beneficial to efficiently search all the JSON documents. To assure that the query picks up the multivalue index, the index must specify the data type to be indexed, and the query predicate must match the type specified by the index. In this case, you can create a multivalue index using the dot notation in the JSON path expression.

```
create multivalue index season_idx on f1_champions f
  (f.season.winner.number())
/
```

The explain plan for the query to find all F1 champions since 2010 is as follows.

```
-----------------------------------------------------------------
| Id | Operation                          | Name         |      |
-----------------------------------------------------------------
|  0 | SELECT STATEMENT                   |              |      |
|  1 |  TABLE ACCESS BY INDEX ROWID BATCHED| F1_CHAMPIONS |      |
|  2 |   HASH UNIQUE                      |              |      |
|  3 |    INDEX RANGE SCAN (MULTI VALUE)  | SEASON_IDX   |      |
-----------------------------------------------------------------
```

The multivalue index can also index scalar values, but a straightforward function-based index would suffice.

Summary

This chapter looked at the different choices you have when you need to store JSON documents in Oracle Database and some techniques to index the JSON documents. Getting familiar with the structure of the JSON document can be done with the JSON data guide, which can aid you with generating views on top of the JSON documents. The best choice for storage depends on the release that you have. When you have an Oracle Database 21 or higher, the choice of a JSON data type is logical. This opens the possibility of creating multivalue indexes on them.

CHAPTER 12

Path Expressions in JSON

To work effectively with JSON, it is important to start with the basic functionality. One of the most important things to learn is the path expressions, navigating, and targeting the correct JSON keys. Path expressions are needed in SQL as well as in PL/SQL. This chapter introduces the path expression and its filtering capabilities and error handling. Finally, you look at the dot notation to extract values from a JSON document with easy-to-understand SQL statements.

Sample Data

For the samples in this chapter, the following table was created.

```
create table f1_drivers_json
    (json_document json)
/
```

Listing 12-1, a JSON document, is stored in this table.

Listing 12-1. The sample JSON document

```
{
    "MRData": {
        "series": "f1",
        "DriverTable": {
            "Drivers": [
                {
                    "driverId": "coulthard",
                    "code": "COU",
                    "givenName": "David",
                    "familyName": "Coulthard",
```

© Alex Nuijten, Patrick Barel 2023
A. Nuijten and P. Barel, *Modern Oracle Database Programming*, https://doi.org/10.1007/978-1-4842-9166-5_12

```
                "dateOfBirth": "1971-03-27",
                "nationality": "British",
                "champion": false,
                "nickname": "DC"
            },
            {
                "driverId": "vettel",
                "permanentNumber": "5",
                "code": "VET",
                "givenName": "Sebastian",
                "familyName": "Vettel",
                "dateOfBirth": "1987-07-03",
                "nationality": "German",
                "champion": true,
                "nickname": null,
                "Constructors": [
                        {
                            "constructorId": "red_bull",
                            "name": "Red Bull",
                            "nationality": "Austrian"
                        },
                        {
                            "constructorId": "aston_martin",
                            "name": "Aston Martin",
                            "nationality": "British"
                        }]
            }
        ]
    }
}
}
```

The script `f1_drivers_json.sql`, which can be found on the GitHub pages for this book, creates the table and inserts the JSON document.

The JSON document contains objects as well as arrays. Notice that the keys in the JSON document contain upper- and lowercase characters. Not all attributes are present for both drivers, like the permanent number. Coulthard doesn't have one, while Vettel does.

JSON Data Types

A JSON document can consist of objects, arrays, and/or scalar values.

The data types for the values within the JSON document can be either an OBJECT, ARRAY, or scalar type: NUMBER, STRING, BOOLEAN, or NULL.

When values are extracted from a JSON document, the JSON data types must be mapped to a comparable SQL data type to be useful. JSON data can't be used for sorting, comparing, or grouping.

How the JSON values are mapped to a SQL data type is up to the developer. For example, a JSON string can be mapped to VARCHAR2, CLOB, BLOB, or even a NUMBER when the value is numerical. How these JSON values are mapped depends on the SQL function you use; for example, with the `returning` clause of the `json_value` function, you can specify to which SQL type you want the JSON value to map.

Because there is no matching data type for the JSON BOOLEAN (only true or false), the developer must determine what to do with it, either map it to 0 and 1 or map it to a "true" or "false" string.

The JSON data type can be inspected with the `type()` item method, more on item methods in the related section in this chapter.

Path Expressions and Filters

Navigating through a JSON document is crucial regardless of when you're using SQL or PL/SQL. This is accomplished with JSON path expressions.

JSON path expressions are somewhat comparable to XQuery or XPath expressions for an XML document. The JSON path expression describes the path to get to the value of interest. The starting point of the JSON path expression is defined by a special symbol—a context-item. The JSON path expression starts with an absolute context-item symbol ($) followed by zero or more steps. In the filter condition, the relative context-item symbol is an at sign (@). The complete JSON document is implied when there is only the absolute context-item symbol in the JSON path expression.

Each step in the JSON path expression can be an object, array, or descendant step. These are called *nonfunction steps* and are separated by a period (.). Each nonfunction step *can* be followed by a filter expression and/or a function step. *Function steps*, also called item methods, are built-in functions that can be applied to the last step of the JSON path expression.

Let's look at a simple path expression with only nonfunction steps. The json_value function in the following query extracts a scalar value from a JSON document as directed by the JSON path expression.

```
select json_value (
          f.json_document
         ,'$.MRData.series'
         ) as series
   from f1_drivers_json f
/

SERIES
------
f1
```

The JSON path expression extracts the value of the field series. The context-item ($) is immediately followed by a period (.) to navigate to the MRData, which is a JSON object.

In the following example, all the driver's codes are extracted. The driver's code is located in the Drivers array. To extract values from an array, square brackets are used. The asterisk (*) in square brackets indicates that you want to extract all values. In this case, the json_value function can't be used as the result is an array of values, not a scalar value, so the json_query function is used instead, with the with array wrapper clause. The result from the query is a JSON array.

```
select json_query (
          f.json_document
         ,'$.MRData.DriverTable.Drivers[*].code'
           with array wrapper
         ) as driver_codes
   from f1_drivers_json f
/
```

314

```
DRIVER_CODES
------------
["COU","VET"]
```

Instead of using the asterisk in square brackets, it is possible to specify a specific entry in the array you want to extract. Since JSON arrays are zero-indexed, extracting the first value by [0], extracting the second value is [1], and so on. It is also possible to specify multiple index values between square brackets or a range of index values, like in the following example.

```
select json_query (
        f.json_document
        ,'$.MRData.DriverTable.Drivers[0 to 1].code'
          with array wrapper
      ) as codes
  from f1_drivers_json f
/
```

```
CODES
------------
["COU","VET"]
```

The same result could have been achieved by specifying [0,1]. When dealing with JSON arrays, this is also possible to state something like [0,2 to 6, 10] to extract the first, third through seventh, and eleventh index values from the array.

Besides the object and array steps taken in the previous examples, there is also a *descendant* step. A descendant step consists of two periods. The descendant step descends recursively into each object or array below the preceding step and gathers all values of the fields that match the field name. The following query extracts all nationalities regardless of where the nationality key appears in the JSON document. Some are within the drivers, and others are within the Constructors object.

```
select json_query (f.json_document
        ,'$..nationality'
          with array wrapper
      ) as nationalities
  from f1_drivers_json f
/
```

```
NATIONALITIES
-------------------------------------------
["British","German","Austrian","British"]
```

Using Filter Conditions

Next to the steps you can take to traverse the JSON document, it is possible to add filters in the JSON path expression. When a value matches the filter, it returns true; otherwise, it returns false.

The filter expression starts with a question mark (?) followed by the filter condition in parentheses. Inside the filter condition, you use relative path expressions, which start with an at sign (@) as the context-item symbol instead of the dollar sign.

A filter condition might look like the following.

```
?(@.code == "COU")
```

The attribute code is compared for equality with the "COU" string. As the filter condition is applied to the previous JSON path expression, whatever JSON path expression is before the filter is important, it can only potentially evaluate to true when the code attribute appears in the selected JSON object. In our sample JSON document, the code attribute only appears in the Drivers array, so the complete JSON path expression is as follows.

```
$.MRData.DriverTable.Drivers[*]?(@.code == "COU")
```

It is possible to specify multiple conditions within the filter condition, each in its own parentheses.

Table 12-1 shows an overview of combining filter conditions.

Table 12-1. *Combining Filter Conditions*

Condition	Meaning
(condition)	Use parentheses for grouping and separating filter conditions from other filter conditions
&&	AND; both conditions on each side must evaluate to true
||	OR; One of the conditions must evaluate to true, or both conditions evaluate to true
! (condition)	Negation of the condition, the condition must not be satisfied
exists (condition)	The target in the condition must exist
==	Equal
<> or !=	Not equal
<	Less than
<=	Less than or equal to
>	Greater than
>=	Greater than or equal to
has substring	The matching data value has the specified string as substring
starts with	The matching data value has the specified string as prefix
like	Similar to SQL `like`; % zero or more characters, _ matches a single character
like_regex	Similar to SQL `regexp_like`. Use a regular expression to match the data value with the specified string
eq_regex	Matches its regular expression syntax against the entire JSON string data value
in (value1, value2)	Matching data value is one of the values specified in a values list, enclosed in parenthesis, separated by commas

The level where the filter expression is applied has effect on the results that are returned. The two following filter expressions look very similar, they both have the same filter condition (code is compared for equality with "COU") but the results are quite different.

```
$.MRData.DriverTable.Drivers[*]?(@.code == "COU")
```

The JSON path expression returns an object of the Drivers array where there is a code attribute whose value is the "COU" string.

The following JSON path expression returns an object of the DriverTable provided that there is a Drivers array with a code attribute whose value is the "COU" string.

```
$.MRData.DriverTable?(@.Drivers[*].code == "COU")
```

When both filter conditions are used in a query, you can see the different results.

```
select json_query (f.json_document
        ,'$.MRData.DriverTable
          ?(@.Drivers[*].code == "COU")
          .Drivers[*].familyName'
        with array wrapper
    ) as drivertable
    ,json_query (f.json_document
        ,'$.MRData.DriverTable
          .Drivers[*]?(@.code == "COU")
          .familyName'
        with array wrapper
    ) as drivers
  from f1_drivers_json f
/

DRIVERTABLE                       DRIVERS
-----------------------------     -----------------------------
["Coulthard","Vettel"]            ["Coulthard"]
```

Filter conditions don't necessarily apply to the same object. Let's examine the following example where the objective is to retrieve the name of a British champion (note that in our small sample JSON, there is only one British driver, but he wasn't a world champion; the other driver is German, and he was a world champion). Using the following filter condition on the DriverTable object gets results, but not the one intended.

```
?(@.Drivers[*].champion == true
  && @.Drivers[*].nationality=="British")
```

318

Both filter conditions must be true. There is an and condition (&&). The first filter tests for the condition that the champion attribute is true within the Drivers array.

The second filter tests for the condition that the nationality attribute is British within the Drivers array. However, it does not test that both conditions are true on the same object within the Drivers array.

When this filter condition is used in a query, you get the following results.

```
select json_query (f.json_document
       ,'$.MRData.DriverTable
         ?(@.Drivers[*].champion == true
         && @.Drivers[*].nationality=="British"
         ).Drivers[*].familyName
         '

         with array wrapper
       ) as champions
  from f1_drivers_json f
/
```

```
CHAMPIONS
----------------------
["Coulthard","Vettel"]
```

The tests are done on the DriverTable object. In the DriverTable object, there is a champion attribute with the value of true, and there is a nationality attribute with a value of British. Both conditions are satisfied, and the complete object is returned.

The correct way to filter for a British driver that was a world champion would be to navigate down an additional level to the Drivers array and then apply the filter.

```
select json_query (f.json_document
        ,'$.MRData.DriverTable
         .Drivers[*]?(@.champion == true
         && @.nationality=="British"
         ).familyName
         '

         with array wrapper
       ) as champions
  from f1_drivers_json f
/
```

```
CHAMPIONS
----------
null
```

Now both filter conditions are applied at the same level, being the individual objects in the Drivers array.

Passing Variables

So far, the filter conditions only contained static values. It is also possible to use bind variables in the filter conditions.

Within the filter condition, a bind variable is prefixed with the dollar sign ($) followed by the name of the variable. The name of the bind variable is case-sensitive. The value that you pass in is defined in the passing clause. In the following example, there is a bind variable $nationality, and the value that is passed in is "British".

```
select json_query (f.json_document
        ,'$.MRData.DriverTable.Drivers[*]
          ?(@.nationality == $nationality).familyName'
          passing 'British' as "nationality"
        ) as lastname
  from f1_drivers_json f
/
LASTNAME
----------------
"Coulthard"
```

The named variable can be used multiple times in the filter condition. In the following example the bind variable is used to compare with the driver's nationality and the nationality of the constructor.

```
select json_query (f.json_document
        ,'$.MRData.DriverTable.Drivers[*]
          ?(@.nationality == $nationality
          || @.Constructors[*].nationality == $nationality
          ).familyName'
          passing 'British' as "nationality"
```

```
      with conditional array wrapper
    ) as lastname
  from f1_drivers_json f
/
LASTNAME
----------------------
["Coulthard","Vettel"]
```

Empty String and NULL

Dealing with NULL is always tricky, and in the JSON realm this is even more true. In JSON a NULL is its own data type. A NULL in JSON is not the same as a SQL NULL, even though they might appear the same. These values are mapped to each other. This becomes obvious when you make a JSON comparison with NULL, with an equality comparison.

```
[*]?(@.nickname == null)
```

However, when passing a NULL as a bind variable, like in the following example, is not allowed, it raises an error.

```
select json_query (f.json_document
        ,'$.MRData.DriverTable.Drivers[*]
          ?(@.nickname == $bind ).code'
          passing null as "bind"
      ) as drivercode
  from f1_drivers_json f
/
```

```
Error at Command Line : 6 Column : 11
Error report -
SQL Error: ORA-40576: Invalid use of bind variable in SQL/JSON path.
40576. 00000 -  "Invalid use of bind variable in SQL/JSON path."
*Cause:    An attempt was made to bind a non-runtime constant to
           a bind variable in SQL/JSON path.
*Action:   Bind either compile time constant or runtime SQL bind variable
value to a bind variable for SQL/JSON path.
```

Passing in an empty string does not raise an error.

```
select json_query (f.json_document
        ,'$.MRData.DriverTable.Drivers[*]
          ?(@.nickname == $bind ).code'
        passing '' as "bind"
      ) as drivercode
  from f1_drivers_json f
/
DRIVERCODE
----------
```

When referencing a bind variable from the calling environment, SQLcl in the following example, does not raise an error either.

```
var b varchar2 (3)

select json_query (f.json_document
        ,'$.MRData.DriverTable.Drivers[*]
          ?(@.nickname == $bind ).code'
.        passing :b as "bind"
      ) as drivercode
  from f1_drivers_json f
/
DRIVERCODE
----------
```

The last two examples do not raise an error, but they do not return the correct results either. When searching for a JSON null, the only option is to do an equality comparison without using a bind variable.

Note   In JSON there is a difference between an empty string and a NULL, this difference does not exist in Oracle SQL. A JSON empty string is equal to a SQL empty string, but not equal to a SQL NULL.

```
select 'empty strings are the equal' as same

  from dual
  where json_exists('{a:""}'
```

```
        ,'$?(@.a == $b)'
        passing '' as "b"
        )
/
SAME
```

```
empty strings are the equal
```

Item Methods

The last query in the section "Using filter condition", where the filter attempts to match a British driver that was champion, returned a JSON data type value of null.

This becomes very clear when materialize the query into a table with a CTAS (**C**reate **T**able **A**s **S**elect).

```
create table champions
as
select json_query (f.json_document
        ,'$.MRData.DriverTable
        .Drivers[*]?(@.champion == true
        && @.nationality=="British"
        ).familyName
        '

        with array wrapper
        ) as champions
    from f1_drivers_json f
/
```

```
Table CHAMPIONS created.
```

A describe of the newly created table reveals that the data type is JSON.

```
desc champions
```

```
Name       Null? Type
--------- ----- ----
CHAMPIONS        JSON
```

This statement was executed in Oracle Database 21c, which has the JSON data type. When the preceding statements are executed in Oracle Database 19c, the data type would be varchar2(4000).

So far, the results from the JSON path expressions have always been JSON data types. Having the query return JSON is not very useful. They can't be compared, ordered, or grouped; instead, it makes more sense to have a SQL scalar data type.

With *item methods,* you can cast the data type returned to a SQL data type, like VARCHAR2, NUMBER, or DATE. It can also provide you with information about the returned value, like the JSON data type or the length of an array.

An item method is applied at the end of the JSON path expression. The following are the most common ones to change to a corresponding SQL data type.

> number(), numberOnly(), string(), stringOnly(), boolean(),
> booleanOnly(), date() and timestamp().

The number() item method converts the matched JSON value to a SQL number, even when the JSON data type is a string. When the numberOnly() item method is used then the JSON data type *must* also be a number, an implicit data type conversion does not take place. The same is true for the other item methods where there is an Only() variation, like stringOnly() and booleanOnly(). It is safe to say that these item methods also act as filters.

In the following example, the permanentNumber attribute of Vettel is extracted from the JSON document and the number() item method is applied to convert it to a SQL NUMBER data type.

```
select json_value (f.json_document
        ,'$.MRData.DriverTable
           .Drivers[1]
           .permanentNumber.number()'
      )  as permanentNumber
  from f1_drivers_json f
/

PERMANENTNUMBER
---------------
             5
```

As you can see in the preceding results, permanentNumber is right-aligned in the column as numbers in SQL do. When instead the numberOnly() item method is applied, the result is null. The data type of the permanentNumber attribute in the JSON document is string that doesn't match the requested data type.

```
select json_value (f.json_document
        ,'$.MRData.DriverTable
           .Drivers[1]
           .permanentNumber.numberOnly()'
       )  as permanentNumber
  from f1_drivers_json f
/
```

```
PERMANENTNUMBER
---------------
```

For date() and timestamp() the targeted JSON value must adhere to the ISO-8601 standard. As the birthdates of the drivers are in the ISO 8601 standard, you can extract it and convert it to a SQL Date.

```
alter session set nls_date_format ='dd-mm-yyyy'
/
Session altered.
```

```
select json_value (f.json_document
        ,'$.MRData.DriverTable
           .Drivers[0]
           .dateOfBirth.date()'
       )  as birthdate
  from f1_drivers_json f
/
```

```
BIRTHDATE
----------
27-03-1971
```

The item method you apply does not raise an error, unlike the JSON path expressions; instead, the returned value is a SQL NULL.

Four item methods give information about the targeted JSON value: `type()`, `size()`, `count()`, and `length()`.

The values that the `type()` method can return are listed in Table 12-2.

Table 12-2. *Data Type Names Returned by type()*

JSON Data Type		Remarks
"array"	Array	
"object"	Object	
"string"	Value that corresponds to `varchar2`	
"null"	`null`	
"boolean"	True or false	
"double"	Number that corresponds to `binary_double`	Only when JSON data type is used
"float"	Number that corresponds to `binary_float`	Only when JSON data type is used
"binary"	Value that corresponds to `raw`	Only when JSON data type is used
"date"	Value that corresponds to `date`	Only when JSON data type is used
"timestamp"	Value that corresponds to `timestamp`	Only when JSON data type is used
"daysecondInterval"	Value that corresponds to `interval day to second`	Only when JSON data type is used
"yearmonthInterval"	Value that corresponds to `interval year to month`	Only when JSON data type is used

The `type()` item method provides information at the level where it is applied. When applying the `type()` item method at the Drivers array, the result is "array". When the same item method is applied to the *content* of the Drivers array, the result is an array of two "objects" because each driver is an object of its own.

```
$.MRData.DriverTable.Drivers.type()
```

```
"array"
```

```
$.MRData.DriverTable.Drivers[*].type()
```

```
["object","object"]
```

Going down another level give information about the attributes.

```
$.MRData.DriverTable.Drivers[*].nickname.type()
```

```
["string","null"]
```

The `size()` item method gives information about the number of elements that are targeted. When the target of the JSON path expression is a scalar, the `size()` is one. The same is true for an object. When an array is targeted, `size()` gives the number of elements in the array.

```
$.MRData.DriverTable.Drivers.size()
```

```
2
```

The `count()` item method gives information about the number of targeted JSON values, regardless of their type. If there is no targeted JSON value, an error is raised.

The `length()` item method gives information about the number of characters in a string, it does not work on any other data type.

A JSON path expression can be at most 32 KB long, but it would be hard pressed to get to this limit.

Handling Errors in JSON Path Expressions

Each step in the JSON path expression is attempted to match. When a matching step fails, the other steps are not evaluated, and the JSON path expression fails. Even though the JSON path expression fails, the query is still executed successfully by default. For the failed JSON path expression, a NULL is returned. This means that when you see a NULL. As a result, it could mean that the JSON path expression fails (there might be an error in it), or it could mean that the attribute *does* exist but has the value of NULL.

Depending on the error clause (available with the json_value, json_query, and json_table functions), the returned value is either a NULL or a specific error message or possibly a default value. Not all SQL functions have the same options; for example, json_query doesn't allow defining a default value.

The following examples attempt to extract a value from a non-existing node in the JSON document with different error clauses. First, with the default error clause, which is null on error, no exception is raised; instead, a NULL is returned.

```
select json_value (
        f.json_document
       ,'$.MRData.non_existing_node'
        null on error
        ) as nothing
  from f1_drivers_json f
/

NOTHING
-------
```

With the error clause set to error on error, the statement fails with an exception stating that the json_value function evaluated to no value.

```
select json_value (
        f.json_document
       ,'$.MRData.non_existing_node'
        error on error
        ) as nothing
  from f1_drivers_json f
/

Error starting at line : 1 in command -
select json_value (
        f.json_document
       ,'$.MRData.non_existing_node'
        error on error
        ) as nothing
```

```
  from f1_drivers_json f
Error report -
ORA-40462: JSON_VALUE evaluated to no value
```

For some SQL functions it is also possible to define a default value when an error is encountered. The default value must be a constant. An example of using default <constant> on error is in the following statement.

```
select json_value (
        f.json_document
       ,'$.MRData.non_existing_node'
        default 'node does not exist' on error
        ) as nothing
  from f1_drivers_json f
/

NOTHING
-------------------
node does not exist
```

An error is also raised when the used function expects a scalar value, but multiple values are targeted by the JSON path expression.

A missing attribute is a special case that is handled by the on error clause but can also be handled by the on empty clause. The on empty clause precedes the on error clause when both are present. The following statement targets a non-existing attribute in the JSON document and has both an on error and a on empty clause.

```
select json_value (
        f.json_document
       ,'$.MRData.non_existing_node'
         default 'node error' on error
         default 'node empty' on empty
        ) as nothing
  from f1_drivers_json f
/

NOTHING
----------
node empty
```

When an item method is applied, and there is an attempt to convert the selected JSON value to an incompatible SQL data type, this could also raise an error. There is also a special clause for this situation: on mismatch. In the following example, the Driver code is attempted to be converted to a SQL NUMBER type using the number() item method. The on mismatch clause overrides the on error clause when both are present.

```
select json_value (f.json_document
        ,'$.MRData.DriverTable.Drivers[0].code.number()'
        default '-10' on error
        error on mismatch
      )
  from f1_drivers_json f
/

Error starting at line : 1 in command -
select json_value (f.json_document
        ,'$.MRData.DriverTable.Drivers[0].code.number()'
        default '-10' on error
        error on mismatch
      )
  from f1_drivers_json f
Error report -
ORA-01722: invalid number
```

Dot Notation

The easiest way to extract values from a JSON document is to use the dot notation syntax. The dot notation syntax uses the table alias, the JSON column name, and one or more field names found in the JSON document, all separated by periods. This can be used for JSON objects as well as JSON arrays.

The returned value depends on the data type of the column holding the JSON document. When the data type of the column is JSON, then the returned value is an instance of JSON data type. In all other cases, it is a VARCHAR2 value.

The dot notation syntax can *only* be used when a JSON document is stored in either of these ways.

- JSON data type

- VARCHAR2, CLOB, BLOB column, and there is an is json check constraint present

- VARCHAR2, CLOB, BLOB column and treat (<column_name> as json) is used in the query.

Let's start with extracting the key "series" value using the dot notation.

```
select f.json_document."MRData"."series"
  from f1_drivers_json f
/
MRData
-----------
"f1"
```

The keys in the JSON document are case-sensitive; in earlier Oracle Database releases, it was therefore necessary that the keys were in quotes. In more recent releases of the Oracle Database (18 and higher), this is no longer needed. The case of the keys in the JSON must be followed. The following query omits the quotation marks and still yields the same results.

```
select f.json_document.MRData.series
  from f1_drivers_json f
/
MRDATA
-----------
"f1"
```

For the remainder of this chapter, quotation marks are not used in the queries unless absolutely necessary. This might be the case when a JSON key has the same name as a reserved word in SQL or when there are special characters that don't work well with SQL, like the asterisk.

Caution When you are using a formatter to format your code, pay attention to what happens with your queries that use JSON path expressions. When all text is converted to, let's say, lowercase, the query might no longer give you the results that it originally did.

The result returned from the query is of data type JSON. The database version used is an Oracle 21c database. The preceding query returned a JSON scalar. When the JSON path expression targets a single value, the returned value could either be a JSON scalar, object, or array. A JSON array is returned when the JSON path expression targets multiple values.

Item methods discussed earlier, such as number(), string(), size(), can be used in the dot notation syntax as well.

You convert the returned value to a corresponding SQL scalar with an item method. In the following query, the series attribute is returned as a string and the drivers' permanentnumber as a number.

```
select f.json_document.MRData.series.string() as serie
      ,f.json_document.MRData.DriverTable
        .Drivers.permanentNumber
        .number() as permanentnumber
  from f1_drivers_json f
/

SERIE       PERMANENTNUMBER
---------- ----------------
f1                        5
```

The preceding query "works" because only one driver in the JSON document has a permanent number—Vettel. This JSON scalar value can be converted to a SQL number data type.

Let's examine what happens when you try to extract the date of birth of both drivers (the drivers are in an array labeled Drivers) and apply the date() item method to the results. The following query shows both the JSON result (in the j_dateofbirth column) and the date() item method application.

```
select f.json_document.MRData
        .DriverTable.Drivers.dateOfBirth as j_dateOfBirth
      ,f.json_document.MRData
        .DriverTable.Drivers.dateOfBirth.date() as dateOfBirth
  from f1_drivers_json f
/
```

```
J_DATEOFBIRTH                          DATEOFBIR
------------------------------ ----------
["1971-03-27","1987-07-03"]
```

Because both drivers have a date of birth, the returned value is an array, and an array can't be converted to a *scalar* SQL data type. To get the birthdate for each driver, you need to amend the query to reflect this and introduce an array step in the dot notation syntax. The array step uses square brackets and an index number to indicate which element you want to retrieve from the array. The index for arrays starts at zero.

```
select f.json_document.MRData
       .DriverTable.Drivers[0]
       .dateOfBirth.date() as dateOfBirth
      ,f.json_document.MRData
       .DriverTable.Drivers[1]
       .dateOfBirth.date() as dateOfBirth
  from f1_drivers_json f
/

DATEOFBIR DATEOFBIR
--------- ---------
27-MAR-71 03-JUL-87
```

Table 12-3 lists some examples of dot notation syntax. In the path expressions, the table alias and column name are omitted. These should be prefixed to the path expression to form the complete path expression: f.json_document.MRData.series.

Table 12-3. *Examples of dot notation syntax*

Path Expression	Meaning
MRData.series	The value of the series field, which is a child of MRData
MRData.DriverTable.Drivers[1]	The second element of the Drivers array
MRData.DriverTable.Drivers[*]	All elements of the Drivers array Asterisk (*) is a wildcard
MRData.DriverTable.Drivers.code	The value of the field code A child occurring in the Drivers array The return value is an array of strings: ["COU","VET"]

Summary

There are many things to learn when dealing with JSON documents. Getting to grips with path expressions and filters might be the most important thing in this chapter. Understanding how path expressions and filters work makes working with JSON documents much simpler. Handling errors in the path expressions clarifies when a null is encountered.

Finally, the dot notation syntax is introduced, an easy way to convert JSON documents into a relational format.

CHAPTER 13

SQL/JSON and Conditions

Having JSON documents stored in the database is one thing, and knowing how to navigate through the document is another, but extracting the data into a relational format is what it is all about.

This chapter focuses on this transformation, creating a relational output from a JSON document using SQL statements.

The examples in this chapter use the sample data from the previous chapter.

SQL/JSON Functions

Four SQL functions can be used to extract values from a JSON document.

- `json_value` extracts a scalar JSON value and returns the SQL equivalent

- `json_query` extracts a fragment of the JSON document

- `json_table` transforms the JSON document into a relational format

- `json_serialize` transforms a JSON document and returns a textual representation

Each of these functions is examined separately in the next sections.

JSON_VALUE

The SQL/JSON `json_value` function *must* target a scalar JSON value. It raises an error when it targets a non-scalar value, an OBJECT, or an ARRAY. By default, an error in the JSON path expression returns a NULL value, which can be overridden in the on error clause.

© Alex Nuijten, Patrick Barel 2023
A. Nuijten and P. Barel, *Modern Oracle Database Programming*, https://doi.org/10.1007/978-1-4842-9166-5_13

There are several reasons an error can occur, which can be handled in the on error clause.

- The JSON document is not well-formed.

- A non-scalar value is found when the JSON data is evaluated by the JSON path expression.

- No match is found when the JSON data is evaluated, like when an attribute doesn't exist; this case can also be handled by the on empty clause, which has precedence over on error.

- The return value data type is not large enough to hold the returned value.

The first argument to pass into the json_value function can be any text literal, BLOB, or JSON. An error is raised when the text literal or BLOB is not well-formed JSON.

The second argument is the JSON path expression which targets the value of interest. This JSON path expression can include filter conditions as well as item methods. An item method can influence the data type retrieved from the JSON document; however, it is also possible to specify the data type that the json_value should return in the returning clause.

In the returning clause, the SQL data type can be specified how the JSON value needs to be returned. By default, when the returning clause is omitted, a varchar2(4000) is returned.

Tip   You have more control over the returned data type with the returning clause. It is possible to specify the length of a string, for example, varchar2(10). This is not possible with the string() item method.

This section covers the most common data types, like STRING, NUMBER, DATE, and BOOLEAN, but it is also possible to return other data types, like TIMESTAMP (with or without timezone), INTERVAL, CHAR, BLOB, CLOB, or SDO_GEOMETRY.

In the following query, the family name of a driver is targeted, and a varchar2(6) is returned.

```
select json_value (f.json_document
        ,'$.MRData.DriverTable.Drivers[1].familyName'
        returning varchar2(6)
      ) as familyname
  from f1_drivers_json f
/

FAMILY
------
Vettel
```

The driver's name is six characters, and the returning clause specifies varchar2(6). The preceding query works fine. When the JSON path expression targets the other driver, whose name is nine characters, an error is raised (the default is to return null when an error occurs).

```
select json_value (f.json_document
        ,'$.MRData.DriverTable.Drivers[0].familyName'
        returning varchar2(6)
      ) as familyname
  from f1_drivers_json f
/

FAMILY
------
```

Instead of increasing the size of the returning value, it is also possible to add the truncate clause to the returning clause. The returned value is truncated whenever the targeted value exceeds the requested length.

```
select json_value (f.json_document
        ,'$.MRData.DriverTable.Drivers[0].familyName'
        returning varchar2(6) truncate
      ) as familyname
  from f1_drivers_json f
/

FAMILY
------
Coulth
```

The permanent number of the driver is numeric, but in the JSON document, it is a string. With the returning clause, this can be converted to a number. The right alignment in the result set indicates that it is a true number.

```
select json_value (f.json_document
        ,'$.MRData.DriverTable.Drivers[1].permanentNumber'
        returning number
      ) as permanentNumber
  from f1_drivers_json f
/

PERMANENTNUMBER
---------------
              5
```

The date of birth in the JSON document is a string. JSON doesn't have a date data type. The dateOfBirth string is in the ISO 8601 format, so this can be converted into a SQL date data type.

```
select json_value (f.json_document
        ,'$.MRData.DriverTable.Drivers[0].dateOfBirth'
        returning date
      ) as dateofbirth
  from f1_drivers_json f
/

DATEOFBIR
---------
27-MAR-71
```

The ISO 8601 format can have a time component, but the sample JSON that is used does not. In the returning clause, you can specify what to do with the time portion of the date, keep it or remove it. As the sample JSON document doesn't have any dates with a time component, the following example use SYSDATE, converted to a JSON value by using the json_scalar function in the subquery factoring clause (with clause, named datesampler). The date-format in this session is changed to show the time component of dates.

```
alter session set nls_date_format = 'dd-mm-yyyy hh24:mi:ss'
/

Session altered.

with datesampler
as
(select json_scalar (sysdate) as dt
  from dual)
select json_value (dt, '$' returning date) as d1
     ,json_value (dt, '$' returning date truncate time) as d2
     ,json_value (dt, '$' returning date preserve time) as d3
  from datesampler
/

D1                   D2                   D3
-------------------- -------------------- --------------------
05-08-2022 00:00:00 05-08-2022 00:00:00 05-08-2022 12:33:07
```

By default, when returning a date, the time is truncated (column D1). This can also be done explicitly with the truncate time addition (column D2). When the time component needs to be preserved, add preserve time when returning the JSON value as a date (column D3).

The other data type that JSON has and needs to be mapped to a SQL data type is boolean. Currently, there is no native SQL boolean data type. Depending on your preference, a boolean can be represented as numeric (0 or 1) or as a string (true or false). Both notational formats can be specified in the returning clause.

The driver information in the sample specifies in a boolean value if he has been a champion. When using returning varchar2 and a boolean is the target, true or false is returned.

```
select json_value (f.json_document
        ,'$.MRData.DriverTable.Drivers[0].champion'
         returning varchar2
        ) as champion
  from f1_drivers_json f
/
```

```
CHAMPION
--------
false
```

When the preference is to return a numeric value, simply specifying `returning number` doesn't work.

```
select json_value (f.json_document
        ,'$.MRData.DriverTable.Drivers[0].champion'
        returning number
      ) as champion
  from f1_drivers_json f
/

   CHAMPION
----------

```

The null returned in the preceding query indicates something wrong; adding the on error clause reveals the following.

```
select json_value (f.json_document
        ,'$.MRData.DriverTable.Drivers[0].champion'
        returning number
        error on error
      ) as champion
  from f1_drivers_json f
/

Error report -
ORA-40799: cannot convert Boolean value to number
```

It must be explicitly stated that this is allowed to convert the JSON boolean to a number.

```
select json_value (f.json_document
        ,'$.MRData.DriverTable.Drivers[0].champion'
        returning number
        allow boolean to number conversion
      ) as champion
```

```
from f1_drivers_json f
/

    CHAMPION
----------
         0
```

Prior to Oracle Database 21, the boolean keyword in the preceding query *must* be omitted.

JSON_QUERY

With the `json_query` you can extract a fragment of a JSON document. The biggest difference with `json_value` is that `json_query` can return multiple targeted values as a JSON snippet.

By default, the returned value's data type is a `varchar2(4000)`, but this can be changed in the `returning` clause and is always well-formed JSON. Truncating the returned value might give the appearance of JSON that is not well-formed, but this is not the case. Truncating is done after the value is targeted by `json_query`. The only allowed return types are VARCHAR2, CLOB, BLOB, or JSON.

With `json_query` it is possible to mimic `json_value` to extract a scalar value, but there is a subtle difference. The `json_query` function returns a stringified version of a JSON snippet, and when a scalar is targeted, it is enclosed in quotation marks so that it is well-formed JSON. The length of the drivers code in the following query is five characters long.

```
select json_query (f.json_document
       ,'$.MRData.DriverTable.Drivers[0].code'
       ) as drivercode
  from f1_drivers_json f
/

DRIVERCODE
----------
"COU"
```

When a different SQL data type than the JSON type is requested, implicit conversion is attempted and, when successful, returned. The following example returns the permanent number of a driver (a string in the JSON sample) and converts it to a number.

```
select json_value (f.json_document
        ,'$.MRData.DriverTable.Drivers[1].permanentNumber'
        returning number
      ) as permanentnumber
  from f1_drivers_json f
/
```

```
PERMANENTNUMBER
----------------
              5
```

The right alignment of the query result reveals that it is a numeric SQL data type. The same query results can be achieved using the number() item method in the JSON path expression.

Unlike json_value, json_query can return an object or array. In the following example, the driver object of the first driver is returned. By adding returning varchar2 pretty, the result is easier to read by adding new lines and indentation.

```
select json_query (f.json_document
        ,'$.MRData.DriverTable.Drivers[0]'
          returning varchar2 pretty
      ) as drivercode
  from f1_drivers_json f
/
```

```
DRIVERCODE
-----------------------------
{
  "driverId" : "coulthard",
  "code" : "COU",
  "givenName" : "David",
  "familyName" : "Coulthard",
  "dateOfBirth" : "1971-03-27",
  "nationality" : "British",
```

```
    "champion" : false,
    "nickname" : "DC"
}
```

When multiple values are targeted and to have the result as well-formed JSON, it might be necessary that these values require an array wrapper. This means that the result is wrapped in square brackets. In the following query, the driver codes are targeted. There are two codes in the sample JSON. Two scalar values must be wrapped in square brackets, making the result valid JSON again.

```
select json_query (f.json_document
        ,'$.MRData.DriverTable.Drivers[*].code'
        with array wrapper
       ) as drivercode
  from f1_drivers_json f
/

DRIVERCODE
-------------
["COU","VET"]
```

The default wrapper clause is `without array wrapper,` and when multiple values are targeted, an error is raised, resulting (by default) in null.

Tip   When you don't want to *always* enclose the results in an array, you can also use `with conditional array wrapper` and leave it to Oracle Database to figure out when it is needed to wrap the results in an array.

There are several reasons an error can occur, which can be handled in the on error clause.

- The input to the function is not well-formed JSON data.

- No match is found by the JSON path expression. An attribute might not exist. This error can also be handled by the on empty clause, which has precedence over the on error clause.

- Return value data type is not large enough to hold the return value.

- Return value data type cannot be implicitly converted to the return requested. This error can also be handled by the on mismatch clause, which has precedence over the on error clause.

- Multiple values are targeted, and the with array wrapper is omitted.

The default handling method is to return a null. This can be made explicitly with null on error, null on empty, and null on mismatch.

Besides propagating the error with error on error and error on empty, it is also possible to return an empty object or array by specifying empty object on error, empty array on error, empty object on empty or empty array on empty.

When a return value exceeds the returning clause, it raises an error. Besides adjusting the return data type, it is possible to truncate the results.

```
select json_query (f.json_document
        , '$.MRData.DriverTable.Drivers[0].familyName'
        returning varchar2(3) truncate
      ) as familyname
  from f1_drivers_json f
/

FAM
---
"Co
```

To demonstrate the on mismatch clause, the following query targets the drivers code and requests a SQL number in the query results. This cannot work because the code is not numeric. By default, a null is returned.

```
select json_value (f.json_document
        ,'$.MRData.DriverTable.Drivers[1].code'
        returning number
      ) as numericCode
  from f1_drivers_json f
/

NUMERICCODE
-----------
```

Both the on error clause and the on mismatch clause can be used. The on mismatch clause has precedence.

```
select json_value (f.json_document
        ,'$.MRData.DriverTable.Drivers[0].code'
        returning number
        default -99 on error
        error on mismatch
      )
  from f1_drivers_json f
/
```

```
ORA-01722: invalid number
```

When the on mismatch clause is omitted, –99 is returned. The on mismatch clause can handle the returning clause data type mismatch and the number() item method in the preceding case.

JSON_TABLE

With the json_table function, a relational view of JSON data is created. This function can only appear in the from clause of a SQL statement.

The JSON path expression determines the row source used to project the JSON data in a relational format. Within the json_table function, the columns clause evaluates the row source to find the JSON values and returns them as SQL values as columns in a row of relational data.

In the following example, part of the Drivers array is projected in a relational format.

```
select d.*
from    f1_drivers_json f
cross
apply  json_table
      ( f.json_document
      , '$.MRData.DriverTable.Drivers[*]'
      columns
        ( driverid  varchar2(10) path '$.driverId'
        , code      varchar2(3)  path '$.code'
```

```
        , firstname varchar2(10) path '$.givenName'
        , lastname  varchar2(10) path '$.familyName'
        , dob        date         path '$.dateOfBirth'
        )
      ) d
/

DRIVERID    COD FIRSTNAME  LASTNAME    DOB
----------  --- ---------- ---------- -------------------
coulthard   COU David      Coulthard  27-03-1971 00:00:00
vettel      VET Sebastian  Vettel     03-07-1987 00:00:00
```

The f1_drivers_json relational table is joined with json_table to create a cartesian product. The JSON path expression targets the Drivers array as the row source. In the columns clause, the path expression indicates where the JSON values can be found relative to the row source. The $ context item in the columns clause refers to the output of the path expression at the json_table level.

Tip   Besides using a cross apply, it is also possible to use a cross join to project the JSON document in a relational format. Using a cross apply reflects that the join is lateral, as there is a correlation between the relational table and the json_table.

In current Oracle Database releases, it is also possible to only specify the keys of the row source. The values can be returned as long as the names of the keys in the JSON document match (case-sensitive!). The following query returns the same data as previously, but some significant differences exist.

```
select d.*
from   f1_drivers_json f
cross
apply  json_table
       ( f.json_document
       , '$.MRData.DriverTable.Drivers[*]'
```

```
      columns
        ( driverId
        , code
        , givenName
        , familyName
        , dateOfBirth
        )
      ) d
/
```

```
DRIVERID    COD GIVENNAME   FAMILYNAME DATEOFBIRT
----------  --- ----------  ---------- ----------
coulthard   COU David       Coulthard  1971-03-27
vettel      VET Sebastian   Vettel     1987-07-03
```

The SQL data type returned for each column is a varchar2(4000), and the column names are derived from the JSON keys.

Changing the SQL data type for a specific column can be done by adding the required type in the columns clause. In the following example, the data types are specified, like a SQL date for the date of birth, and instead of the driver's first name, only the first initial is returned by truncating the rest of the givenName attribute.

```
select d.*
from    f1_drivers_json f
cross
apply   json_table
        ( f.json_document
        , '$.MRData.DriverTable.Drivers[*]'
        columns
          ( driverId     varchar2(10)
          , code         varchar2(3)
          , givenName    varchar2(1) truncate
          , familyName   varchar2(10)
          , dateOfBirth  date
          )
        ) d
/
```

```
DRIVERID    COD G FAMILYNAME DATEOFBIR
---------- --- - ---------- ----------
coulthard  COU D Coulthard  27-MAR-71
vettel     VET S Vettel     03-JUL-87
```

For each column it is possible to use all options that are available with the json_
value and json_query functions, like the on error or on empty clauses. As they have
been discussed before, they are omitted from this section.

Instead of specifying error on error for each column, it is also possible to define
this once at the highest level. This needs to be done before the columns clause. Error
clauses in the column have precedence over table-level clauses. The following query
demonstrates the use of error on error at the table level and the override at the
column level.

```
select d.*
from    f1_drivers_json f
cross
apply   json_table
        ( f.json_document
        , '$.MRData.DriverTable.Drivers[*]'
        error on error
        columns
          ( driverId
          , does_not_exist default 'x' on empty
          )
        ) d
/

DRIVERID    DOES_
---------- -----
coulthard  x
vettel     x
```

Only one of the drivers (Vettel) has an permanentNumber attribute. Coulthard
doesn't have the attribute. Both have the nickname attribute, but only Coulthard has
a non-null value. When you extract the familyName attribute, Coulthard has a null for
permanentNumber (missing attribute), and Vettel has a null for the nickname (because it
has a null JSON value).

```
select d.*
from   f1_drivers_json f
cross
apply  json_table
       ( f.json_document
       , '$.MRData.DriverTable.Drivers[*]'
       columns
         ( familyName
         , permanentNumber
         , nickname
         )
       ) d
/
FAMILYNAME       PERM NICKN
---------------- ---- -----
Coulthard             DC
Vettel           5
```

In the query results, it is not immediately clear what causes the NULL values. At the column level, it is possible to test for attribute existence with the exists clause. In the following example, two extra columns are added to test for the existence of the attribute specified on the path. The existence test for the permanentNumber attribute returns a VARCHAR2 (true or false), and the test for "nickname" returns a number (0 or 1). Right after the column name (has_nickname), the data type you want to be returned is specified before the exists keyword.

```
select d.*
from   f1_drivers_json f
cross
apply  json_table
       ( f.json_document
       , '$.MRData.DriverTable.Drivers[*]'
       columns
         ( familyName
         , permanentNumber
         , has_permanentNumber exists path permanentNumber
```

```
        , nickname
        , has_nickname number exists path nickname
        )
      ) d
/

FAMILYNAME       PERM HAS_P NICKN HAS_N
---------------- ---- ----- ----- -----
Coulthard             false DC        1
Vettel           5    true            1
```

In the results, the null for permanentNumber is caused by the missing attribute for Coulthard (the has_permanentnumber column is false), while the nickname for Vettel has a NULL JSON value (the has_nickname column is 1).

The sample JSON document has two arrays: Drivers and Constructors. The nested path clause, with its own columns clause, transforms the data in the nested array into a relational format.

The following query shows the use of nested path in the columns clause.

```
select d.*
from   f1_drivers_json f
cross
apply  json_table
       ( f.json_document
       , '$.MRData.DriverTable.Drivers[*]'
       columns
         ( code
         , nested path '$.Constructors[*]'
           columns
             ( constructorId
             , name
             , nationality
             )
         )
       ) d
/
```

```
CODE   CONSTRUCTORID    NAME                NATIONALITY
-----  ---------------  ------------------  ------------
COU
VET    red_bull         Red Bull            Austrian
VET    aston_martin     Aston Martin        British
```

Take special precautions when an attribute in the JSON document occurs multiple times and needs to be shown in a relational format. The `nationality` attribute appears in the Drivers array and the Constructors array in the sample JSON document. Adding both to the query leads to an error.

```
00918. 00000 -  "column ambiguously defined"
```

When this occurs, one of the columns needs to be assigned a different name. In the following example, the nationality of the Constructor is renamed to `cnationality`.

```
select d.*
from    f1_drivers_json f
cross
apply   json_table
        ( f.json_document
        , '$.MRData.DriverTable.Drivers[*]'
        columns
          ( code
          , nationality
          , nested path '$.Constructors[*]'
            columns
              ( name
              , cnationality path '$.nationality'
              )
          )
        ) d
/
```

```
CODE   NATIONALITY       NAME              CNATIONALITY
-----  ----------------  ----------------  ----------------
COU    British
VET    German            Red Bull          Austrian
VET    German            Aston Martin      British
```

Note that the driver's code VET appears twice in the result set in the preceding query results. This is because there are two entries in the Constructors array.

Because of the limited size of the sample JSON document, it is easy to see which data belongs together, but this might not always be the case.

The for ordinality clause can be added to generate row numbers to clarify which records in the relational view belong together. There can only be one ordinality column per json_table or nested clause. The following example adds an ordinality column for the drivers and the constructors.

```
select d.*
from   f1_drivers_json f
cross
apply  json_table
       ( f.json_document
       , '$.MRData.DriverTable.Drivers[*]'
       columns
         ( dseq for ordinality
         , code
         , nationality
         , nested path '$.Constructors[*]'
           columns
             ( cseq for ordinality
             , name
             )
         )
       ) d
/
```

```
    DSEQ CODE   NATIONALITY            CSEQ NAME
---------- ----- ---------------- ---------- ----------------
       1 COU    British
       2 VET    German                    1 Red Bull
       2 VET    German                    2 Aston Martin
```

There are circumstances where there is a need to extract a fragment of the JSON document for processing later. For example, when the delivered JSON document contains customer information (multiple customers) with all their related orders. To distribute this JSON document over several database tables, it might be prudent to extract the customer data first and store it in the customer table while also extracting the related order data in JSON format so it can be passed to the next `json_table` function to parse the order data for this customer. This way, it is unnecessary to parse the complete JSON document several times but only parse the part needed for a specific task.

The following query extracts the constructors JSON fragment, with `format json` added in the `columns` clause.

```
select d.*
from   f1_drivers_json f
cross
apply  json_table
       ( f.json_document
       , '$.MRData.DriverTable.Drivers[*]'
       columns
         ( code
         , constructors format json path '$.Constructors'
         )
       ) d
/

CODE  CONSTRUCTORS
----- ------------------------------------------------------
COU
VET   [{"constructorId":"red_bull","name":"Red Bull","na
      tionality":"Austrian"},{"constructorId":"aston_mar
      tin","name":"Aston Martin","nationality":"British"
      }]
```

Only one of the drivers has a Constructors array associated with it.

Caution   The Constructors array does not exist for Coulthard and the results in the preceding query reflect this. When only the `error on error` clause is used at the table level or column level with `format json`, an error is raised. The error states that no value is targeted, which is correct in this situation. In situations like these, also add the `null on empty` clause. This also occurs when the `nested path` is used in the `columns` clause.

JSON_SERIALIZE

The `json_serialize` function can transform a JSON document into a textual representation. This is especially useful when the JSON document is stored in a BLOB, and the contents need to be read.

The sample JSON table is copied to demonstrate how `json_serialize` can convert the JSON document to a different data type, but this time with JSON in a binary format.

```
create table f1_drivers_blob
as
select json_serialize
       ( json_document returning blob ) as json_document
from   f1_drivers_json
/
```

In this case, the `returning` clause dictates the data type wanted for a BLOB.

Adding `pretty` after the `returning` clause makes the textual representation easier to read.

```
select json_serialize
       ( json_document returning clob pretty ) as json_document
  from f1_drivers_blob
/
```

```
JSON_DOCUMENT
--------------------------------------
{
  "MRData" :
  {
    "series" : "f1",
    "DriverTable" :
    {
      "Drivers" :
      [
        {
          "driverId" : "coulthard",
< rest of the JSON document omitted >
```

When the JSON document contains non-ASCII characters, these can be escaped by adding ascii after the returning clause. As our sample data doesn't contain special characters like these, the following example uses a select from dual to demonstrate what the ascii clause does.

```
select json_serialize
       ( '{"racecar":"🏎"}' returning varchar2 ) as rc
  from dual
/
RC
----------------
{"racecar":"🏎"}

select json_serialize
       ( '{"racecar":"🏎"}' returning varchar2 ascii ) as rc
  from dual
/
RC
--------------------------------
{"racecar":"\uD83C\uDFCE\uFE0F"}
```

SQL Conditions

Filtering out rows that meet specific conditions is done in the where clause of a query. When these conditions involve JSON documents, a few options are available.

When there is a table that contains JSON documents and other non-JSON documents, you can use the is json and is not json conditions.

The following example creates a staging table (f1_staging) to store all the data. The idea is that this data is processed later.

```
create table f1_staging
(all_data clob)
/
```

Two records are inserted: one non-JSON and the other JSON.

```
insert into f1_staging
values ('David Marshall Coulthard MBE born 27 March 1971) is a British
former racing driver from Scotland, later turned presenter, commentator
and journalist. Nicknamed "DC", he competed in 15 seasons of Formula
One between 1994 and 2008, taking 13 Grand Prix victories and 62 podium
finishes. He was runner-up in the 2001 championship, driving for McLaren.')
/
insert into f1_staging
values ('{"driverId":"coulthard","code":"COU","give
nName":"David","familyName":"Coulthard","dateOfBir
th":"1971-03-27","nationality":"British","champion"-
:false,"nickname":"DC"}')
/
commit
/
```

Filtering out the non-JSON data is done with the following statement.

```
select *
from   f1_staging
where  all_data is not json
/
ALL_DATA
----------------------------------
```

David Marshall Coulthard MBE born 27 March 1971) is a British
<rest omitted for brevity>

The following statement is used to filter out the JSON data.

```
select *
from   f1_staging
where  all_data is json
/
ALL_DATA
------------------------------------
{"driverId":"coulthard","code":"COU","givenName":"David","familyName":"Co
ulthard
<rest omitted for brevity>
```

You can use json_exists to filter in a JSON document for a specific attribute and/or value associated with the attribute.

For the following examples, the driver objects have been separated into two rows in the f1_drivers_obj table. There is one row for Coulthard and one for Vettel.

The JSON path expression targets the attribute to test for the existence of an attribute. The following query tests for the existence of the driverId attribute.

```
select f.driver.givenName.string() as firstname
from   f1_drivers_obj f
where  json_exists ( f.driver
                   , '$.driverId'
                   )
/
FIRSTNAME
---------
David
Sebastian
```

Both drivers have the driverId attribute, so both rows are returned.

The following example uses the json_exists condition to filter the correct JSON document from the table. A filter condition is used to test the driverId for the name "coulthard".

```
select f.driver.givenName.string() as firstname
from    f1_drivers_obj f
where   json_exists ( f.driver
                    , '$?(@.driverId == "coulthard")'
                    )
/
FIRSTNAME
---------
David
```

Both drivers have a nickname attribute, one with a value of DC, and the other has a value of JSON NULL (not SQL NULL). The following filter condition finds the driver whose nickname is null.

```
select f.driver.givenName.string() as firstname
from    f1_drivers_obj f
where   json_exists ( f.driver
                    , '$?(@.nickname == null)'
                    )
/
FIRSTNAME
---------
Sebastian
```

The json_exists condition can also be used in a CASE expression, like in the following example.

```
select case
       when json_exists ( f.driver
                        , '$?(@.champion ==true)'
                        )
       then
         'We''ve got a winner'
       end as champion
from    f1_drivers_obj f
/
```

```
CHAMPION
-------------------

We've got a winner
```

Two rows are returned, one for each driver, but because the condition is only satisfied for one of the drivers, only one row has the "We've got a winner" text, whereas the other is null.

Multiple conditions can be tested by combining JSON path filter conditions (see Chapter 12). However, testing for an attribute having a certain value *and* the existence of another attribute requires an `exists` filter.

The following condition attempts to filter for a driver whose nationality is Finnish *or* there is a Constructors array present.

```
$?(@.nationality == "Finnish" || @.Constructors[*])
```

This leads to the following error.

```
SQL Error: ORA-40597: JSON path expression syntax error ('$?(@.nationality
== "Finnish" || @.Constructors[*])')
JZN-00224: Unexpected characters in comparison operator
at position 51
40597. 00000 -  "JSON path expression syntax error ('%s')%s\nat
position %s"
*Cause:    The specified JavaScript Object Notation (JSON) path expression
           had invalid syntax and could not be parsed.
*Action:   Specify JSON path expression with the correct syntax.
```

The following is the correct JSON path expression to test for these conditions.

```
$?(@.nationality == "Finnish" || exists(@.Constructors[*]))
```

Using this in a `json_exists` condition returns the following result. Even though the driver is German, not Finnish, a Constructors array exists for him.

```
select f.driver.familyName.string() as lastname
     , f.driver.nationality.string() as nationality
     , f.driver.Constructors[*].nationality as c_nationalities
from   f1_drivers_obj f
```

```
where   json_exists ( f.driver
                    , '$?(@.nationality == "Finnish"
                    || exists(@.Constructors[*]))'
                    )
/
LASTNAME            NATIONALITY      C_NATIONALITIES
---------------     ---------------  ----------------------
Vettel              German           ["Austrian","British"]
```

Of course, it is also possible to pass bind variables to the json_exists clause. The following query shows all drivers where *either* their nationality is British *or* the nationality of the constructor is British, *or* both conditions are true.

```
select  f.driver.familyName.string() as lastname
     , f.driver.nationality.string() as nationality
     , f.driver.Constructors[*].nationality as c_nationalities
from    f1_drivers_obj f
where   json_exists ( f.driver
                    , '$?(@.nationality == $nationality
                    || @.Constructors[*].nationality
                    == $nationality)'
                    passing 'British' as "nationality"
                    )
/
LASTNAME            NATIONALITY      C_NATIONALITIES
---------------     ---------------  ----------------------
Coulthard           British          null
Vettel              German           ["Austrian","British"]
```

A JSON search index can be created for full-text searches of the JSON document. The JSON search index is comparable to an Oracle Text index. For more information about the JSON search index and how to create and use it, see Chapter 11.

Summary

This chapter focused on SQL/JSON functions. The `json_value` function can extract scalar values from a JSON document. The `json_query` function allows you to extract JSON snippets from a JSON document. The `json_table` function plays a crucial role in projecting a JSON document in a relational format. The `json_serialize` function can change a JSON document to a textual format.

Finally, the usage of `json_exists` and how to apply it in a `where` clause or a CASE expression were explained.

CHAPTER 14

Generate, Compare, and Manipulate JSON

Generating JSON documents from relational data is a common requirement, and Oracle Database offers the necessary tools. This chapter looks at these possibilities in SQL and PL/SQL.

There is also information about working with JSON documents in PL/SQL, like extracting data and making changes to a JSON document.

Generating JSON Documents

To generate JSON documents in SQL, there are several functions available.

- `json` is a very flexible way to generate JSON documents newly introduced in Oracle Database 21c. The JSON constructor can accept any well-formed JSON string and returns a JSON data type, including JSON scalars. It can also be used with curly braces to construct a JSON object or with square brackets to generate a JSON array.

- `json_scalar` accepts a SQL value and returns a JSON equivalent. This is especially useful when converting dates, timestamps, or intervals in the correct ISO 8601 format, which is new in Oracle Database 21c.

- `json_object` accepts key-value pairs and returns a JSON object. You can use wildcard or column names as input.

- `json_objectagg` is an aggregate function that accepts key-value pairs and returns a single JSON object. Typically, the key or value are columns from a table.

© Alex Nuijten, Patrick Barel 2023
A. Nuijten and P. Barel, *Modern Oracle Database Programming*, https://doi.org/10.1007/978-1-4842-9166-5_14

- `json_array` accepts one or more scalar SQL expressions or columns turns them into JSON scalar, and returns an array.

- `json_arrayagg` is an aggregate function that accepts a column or SQL expression and returns a single JSON array.

All these functions allow you to generate JSON documents from relational data from simple to complex.

The `json_scalar` function is especially useful when converting `date`, `timestamp`, and `interval` to their JSON equivalent. The following example converts these data types to JSON in ISO-8601 format.

```
select json_scalar (current_date) as now
  from dual
/
NOW
--------------------
"2022-08-24T08:53:29"
```

The `json_scalar` function knows the SQL data type from which it was derived. The appropriate item method with the `json_value` function converts it back to its original data type. The following example shows the conversion to a JSON scalar, as VARCHAR2 in ISO-8601 format, and the data type is preserved.

```
select json_value
        ( json_scalar (current_timestamp)
        , '$'
        ) as now
     , json_value
        ( json_scalar (current_timestamp)
        , '$.type()'
        ) as now_datatype
from    dual
/
NOW                             NOW_DATATYPE
------------------------------  -------------------------
2022-08-24T07:13:42.365662Z     timestamp with time zone
```

The following example converts the interval to the JSON equivalent using the ISO-8601 standard.

```
select json_scalar ( to_dsinterval ( '1 2:45:15' ) ) as ds
     , json_scalar ( to_yminterval ( '2-3' ) ) as ym
from    dual
/
DS                       YM
-------------------- -------
"P1DT2H45M15S"           "P2Y3M"
```

> **Tip**   It is also possible in Oracle Database 21c to use the ISO-8601 interval notation in the to_dsinterval and to_yminterval functions.
>
> ```
> select to_dsinterval ('P1DT2H45M15S') as ds
>
> from    dual
> /
>
> DS
> --------------------
> +01 02:45:15.000000
> ```

In the following example, four different methods are used to generate a simple object. The first column uses an explicit "key" and "value" keyword, and the second column uses a colon (:) to separate the key and value. The third column uses the name of the column to generate a JSON object. Finally, the json operator uses curly braces and a colon to define the JSON object.

Each method generates the same JSON object (so it is only shown once).

```
select json_object ( key 'driverid' value driverid ) as verbose
     , json_object ( 'driverid' : driverid )  as colon
     , json_object ( driverid ) as col
     , json {'driverid' : driverid} as curly_braces
from    f1_drivers
where   givenname = 'David'
```

```
and     familyname = 'Coulthard'
/
{"driverid":"coulthard"}
```

It should be noted that it is possible to pass multiple column names in to generate a JSON object or even an asterisk to select all columns.

```
select json_object ( familyname
                    , nationality
                    ) as estebans
from    f1_drivers
where   givenname = 'Esteban'
/
ESTEBANS
--------
{"familyname":"Tuero","nationality":"Argentine"}
{"familyname":"Gutiérrez","nationality":"Mexican"}
{"familyname":"Ocon","nationality":"French"}
```

A JSON object is returned for each record in the f1_drivers table. When it is desirable to have a single JSON object instead of three separate ones, the json_objectagg function can be used.

```
select json_objectagg
        ( key familyname value nationality ) as estebans
from    f1_drivers
where   givenname = 'Esteban'
/
ESTEBANS
--------
{"Tuero":"Argentine","Gutiérrez":"Mexican","Ocon":"French"}
```

The json_objectagg function can only aggregate a single key-value pair, but this pair can be another JSON object to create an object of objects (the JSON output has been formatted for readability).

```
select json_objectagg
        ( key givenname value json_object ( familyname
                                          , nationality
                                          )
        ) as estebans
from    f1_drivers
where   givenname = 'Esteban'
/
ESTEBANS
--------
{
   "Esteban": {
     "familyname": "Tuero",
     "nationality": "Argentine"
   },
   "Esteban": {
     "familyname": "Gutiérrez",
     "nationality": "Mexican"
   },
   "Esteban": {
     "familyname": "Ocon",
     "nationality": "French"
   }
}
```

Generating JSON arrays can be done by using the json_array function. With the new json constructor, this can also be achieved when square brackets are used. Both notations are shown in the following example. An array is shown for each row.

```
select json_array ( familyname, nationality ) as estebans
    , json [familyname, nationality] as estebans
  from f1_drivers
 where givenname = 'Esteban'
/
```

367

```
ESTEBANS                ESTEBANS
----------------------  ----------------------
["Tuero","Argentine"]   ["Tuero","Argentine"]
["Gutiérrez","Mexican"] ["Gutiérrez","Mexican"]
["Ocon","French"]       ["Ocon","French"]
```

To generate a single JSON array, use json_arrayagg. The following example shows a single array with objects.

```
select json_arrayagg
        ( json {key familyname value nationality} ) as estebans
from    f1_drivers
where   givenname = 'Esteban'
/
ESTEBANS
--------
[{"Tuero":"Argentine"},{"Gutiérrez":"Mexican"},{"Ocon":"French"}]
```

Tip   When creating larger, more complex JSON documents which might exceed the default 4000 bytes, use the returning CLOB/BLOB or returning JSON (Oracle Database 21c and up) at every object and array level. This is especially true when the following error is encountered: ORA-40478: output value too large

---

The following example shows the combined use of json_object, json_array, and json_arrayagg to generate a more complex JSON document. The first part of the JSON document is also shown (in formatted form). In the resulting JSON document, there are a few things to note.

- The rounds are ordered by round number within the array (order by rce.round).

- The top three are determined by a correlated subquery.

- When there is no top three when a race is planned in the future, the top three attributes are not included in the JSON document (absent on null).

- Because of the size of the JSON document, it is returned as a CLOB. When at least Oracle Database 21c is used, it can also be returned as JSON.

- A JSON document for each year is created. When a single document is needed for all years, change `json_array` for the `'raceresults'` attribute to `json_arrayagg` and remove the final where clause.

```
select json_object (
     'raceresults' value json_array(
       json_object (
           rce.year
          , 'races' value (json_arrayagg(
             json_object(
                 rce.round
                ,key 'circuit' value cct.name
                ,rce.race_date
                ,key 'top3' value(
                   select
                      json_arrayagg(winners returning clob)
                   from
                      (select json_object(
                             rst.position
                            ,'driver' value dvr.forename
                                            ||' '
                                            || dvr.surname
                            ,'constructor' value csr.name
                            ,dvr.nationality
                            ) as winners
                       from results rst
                       join drivers       dvr
                         on rst.driverid = dvr.driverid
                       join constructors csr
                         on csr.constructorid = rst.constructorid
                      where rst.raceid = rce.raceid
                      order by rst.position
```

```
                          fetch first 3 rows only
                    )
                )
            absent on null returning clob)
        order by rce.round
        returning clob))
      returning clob)
    returning clob)
  returning clob)
 from races rce
 join circuits cct
   on rce.circuitid = cct.circuitid
 where rce.year = 2022
 group by rce.year
/
{
   "raceresults": [
      {
         "year": 2022,
         "races": [
            {
               "round": 1,
               "circuit": "Bahrain International Circuit",
               "race_date": "2022-03-20T00:00:00",
               "top3": [
                  {
                     "position": 1,
                     "driver": "Charles Leclerc",
                     "constructor": "Ferrari",
                     "nationality": "Monegasque"
                  },
                  {
                     "position": 2,
                     "driver": "Carlos Sainz",
                     "constructor": "Ferrari",
```

```
                    "nationality": "Spanish"
                },
                {
                    "position": 3,
                    "driver": "Lewis Hamilton",
                    "constructor": "Mercedes",
                    "nationality": "British"
                }
            ]
        },
<shortened for brevity>
        {
            "round": 15,
            "circuit": "Circuit Park Zandvoort",
            "race_date": "2022-09-04T00:00:00"
        },
<rest of the JSON document omitted>
```

Comparing JSON Documents

For JSON documents, whitespace and attribute order is irrelevant. So even though the following JSON snippets look different from a textual perspective, they are the same from a JSON perspective.

```
{"code":"COU","givenName":"David","familyName":"Coulthard"}
```

```
{
  "givenName" : "David",
  "familyName" : "Coulthard",
  "code" : "COU"
}
```

The json_equal function can compare JSON documents. It is not possible to compare a part of the JSON document using a JSON path expression directly; only complete JSON documents are comparable. It is possible to use json_query to pass in a snippet of a JSON document. In the following example, the JSON snippets are compared.

371

```
select *
from    dual
where   json_equal ('{"code":"COU","givenName":"David","familyName":"Coulth
ard"}'
,'
{
  "givenName" : "David",
  "familyName" : "Coulthard",
  "code" : "COU"
}')
/

D
-
X
```

The comparison works even when the JSON document is in a binary format, like stored in a BLOB column. The following query compares a JSON string and a binary representation of the same JSON document.

```
with test as
(
select utl_raw.cast_to_raw
 ('{"code":"COU","givenName":"David","familyName":"Coulthard"}') as
 bin_json
     , json ('{"code":"COU","givenName":"David","familyName":"Coulthard"}')
     as j_json
from    dual)
select 'The JSON documents are the same' as result
from    test t
where   json_equal ( t.bin_json, t.j_json )
/
RESULT
--------------------------------
The JSON documents are the same
```

When this function is used in the SELECT clause, the following error might be encountered: ORA-40600: JSON_EQUAL used outside predicate. This might give the impression that it can only be used in the WHERE clause of a query, this is not the case. It can also be used in a CASE expression.

Changing a JSON Document

Changing the structure of a JSON document can be done with the json_transform function. This function is like a Swiss-army knife; almost all possible manipulations of a JSON document are possible. The most common usage is in combination with an UPDATE statement to persist the changed JSON document. There is also the json_mergepatch function to change JSON documents, but this is not covered because of its limited functionality.

Table 14-1 shows the possible modifications that can be done.

***Table 14-1.** Modifications with json_transform*

Modification	Description
Remove	Remove the input data that is targeted by the path expression.
Append	Append the value to a targeted array. It raises an error if the target is not an array.
Keep	Remove all inputs that are not targeted by the path expression. It is possible to specify multiple path expressions.
Rename	Rename the attribute targeted by the path expression.
Set	Replace existing target data with a new value or creates a new attribute when it doesn't exist.
Replace	Replace existing target data. Similar to set ignore on missing.
Insert	Add new value when it doesn't exist. Raises an error when it already exists. Similar to set create on missing.

The following example shows a modified JSON document. The input is the sample JSON document defined in Chapter 12, Listing 12-1.

```
select json_transform (f.json_document
    , remove  '$.MRData.DriverTable.Drivers[1]'
```

```
      , replace '$.MRData.series' = 'Formula 1'
      , set '$.FIA' = 'Fédération Internationale de l''Automobile'
      , append  '$.MRData.DriverTable.Drivers' =
          json { 'code': 'RIC'
               , 'givenName':'Daniel'
               , 'familyName':'Ricciardo'
               , 'nickname':'Honey Badger'
               }
      , insert  '$.MRData.Constructors' =
              json ['Red Bull', 'Ferrari', 'Mercedes', 'Renault']
      , rename  '$.MRData' = 'F1Data'
      )
   from f1_drivers_json f
/
{
    "FIA": "Fédération Internationale de l'Automobile",
    "F1Data": {
       "series": "Formula 1",
       "DriverTable": {
          "Drivers": [
              {
                 "driverId": "coulthard",
                 "code": "COU",
                 "givenName": "David",
                 "familyName": "Coulthard",
                 "dateOfBirth": "1971-03-27",
                 "nationality": "British",
                 "champion": false,
                 "nickname": "DC"
              },
              {
                 "code": "RIC",
                 "givenName": "Daniel",
                 "familyName": "Ricciardo",
                 "nickname": "Honey Badger"
```

```
        }
      ]
    },
    "Constructors": [
      "Red Bull",
      "Ferrari",
      "Mercedes",
      "Renault"
    ]
  }
}
```

The modifications that were done in the preceding query.

- The second driver (array 1) is removed from the Drivers array.

- The value of the series attribute is changed to Formula 1.

- An extra FIA attribute is added at the root level with the full name as the value.

- A new driver is added to the Drivers array.

- An array of Constructors is added.

- The name of the MRData attribute is changed to F1Data.

With the keep modification, you specify the sections of the JSON document that should be preserved. All other keys are removed. The following example modifies the JSON document, so that only the Driver object is preserved when the nickname equals DC. The output is formatted for readability.

```
select json_transform
        ( f.json_document
        , keep
          '$.MRData.DriverTable.Drivers[*]?(@.nickname=="DC")'
        ) with_nickname
from    f1_drivers_json f
/
WITH_NICKNAME
-------------
```

```
{
    "MRData": {
        "DriverTable": {
            "Drivers": [
                {
                    "driverId": "coulthard",
                    "code": "COU",
                    "givenName": "David",
                    "familyName": "Coulthard",
                    "dateOfBirth": "1971-03-27",
                    "nationality": "British",
                    "champion": false,
                    "nickname": "DC"
                }
            ]
        }
    }
}
```

The keep modification is the only one that can handle multiple JSON path expressions. The following example preserves the nickname of all drivers and the code of the first driver in the Drivers array.

```
select json_transform
        ( f.json_document
        , keep '$.MRData.DriverTable.Drivers[*].nickname'
            , '$.MRData.DriverTable.Drivers[0].code'
        ) nickname_code
from    f1_drivers_json f
/

NICKNAME_CODE
--------------

{
    "MRData": {
        "DriverTable": {
            "Drivers": [
```

```
        {
          "code": "COU",
          "nickname": "DC"
        },
        {
          "nickname": null
        }
      ]
    }
  }
}
```

Making more complex changes, like adding a fullname attribute for each driver and populating it with the values of the givenName and familyName attributes, takes more effort. In the next example, it is done as follows: with json_table each givenname and familyname is extracted, as well as the Driver objects from the Drivers array. The json_transform function adds a new attribute, fullName, to the Driver objects and populates it with the concatenated givenname and familyname. Finally, a combination of json_arrayagg and json_object finalizes the JSON document. To keep the output short, only the new fullName attribute is kept.

```
select json_object
        ( 'DriversList' value json_arrayagg
          ( json_transform ( jt.driver
                            , insert '$.fullName' =
                              jt.givenname||' '||jt.familyname
                            , keep '$.fullName'
                            )
          )
        ) as just_names
from    f1_drivers_json f
cross
join    json_table
        ( f.json_document
        , '$.MRData.DriverTable.Drivers[*]'
        columns
```

```
        ( givenName
        , familyName
        , driver json path '$'
        )
      ) jt
/
JUST_NAMES
----------
{
   "DriversList": [
     {
        "fullName": "David Coulthard"
     },
     {
        "fullName": "Sebastian Vettel"
     }
   ]
}
```

JSON and PL/SQL

To support JSON in PL/SQL, several object types are specifically designed to read and write JSON documents. This can increase performance, especially when a document needs to be parsed multiple times.

With the object types, it is possible to programmatically manipulate JSON in memory to validate, construct or transform JSON documents.

The PL/SQL object types are listed in Table 14-2.

Table 14-2. *JSON-Related PL/SQL Object Types*

Object Type	Description
json_ element_t	Supertype of all other types This type is instantiable With the `treat` function, a variable of `json_element_t` can be instantiated as one of the subtypes
json_object_t	Subtype of `json_element_t` Corresponds to a JSON object type
json_array_t	Subtype of `json_element_t` Corresponds to a JSON array type
json_scalar_t	Subtype of `json_element_t` Corresponds to a JSON scalar type
json_key_list	Subtype of `json_element_t` Varray of VARCHAR2(4000) designed to hold the keys of a json_object_t

For the coming examples, the same JSON document is used as in Listing 12-1 from Chapter 12, this time as a local variable named `l_f1data` with data type `CLOB`.

When the structure of the JSON document is known, the driver's information is contained in a JSON object. It is possible to parse it directly to the appropriate data type.

```
declare
  l_f1data clob := '<the sample JSON document>';
  l_object json_object_t;
begin
  l_object := json_object_t.parse ( l_f1data );
end;
/
```

Once the textual representation is parsed as a JSON document, you can extract the object and arrays as needed. The top-level object in the sample is named MRData; to extract this object, the `get_object` method function is used in the following example.

```
declare
  l_f1data clob := '<the sample JSON document>';
  l_object json_object_t;
```

```
  l_mrdata json_object_t;
begin
  l_object := json_object_t.parse ( l_f1data );
  l_mrdata := l_object.get_object ( 'MRData' );
end;
/
```

The same methodology can be used to extract the Drivers array, declare the appropriate data type for each level in the JSON document and use the get_object and get_array method functions.

```
declare
  l_f1data clob := '<the sample JSON document>';
  l_object json_object_t;
  l_mrdata json_object_t;
  l_drivertable json_object_t;
  l_drivers_array json_array_t;
begin
  l_object := json_object_t.parse ( l_f1data );
  l_mrdata := l_object.get_object ( 'MRData' );
  l_drivertable := l_mrdata.get_object ( 'DriverTable' );
  l_drivers_array := l_drivertable.get_array( 'Drivers' );
end;
/
```

It can also be condensed to apply the method functions in succession, the result would be the same.

```
declare
  l_f1data clob := '<the sample JSON document>';
  l_drivers_array json_array_t;
begin
  l_drivers_array := json_object_t.parse (l_f1data)
                              .get_object ('MRData')
                              .get_object ('DriverTable')
                              .get_array  ('Drivers');
end;
/
```

When the structure of the JSON document is unknown, it is possible to examine the content of the JSON document. In the following example, the JSON document is parsed. The json_element_t supertype and the is_object and is_array introspection functions determine the JSON data type.

```
declare
  l_f1data clob := '<the sample JSON document>';
  l_element json_element_t;
begin
  l_element := json_element_t.parse ( l_f1data );
  if l_element.is_object
  then
    sys.dbms_output.put_line ( 'It is an Object' );
  elsif l_element.is_array
  then
    sys.dbms_output.put_line ( 'It is an Array' );
  end if;
end;
/
```

```
It is an Object
```

Contained within the Drivers array are JSON objects representing the drivers. Extracting these JSON objects can be done with the get method function. Note that the get method function returns the supertype json_element_t. Therefore, it needs to be converted to a JSON object using the treat function.

After converting it to a JSON object, the individual attributes can be retrieved using the get_string, get_number, get_date, and similar method functions. The following example shows how to get the value of a specific key in the JSON object.

```
declare
  l_f1data clob := '<the sample JSON document>';
  l_drivers_array json_array_t;
  l_driver json_object_t;
begin
  l_drivers_array := json_object_t.parse (l_f1data)
                              .get_object ('MRData')
```

```
                              .get_object ('DriverTable')
                              .get_array  ('Drivers');
  for i in 0 .. l_drivers_array.get_size -1
  loop
    l_driver := treat (l_drivers_array.get (i)
                       as json_object_t);
    sys.dbms_output.put_line (l_driver.get_string ('driverId'));
    sys.dbms_output.put_line (l_driver.get_string ('code'));
    sys.dbms_output.put_line (l_driver.get_date ('dateOfBirth'));
  end loop;
end;
/
coulthard
COU
27-MAR-71
vettel
VET
03-JUL-87
```

Instead of getting the values of the attributes by looking up each key in the JSON document, it is also possible to get it more generically.

The get_keys method function returns a varray of VARCHAR2, best stored in a variable of type json_key_list. In the following example, get_keys is used to extract the attribute names and the related values.

```
declare
  l_f1data clob := '<the sample JSON document>';
  l_drivers_array json_array_t;
  l_driver json_object_t;
  l_driver_keys json_key_list;
begin
  l_drivers_array := json_object_t.parse (l_f1data)
                              .get_object ('MRData')
                              .get_object ('DriverTable')
                              .get_array  ('Drivers');
```

```
  for i in 0 .. l_drivers_array.get_size -1
  loop
    l_driver := treat (l_drivers_array.get (i)
                          as json_object_t);
    l_driver_keys := l_driver.get_keys;
    for key_idx in 1 .. l_driver_keys.count
    loop
      sys.dbms_output.put_line (
         l_driver_keys (key_idx)||' : '||
         l_driver.get_string (l_driver_keys (key_idx))
      );
    end loop;
  end loop;
end;
/
driverId : coulthard
code : COU
givenName : David
familyName : Coulthard
dateOfBirth : 1971-03-27
nationality : British
champion : false
nickname : DC
driverId : vettel
permanentNumber : 5
code : VET
givenName : Sebastian
familyName : Vettel
dateOfBirth : 1987-07-03
nationality : German
champion : true
nickname :
Constructors :
```

In the preceding output, the Constructors attributes don't show a value associated with it. When looking closer at this attribute in the sample JSON, the value is an array of objects. To make these values visible as well, a similar nested loop construction can be created; one loop to get the objects and one to get the key-value pairs from the object.

```
l_constructor_array := l_driver.get_array (
                          l_driver_keys (key_idx));
for ci in 0 .. l_constructor_array.get_size -1
loop
  l_constructor := treat (l_constructor_array.get (ci)
                    as json_object_t);
  l_constructor_keys := l_constructor.get_keys;
  for constructor_idx in 1 .. l_constructor_keys.count
  loop
    sys.dbms_output.put_line (
     l_constructor.get_string (
         l_constructor_keys (constructor_idx))
    );
  end loop;
end loop;
```

You can determine which JSON data type is encountered using the get_type method function.

The following code makes the sample JSON visible with dbms_output. The output is omitted for brevity.

```
declare
  l_f1data clob := '<the sample JSON document>';
  l_drivers_array json_array_t;
  l_driver         json_object_t;
  l_driver_keys.   json_key_list;
  l_constructor_array json_array_t;
  l_constructor_keys  json_key_list;
  l_constructor        json_object_t;
```

```
begin
  l_drivers_array := json_object_t.parse (l_f1data)
                                 .get_object ('MRData')
                                 .get_object ('DriverTable')
                                 .get_array  ('Drivers');
  for i in 0 .. l_drivers_array.get_size -1
  loop
    l_driver := treat (l_drivers_array.get (i)
                            as json_object_t);
    l_driver_keys := l_driver.get_keys;
    for key_idx in 1 .. l_driver_keys.count
    loop
      case l_driver.get_type (l_driver_keys (key_idx))
      when 'SCALAR'
      then
        sys.dbms_output.put_line (
          l_driver_keys (key_idx)||' : '||
          l_driver.get_string (l_driver_keys (key_idx)));
      when 'ARRAY'
      then
        l_constructor_array := l_driver.get_array (
                               l_driver_keys (key_idx));
        for ci in 0 .. l_constructor_array.get_size -1
        loop
          l_constructor := treat (l_constructor_array.get (ci)
                            as json_object_t);
          l_constructor_keys := l_constructor.get_keys;
          for constructor_idx in 1 .. l_constructor_keys.count
          loop
            sys.dbms_output.put_line (
              l_constructor.get_string (
                  l_constructor_keys (constructor_idx))
            );
          end loop;
        end loop;
```

```
      end case;
    end loop;
  end loop;
end;
```

Using the SQL/JSON functions, like json_value and json_query, is also possible in PL/SQL code. Because there *is* a boolean data type in PL/SQL, it can be mapped from JSON directly. The following example shows the usage of json_value and json_query in PL/SQL.

```
declare
  l_f1data clob := '<the sample JSON document>';
  l_boolean boolean;
begin
  l_boolean := json_value
                  ( l_drivers
                  ,'$.MRData.DriverTable.Drivers[1].champion'
                    returning boolean
                  );
  sys.dbms_output.put_line
          ( json_value
              ( l_drivers
              , '$.MRData.DriverTable.Drivers[1].givenName'
              returning varchar2
              )
          );
  sys.dbms_output.put_line
          ( json_query
              ( l_drivers
              , '$.MRData.DriverTable.Drivers[*].champion'
              returning varchar2
              with conditional array wrapper
              )
          );
end;
/
```

Caution   Pay attention to the data type returned from the SQL/JSON functions. Without the usage of item method functions (like `string()`, `number()`) or the `returning` clause that specifies the data type, they return JSON when using Oracle Database 21c or higher; VARCHAR2(4000) otherwise.

Constructing and Manipulating JSON with PL/SQL

Generating JSON is often based on relational data, but sometimes it is necessary to create or manipulate a JSON document with PL/SQL.

With the constructor functions of the JSON PL/SQL objects, it is trivial to generate a JSON document. In the following example, a string representing a JSON object is passed as an argument to the `json_object_t` constructor function. It returns a `json_object_t` function and is shown using `dbms_output`.

```
declare
  l_driver json_object_t;
begin
  l_driver := new json_object_t (
'{
  "firstname": "Stirling",
  "lastname": "Moss",
  "extra": {
    "dob": "1929-09-17",
    "nationality": "British"
  }
}');
  sys.dbms_output.put_line ( l_driver.to_string );
end;
/
{"firstname":"Stirling","lastname":"Moss","extra":{"dob":"1929-09-17",
"nationality":"British"}}
```

Extracting a nested object or array is done by reference. Making changes to the extracted object or array is reflected in the containing object. The extra object is extracted and modified in the following example by adding an extra key-value pair. The additional key-value pair also appears when the original object is inspected.

```
declare
  l_driver json_object_t;
  l_extra  json_object_t;
begin
  l_driver := new json_object_t (
'{
  "firstname": "Stirling",
  "lastname": "Moss",
  "extra": {
    "dob": "1929-09-17",
    "nationality": "British"
  }
}');
  l_extra := l_driver.get_object ( 'extra' );
  l_extra.put ( 'notRelated', 'Bill' );
  sys.dbms_output.put_line ( l_extra.to_string );
  sys.dbms_output.put_line ( l_driver.to_string );
end;
/
{"dob":"1929-09-17","nationality":"British","notRelated":"Bill"}

{"firstname":"Stirling","lastname":"Moss","extra":{"dob":"1929-09-17",
"nationality":"British","notRelated":"Bill"}}
```

The clone function makes a copy when extracting the nested object or array; changes done on this object or array are not reflected in the containing object. The following example shows this behavior. The extra nested object is not changed in the containing object.

```
declare
  l_driver json_object_t;
  l_extra  json_object_t;
```

```
begin
  l_driver := new json_object_t (
'{
  "firstname": "Stirling",
  "lastname": "Moss",
  "extra": {
    "dob": "1929-09-17",
    "nationality": "British"
  }
}');
  l_extra := l_driver.get_object ( 'extra' ).clone;
  l_extra.put ( 'notRelated', 'Bill' );
  sys.dbms_output.put_line ( l_extra.to_string );
  sys.dbms_output.put_line ( l_driver.to_string );
end;
/
{"dob":"1929-09-17","nationality":"British","notRelated":"Bill"}

{"firstname":"Stirling","lastname":"Moss","extra":{"dob":"1929-09-17",
"nationality":"British"}}
```

The put procedure sets the value of a specific key in a JSON object. When the key is not present in the object, it is added. When the key is already present, the value is overwritten. With JSON arrays the put procedure works slightly different, it is required to specify where the value needs to be added and by default it does not overwrite the value at that location. It is possible to direct that the value is overwritten when it exists.

Removing and renaming keys in an object are done with the remove and rename_ key procedures. The next example removes the "extra" nested object, constructs a placeholder based on the first- and last name and renames the key to fullName.

```
declare
  l_driver json_object_t;
begin
  l_driver := new json_object_t (
'{
  "firstname": "Stirling",
  "lastname": "Moss",
```

```
  "extra": {
    "dob": "1929-09-17",
    "nationality": "British"
  }
}');
  l_driver.remove ( 'extra' );
  l_driver.put ( 'placeholder'
              , 'Sir '||
                l_driver.get_string ('firstname')
                ||' '||
                l_driver.get_string ('lastname')
              );
  l_driver.remove ( 'firstname' );
  l_driver.remove ( 'lastname' );
  l_driver.rename_key ( 'placeholder', 'fullName' );
  sys.dbms_output.put_line ( l_driver.to_string );
end;
/
{"fullName":"Sir Stirling Moss"}
```

Sir Stirling Moss raced from 1951 to 1961 and won many races. The following example captures the race years in a JSON array using a simple for loop. The append procedure adds values at the end of the array. Using the put procedure, the year 1900 is added at the first position, overwritten with 2022, and finally removed.

```
declare
  l_races   json_array_t;
begin
  l_races := new json_array_t ();
  for i in 1951 .. 1961
  loop
    l_races.append(i);
  end loop;
```

```
sys.dbms_output.put_line
        ( 'Race year count: '
          || l_races.get_size
        );
l_races.put ( 0,1900, false );
sys.dbms_output.put_line
        ( 'First race year in the Array: '
          || l_races.get_string ( 0 )
        );

l_races.put ( 0,2022, true );
sys.dbms_output.put_line
        ( 'First race year in the Array: '
          || l_races.get_string ( 0 )
        );
l_races.remove ( 0 );
sys.dbms_output.put_line
        ( 'First race year in the Array: '
          || l_races.get_string ( 0 )
        );
end;
/
Race year count: 11
First race year in the Array: 1900
First race year in the Array: 2022
First race year in the Array: 1951
```

Summary

In this chapter generation of JSON documents from SQL is discussed. Using various functions (json, json_object, json_objectagg, json_array, json_arrayagg), all JSON documents can be constructed from relational data. Changing JSON documents and removing, adding, or renaming keys is easily done with json_transform. Finally, the focus was JSON and PL/SQL to extract values and manipulate and generate complete JSON documents.

PART III

Oracle-Provided Functionality

CHAPTER 15

Useful APEX Packages

Oracle Application Express (APEX) is a low-code development platform that allows you to build scalable, secure enterprise applications that can be deployed anywhere. Well, almost anywhere; the APEX engine still needs an Oracle database. APEX is a no-cost option with Oracle Database from the Always Free cloud tier to XE to the Enterprise Edition.

All APEX packages are useful when using APEX. However, even if you are not using APEX for what it is intended for—creating front-end applications, you can still benefit from its functionality. And these packages are the subject of this topic.

Because APEX resides inside the Oracle database, you can integrate it seamlessly with your own code. APEX packages are maintained by Oracle. A homegrown solution would have to be maintained by you.

Calling a web service from PL/SQL can be quite challenging, but with the APEX package, this is trivial. Creating a ZIP file and parsing CSV data are easy to do with the functionality that APEX provides out of the box.

APEX Availability

You can only take advantage of APEX if it is available in your database. When it is installed, keep up to date because new features and functionality are always being added, and security fixes are being implemented.

APEX lives in the database in a separate schema, so an easy way to check if APEX is installed is to query for the APEX user.

```
select username
  from all_users
 where username like 'APEX%'
```

© Alex Nuijten, Patrick Barel 2023
A. Nuijten and P. Barel, *Modern Oracle Database Programming*, https://doi.org/10.1007/978-1-4842-9166-5_15

The result that this query produces gives you information about the existence of the APEX schema and, if so, about the installed version.

When you have version 22.1 installed, the result is as follows.

APEX_220100

When you don't get any results from this query, it simply means that APEX is not installed. Installing APEX is beyond the scope of this book, so refer to the documentation. The latest version of APEX is always recommended. The documentation (for the latest version) can be found via this URL.

https://apex.oracle.com/doc

For version-specific documentation, you can suffix the URL with the version you are looking for, such as the following.

https://apex.oracle.com/doc212

Because this chapter focuses on some of the built-in packages that APEX provides, easy access to the documentation is very helpful. There is a URL that directly takes you to the PL/SQL API.

https://apex.oracle.com/api

Note   When it is not possible to take advantage of everything that APEX has to offer because a DBA might argue that "it is too risky to have a web server access the database," it might be possible to ask that *only* the APEX packages be installed *without* setting up a web server. Having the APEX packages available makes PL/SQL development a lot easier.

Calling Web Services

A common requirement is to combine the data in a local database with data available in a different data source. Think of weather information, currency exchange rates, quotes for shipping, or exchange invoice data.

One method that this objective can be achieved is by calling web services. Previously, when interacting with web services, you would have to use UTL_HTTP and do much of the plumbing. Oracle APEX makes it very simple to call web services. The APEX package supports both SOAP web services and REST-style APIs.

The example discussed in this part uses the Ergast Developer API (*http://ergast. com/mrd/*), which provides a historical record of motor racing data. With this web service, it is possible to get the results back in either XML or JSON format. We prefer to work with JSON.

The examples in this chapter use Oracle Database 21c Express Edition. Depending on your database setup, you might need a network ACL configured by your DBA.

Note   Configuring a network ACL is beyond the scope of this book. It is discussed in Chapter 6, "Installing and Configuring Oracle APEX and Oracle REST Data Services," of the *Oracle APEX Installation Guide.*

In the package apex_web_service, there are two procedures to call a REST-style web service; one that returns a CLOB and one that returns a BLOB. In the example, the CLOB variant is called so the results can be easily inspected. When you need to store JSON documents in the database, refer to Chapter 11.

The bare minimum needed to call the web service is the URL and the HTTP method, in this case, a GET request.

```
declare
    l_response clob;
    l_part      varchar2(4000 char);
    l_offset    pls_integer;
begin
    l_response := apex_web_service.make_rest_request
        (p_url          => 'http://ergast.com/api/f1/current.json'
        ,p_http_method => 'GET'
        );
```

The URL specifies what to retrieve: the current year of Formula 1 as a JSON document. Omitting the JSON extension from the URL returns an XML instead. The URL syntax is dictated by the web service that you are using.

After calling a web service, it is good practice to verify that the call was successful. This value can be obtained by inspecting the global variable g_status_code, which is declared in the apex_web_service package. A successful response can differ significantly from an error response, so your parsing method must also be different to extract useful information from a failed response.

A response status ranging from 200 to 299 indicates a successful response.

```
if apex_web_service.g_status_code between 200 and 299 then
```

To show the response's content, let's use another APEX package, apex_string, to get the parts of the CLOB variable and show them with dbms_output.

```
while apex_string.next_chunk (
    p_str    => l_response
   ,p_chunk  => l_part
   ,p_offset => l_offset
   ,p_amount => 4000)
loop
   sys.dbms_output.put_line (l_part);
end loop;
```

Listing 15-1 shows the complete code sample and the first part of the output. The complete message is too long to show here.

Listing 15-1. Get the current season of F1 races from a web service

```
declare
  l_response clob;
  l_part     varchar2(4000 char);
  l_offset   pls_integer;
begin
  l_response := apex_web_service.make_rest_request
        (p_url          => 'http://ergast.com/api/f1/current.json'
        ,p_http_method => 'GET'
        );
  sys.dbms_output.put_line (apex_web_service.g_status_code);
  if apex_web_service.g_status_code between 200 and 299 then
    while apex_string.next_chunk (
```

```
                p_str    => l_response
                ,p_chunk  => l_part
                ,p_offset => l_offset
                ,p_amount => 4000)
    loop
      sys.dbms_output.put_line (l_part);
    end loop;
  end if;
end;
```

{"MRData":{"xmlns":"http:\/\/ergast.com\/mrd\/1.5","series":"f1","url":"ht
tp://ergast.com/api/f1/current.json","limit":"30","offset":"0","total":"22"
,"RaceTable":{"season":"2022","Races":[{"season":"2022","round":"1",...
<rest of the response omitted for brevity>

When the web service requires that you specify request headers, it might not be clear how to do that at first.

Setting request headers is done by assigning values to the global variable g_request_ headers, specified in the apex_web_service package.

Listing 15-2 shows how to set the request header for a Bearer token authorization, concatenating the text "Bearer " (with a trailing space) and a local variable "l_bearer_ token", as well as a request header containing the content type of the body that you send when invoking the web service with an HTTP GET request.

Listing 15-2. Setting request headers

```
apex_web_service.g_request_headers(1).name  := 'Authorization';
apex_web_service.g_request_headers(1).value := 'Bearer ' || l_bearer_token;
apex_web_service.g_request_headers(2).name  := 'Content-Type';
apex_web_service.g_request_headers(2).value := 'application/json';
```

As the request headers are set in a global variable, it is advisable to clear them after the web service call. This prevents other web service invocations from reusing the same request headers meant for a specific web service. Clearing the request headers can be done via the following.

```
apex_web_service.clear_request_headers;
```

While the preceding method of setting the request headers works as expected, a packaged procedure can do it all.

```
apex_web_service.set_request_headers (
    p_name_01  => 'Authorization'
   ,p_value_01 => 'Bearer ' || l_bearer_token
   ,p_name_02  => 'Content-Type'
   ,p_value_02 => 'application/json'
);
```

Invoking this procedure has the advantage of resetting request headers by default; you don't have to worry about them. They are only used for the current web service call. Up to five request headers can be set via the set_request_headers procedure.

Much more is possible with the APEX_WEB_SERVICE package, such as basic authentication, OAuth authentication, specifying which Oracle Wallet to use, and sending a multipart/form request body to a web service.

A common requirement is to have multiple endpoints that the web service needs to point to, depending on the environment. For development, you want to point to endpoint A, while production should point to endpoint B. This can be achieved using conditional compilation (see Chapter 6 for more details).

Listing 15-3 is an example of a variable declaration that points to different endpoints depending on the static boolean values in the environment_pkg.

Listing 15-3. One variable, different endpoints per environment

```
l_url constant varchar2(50) :=
   $if environment_pkg.development
   $then 'url to endpoint A'
   $elsif environment_pkg.production
   $then 'url to endpoint B'
   $end;
```

The declarations of the static booleans in environment_pkg look something like the following.

```
development constant boolean := TRUE;
production  constant boolean := FALSE;
```

Getting Data from JSON

When working with Oracle Database 12 or higher, you are better off using the built-in JSON functionality (see Chapters 11, 12, 13 and 14) over APEX's functionality. The performance of built-in JSON functionality is far superior to apex_json.

You already retrieved a JSON document containing Formula 1 data. Listing 15-4 is a small sample of this response, nicely formatted.

Listing 15-4. Formatted JSON response

```
{
    "MRData": {
        "xmlns": "http:\/\/ergast.com\/mrd\/1.5",
        "series": "f1",
        "url": "http://ergast.com/api/f1/current.json",
        "limit": "30",
        "offset": "0",
        "total": "22",
        "RaceTable": {
            "season": "2022",
            "Races": [
                {
                    "season": "2022",
                    "round": "1",
                    "url": "http:\/\/en.wikipedia.org\/wiki\/2022_Bahrain_
                    Grand_Prix",
                    "raceName": "Bahrain Grand Prix",
                    // omitted for brevity
                    // there are details of 22 races
                    // in this section, such as circuits
                }
            ]
        }
    }
}
```

Before you can extract data from this JSON document, you need to parse the JSON document into an internal format.

```
apex_json.parse (p_values => races
                ,p_source => l_races
                );
```

Where `races` is a local variable of type `apex_json.t_values` is the internal format needed. In the local variable, `l_races` is the response from the call to the web services, which data type is CLOB.

The number of races in this season is stored in the `total` attribute in the `MRData` object. Because this value is expected to be a number, you can extract it using the `get_number` function.

```
apex_json.get_number (
    p_path   => 'MRData.total'
    ,p_values => races
    );
```

Using a dot notation, you indicate the path that leads to the total number of races. Similarly, you can extract the season, located one level deeper in the `RaceTable` object.

```
apex_json.get_number (
    p_path   => 'MRData.RaceTable.season'
    ,p_values => races
    );
```

Note   Names in a path are case-sensitive. You cannot find the node you are looking for if you use the wrong case.

The names of all the season races are located in an array of objects in the `Races` attribute. Getting the first race name of the season can be done by adjusting the path accordingly.

```
apex_json.get_varchar2
    (p_path => 'MRData.RaceTable.Races[1].raceName'
    ,p_values => races
    );
```

Listing 15-5 is a full-fledged example with the call to the web service and showing different values from the JSON document.

Listing 15-5. Extracting values from JSON document

```
declare
    races apex_json.t_values;
    l_races clob;
    l_elements apex_t_varchar2;
begin
    l_races := apex_web_service.make_rest_request
                (p_url=> 'http://ergast.com/api/f1/current.json'
                ,p_http_method => 'GET'
                );
    if apex_web_service.g_status_code between 200 and 299
    then
        apex_json.parse (p_values => races
                        ,p_source => l_races
                        );
        sys.dbms_output.put_line (
            'Season: '||
            apex_json.get_number
                (p_path   => 'MRData.RaceTable.season'
                ,p_values => races)
        );
        sys.dbms_output.put_line (
            'Nr of races: '||
            apex_json.get_number
                (p_path   => 'MRData.total'
                ,p_values => races)
        );
        sys.dbms_output.put_line (
            'First Race: '||
            apex_json.get_varchar2
                (p_path => 'MRData.RaceTable.Races[1].raceName'
                ,p_values => races)
        );
```

```
    end if;
end;
```

```
Season: 2022
Nr of races: 22
First Race: Bahrain Grand Prix
```

Basic Spatial Functionality

The web service used in this chapter also includes the circuits' coordinates—latitude (lat) and longitude (long). These values can be seen in the following JSON snippet, which is not a complete JSON document, in the Location object.

```
"Races": [
            {
                "season": "2022",
                "round": "15",
                "url": "http:\/\/en.wikipedia.org\/wiki\/2022_Dutch_
                Grand_Prix",
                "raceName": "Dutch Grand Prix",
                "Circuit": {
                    "circuitId": "zandvoort",
                    "url": "http:\/\/en.wikipedia.org\/wiki\/Circuit_
                    Zandvoort",
                    "circuitName": "Circuit Park Zandvoort",
                    "Location": {
                        "lat": "52.3888",
                        "long": "4.54092",
                        "locality": "Zandvoort",
                        "country": "Netherlands"
                    }
                },
```

The following expression extracts the latitude, located in the Location object, for the 15th race (Zandvoort), which is also the 15th object in the array.

```
apex_json.get_number (p_path => 'MRData.RaceTable.Races[15].Circuit.
Location.lat'
                        ,p_values => races)
```

And a similar expression for the longitude.

To work with all spatial functions that Oracle Database offers, the coordinates need to be altered into the correct data type, mdsys.sdo_geometry.

This is done in the following code fragment, where l_circuit is a local variable.

```
l_circuit := apex_spatial.point
  (p_lon =>  apex_json.get_number
    (p_path => 'MRData.RaceTable.Races[15].Circuit.Location.long'
    ,p_values => races)
  ,p_lat => apex_json.get_number
    (p_path => 'MRData.RaceTable.Races[15].Circuit.Location.lat'
    ,p_values => races)
  );
```

Now that the values from the JSON document are converted to a real geometry, let's use spatial functions to determine the distance between Oosterhout in the Netherlands and the circuit in Zandvoort. Listing 15-6 is the complete code sample where two geometries are constructed with apex_spatial. The sdo_distance spatial function determines the distance (in kilometers) between the two. For example, you can look up the coordinates for your hometown using Google Maps.

Listing 15-6. How far is my hometown from the Zandvoort circuit?

```
declare
    l_circuit   mdsys.sdo_geometry;
    l_hometown mdsys.sdo_geometry;
    races       apex_json.t_values;
    l_races     clob;
begin
    l_hometown := apex_spatial.point
                    (p_lon => 4.861316883708699
                    ,p_lat => 51.64485385756768
                    );
```

```
    l_races := apex_web_service.make_rest_request
                (p_url         => 'http://ergast.com/api/f1/current.json'
                ,p_http_method => 'GET'
                );
    apex_json.parse (p_values => races
                    ,p_source => l_races
                    );
    l_circuit := apex_spatial.point
                    (p_lon =>  apex_json.get_number (p_path => 'MRData.
                    RaceTable.Races[15].Circuit.Location.long'
                                          ,p_values => races)
                    ,p_lat => apex_json.get_number (p_path => 'MRData.
                    RaceTable.Races[15].Circuit.Location.lat'
                                          ,p_values => races)
                    );
    sys.dbms_output.put_line (
        'The distance from my hometown to the circuit is '
        ||sdo_geom.sdo_distance
            (geom1 => l_hometown
            ,geom2 => l_circuit
            ,unit  => 'unit=KM')
        ||' km'
    );
end;
```

```
The distance from my hometown to the circuit is 85.64951103008 km
```

Utilities for Text Manipulations

You learned how to display a CLOB by taking advantage of the apex_string.next_chunk
packaged function, but there are many more cool functions worth investigating.

One of our personal favorites is split. Listing 15-7 shows an example of this
function.

Listing 15-7. Example usage of apex_string.split

```
select column_value
  from apex_string.split
         (p_str => 'this:should:be:shown:as:a:table'
         ,p_sep => ':')

COLUMN_VALUE
------------
this
should
be
shown
as
a
table
```

As you can see in Listing 15-7, the split function turns a character-separated string, which can also be a CLOB, into a nested table type.

There must also be a join function when there is a split function. The input nested table is of type apex_t_varchar2. You can see an example of this functionality and the output in Listing 15-8.

Listing 15-8. Example usage of apex_string.join

```
declare
   l_ename_t apex_t_varchar2;
begin
   select ename
     bulk collect
     into l_ename_t
     from emp;
   sys.dbms_output.put_line (
     apex_string.join (p_table => l_ename_t
                      ,p_sep   => '~'
                      )
   );
end;
```

SMITH~ALLEN~WARD~JONES~MARTIN~BLAKE~CLARK~SCOTT~KING~TURNER~ADAMS~JAMES~FOR
D~MILLER

It must be noted that the above apex_string.join function can also be achieved
with the SQL function listagg. The maximum size that the listagg function can handle
depends on the setting of the max_string_size initialization parameter. When the listagg
function doesn't suffice, it exceeds the length limits, apex_string.join_clobs can fill
this void.

Formatting a Message

When you need to format a message, the `format` function is really helpful. This function
allows you to create a message with up to 19 substitution variable placeholders.
Listing 15-9 is an example of a formatted error message with substitution parameters.

Listing 15-9. A nicely formatted error message with variables

```
raise_application_error
   (-20000
   ,apex_string.format (p_message => q'{The combination %0, %1, and %2 is
   not allowed}'
                        ,p0 => 'A'
                        ,p1 => 'B'
                        ,p2 => 'C'
                        )
   );

Error report -
ORA-20000: The combination A, B, and C is not allowed
ORA-06512: at line 2
```

This function also provides an argument, p_max_length, which can prevent the
message from becoming too long. The default value for this argument is 1000.

When you need to preserve the layout of a multiline message, then the p_prefix
argument is very useful. The given prefix and the leading whitespace are removed from
each line. Listing 15-10 shows an example of a multiline message and the output. Note
that all the leading whitespace is removed, but the resulting text is indented as intended.

Listing 15-10. Preserve the layout of a multiline message

```
begin
   sys.dbms_output.put_line (
      apex_string.format (
         p_message => q'{Things you should do:
                        !   * Get quality sleep
                        !   * Eat Healthy
                        !   * Exercise regularly
                        !and all will be well}'
         ,p_prefix => '!'
      ));
end;
/

Things you should do:
   * Get quality sleep
   * Eat Healthy
   * Exercise regularly
and all will be well
```

Please Initial Here

A nice little utility in the APEX_STRING package is `get_initials`. This function transforms names into initials. It outputs the first letter of each word, in uppercase, with a maximum that you specify. The default is to get two letters back. If there are more words than `p_cnt`, you get the initials from the *first* `p_cnt` words. Listing 15-11 is an example of this function. Note that the name input is in lowercase and specified to get a maximum of four letters back. The result is two letters, only two words in the input string, changed to uppercase.

Listing 15-11. Retrieving initials

```
begin
   sys.dbms_output.put_line (
      apex_string.get_initials (
         p_str => 'alex nuijten'
```

```
        ,p_cnt => 4
    )
  );
end;
```

AN

A more dynamic way to get all the initials from a given name can be obtained by using a regular expression to count the number of words there are in a name, something along the lines of the following example:

```
declare
  l_str varchar2(140) := 'Willem-Alexander Claus George Ferdinand';
begin
  sys.dbms_output.put_line (
    apex_string.get_initials (
      p_str => l_str
      ,p_cnt => regexp_count (l_str, '[[:punct:][:space:]]') + 1
    )
  );
end;
```

WACGF

Parsing Data

A common requirement is to upload a file to the database, let's say an Excel or CSV file, and parse it to get the content and store it in database tables. This requirement can be quite challenging, especially when you need to escape certain values when there are multiple sheets in the Excel file, and so on. This is where apex_data_parser shines and can make your programs elegant.

Business Case

The examples in this section are part of a business case. Users of our application can upload CSV files to the database. These files are stored in a BLOB column. In this case, the TEMP_FILES table that holds the uploaded files have the columns outlined in Table 15-1.

Table 15-1. *Columns in the TEMP_FILES Table*

Column Name	Purpose
ID	Primary key to identify which file to process
Filename	Name of the uploaded file, should include the file extension
Mime_type	Mime type, in this case, should be "text/csv"
Blob_content	The uploaded file in binary format

Caution   The filename extension is used by the APEX_DATA_PARSER package to identify how the file should be parsed. In this case, the filename should be suffixed with .csv.

The files contain payment data, such as payment_date, payment_method, currency, amount, and so on. The delimiter used in the CSV file can vary from one to the other; sometimes it's a comma, sometimes a semi-colon. In some of the files, the headers are in quotes; in others, they are not.

As the application allows different files to be uploaded, the signatures of each file can be quite different. The header in the file determines how you should use the data within. There can be many more columns in the file that you need, but these can be ignored.

For each file, you know where the relevant information can be found.

A target table, called DESTINATION_TBL, stores the parsed data.

You must deal with many variations; implementing this is certainly not trivial.

Let's Parse!

The first step to implementing the requirements is to determine which variation of the payment file you are dealing with.

Because there are a finite set of file variations, in this case, you can define constants with the known structure of each header line. Listing 15-12 defines the constants for two different headers: one for a Mollie file and one for a PayPal file. The data type for the constants is apex_t_varchar2, a nested table type. Even though every column in the file isn't used to extract data from, later on, you still need to declare them in the constant. As you can see, the structure of both files is quite different.

Listing 15-12. Constants for the different file headers

```
l_mollie_headers constant apex_t_varchar2
     := apex_t_varchar2
        ('DATE_'
        ,'PAYMENT_METHOD'
        ,'CURRENCY'
        ,'AMOUNT'
        ,'STATUS'
        ,'ID'
        ,'DESCRIPTION'
        ,'CONSUMER_NAME'
        ,'CONSUMER_BANK_ACCOUNT'
        ,'CONSUMER_BIC'
        ,'SETTLEMENT_CURRENCY'
        ,'SETTLEMENT_AMOUNT'
        ,'SETTLEMENT_REFERENCE'
        ,'AMOUNT_REFUNDED'
        );
l_paypal_headers constant apex_t_varchar2
    := apex_t_varchar2
       ('DATE_'
       ,'TIME'
       ,'TIME_ZONE'
       ,'DESCRIPTION'
       ,'CURRENCY'
       ,'GROSS'
       ,'FEE'
       ,'NET'
       ,'BALANCE'
       ,'TRANSACTION_ID'
       ,'FROM_EMAIL_ADDRESS'
       ,'NAME'
       ,'BANK_NAME'
       ,'BANK_ACCOUNT'
       ,'SHIPPING_AND_HANDLING_AMOUNT'
```

```
  ,'SALES_TAX'
  ,'INVOICE_ID'
  ,'REFERENCE_TXN_ID'
  );
```

The next step would be to extract the first line, the header, from the uploaded CSV file. This file header is stored in a local variable, also an `apex_t_varchar2`.

You can use the `discover` function in the APEX_DATA_PARSER package to discover the file you are dealing with. This function returns a CLOB value with the column profile of the file. You can retrieve information about the columns by feeding this profile into the `get_columns` function, such as the following.

- Column position

- Column name

- Data type

- Format mask

With a single select statement, you can extract this information shown in Listing 15-13. As an argument, it is P_ID. It needs the primary key of the uploaded file you want to process.

Listing 15-13. Extract the column names from the file

```
select column_name
  bulk collect
  into l_file_headers
  from temp_files tf
 cross
  join table (apex_data_parser.get_columns
                (apex_data_parser.discover
                    (p_content   => tf.blob_content
                    ,p_file_name => tf.filename
                )))
    where tf.id = p_id;
```

Tip   The `table` operator in Listing 15-13 has been optional since Oracle Database 12.2. You are no longer required to use it. But it can make your code more legible and easier to understand.

Once you have the profile of the file and the names of the columns in that file, you can compare this with the predefined file patterns (the constants declared earlier).

```
case l_file_headers
when l_mollie_headers
then
    process_mollie;
when l_paypal_headers
then
    process_paypal;
end case;
```

We prefer to use a searched case statement. When there is no match (an unknown file was uploaded), it raises a CASE_NOT_FOUND exception. This can be handled and provide feedback to the application that an incorrect file was uploaded.

After a match is found, the file can finally be processed. You need a separate procedure to extract the relevant information for each file type.

You can retrieve all data from the uploaded file using the `parse` function from the APEX_DATA_PARSER package. Up to 300 columns are supported.

Listing 15-14 shows how to use the `parse` function to insert the relevant data into DESTINATION_TBL.

Listing 15-14. Move the data from the file into the table

```
insert into destination_tbl
    (date_
    ,payment_method
    ,currency
    ,amount
    ,status
    ,description
    )
```

```
select to_date (col001, 'yyyy-mm-dd hh24:mi:ss')
          ,col002
          ,col003
          ,col004
          ,col005
          ,col007
      from temp_files tf
    cross
    join table (apex_data_parser.parse
            (p_content    => tf.blob_content
            ,p_file_name => tf.filename
            ,p_skip_rows => 1 -- skip the header line
            ))
  where tf.id = p_id;
```

This gives you an impression of what is possible with the `apex_data_parser,` but it can be even more flexible. In the file profile, which you get from the `discover` function, there is also information about the format mask used in the column and the decimal character used. This information can convert the data from the file into the correct data in the database.

Tip   Using the `validate_conversion` function, you can determine if an expression can be converted to a specified data type. Also, the `default on conversion error` of `to_date` and `to_number` can help in this respect.

Working with ZIP Files

The previous section discussed uploading files to the database, but for a user of the application, this can be quite tedious. In those situations, it might be beneficial that the user can upload ZIP files containing all the files that need to be uploaded to the database.

The other way around is also true. When the user wants to download multiple files from the database, it is more efficient to download a single ZIP file instead of ten separate files.

Unzipping Files

Once the uploaded ZIP file is in the database, extracting the files from it is straightforward. It is good practice to upload the files into a separate table.

To unzip the file, you first need to fetch it into a local BLOB variable based on the name of the ZIP file. This local BLOB variable is being passed as an argument into the get_files function. The return value is of data type apex_zip.t_files, which is an associative array. It is a list of file names inside the ZIP file.

```
declare
    l_zip_file      blob;
    l_unzipped_file blob;
    l_files         apex_zip.t_files;
begin
    select blob_content
      into l_zip_file
      from zip_files
    where filename = 'archive.zip';
    l_files := apex_zip.get_files
                 (p_zipped_blob => l_zip_file);
```

The next step is to get the actual files from the ZIP file. To do this, use the get_file_content function, which takes the name of the files inside the ZIP file. This example uses a simple for loop to insert the files inside the ZIP into the table created earlier.

```
    for i in 1 .. l_files.count
    loop
        l_unzipped_file := apex_zip.get_file_content
                            (p_zipped_blob => l_zip_file
                            ,p_file_name   => l_files(i)
                            );
        insert into temp_files
            (filename
            ,blob_content
            )
        values
            (l_files (i)
```

```
            ,l_unzipped_file
            );
    end loop;
end;
```

And that is all that is needed to extract a ZIP file and store the files in a database table.

When the ZIP file contains folders, the filenames reflect that in the form of dir/subdir/filename.

Zipping Files

Creating a ZIP file inside the database, which the application can download, can be useful for the user.

First, you must retrieve the files you want to compress into a ZIP file. For this example, a cursor for loop is used; it does an implicit bulk fetch for 100 rows. The local variable, data type BLOB, is the ZIP file.

```
declare
    l_zip_file blob;
begin
    for r in (select tf.filename
                    ,tf.blob_content
                from temp_files tf
            )
    loop
```

The add_file procedure takes three arguments: the local variable (a ZIP file), the name of the file, and the file content.

```
        apex_zip.add_file (p_zipped_blob => l_zip_file
                          ,p_file_name   => r.filename
                          ,p_content     => r.blob_content
                          );
    end loop;
```

To complete the ZIP file, you need to tell the zipping process that you no longer want to add files to the zip.

```
apex_zip.finish (p_zipped_blob => l_zip_file);
```

The following example stores the result in an existing table.

```
insert into zip_files
    (filename
    ,mime_type
    ,blob_content
    )
values
    ('all_files.zip'
    ,'application/zip'
    ,l_zip_file
    );
end;
```

Summary

This chapter took a closer look at APEX packages. Even when you are not using APEX to develop applications, you can still take advantage of some of its functionality.

You learned about calling a web service and extracting information from a JSON document. The JSON document contained spatial information, so APEX functions could be used to convert them to real spatial geometries. Formatting strings and extracting initials are made easy with apex_string.

Parsing data from files and extracting the relevant information is easy with apex_data_parser.

Finally, you saw how to zip and unzip files from a database.

CHAPTER 16

Processing Data in the Background

Processing data can be quite time-consuming; for instance, when a file is uploaded to the database, and it needs to be parsed and loaded into several tables. As an end user, working with the application grinds to a halt until the process has been completed.

Often the processing of a file (or any other type of data influx—like a web service) can be delayed until later. Moving the process to the background gives the control of the application back to the user, giving the appearance of a fast-responding application, which improves the user experience.

Resource Intensive

Processing data can be resource-intensive, which could hinder the application's users. Postponing data processing later when the peak load on the system is less would be beneficial as it doesn't hinder any users.

Any process that is not time-dependent, generating documents by an external web service or sending out emails from the database, can be offloaded to a background process. You are the best judge of your system if a process can be offloaded to the background.

Queuing

The Merriam-Webster dictionary defines *queuing* as "a data structure that consists of a list of records such that records are added at one end and removed from the other."

© Alex Nuijten, Patrick Barel 2023
A. Nuijten and P. Barel, *Modern Oracle Database Programming*, https://doi.org/10.1007/978-1-4842-9166-5_16

At the most basic level, messages are enqueued into a queue, and each message is dequeued and processed once by a consumer. The message stays on the queue until it is removed by dequeuing or if the message is expired. The producer of the message determines when a message expires. Messages are not necessarily dequeued in the order that they were enqueued.

Within Oracle Database, queuing is a full-featured messaging solution. Point-to-point, publish/subscribe, persistent, and non-persistent messaging. There are many ways to interact with the queuing functionality, including PL/SQL, JMS, JDBC, .NET, Python, and Node.js.

Oracle Database offers two types of queuing systems: Transactional Event Queues (TEQ) and Advanced Queuing (AQ). TEQ is a high-performance partitioned implementation with multiple event streams per queue. AQ is a disk-based implementation for simpler workflow use cases. In this chapter, the focus is on AQ.

The Use Case

Several CSV files with the latest details are uploaded through an application to keep the Formula 1 database up to date. There are many details to store, like lap times, pit stop information, qualifications results, and so on.

Processing all the different results from the files takes a considerable amount of time and can be resource-intensive. While these files are parsed and processed, the application doesn't respond, and users complain about this.

By moving the parsing and processing of the files to a later moment in time, the control of the application can be returned to the user.

At a high level, the plan is to store the files in a database table. A message with the primary key of the newly created record is placed on a queue. When this is done, the control is passed back to the user.

Later, the messages on the queue are retrieved, indicating which files still need to be processed. When the processing is done, the message from the queue can be removed, and the record from the staging table can be removed (but this is not necessary for the process, it might be useful to keep them just in case).

Reading the messages from the queue can be done at a timed interval with a scheduler job, but AQ has a better method for it, which is explored later.

Setup

To be able to work with AQ, extra privileges are required. The privileges related to working with AQ are outlined in Table 16-1.

Table 16-1. *Privileges*

Operations	Privileges
Create, drop, and monitor own queues	Execute privileges on DBMS_AQADM
Create, drop, and monitor any queues	Execute privileges on DBMS_AQADM and the role AQ_ADMINISTRATOR_ROLE
Enqueue and dequeue own queues	Execute privileges on DBMS_AQ
Enqueue and dequeue another queue	Execute privileges on DBMS_AQ The owner of the other queue can grant privileges with DBMS_AQADM.GRANT_QUEUE_PRIVILEGE
Enqueue and Dequeue any queue	Execute privileges on DBMS_AQ The AQ admin must grant ENQUEUE ANY QUEUE and DEQUEUE ANY QUEUE using DBMS_AQADM.GRANT_SYSTEM_PRIVILEGE

For the use case, execute privileges on dbms_aqadm and dbms_aq. This allows you to create and drop queues and enqueue and dequeue messages.

As described in the high-level plan, a staging table is needed to hold the uploaded files. The table includes the columns outlined in Table 16-2.

Table 16-2. *Structure of the Staging table*

Column Name	Purpose
FileID	Primary key to identify which file to process
Filename	Name of the uploaded file, should include the file extension
Mime_type	Mime type, in our case, should be "text/csv"
Blob_content	The uploaded file in binary format
Processed	A yes/no flag indicating if the file has been processed
Uploaded_ts	A timestamp to register when the file was uploaded, default: `systimestamp`
Processed_ts	A timestamp that records the completion of the processing

Queue Table and Queue

The message (also called the *payload*) to be placed in the queue is defined by an object type. In this case, the object type is defined as follows.

```
create noneditionable
type file_payload_ot as object
(fileid number)
/
```

This use case is very straightforward, but you can create an object type with many more attributes.

Based on this object type, a queue table can be created using the DBMS_AQADM package.

```
begin
  sys.dbms_aqadm.create_queue_table (
    queue_table        => 'file_process_qt'
  , queue_payload_type => 'file_payload_ot'
    );
end;
/
```

This creates a queue table based on the payload object type that was created earlier.

In this queue table, a queue is needed where the messages are placed and removed. It is possible to have multiple queues in a single queue table, but that's beyond the scope of the use case. The queue is created and started with the following statement.

```
begin
    sys.dbms_aqadm.create_queue
        ( queue_name  => 'file_process_q'
        , queue_table => 'file_process_qt'
        );
    sys.dbms_aqadm.start_queue
        ( queue_name => 'file_process_q' );
end;
/
```

When a queue is started, it is ready to accept messages to be enqueued.

After these actions, several new extra objects are in the database to support the queue functionality.

```
select object_name
     , object_type
from   user_objects
where  object_name like 'AQ%'
/
OBJECT_NAME                OBJECT_TYPE
------------------------    ------------------------
AQ$FILE_PROCESS_QT          VIEW
AQ$_FILE_PROCESS_QT_E       QUEUE
AQ$_FILE_PROCESS_QT_F       VIEW
AQ$_FILE_PROCESS_QT_H       TABLE
AQ$_FILE_PROCESS_QT_I       INDEX
AQ$_FILE_PROCESS_QT_T       INDEX

6 rows selected.
```

Enqueue and Dequeue

Placing a message on the queue is done by calling dbms_aq.enqueue. While enqueuing a message, many properties can be set, such as specifying a delay or when a message should expire, but for the straightforward enqueue, the defaults are perfectly fine. For example, by default, the enqueuing follows the main transaction. When the session that enqueues a message rolls back the transaction, the message is removed from the queue. This behavior can be overruled; the message stay enqueued even if the main transaction rolls back.

The options for enqueuing are set through a variable of the following type.

```
sys.dbms_aq.enqueue_options_t
```

The following code enqueues a message.

```
declare
    l_enqueue_options     sys.dbms_aq.enqueue_options_t;
    l_message_properties  sys.dbms_aq.message_properties_t;
    l_msgid               raw( 16 );
    l_payload             file_payload_ot;
begin
    l_payload := file_payload_ot (1234);
    sys.dbms_aq.enqueue
        ( queue_name           => 'file_process_q'
        , enqueue_options      => l_enqueue_options
        , message_properties => l_message_properties
        , payload              => l_payload
        , msgid                => l_msgid
        );
end;
/
```

Caution   The queue_name argument for enqueuing and dequeuing refers to the name of the queue, not the queue table.

The message appears in the result set when the file_process_qt queue table is queried.

```
select user_data
  from file_process_qt
/

USER_DATA(FILEID)
--------------------------
FILE_PAYLOAD_OT(1234)
```

Rolling back the transaction removes it again.

```
rollback
/
Rollback complete.
```

```
select user_data
  from file_process_qt
/
no rows selected
```

To dequeue a message from a queue, the dbms_aq.dequeue procedure is used. Like with the enqueue procedure, the default settings for dequeuing are well-chosen and suffice in most situations. By default, the dequeue procedure follows the main transaction. When a message is dequeued and the transaction is rolled back, the message is not removed from the queue.

Dequeuing options are set through a local variable of the following type.

```
sys.dbms_aq.dequeue_options_t;
```

The following code dequeues a message from the queue.

```
declare
    l_dequeue_options     sys.dbms_aq.dequeue_options_t;
    l_message_properties sys.dbms_aq.message_properties_t;
    l_msgid               raw( 16 );
    l_payload             file_payload_ot;
begin
    sys.dbms_aq.dequeue
```

```
    ( queue_name            => 'file_process_q'
    , dequeue_options       => l_dequeue_options
    , message_properties    => l_message_properties
    , payload               => l_payload
    , msgid                 => l_msgid
    );
  sys.dbms_output.put_line
    ( 'File to be processed is [' || l_payload.fileid || ']' );
end;
/
File to be processed is [1234]
```

When there is no message to dequeue, the procedure waits until there is a message. The default setting for wait is *forever*. This can be overruled by setting the wait dequeue option to no_wait or a specific number of seconds to wait.

```
l_dequeue_options.wait := dbms_aq.no_wait;
```

Wait a maximum time of three seconds.

```
l_dequeue_options.wait := 3;
```

When the wait time is elapsed, or no_wait is specified, an exception is raised when there is no message on the queue.

```
ORA-25228: timeout or end-of-fetch during message dequeue from BOOK.FILE_
PROCESS_Q
```

Wrapper Procedures

For this use case, a procedure is needed to store the file in the staging table and place a message on the queue. The wrapper procedure to enqueue a message is defined as follows.

```
procedure process_later (p_fileid in staging.fileid%type)
is
   l_enqueue_options    sys.dbms_aq.enqueue_options_t;
   l_message_properties sys.dbms_aq.message_properties_t;
```

```
  l_msgid                  raw( 16 );
  l_payload                file_payload_ot;
begin
  l_payload := file_payload_ot( p_fileid );
  sys.dbms_aq.enqueue
    ( queue_name          => 'file_process_q'
    , enqueue_options     => l_enqueue_options
    , message_properties  => l_message_properties
    , payload             => l_payload
    , msgid               => l_msgid
    );
end process_later;
```

The procedure called by the application to store the file in the staging table is defined
as follows.

```
procedure upload_file
            ( p_filename     in staging.filename%type
            , p_mime_type    in staging.mime_type%type
            , p_blob_content in staging.blob_content%type
            )
is
  l_fileid staging.fileid%type;
begin
  insert into staging
    ( filename
    , mime_type
    , blob_content
    , upload_ts
    , processed)
  values
    ( p_filename
    , p_mime_type
    , p_blob_content
    , systimestamp
    , 'N')
```

```
        returning fileid
            into l_fileid;
        -- When the file is stored in the table
        -- place a message on the queue to
        -- initiate the processing at a later time
        process_later( p_fileid => l_fileid );
end;
/
```

There also needs to be a procedure to process the file and distribute the data to the correct tables. For this chapter, the implementation of that procedure is irrelevant. The following procedure is implemented to simulate the processing of the file.

```
procedure process_file (p_fileid in staging.fileid%type)
is
begin
    sys.dbms_session.sleep( 3 ); -- simulate hard work
    update staging
    set    processed = 'Y'
         , processed_ts = systimestamp
    where   fileid = p_fileid;
end process_file;
/
```

This procedure first waits three seconds, after which the processed flag is set to 'Y', and the processed timestamp is populated with the current timestamp.

PL/SQL Callback Notification

Once the file is uploaded to a staging table, and a message is placed in the queue, how do you kick off the processing?

One method is to have a scheduled job run, let's say, every day at a specified time. The downside of a scheduled job is that it would mean that the job also runs when there are no files to be processed. The files could also be uploaded after running the job, resulting in delayed processing. It would also mean that the job runs even if the system is really busy at that time, which would hinder the system's users.

Queues have a better trick up their sleeve; PL/SQL callback notification. Callback notification can initiate a PL/SQL procedure when a message is added to the queue. When a message is enqueued, the callback procedure is started automatically. When this happens, it is handled by the database, most likely when it is "quiet." The downside is that there is no control over *when* the file is processed.

Some steps must be taken to set up the PL/SQL callback notification. First, the queue table must allow multiple consumers to dequeue messages. A consumer is an agent that reads messages in the queue.

Unfortunately, the queue table can't be altered to allow multiple consumers. This can only be specified at creation time. To remove the queue table and queue, execute the following code.

```
begin
    dbms_aqadm.stop_queue
        ( queue_name => 'file_process_q' );
    dbms_aqadm.drop_queue
        ( queue_name => 'file_process_q' );
    dbms_aqadm.drop_queue_table
        ( queue_table => 'file_process_qt' );
end;
/
```

A queue can't be dropped when it has been started. It must be stopped first.

The following code creates a new queue table with multiple consumers enabled and based on the same object type.

```
begin
    sys.dbms_aqadm.create_queue_table
        ( queue_table       => 'file_process_qt'
        , queue_payload_type => 'file_payload_ot'
        , multiple_consumers => true
        );
end;
/
```

After the queue table is re-created, the queue must also be reinstated.

```
begin
   sys.dbms_aqadm.create_queue
      ( queue_name  => 'file_process_q'
      , queue_table => 'file_process_qt'
      );
   sys.dbms_aqadm.start_queue
      ( queue_name => 'file_process_q' );
end;
/
```

These actions lead to additional objects being created in the database.

```
select object_name
     , object_type
from   user_objects
where  object_name like 'AQ%'
/
OBJECT_NAME                  OBJECT_TYPE
------------------------     ----------------------
AQ$FILE_PROCESS_QT           VIEW
AQ$FILE_PROCESS_QT_R         VIEW
AQ$FILE_PROCESS_QT_S         VIEW
AQ$_FILE_PROCESS_QT_E        QUEUE
AQ$_FILE_PROCESS_QT_F        VIEW
AQ$_FILE_PROCESS_QT_G        TABLE
AQ$_FILE_PROCESS_QT_H        TABLE
AQ$_FILE_PROCESS_QT_I        TABLE
AQ$_FILE_PROCESS_QT_L        TABLE
AQ$_FILE_PROCESS_QT_N        SEQUENCE
AQ$_FILE_PROCESS_QT_S        TABLE
AQ$_FILE_PROCESS_QT_T        TABLE
AQ$_FILE_PROCESS_QT_V        EVALUATION CONTEXT

13 rows selected.
```

Before the consumer can subscribe to the queue and specify which PL/SQL routine to call, the PL/SQL callback procedure must be created.

The PL/SQL callback procedure *must* adhere to the following signature.

```
procedure plsqlcallback(
  context  IN  RAW
, reginfo  IN  SYS.AQ$_REG_INFO
, descr    IN  SYS.AQ$_DESCRIPTOR
, payload  IN  RAW
, payloadl IN  NUMBER
);
```

For this simple use case, the descr argument contains all the information that is needed. The other arguments can be used for more advanced use cases.

The main purpose of the PL/SQL callback procedure is to dequeue the message and call the file processing functionality.

```
procedure process_file_callback( context  in raw
                               , reginfo  in sys.aq$_reg_info
                               , descr    in sys.aq$_descriptor
                               , payload  in raw
                               , payloadl in number)
is
   l_dequeue_options     sys.dbms_aq.dequeue_options_t;
   l_message_properties sys.dbms_aq.message_properties_t;
   l_msgid              raw(16);
   l_payload            file_payload_ot;
begin
   -- Retrieve the message from the queue
   l_dequeue_options.msgid := descr.msg_id;
   l_dequeue_options.consumer_name := descr.consumer_name;
   sys.dbms_aq.dequeue
      ( queue_name          => descr.queue_name
      , dequeue_options     => l_dequeue_options
      , message_properties  => l_message_properties
      , payload             => l_payload
```

```
    , msgid                    => l_msgid
    );
    -- Once the message is dequeued, the real
    -- work can be done in the process file
    -- procedure to parse and process
    -- the file contents
    process_file (p_fileid => l_payload.fileid);
    -- The transaction must be committed to
    -- make sure that the message is removed
    -- from the queue
    commit;
end process_file_callback;
/
```

The procedure should complete the transaction with a commit so that the message is definitively removed from the queue.

With this PL/SQL callback notification in place, a consumer can be created to subscribe to the queue. The name of the subscriber is file_process_subscriber and is added to the file_process_q.

```
begin
    sys.dbms_aqadm.add_subscriber
        ( queue_name => 'file_process_q'
        , subscriber => sys.aq$_agent
                        ( name     => 'file_process_subscriber'
                        , address  => null
                        , protocol => null
                        )
        );
end;
/
```

The final piece of the puzzle is to register the actual callback procedure.

```
begin
    sys.dbms_aq.register
    ( reg_list =>
```

```
      sys.aq$_reg_info_list
      ( sys.aq$_reg_info
        ( name       => 'file_process_q:file_process_subscriber'
        , namespace => dbms_aq.namespace_aq
        , callback  => 'plsql://process_file_callback'
        , context   => null
        )
      )
    , reg_count => 1
    );
end;
/
```

The context argument can be used to pass information (in RAW format) to the callback procedure. In the callback procedure you can use this information, for example, to distinguish between different subscribers to the queue. For this use case this is not needed as there is only one subscriber.

Seeing It in Action

Once all components are in place, the code that the application uses to upload the files to the database initiates the whole process. As the files are not parsed and processed, the control returns immediately back to the user of the application.

```
begin
  upload_file
    ( p_filename     => 'latest.csv'
    , p_mime_type    => 'text/csv'
    , p_blob_content => :file
    );
end;
/
```

The front-end application manages the transactions. The user is in control of ending a transaction with either a commit or rollback.

Once the transaction is ended with a commit, the message on the queue is stored, and the callback procedure is called.

Right after a file is uploaded using the preceding routine, the following can be observed in the staging table.

```
select  to_char (upload_ts,    'hh24:mi:ss.ff9')    as upload_ts
    ,   to_char (processed_ts, 'hh24:mi:ss.ff9')  as processed_ts
    ,   processed_ts - upload_ts                   as elapsed_time
from    staging
/
UPLOAD_TS            PROCESSED_TS         ELAPSED_TIM
------------------  ------------------  -----------
12:28:54.873961000
```

After waiting for a few seconds, the following results can be seen.

```
UPLOAD_TS           PROCESSED_TS         ELAPSED_TIME
------------------  ------------------  --------------------
12:28:54.873961000 12:28:58.108458000 +00 00:00:03.234497
```

Of course, this strongly depends on how "busy" or "quiet" the database is. When the database is busy, the callback function is executed later. There is no API to control or define the number of concurrent PL/SQL notification dequeue processes. This is because AQ messages can come in bursts, and having a fixed number of processes may not always work efficiently. AQ notification automatically starts the appropriate number of background processes (a.k.a. EMON slaves), depending on the total workload and time it takes to execute the user-defined PL/SQL callback procedure.

When a message is enqueued, user SYS starts a new session in the background. The module is DBMS_SCHEDULER, so there must be some involvement of this package in relation to the mechanism. The action is set to something to the effect of "AQ$_PLSQL_NTFN_" followed by a number. The action signals involve AQ and PL/SQL notification. This can be observed by querying gv$session.

```
select  username
    ,   module
    ,   action
from    gv$session
/
```

```
USERNAME      MODULE              ACTION
-----------   ------------------  ---------------------------
SYS           DBMS_SCHEDULER      AQ$_PLSQL_NTFN_4107371948
```

Exception Queue

An exception queue is automatically added when a queue table is created. When an unexpected exception occurs during the execution of the callback procedure, the message that is on the queue is moved to an exception queue.

Querying the user_queues data dictionary view shows two queues in the file_process_qt queue table: one normal and one exception.

```
select name
     , queue_table
     , queue_type
from   user_queues
/
NAME                     QUEUE_TABLE      QUEUE_TYPE
---------------------    ---------------  --------------------
FILE_PROCESS_Q           FILE_PROCESS_QT  NORMAL_QUEUE
AQ$_FILE_PROCESS_QT_E FILE_PROCESS_QT  EXCEPTION_QUEUE
```

For demonstration purposes, the process_file procedure, which is eventually called from the callback procedure, is modified to *always* raise an exception by including the following line in the procedure body.

```
raise zero_divide;
```

This exception goes unhandled in the process_file procedure and is propagated to the calling process_file_callback procedure. As the callback procedure is being called *headless*, there is no client to observe this exception. The message is moved to the exception queue.

This doesn't happen immediately; several attempts are made to execute the procedure successfully. How often these attempts are made and how much delay should be between attempts can be controlled when the queue is created. Two arguments control these settings: max_retries and retry_delay. When these arguments are not filled out, the callback procedure is tried six times before the message is moved to the exception queue. Each attempt is tried immediately. There is no delay.

The movement of the message from the normal queue to the exception queue can be observed when querying the queue table `file_process_qt` in succession.

```
select qt.q_name
     , qt.msgid
     , to_char (systimestamp, 'hh24:mi:ss.ff9') as ts
from   file_process_qt qt
/

Q_NAME                 MSGID                    TS
-------------------- ------------------------ -------------------
FILE_PROCESS_Q         ECA2CF1D94B3043FE0539518 13:45:55.842533000

<< re-execute query from above >>
Q_NAME                 MSGID                    TS
-------------------- ------------------------ -------------------
FILE_PROCESS_Q         ECA2CF1D94B3043FE0539518 13:46:12.811844000

<< re-execute query from above >>
Q_NAME                 MSGID                    TS
-------------------- ------------------------ -------------------
AQ$_FILE_PROCESS_QT_E ECA2CF1D94B3043FE0539518 13:46:15.315077000
```

Once the situation has been remedied and the exceptional situation is gone, the messages from the exception queue can be placed back into the normal queue, which triggers the callback procedure to be executed again.

Before messages can be dequeued from an exception queue, the exception queue must be started for dequeue operations. The following code must be executed to start the exception queue for dequeuing operations.

```
begin
   sys.dbms_aqadm.start_queue
      ( queue_name => 'AQ$_FILE_PROCESS_QT_E'
      , enqueue    => false
      , dequeue    => true
      );
end;
/
```

The exception queue can't be started for enqueue operations.

Moving the messages from the exception to the normal queue can be done by dequeuing them from the exception queue and enqueuing them on the normal queue. The following code shows this for all messages on the exception queue with a simple for-loop construct.

```
declare
    l_dequeue_options     sys.dbms_aq.dequeue_options_t;
    l_message_properties sys.dbms_aq.message_properties_t;
    l_message_handle      raw(16);
    l_payload             file_payload_ot;
    l_enqueue_options     sys.dbms_aq.enqueue_options_t;
begin
    for r in (select qt.msgid
              from   file_process_qt qt
              where  qt.q_name = 'AQ$_FILE_PROCESS_QT_E')
    loop
        l_dequeue_options.msgid := r.msgid;
        sys.dbms_aq.dequeue
            ( queue_name          => 'AQ$_FILE_PROCESS_QT_E'
            , dequeue_options     => l_dequeue_options
            , message_properties => l_message_properties
            , payload             => l_payload
            , msgid               => l_message_handle
            );
        sys.dbms_aq.enqueue
            ( queue_name          => 'file_process_q'
            , enqueue_options     => l_enqueue_options
            , message_properties => l_message_properties
            , payload             => l_payload
            , msgid               => l_message_handle
            );
    end loop;
    commit;
end;
/
```

There are situations where messages are on the exception queue and need to be removed. When this is the case, the exception queue can be purged using the purge_ queue_table procedure from the DBMS_AQADM package.

```
declare
    l_purge_options sys.dbms_aqadm.aq$_purge_options_t;
begin
    sys.dbms_aqadm.purge_queue_table
        ( 'file_process_qt'
        , 'qtview.queue = ''AQ$_FILE_PROCESS_QT_E'''
        , l_purge_options
        );
end;
/
```

Advanced Queuing and JSON

Since Oracle Database 21c, AQ also supports native JSON payloads. This release introduced a native JSON data type. Before this release, working with a JSON payload was possible but was always text-based; for example, with sys.aq$_jms_text_message as the payload data type.

To create a queue table that handles a JSON payload, specify JSON for the queue_ payload_type argument.

```
begin
  sys.dbms_aqadm.create_queue_table (
      queue_table         => 'json_qt'
      ,queue_payload_type => 'json'
      );
end;
/
```

Creating and starting the queue in the queue table is the same as before.

```
begin
    sys.dbms_aqadm.create_queue (
        queue_name   => 'jq'
```

```
        ,queue_table => 'json_qt'
        );
    sys.dbms_aqadm.start_queue (
        queue_name => 'jq'
        );
end;
/
```

The message placed on the queue should be JSON, of course.

```
declare
    l_enqueue_options      sys.dbms_aq.enqueue_options_t;
    l_message_properties sys.dbms_aq.message_properties_t;
    l_msgid                raw (16);
    l_payload              json;
begin
    l_payload := json ('{"Hello" : "World"}');
    sys.dbms_aq.enqueue
        (queue_name          => 'jq'
        ,enqueue_options     => l_enqueue_options
        ,message_properties => l_message_properties
        ,payload             => l_payload
        ,msgid               => l_msgid
        );
    commit;
end;
/
```

When the message is dequeued, keep in mind that the payload is JSON. This means that it should be treated as such when used in dbms_output. In the following example, the returned value should be converted to a string.

```
set serveroutput on
declare
    l_dequeue_options      sys.dbms_aq.dequeue_options_t;
    l_message_properties sys.dbms_aq.message_properties_t;
    l_msgid                raw(16);
```

```
    l_payload              json;
begin
    sys.dbms_aq.dequeue(
        queue_name          => 'jq',
        dequeue_options     => l_dequeue_options,
        message_properties  => l_message_properties,
        payload             => l_payload,
        msgid               => l_msgid
        );
    sys.dbms_output.put_line(
        'Retrieved from the JSON-payload ['
          || json_value (l_payload, '$.Hello' returning varchar2 )
          || ']'
        );
end;
/

Retrieved from the JSON-payload [World]
```

Summary

This chapter examined a common use case to increase the user experience and discussed how AQ plays a role. Offloading processing to a background process gives the impression that the application is very responsive when control is passed back to the user.

Generating PDF documents can take time and be resource-intensive. When this generation is offloaded to a background process, it does not hinder any users by excessive resource consumption.

Because callback procedures run in the background, any exceptions that lead to the message being propagated to the exception queue must be monitored to ensure that the work it was supposed to do is done.

The chapter also included a short example showcasing the native JSON data type introduced in Oracle Database 21c.

CHAPTER 17

Introspecting PL/SQL

Knowing what is going on in an executing PL/SQL block can provide valuable information. Setting client_identifier, module, and action from within a PL/SQL block can help track what each session is doing. In the DBMS_SESSION package, there are supporting procedures and functions for this.

Within the DBMS_UTILITY package are procedures and functions that can identify the call stack in case of an unexpected exception. Even more information about the call stack can be retrieved with `utl_call_stack`, also covered in this chapter.

DBMS_SESSION

Using DBMS_SESSION, you can execute `alter session` commands from PL/SQL. Settings you normally would do in your SQL*Plus or SQLcl session have been made available to your PL/SQL procedures and functions.

current_is_role_enabled

If a certain part of your program needs you to have a certain role enabled, you can use `dbms_session.current_is_role_enabled` to check if the named role is currently enabled. You supply the function with the name of the role you want to check. The function returns `TRUE` if the role is enabled; it returns `FALSE` if it is not.

```
function current_is_role_enabled(rolename varchar2)
   return boolean;
```

© Alex Nuijten, Patrick Barel 2023
A. Nuijten and P. Barel, *Modern Oracle Database Programming*, https://doi.org/10.1007/978-1-4842-9166-5_17

set_role

If the role needed is not enabled but has been granted to you, you can use dbms_ session.set_role to set the role a run time. If the role is already enabled, issuing a set role command again executes without error. The text in the parameter is appended to the "SET ROLE" SQL statement and then executed as dynamic SQL.

```
procedure set_role(role_cmd varchar2);
```

set_nls

Sometimes your programs rely on specific NLS settings; for instance, when converting a string to a date or the other way around. If you want to be sure the NLS settings are done correctly, independent of the user's settings, you can use dbms_session.set_nls to set these specific settings. The procedure takes two parameters, the param name, and its value.

```
procedure set_nls(param varchar2, value varchar2);
```

Calling this procedure is equivalent to issuing alter session set <nls_parameter> = <value>.

The parameter name must begin with NLS. If the value is a text literal, it needs to be embedded in single quotes. The following is an example.

```
set_nls('nls_date_format','''DD-MON-YY''')
```

If the parameter needs a lot of quotes, you might want to use alternative quoting.

```
dbms_session.set_nls('nls_date_format', q'['DD-MON-YY']')
```

Note   Using execute immediate 'alter session ...' has better performance. Also, execute immediate permits multiple parameters in one statement, which is more efficient than calling dbms_session.set_nls multiple times.

---

set_context

To work with context settings, you must create a context using the SQL command in Listing 17-1.

Listing 17-1. Creating an application context

```
create or replace context modp_ctx using modp_pkg
/
```

If you want to set or clear values in this context, you cannot call the DBMS_SESSION package directly.

```
begin
  dbms_session.set_context( namespace => 'modp_ctx'
                          , attribute => 'author1'
                          , value     => 'Alex Nuijten'
                          );
  dbms_session.set_context( namespace => 'modp_ctx'
                          , attribute => 'author2'
                          , value     => 'Patrick Barel'
                          );
end;
/

ORA-01031: insufficient privileges
ORA-06512: at "SYS.DBMS_SESSION", line 141
ORA-06512: at line 2
```

You must create a package to access the procedures in the DBMS_SESSION package. This can be a simple wrapper package, as shown in Listing 17-2. As you can see in the statement in Listing 17-1 creating the application context, this package is connected to the context.

Listing 17-2. modp_pkg to communicate to the context

```
create or replace package modp_pkg as
  procedure set_context
  ( namespace_in in varchar2
```

```
  , attribute_in in varchar2
  , value_in     in varchar2
  , username_in  in varchar2 default null
  , client_id_in in varchar2 default null
  );
  procedure clear_context
  ( namespace_in in varchar2
  , client_id_in in varchar2 default null
  , attribute_in in varchar2 default null
  );
  procedure clear_all_context
  ( namespace_in in varchar2 );
end modp_pkg;
/

create or replace package body modp_pkg as
  procedure set_context
  ( namespace_in in varchar2
  , attribute_in in varchar2
  , value_in     in varchar2
  , username_in  in varchar2 default null
  , client_id_in in varchar2 default null
  ) is
  begin
    dbms_session.set_context(namespace => namespace_in
                            ,attribute => attribute_in
                            ,value     => value_in
                            ,username  => username_in
                            ,client_id => client_id_in);
  end set_context;

  procedure clear_context
  ( namespace_in in varchar2
  , client_id_in in varchar2 default null
  , attribute_in in varchar2 default null
  ) is
```

```
begin
  dbms_session.clear_context(namespace => namespace_in
                            ,client_id => client_id_in
                            ,attribute => attribute_in);
end clear_context;

procedure clear_all_context
( namespace_in in varchar2 ) is
begin
  dbms_session.clear_all_context(namespace => namespace_in);
end clear_all_context;
end modp_pkg;
/
```

Now, when you try to run the same block as before, only now calling the wrapper packages, you can set the context values.

```
begin
  modp_pkg.set_context( namespace_in => 'modp_ctx'
                      , attribute_in => 'author1'
                      , value_in     => 'Alex Nuijten'
                      );
  modp_pkg.set_context( namespace_in => 'modp_ctx'
                      , attribute_in => 'author2'
                      , value_in     => 'Patrick Barel'
                      );
end;
/
PL/SQL procedure successfully completed
```

Note   The wrapper package can be used for multiple contexts. If the package is used for a single context only, it would be better to remove the namespace_in parameter.

You can check the values in the context using a simple select, as follows.

```
select sys_context('modp_ctx','author1') author1
     , sys_context('modp_ctx','author2') author2
from   dual
/
```

```
AUTHOR1              AUTHOR2
-------------------- --------------------
Alex Nuijten         Patrick Barel
```

But you can also use the context values in a predicate in your where clause.

```
select 'author2 = Patrick Barel'
from   dual
where  sys_context('modp_ctx','author2') = 'Patrick Barel'
/
```

```
'AUTHOR2=PATRICKBAREL'
-----------------------
author2 = Patrick Barel
```

Note   This technique is sometimes used for a *parameterized view*, where the context predicate is used as a filter.

---

clear_context

You can call the dbms_session.clear context procedure to clear an attribute in the context. Just as with the set_context procedure, you have to write a wrapper procedure to call this procedure.

```
begin
  dbms_session.clear_context( namespace => 'modp_ctx'
                            , attribute => 'author1' );
  dbms_session.clear_context( namespace => 'modp_ctx'
                            , attribute => 'author2' );
```

```
end;
/
```

```
ORA-01031: insufficient privileges
ORA-06512: at "SYS.DBMS_SESSION", line 155
ORA-06512: at line 2
```

You can clear the attributes using the package shown in Listing 17-2.

```
begin
  modp_pkg.clear_context( namespace_in => 'modp_ctx'
                        , attribute_in => 'author1' );
  modp_pkg.clear_context( namespace_in => 'modp_ctx'
                        , attribute_in => 'author2' );
end;
/
PL/SQL procedure successfully completed
```

clear_all_context

If you want to clear all the attributes in a context, use the dbms_session.clear_all_ context procedure. As with the other context procedures, this cannot be called directly, only through a user-defined package.

set_identifier

When you want to identify the connected session in the v$session data dictionary view, you can use the dbms_session.set_identifier procedure. You can set anything in the parameter, but only the first 64 characters are used.

```
begin
  dbms_session.set_identifier
    ( client_id => 'Whatever you want, whatever you need.' );
end;
/
```

You can see the identifier if you have access to the v$session view.

```
select username
      ,client_identifier
from   v$session
/

USERNAME    CLIENT_IDENTIFIER
---------- ----------------------------------------
BOOK
BOOK        Whatever you want, whatever you need.
```

clear_identifier

To clear the identifier, you can call the set_identifier procedure with an empty string, but it makes more sense to call the dbms_session.clear_identifier procedure.

```
begin
  dbms_session.clear_identifier;
end;
/
```

As you can see, the identifier is cleared.

```
select username
      ,client_identifier
from   v$session
/

USERNAME    CLIENT_IDENTIFIER
---------- ----------------------------------------
BOOK
BOOK
```

sleep

Sometimes you want your session to hold for a short time. You can use the dbms_session.sleep procedure for this.

```
procedure sleep(seconds in number);
```

The parameter also accepts fractions of seconds. The maximum resolution is hundredths of seconds; for example, 1.5, 1.01, and 0.99 are legal values.

Calling this procedure is preferable over calling `dbms_lock.sleep`, which does the same, but this procedure avoids having to grant `dbms_lock` permissions and exposes more sensitive methods.

DBMS_APPLICATION_INFO

Use the procedures in DBMS_APPLICATION_INFO to set runtime information about your program. You can use this information in your generic logging procedures and functions. The module and action are also used by database instrumentation. They are logged for tracing and in various Enterprise Manager reports, unlike `set_client_info,` which is not used by the database, only in your custom code.

set_module

This procedure sets the name of the current module to a new module. When using this procedure in a logging framework, you should note the following: If the procedure or function terminates, it should be set to the previous value, so when the calling program resumes, it is set to the correct value. If there is no previous value, it should be set to `NULL`.

```
procedure set_module(module_name varchar2, action_name varchar2);
```

The maximum length of the parameters is 64 bytes. Longer names are truncated.

set_action

This procedure sets the name of the current action within the current module. The module can be set using the `set_module` procedure.

```
procedure set_action(action_name varchar2);
```

The maximum length of the parameter is 64 bytes. Longer names are truncated.

read_module

This procedure reads the values currently in the module and action fields.

```
procedure read_module( module_name out varchar2
                     , action_name out varchar2);
```

Listing 17-3 shows the general usage of these procedures.

Listing 17-3. module and action usage

```
declare
  l_old_module_name varchar2(64);
  l_old_action_name varchar2(64);
begin
  sys.dbms_application_info.read_module
  ( module_name => l_old_module_name
  , action_name => l_old_action_name
  );
  sys.dbms_application_info.set_module
  ( module_name => 'ModernOracleDatabaseProgramming'
  , action_name => 'DemoDBMS_Application_Info'
  );
  -- do the real work of this program
  --
  -- at the end, reset the module and action
  sys.dbms_application_info.set_module
  ( module_name => l_old_module_name
  , action_name => l_old_action_name
  );
end;
/
```

DBMS_UTILITY

The utility package contains various utility routines, like compile_schema, format_ call_stack, and expand_sql_text. The compile_schema is useful after upgrading the application to ensure that the code base is recompiled when needed. Inspecting related to a view or nested views can easily be done with expand_sql_text. This eliminates the need to inspect the source code manually.

compile_schema

The compile_schema procedure is not a procedure you want to call during the execution of your program but rather a procedure you want to call after installing a new version of your codebase. It compiles all procedures, functions, packages, and triggers in the specified schema. Since it is not necessary to recompile already valid objects, it is recommended to set the flag compile_all to FALSE.

After calling this procedure, you can use the ALL_OBJECTS or USER_OBJECTS view to check if all objects were successfully compiled. The parameters are described in Table 17-1.

Table 17-1. *Parameters for the compile_schema Procedure*

Parameter	Mandatory	Description
schema	Y	The schema that is to be (re)compiled
compile_all		A boolean flag indicating whether all schema objects should be compiled, regardless of whether the object is currently invalid The default value is TRUE
reuse_settings		A boolean flag indicating whether the session settings in the objects should be reused or whether the current session settings should be used instead Default value is FALSE

format_call_stack

It can be very useful to retrieve the call stack, especially during debugging. The dbms_utility.format_call_stack procedure returns a formatted string of the current call stack, including the names of private package procedures and functions. This string can be up to 2000 bytes in size. To demonstrate this, look at the package in Listing 17-4.

Note   Instead of writing your own parser for the call stack, look at the functionality available in utl_call_stack, later in this chapter.

Listing 17-4. Package to demonstrate dbms_utility.format_call_stack

```
create or replace package call_stack_demo is

  procedure packageprocedure;

end call_stack_demo;
/

create or replace package body call_stack_demo is

  procedure privateprocedure is
  begin
    dbms_output.put_line('-- call stack in PRIVATEPROCEDURE --');
    dbms_output.put_line( dbms_utility.format_call_stack );
    dbms_output.put_line('------------------------------------');
  end privateprocedure;

  procedure packageprocedure is
  begin
    dbms_output.put_line('-- call stack in PACKAGEPROCEDURE --');
    dbms_output.put_line( dbms_utility.format_call_stack );
    dbms_output.put_line('------------------------------------');
    privateprocedure;
  end packageprocedure;

end call_stack_demo;
/
```

The following is the output from calling the package procedure.

```
begin
  dbms_output.put_line( '-- call stack in ANONYMOUS BLOCK    --' );
  dbms_output.put_line( dbms_utility.format_call_stack );
  dbms_output.put_line( '-------------------------------------' );
  call_stack_demo.packageprocedure;
end;
/

-- call stack in ANONYMOUS BLOCK    --
----- PL/SQL Call Stack -----
object  line    object
handle  number  name
0x2138aa190   3 anonymous block

-------------------------------------
-- call stack in PACKAGEPROCEDURE --
----- PL/SQL Call Stack -----
object  line    object
handle  number  name
0x6863c2600 13 package body BOOK.CALL_STACK_DEMO.PACKAGEPROCEDURE
0x2138aa190   5 anonymous block

-------------------------------------
-- call stack in PRIVATEPROCEDURE --
----- PL/SQL Call Stack -----
object  line    object
handle  number  name
0x6863c2600   6 package body BOOK.CALL_STACK_DEMO.PRIVATEPROCEDURE
0x6863c2600 15 package body BOOK.CALL_STACK_DEMO.PACKAGEPROCEDURE
0x2138aa190   5 anonymous block

-------------------------------------

PL/SQL procedure successfully completed
```

format_error_stack

Knowing the error stack when an exception occurs may be more important than retrieving the call stack. There are two procedures to retrieve this, dbms_utility.format_error_stack, which includes the error code and description that occurred, and dbms_utility.format_error_backtrace, which doesn't give you the error code, but it returns the full call stack. Not the procedure or function names but the line numbers where the error occurred or where the next procedure or function was called. To demonstrate this, look at the package in Listing 17-5.

Listing 17-5. Package to demonstrate the error stack procedures

```
create or replace package body error_stack_demo is

  procedure privateprocedure is
  begin
    raise no_data_found;
  end privateprocedure;

  procedure packageprocedure is
  begin
    privateprocedure;
  exception
    when others
    then
    dbms_output.put_line('-- error stack in PACKAGEPROCEDURE--');
    dbms_output.put_line( dbms_utility.format_error_stack );
    dbms_output.put_line('------------------------------------');
    dbms_output.put_line('-error backtrace in PACKAGEPROCEDURE');
    dbms_output.put_line( dbms_utility.format_error_backtrace );
    dbms_output.put_line('------------------------------------');
  end packageprocedure;

end error_stack_demo;
/
```

The following is the output from calling the package procedure.

```
begin
  error_stack_demo.packageprocedure;
end;
/

-- error stack in PACKAGEPROCEDURE--
ORA-01403: no data found
ORA-06512: at "BOOK.ERROR_STACK_DEMO", line 5

------------------------------------

-- error backtrace in PACKAGEPROCEDURE--
ORA-06512: at "BOOK.ERROR_STACK_DEMO", line 5
ORA-06512: at "BOOK.ERROR_STACK_DEMO", line 10

------------------------------------

PL/SQL procedure successfully completed
```

Depending on your needs, you can use either one of these procedures.

comma_to_table

Using comma_to_table, you can split a comma-separated string into values in an associative array. This can be useful if a column in your database consists of comma-separated values you want to process individually, especially when the number of elements can differ in every row.

Note dbms_utility.comma_to_table is intended for comma-separated list of identifiers, so the uncl_array used as an example in this section is table of varchar2(227), where 227 is the max length possible for "user"."name"."column"@link format identifiers. You cannot use comma_to_table for any generic list of values, only with a maximum length of 227. If a more generic solution is needed, look into apex_string.split (see Chapter 15).

Let's say you have a view with a column containing all the drivers for a certain constructor, as shown in Listing 17-6.

Listing 17-6. A view containing all the drivers per constructor

```
create or replace view drivers_for_constructors
as
select dcr.constructorid                        as constructorid
    , ctr.name                                  as name
    , listagg( distinct( drv.driverref ), ',' ) as drivers
from    driverconstructors  dcr
join    f1data.constructors ctr
  on ( dcr.constructorid = ctr.constructorid )
join    f1data.drivers      drv
  on ( dcr.driverid      = drv.driverid )
group   by dcr.constructorid
         , ctr.name
/
```

Some constructors only have two drivers, for example, because they only participated for a single season. Some have a plethora of drivers because they have participated since Formula 1 started.

If you want to display the separate drivers for every constructor, you can build a script as you see in Listing 17-7.

Listing 17-7. Display drivers per constructor

```
declare
  l_tablen binary_integer;
  l_tab dbms_utility.uncl_array;
  l_drivername varchar2( 32767 );
begin
  for rec in (select distinct ctr.name
                  , dfc.drivers
            from    drivers_for_constructors dfc
            join    driverconstructors as of period
            for     drivercontract to_date( '20220320'
```

```
                                      , 'YYYYMMDD') dcr
            on     ( dfc.constructorid = dcr.constructorid )
            join   f1data.constructors ctr
            on     ( dfc.constructorid = ctr.constructorid )
            )
 loop
   dbms_output.put_line( rec.name );
   dbms_utility.comma_to_table( list   => rec.drivers
                              , tablen => l_tablen
                              , tab    => l_tab );
   dbms_output.put_line( 'Nr of drivers: '
                       || to_char( l_tablen )
                       );
   for indx in 1 .. l_tablen
   loop
     select d.forename || ' ' || d.surname as drivername
     into   l_drivername
     from   f1data.drivers d
     where  d.driverref = l_tab( indx );
     dbms_output.put_line( to_char( indx )
                         || ') '
                         || l_drivername
                         );
   end loop;
 end loop;
end;
/

Aston Martin
Nr of drivers: 3
1) Nico Hülkenberg
2) Lance Stroll
3) Sebastian Vettel
Mercedes
Nr of drivers: 5
1) Valtteri Bottas
```

2) Lewis Hamilton

3) Michael Schumacher

4) Nico Rosberg

5) George Russell

Red Bull

Nr of drivers: 12

1) Alexander Albon

2) David Coulthard

3) Robert Doornbos

4) Pierre Gasly

5) Christian Klien

6) Daniil Kvyat

7) Vitantonio Liuzzi

8) Max Verstappen

9) Sergio Pérez

10) Daniel Ricciardo

11) Sebastian Vettel

12) Mark Webber

<<Results removed for brevity>>

Haas F1 Team

Nr of drivers: 6

1) Romain Grosjean

2) Esteban Gutiérrez

3) Kevin Magnussen

4) Nikita Mazepin

5) Mick Schumacher

6) Pietro Fittipaldi

PL/SQL procedure successfully completed

Note   This code is not optimized; it only shows the use of dbms_utility. comma_to_table.

---

expand_sql_text

If you want to see what SQL is executed, you can use dbms_utility.expand_sql_text. This recursively replaces any view references in the input SQL with the actual subquery from the view. This procedure is also very useful when debugging SQL Macros.

```
procedure expand_sql_text( input_sql_text  in  clob,
                           output_sql_text out nocopy clob );
```

The view returns all the drivers for a constructor (see Listing 17-6). Using this view, you can query all the drivers for the constructors in the 2022 championship.

```
select distinct c.name
            , dfc.drivers
from    drivers_for_constructors dfc
join    driverconstructors as of period
for     drivercontract to_date('20220320', 'YYYYMMDD') dc
on      ( dfc.constructorid = dc.constructorid )
join    f1data.constructors c
on      ( dfc.constructorid = c.constructorid )
/
```

```
NAME                    DRIVERS
----------------------  ----------------------------------------
Aston Martin            hulkenberg,stroll,vettel
Mercedes                bottas,hamilton,michael_schumacher,
                        rosberg,russell
Red Bull                albon,coulthard,doornbos,gasly,klien,
                        kvyat,liuzzi,max_verstappen,perez,ricciardo
                        ,vettel,webber
Alpine F1 Team          alonso,ocon
Ferrari                 adamich,alboreto,alesi,alonso,amon,
                        arnoux,badoer,baghetti,bandini,barrichello,
                        bell,berger,bondurant,capelli,fisichella,
                        galli,gilles_villeneuve,giunti,ickx,
                        irvine,johansson,larini,lauda,leclerc,
                        mansell,mario_andretti,massa,merzario,
                        michael_schumacher,morbidelli,parkes,pironi,
```

	prost,raikkonen,regazzoni,reutemann, rodriguez,sainz,salo,scarfiotti,scheckter, surtees,tambay,vaccarella,vettel,williams
Alfa Romeo	baldi,bottas,brambilla,cesaris,cheever, depailler,giacomelli,giovinazzi,kubica, mario_andretti,patrese,raikkonen,zhou
McLaren	alliot,alonso,andretti,berger,blundell, bonnier,brundle,button,cesaris,charlton, coulthard,donohue,emerson_fittipaldi, gethin,giacomelli,gilles_villeneuve, hailwood,hakkinen,hamilton,hobbs,hulme,hunt, ickx,johansson,keke_rosberg,kevin_magnussen, kovalainen,lauda,lunger,magnussen,mansell, mass,mclaren,montoya,norris,oliver,perez, piquet,prost,raikkonen,redman,revson, ricciardo,rosa,sainz,scheckter,senna, south,tambay,trimmer,vandoorne,villota, watson,wurz
Williams	aitken,albon,ashley,barrichello,bottas, boutsen,brise,brundle,bruno_senna,button, cogan,coulthard,daly,damon_hill, desire_wilson,frentzen,gene,heidfeld, hulkenberg,ian_scheckter,jones,keegan, keke_rosberg,kubica,laffite,latifi,lees, lombardi,magee,maldonado,mansell, mario_andretti,massa,merzario,migault, montoya,nakajima,palmer,patrese,piquet, pizzonia,prost,ralf_schumacher,regazzoni, resta,reutemann,rosberg,russell,schlesser, senna,sirotkin,stroll,villeneuve,vonlanthen, webber,wurz,zanardi,zapico,zorzi
AlphaTauri	gasly,kvyat,tsunoda
Haas F1 Team	grosjean,gutierrez,kevin_magnussen,mazepin, mick_schumacher,pietro_fittipaldi

```
10 rows selected
<<result formatted manually>>
```

If you want to see the SQL that was executed, use the statement as input for the dbms_utility.expand_sql_text procedure.

```
declare
  l_input_sql  clob;
  l_output_sql clob;
begin
  l_input_sql := q'[
select distinct c.name
              , dfc.drivers
from    drivers_for_constructors dfc
join    driverconstructors as of period
for     drivercontract to_date('20220320', 'YYYYMMDD') dc
on      ( dfc.constructorid = dc.constructorid )
join    f1data.constructors c
on      ( dfc.constructorid = c.constructorid )
  ]';
  dbms_utility.expand_sql_text
  ( input_sql_text => l_input_sql
  , output_sql_text => l_output_sql );
  dbms_output.put_line( l_output_sql );
end;
/

select distinct "A1"."NAME_4"     "NAME"
              , "A1"."DRIVERS_1" "DRIVERS"
from
  (select "A3"."QCSJ_C000000000300000_0" "QCSJ_C000000000300000"
      , "A3"."DRIVERS_1"                 "DRIVERS_1"
      , "A3"."QCSJ_C000000000300001_2" "QCSJ_C000000000300001"
      , "A2"."CONSTRUCTORID"           "CONSTRUCTORID"
      , "A2"."NAME"                    "NAME_4"
```

```
from
 (select "A5"."CONSTRUCTORID" "QCSJ_C000000000300000_0"
       , "A5"."DRIVERS"        "DRIVERS_1"
       , "A4"."CONSTRUCTORID" "QCSJ_C000000000300001_2"
   from
    (select "A6"."CONSTRUCTORID_1" "CONSTRUCTORID"
          , listagg( distinct "A6"."DRIVERREF_5", ',') "DRIVERS"
      from
       (select "A8"."DRIVERID"       "QCSJ_C000000000900000"
             , "A8"."CONSTRUCTORID" "CONSTRUCTORID_1"
             , "A8"."STARTCONTRACT" "STARTCONTRACT"
             , "A8"."ENDCONTRACT"   "ENDCONTRACT"
             , "A7"."DRIVERID"      "QCSJ_C000000000900001"
             , "A7"."DRIVERREF"     "DRIVERREF_5"
        from    "BOOK"."DRIVERCONSTRUCTORS" "A8"
              , "F1DATA"."DRIVERS"          "A7"
        where "A8"."DRIVERID" = "A7"."DRIVERID") "A6"
        group by "A6"."CONSTRUCTORID_1"
   ) "A5"

   ,
   (select "A9"."DRIVERID"       "DRIVERID"
         , "A9"."CONSTRUCTORID" "CONSTRUCTORID"
         , "A9"."STARTCONTRACT" "STARTCONTRACT"
         , "A9"."ENDCONTRACT"   "ENDCONTRACT"
    from    "BOOK"."DRIVERCONSTRUCTORS" "A9"
    where  (   "A9"."STARTCONTRACT" is null
            or "A9"."STARTCONTRACT" <= to_date( '20220320'
                                              , 'YYYYMMDD' )
           )
    and    (   "A9"."ENDCONTRACT" is null
            or "A9"."ENDCONTRACT" > to_date( '20220320'
                                            , 'YYYYMMDD' )
           )
   ) "A4"
   where "A5"."CONSTRUCTORID" = "A4"."CONSTRUCTORID"
```

```
) "A3"
,
"F1DATA"."CONSTRUCTORS" "A2"
where  "A3"."QCSJ_C000000000300000_0" = "A2"."CONSTRUCTORID"
) "A1"
<<formatted manually for readability>>
```

If you don't have all the required privileges, for example select on the tables, execute on the types and functions, then ORA-24256 is raised.

If the input_sql text is not a select statement, then ORA-24251 is raised.

If the input is not valid, then ORA-00900 is raised.

If the input lob size exceeds the maximum size of 4 GB, then ORA-29477 is raised.

The expanded and merged SQL statement text is copied to output_sql_text on successful completion. This query only contains references to the table and is semantically equivalent to the input with some caveats.

- If invoker rights functions are called from any of the views, they may get called as a different user in the resulting query text if the view owner is different from the user who eventually compiles/runs the expanded SQL text.

- If there are VPD policies on any of the views that produce different expansions depending on who the user is.

- If there are references to remote objects, the resulting query may not work.

UTL_CALL_STACK

To demonstrate the outcome of the following functions, let's use the template of the code in Listing 17-8. The code (specific to the different functions) must be between the lines.

```
-----8<-replace-start------
```

and

```
------8<-replace-end------
```

Listing 17-8. utl_call_stack_demo template

```
create or replace package utl_call_stack_demo
is
  procedure public_procedure;
end utl_call_stack_demo;
/

create or replace package body utl_call_stack_demo is
  procedure private_procedure is
    l_subprogram utl_call_stack.unit_qualified_name;

    procedure local_procedure_in_private_procedure is
      l_subprogram utl_call_stack.unit_qualified_name;

      procedure local_procedure_in_local_procedure is
        l_subprogram utl_call_stack.unit_qualified_name;
      begin
        -----8<-replace-start------
        null;
        ------8<-replace-end------
      end local_procedure_in_local_procedure;

    begin
      -----8<-replace-start------
      null;
      ------8<-replace-end------
      dbms_output.put_line( 'Call the local in local procedure');
      local_procedure_in_local_procedure;
    end local_procedure_in_private_procedure;
  begin
    -----8<-replace-start------
    null;
    ------8<-replace-end------
    dbms_output.put_line( 'Call the local in private procedure');
    local_procedure_in_private_procedure;
  end private_procedure;
```

```
  procedure public_procedure is
    l_subprogram utl_call_stack.unit_qualified_name;

    procedure local_procedure_in_public_procedure is
      l_subprogram utl_call_stack.unit_qualified_name;

      procedure local_procedure_in_local_procedure is
        l_subprogram utl_call_stack.unit_qualified_name;
      begin
        -----8<-replace-start------
        null;
        ------8<-replace-end------
      end local_procedure_in_local_procedure;

    begin
      -----8<-replace-start------
      null;
      ------8<-replace-end------
      dbms_output.put_line( 'Call the local in local procedure');
      local_procedure_in_local_procedure;
    end local_procedure_in_public_procedure;
  begin
    -----8<-replace-start------
    null;
    ------8<-replace-end------
    dbms_output.put_line( 'Call the local procedure' );
    local_procedure_in_public_procedure;
    dbms_output.put_line( 'Call the private procedure' );
    private_procedure;
  end public_procedure;
end utl_call_stack_demo;
/
```

subprogram

The utl_call_stack.subprogram function returns a varray with all the individual names of programs starting at the level you pass as a parameter. Level 1 is the current program, level 2 is the "parent" program, and so on. The varray is filled from the bottom up, where the current program is the last item in the varray.

To demonstrate the workings of this function, replace

```
-----8<-replace-start------
null;
------8<-replace-end------
```

with

```
-----8<-replace-start------
l_subprogram := utl_call_stack.subprogram( 1 );
dbms_output.put_line('subprograms ');
for indx in l_subprogram.first .. l_subprogram.last
loop
  dbms_output.put_line(to_char(indx) || ')' ||
                       l_subprogram(indx));
end loop;
------8<-replace-end------
```

The following is the output if you call the public procedure.

```
begin
  utl_call_stack_demo_subprogram.public_procedure;
end;
/

subprograms
1)UTL_CALL_STACK_DEMO
2)PUBLIC_PROCEDURE
Call the local procedure
subprograms
1)UTL_CALL_STACK_DEMO
2)PUBLIC_PROCEDURE
3)LOCAL_PROCEDURE_IN_PUBLIC_PROCEDURE
```

```
Call the local in local procedure
subprograms
1)UTL_CALL_STACK_DEMO
2)PUBLIC_PROCEDURE
3)LOCAL_PROCEDURE_IN_PUBLIC_PROCEDURE
4)LOCAL_PROCEDURE_IN_LOCAL_PROCEDURE
Call the private procedure
subprograms
1)UTL_CALL_STACK_DEMO
2)PRIVATE_PROCEDURE
Call the local in private procedure
subprograms
1)UTL_CALL_STACK_DEMO
2)PRIVATE_PROCEDURE
3)LOCAL_PROCEDURE_IN_PRIVATE_PROCEDURE
Call the local in local procedure
subprograms
1)UTL_CALL_STACK_DEMO
2)PRIVATE_PROCEDURE
3)LOCAL_PROCEDURE_IN_PRIVATE_PROCEDURE
4)LOCAL_PROCEDURE_IN_LOCAL_PROCEDURE

PL/SQL procedure successfully completed
```

concatenate_subprogram

Instead of retrieving all the individual subprogram names, you can also get the varray
conveniently concatenated into a VARCHAR2 comprising the names in the unit-
qualified name, separated by dots. The input to the utl_call_stack.concatenate_
subprogram procedure is a varray that you can retrieve using the utl_call_stack.
subprogram procedure.

The following is an example of a call to this procedure.

```
utl_call_stack.concatenate_subprogram
  ( utl_call_stack.subprogram( 1 ) );
```

To demonstrate the workings of this function, replace

```
-----8<-replace-start------
null;
------8<-replace-end------
```

with

```
-----8<-replace-start------
dbms_output.put_line
  ( utl_call_stack.concatenate_subprogram
    ( utl_call_stack.subprogram( 1 ) )
  );
------8<-replace-end------
```

The following is the output if you call the public procedure.

```
begin
  utl_call_stack_demo_concatenate_subprogram.public_procedure;
end;
/

UTL_CALL_STACK_DEMO.PUBLIC_PROCEDURE
Call the local procedure
UTL_CALL_STACK_DEMO.PUBLIC_PROCEDURE.LOCAL_PROCEDURE_IN_PUBLIC_PROCEDURE
Call the local in local procedure
UTL_CALL_STACK_DEMO.PUBLIC_PROCEDURE.LOCAL_PROCEDURE_IN_PUBLIC_PROCEDURE.
LOCAL_PROCEDURE_IN_LOCAL_PROCEDURE
Call the private procedure
UTL_CALL_STACK_DEMO.PRIVATE_PROCEDURE
Call the local in private procedure
UTL_CALL_STACK_DEMO.PRIVATE_PROCEDURE.LOCAL_PROCEDURE_IN_PRIVATE_PROCEDURE
Call the local in local procedure
UTL_CALL_STACK_DEMO.PRIVATE_PROCEDURE.LOCAL_PROCEDURE_IN_PRIVATE_PROCEDURE.
LOCAL_PROCEDURE_IN_LOCAL_PROCEDURE

PL/SQL procedure successfully completed
```

owner

The utl_call_stack.owner function returns the owner name of the subprogram. The parameter is the same as you would use for the utl_call_stack.subprogram function. The return value of this function is a single VARCHAR2 with the owner of the given level, not the entire stack in a varray.

unit_line

Using the utl_call_stack.unit_line, you can get the line numbers of where the calls to the programs occurred. The line numbers are the line numbers in the different programs in the call stack, not just the current program.

To demonstrate the workings of this function, replace

```
-----8<-replace-start------
null;
------8<-replace-end------
```

with

```
-----8<-replace-start------
for indx in reverse 1 .. utl_call_stack.dynamic_depth
loop
  dbms_output.put
    ( utl_call_stack.unit_line( indx ) );
  if indx <> 1
  then
    dbms_output.put('->');
  end if;
end loop;
dbms_output.put_line('');
------8<-replace-end------
```

The following is the output if you call the public procedure.

```
begin
  utl_call_stack_demo_unit_line.public_procedure;
end;
/
```

```
2->97
Call the local procedure
2->107->81
Call the local in local procedure
2->107->91->66
Call the private procedure
2->109->44
Call the local in private procedure
2->109->54->28
Call the local in local procedure
2->109->54->38->13

PL/SQL procedure successfully completed
```

Summary

There are a lot of utility packages available. Using the procedures and functions in DBMS_SESSION, you can ensure the correct role is set and the NLS settings are correct. To make debugging easier, set the session identifier. Using the procedures and functions in DBMS_UTILITY and UTL_CALL_STACK, you can inquire exactly where your program is at and what path it has taken to get there. Use these procedures and functions to instrument your code so you can figure out what, when, and why if something unanticipated happens.

CHAPTER 18

See What You Need to See

If you store data in the database, it does not have to be visible to everyone at any time. Sometimes you don't want people to see your data. Sometimes you want certain groups to see your data and others not. And sometimes you want your data to be available at a certain period. Oracle Database provides different mechanisms for these issues.

Temporal Validity

Sometimes the data in our database is only valid for a certain period of time. You can simply update the rows to their new values for the new period. But what if you need to be able to retrieve the data as it was at a certain point in time? This means introducing history tables where all the updates to the table are logged and then creating queries to retrieve the data needed.

Setup

Oracle Database 12c (12.1) introduces the concept of *temporal validity*. Using two DATE or TIMESTAMP columns in your table, Oracle Database can determine if a record should be returned in the result set of a query or not. They can be existing columns, or they can be created automatically when creating the validity period.

Suppose you create a table of Formula 1 drivers and their contracts. Create a table using the data available. This doesn't mean the result is correct, but it does for the example.

Our assumptions are as follows.

- The first race of a driver for a certain constructor is the start of the contract.

- The last race of a driver for a certain constructor is the end of the contract.

© Alex Nuijten, Patrick Barel 2023
A. Nuijten and P. Barel, *Modern Oracle Database Programming*, https://doi.org/10.1007/978-1-4842-9166-5_18

- Only show contracts since 1965 (before that, the data available is not accurate enough).

You can take two approaches in this case. Create a table with `driverid` and `constructorid`, add a period for the contract, which automatically adds a start and an end date column, and then use the query to fill the table.

The other possibility is to create the table with the start and end date columns already in place (e.g., by running a **C**reate **T**able **A**s **S**elect statement) and then add the period for the contract using the existing columns.

The main difference between these two approaches is that when the columns are automatically created, they are created as invisible columns, which are not visible when describing the table. The names of the newly created columns are `<periodname>_start` and `<periodname>_end`.

The check constraint created when adding a period to a table checks if the period's start date is less than the end date. If either one of the values is NULL, then the constraint is also considered to be valid.

Using the script in Listing 18-1, create the table and add the validity period.

Listing 18-1. Create drivercontracts table

```
create table driverconstructors as
with resultrace as
( select rsl.driverid
       , rsl.constructorid
       , rcs.year
       , rcs.round
       , rcs.race_date
  from   f1data.results rsl
  join   f1data.races   rcs
  on     ( rsl.raceid = rcs.raceid )
  where  1 = 1
  and    rcs.race_date > to_date('19650101', 'YYYYMMDD')
)
, contractinfo as
( select rrc.driverid
       , rrc.constructorid
       , rrc.year
```

```
        , rrc.round
        , case
            when lag( rrc.constructorid )
                over( partition by rrc.driverid order by year
                        ,round ) = rrc.constructorid
            then
                null
            else
                rrc.race_date
          end begincontract
        , case
            when lead( rrc.constructorid )
                over( partition by rrc.driverid order by year
                        ,round ) = rrc.constructorid
            then
                null
            else
                rrc.race_date
          end endcontract
    from    resultrace rrc
)
, contracts as
( select cif.driverid
        , cif.constructorid
        , cif.year
        , cif.round
        , cif.begincontract
        , cif.endcontract
        , sum( case
                    when cif.begincontract is null
                    then
                        0
                    else
                        1
                end )
```

```
                        over ( partition by driverid order by year
                                             , round) contractnumber
   from    contractinfo cif
)
, all_contracts as
( select con.contractnumber
        , con.driverid
        , con.constructorid
        , min(con.begincontract) as startcontract
        , max(con.endcontract) as endcontract
   from    contracts con
   group   by con.driverid
             , con.constructorid
             , con.contractnumber)
select act.driverid
      , act.constructorid
      , act.startcontract
      , greatest( act.startcontract + 1 / 24 / 60 / 60
                  , act.endcontract) as endcontract
from    all_contracts act
/
```

After creating the table, add a validity period to this table, using the two existing columns: startcontract and endcontract.

```
alter table driverconstructors add period for drivercontract
(startcontract, endcontract)
/
```

A record falls within the validity period if the period's start date is less than or equal to the appointed date *and* the period's end date is greater than the appointed date. NULL values for dates are considered infinitely small. For the start date, that would be the beginning of time, or infinitely large. For the end date, that would be the end of time.

as of Queries

The following lets you retrieve only those records from the table valid on the date supplied.

```
select ... from <table> as of period for <periodname> <date>
```

Using the period defined on the DRIVERCONSTRUCTORS table, you can find the drivers having a contract at a certain point in time. Let's look at the start of the 2022 season.

```
select d.forename as firstname
     , d.surname  as lastname
     , c.name     as constructorname
from   driverconstructors as of period
for    drivercontract to_date( '20220320', 'YYYYMMDD' ) dc
join   f1data.drivers d
on     (dc.driverid = d.driverid)
join   f1data.constructors c
on     (dc.constructorid = c.constructorid)
order  by constructorname, lastname, firstname
/
```

FIRSTNAME	LASTNAME	CONSTRUCTORNAME
Valtteri	Bottas	Alfa Romeo
Guanyu	Zhou	Alfa Romeo
Pierre	Gasly	AlphaTauri
Yuki	Tsunoda	AlphaTauri
Fernando	Alonso	Alpine F1 Team
Esteban	Ocon	Alpine F1 Team
Nico	Hülkenberg	Aston Martin
Lance	Stroll	Aston Martin
Sebastian	Vettel	Aston Martin
Charles	Leclerc	Ferrari
Carlos	Sainz	Ferrari
Kevin	Magnussen	Haas F1 Team
Mick	Schumacher	Haas F1 Team

Lando	Norris	McLaren
Daniel	Ricciardo	McLaren
Lewis	Hamilton	Mercedes
George	Russell	Mercedes
Sergio	Pérez	Red Bull
Max	Verstappen	Red Bull
Alexander	Albon	Williams
Nicholas	Latifi	Williams

```
21 rows selected
```

You can use any date for the "as of" period, so if you would like to see the drivers at the start of the 1998 season, the query would look like the following.

```
select d.forename as firstname
     , d.surname   as lastname
     , c.name      as constructorname
from   driverconstructors as of period
for    drivercontract to_date( '19980308', 'YYYYMMDD' ) dc
join   f1data.drivers d
on     (dc.driverid = d.driverid)
join   f1data.constructors c
on     (dc.constructorid = c.constructorid)
order  by constructorname, lastname, firstname
/
```

FIRSTNAME	LASTNAME	CONSTRUCTORNAME
Pedro	Diniz	Arrows
Mika	Salo	Arrows
Giancarlo	Fisichella	Benetton
Alexander	Wurz	Benetton
Eddie	Irvine	Ferrari
Michael	Schumacher	Ferrari
Damon	Hill	Jordan
Ralf	Schumacher	Jordan
David	Coulthard	McLaren

Mika	Häkkinen	McLaren
Tarso	Marques	Minardi
Shinji	Nakano	Minardi
Esteban	Tuero	Minardi
Olivier	Panis	Prost
Jarno	Trulli	Prost
Jean	Alesi	Sauber
Johnny	Herbert	Sauber
Rubens	Barrichello	Stewart
Jan	Magnussen	Stewart
Ricardo	Rosset	Tyrrell
Toranosuke	Takagi	Tyrrell
Heinz-Harald	Frentzen	Williams
Jacques	Villeneuve	Williams

23 rows selected

Tip   One typical use of "as of" is to query "as of period for … sysdate" to retrieve currently valid data.

Versions Between Queries

If you want to see for which constructor a certain driver has driven, you can use the versions between construction. If you want to see the contracts for Kimi Räikkönen, use the following query.

```
select d.forename as firstname
     , d.surname  as lastname
     , c.name     as constructorname
     , dc.startcontract
     , dc.endcontract
from   driverconstructors versions period for drivercontract
       between to_date( '19900101', 'YYYYMMDD' )
       and     to_date( '20230101', 'YYYYMMDD' ) dc
join   f1data.drivers d
```

```
on      (dc.driverid = d.driverid)
join    f1data.constructors c
on      (dc.constructorid = c.constructorid)
where   d.surname = 'Räikkönen'
order   by dc.startcontract
        , dc.endcontract
/
```

FIRSTNAME	LASTNAME	CONSTRUCTORNAME	STARTCONTRACT	ENDCONTRACT
Kimi	Räikkönen	Sauber	04/03/2001	14/10/2001
Kimi	Räikkönen	McLaren	03/03/2002	22/10/2006
Kimi	Räikkönen	Ferrari	18/03/2007	01/11/2009
Kimi	Räikkönen	Lotus F1	18/03/2012	03/11/2013
Kimi	Räikkönen	Ferrari	16/03/2014	25/11/2018
Kimi	Räikkönen	Alfa Romeo	17/03/2019	12/12/2021

```
6 rows selected
```

You can also check which drivers drove for a certain constructor.

```
select d.forename as firstname
     , d.surname  as lastname
     , c.name     as constructorname
     , dc.startcontract
     , dc.endcontract
from    driverconstructors versions period for drivercontract
        between to_date( '19900101', 'YYYYMMDD' )
and     to_date( '20230101', 'YYYYMMDD' ) dc
join    f1data.drivers d
on      (dc.driverid = d.driverid)
join    f1data.constructors c
on      (dc.constructorid = c.constructorid)
where   c.name = 'Red Bull'
order   by dc.startcontract
        , dc.endcontract
/
```

```
FIRSTNAME     LASTNAME    CONSTRUCTORNAME STARTCONTRACT ENDCONTRACT
------------  ----------  --------------- ------------- -----------
Christian     Klien       Red Bull        06/03/2005    10/09/2006
David         Coulthard   Red Bull        06/03/2005    02/11/2008
Vitantonio    Liuzzi      Red Bull        24/04/2005    29/05/2005
Robert        Doornbos    Red Bull        01/10/2006    22/10/2006
Mark          Webber      Red Bull        18/03/2007    24/11/2013
Sebastian     Vettel      Red Bull        29/03/2009    23/11/2014
Daniel        Ricciardo   Red Bull        16/03/2014    25/11/2018
Daniil        Kvyat       Red Bull        15/03/2015    01/05/2016
Max           Verstappen  Red Bull        15/05/2016    03/07/2022
Pierre        Gasly       Red Bull        17/03/2019    04/08/2019
Alexander     Albon       Red Bull        01/09/2019    13/12/2020
Sergio        Pérez       Red Bull        28/03/2021    03/07/2022

12 rows selected
```

DBMS_FLASHBACK_ARCHIVE

Using the dbms_flashback_archive.enable_at_valid_time you can set the validity
date to a fixed date, so you don't have to add the as of period clause to every query.
The parameters of this procedure are described in Table 18-1.

Table 18-1. *enable_at_valid_time Procedure Parameters*

Parameter	Mandatory	Description

level	Y	Options:
		— ALL
		  Displays all the data, the default
		— CURRENT
		  This displays only the data that is valid at the current timestamp. Data becomes visible and invisible as time passes.
		— ASOF
		  This displays the data valid at the timestamp set in the next parameters.

query_ time		Used only if the level is ASOF Only valid data is shown

Set the flashback archive to the start of the 2022 season.

```
begin
  dbms_flashback_archive.enable_at_valid_time
    ( level      => 'ASOF'
    , query_time => to_date( '20220320','YYYYMMDD' )
    );
end;
/
```

You can use a simple query, note the absence of the as of period clause, to get the same result as in the first example.

```
select d.forename as firstname
     , d.surname   as lastname
     , c.name      as constructorname
from   driverconstructors  dc
join   f1data.drivers      d
on     (dc.driverid = d.driverid)
join   f1data.constructors c
on     (dc.constructorid = c.constructorid)
order  by constructorname, lastname, firstname
/
```

```
FIRSTNAME     LASTNAME      CONSTRUCTORNAM
------------  ------------  ---------------
Valtteri      Bottas        Alfa Romeo
Guanyu        Zhou          Alfa Romeo
Pierre        Gasly         AlphaTauri
Yuki          Tsunoda       AlphaTauri
Fernando      Alonso        Alpine F1 Team
Esteban       Ocon          Alpine F1 Team
Nico          Hülkenberg    Aston Martin
Lance         Stroll        Aston Martin
Sebastian     Vettel        Aston Martin
Charles       Leclerc       Ferrari
Carlos        Sainz         Ferrari
```

```
Kevin        Magnussen    Haas F1 Team
Mick         Schumacher   Haas F1 Team
Lando        Norris       McLaren
Daniel       Ricciardo    McLaren
Lewis        Hamilton     Mercedes
George       Russell      Mercedes
Sergio       Pérez        Red Bull
Max          Verstappen   Red Bull
Alexander    Albon        Williams
Nicholas     Latifi       Williams

21 rows selected
```

To return to a "normal" operation, call the `dbms_flashback_archive.enable_at_valid_time` with the level set to ALL or call the `dbms_flashback_archive.disable_asof_valid_time` procedure

```
begin
  dbms_flashback_archive.disable_asof_valid_time;
end;
/
```

Virtual Private Database

Virtual Private Database (VPD) gives the impression that each end user has their own database while still having a single code base and set of tables. Let's assume that the Formula1 teams are not allowed to see the results of the other constructors (this is not the case, but for this example, assume it is). You could build different schemas in the database, each with its own tables. When adding the results for a race, you must add the data to the correct schema. It is easier to create one table in one schema and have Oracle Database show the correct data.

When the table is part of the VPD, Oracle Database under the hood adds an extra predicate to any SQL statement issued against this table. This can be a single select from this table, but also when the table is used in a join or a subselect. To define this extra predicate, you have to define a policy function and then connect this function to the table.

The Policy Function

Oracle Database calls this procedure with two parameters—schemaname and tablename—in that order. The signature of the policy function VPD uses is as follows.

```
function <functionname>
( <schemaname> in varchar2
, <tablename>  in varchar2)
return varchar2
```

The function has to return a valid predicate that is added to any SQL statement issued against this table.

You can do whatever you want in the policy function, but it is called very often, and if the function takes a lot of time to complete, then every SQL statement against the table takes a lot of time.

Listing 18-2 shows a policy function to ensure a constructor can only see its own data.

Listing 18-2. Policy function thisconstructoronly

```
create or replace function thisconstructoronly
( schemaname_in in varchar2
, tablename_in  in varchar2
) return varchar2
is
begin
  return q'[constructorid = sys_context
                            ( 'CONSTRUCTOR_CTX'
                            , 'CONSTRUCTORID'
                            )]';
end;
/
```

This function returns a VARCHAR2 with these contents.

```
constructorid = sys_context( 'CONSTRUCTOR_CTX', 'CONSTRUCTORID' )
```

Context

The easiest (and fastest) way to communicate settings from outside the policy function to the policy function or the predicate it results in is using application context.

You can create a context by using this command.

```
create or replace context constructor_ctx using context_pkg
/
```

Then you build a package to set (or clear) properties within the context. They must be set using the associated package. Listing 18-3 features the package to communicate with the context.

Listing 18-3. context_pkg to communicate with the constructor_ctx

```
create or replace package context_pkg as
  procedure set_constructor( constructorid_in in number );
  procedure unset_constructor;
end;
/

create or replace package body context_pkg as
  procedure set_constructor(constructorid_in in number)
  is
  begin
    dbms_session.set_context( namespace => 'CONSTRUCTOR_CTX'
                            , attribute => 'CONSTRUCTORID'
                            , value     => constructorid_in
                            );
  end set_constructor;

  procedure unset_constructor
  is
  begin
    dbms_session.clear_context( namespace => 'CONSTRUCTOR_CTX' );
  end unset_constructor;
end context_pkg;
/
```

Policy

This predicate must now be added to every statement issued against the table. You must create a VPD policy to connect the policy function to the table.

add_policy

The dbms_rls.add_policy procedure can take the parameters described in Table 18-2.

Table 18-2. *Parameters for the Add Policy Procedure*

Parameter	Mandatory	Description
object_schema		The schema in which the object to be protected resides If null, then the current schema is assumed
object_name	Y	The name of the object that is to be protected
policy_name	Y	An arbitrarily chosen name Use this name to enable/disable and drop the policy
function_schema		The schema in which the policy function resides If null, then the current schema is assumed
policy_function	Y	The name of the policy function
statement_types		Statement type that the policy applies to, select, insert, update, delete, or index Default is any type, except index
update_check		Policy is checked against the updated or inserted value Ability to see the information after the statement is executed, based on the policy
Enable		Is the policy enabled?
static_policy		Will the policy always result in the same predicate?

(continued)

Table 18-2. (*continued*)

Parameter	Mandatory	Description
policy_type		Choose from these options: DYNAMIC STATIC SHARED_STATIC CONTEXT_SENSITIVE SHARED_CONTEXT_SENSITIVE Overwrites static_policy if non-null (See Table 18-3 for an explanation of these types.)
long_predicate		Predicate returned has a maximum length of 4000 bytes (default) or 32K
sec_relevant_cols		List of security-relevant columns The policy function is executed when one of these columns is referenced
sec_relevant_cols_opt		If set to dbms_rls.all_rows, all rows returned, but with the columns specified in the security relevant column option nullified
namespace		The name of application context namespace
attribute		The name of application context attribute

Table 18-3. *Policy Types*

Type	Description
DYNAMIC	This policy type runs the policy function each time a user accesses the VPD-protected database objects.
STATIC	This policy type runs the policy function once, then shares the outcome in the SGA. The static policy type enforces the same predicate for all users in the instance.
SHARED_STATIC	You can use the same policy function for multiple tables.
CONTEXT_SENSITIVE	If there is no change in the local application context, Oracle Database does not rerun the policy function within the user session. If there is a change in any application context attribute during the user session, it doesn't even have to be referenced; by default, the database re-executes the policy function to ensure that it captures all changes to the predicate since the initial parsing.
SHARED_CONTEXT_SENSITIVE	This is used when there is the same policy function for multiple tables.

If you query the constructors table you see information of all constructors.

```
select c.constructorid
     , c.name
     , c.nationality
from   f1data.constructors c
/

CONST NAME            NATIONALITY
----- --------------- ---------------
    1 McLaren         British
    2 BMW Sauber      German
    3 Williams        British
    4 Renault         French
    5 Toro Rosso      Italian
    6 Ferrari         Italian
```

```
 7 Toyota          Japanese
 8 Super Aguri     Japanese
 9 Red Bull        Austrian
10 Force India     Indian
...

select cr.constructorresultsid as crid
     , cr.constructorid       as cid
     , cr.raceid              as rid
     , cr.points              as points
from   f1data.constructorresults cr
/

CRID   CID   RID POINT
-----  ----- ----- -----
 1197      6   133    16
 1198      3   133     4
 1199     16   133     5
 1200     15   133     1
 1201     17   133     0
 1202      1   133     0
 1203     19   133     0
 1204      4   133     0
 1205     21   133     0
 1206      7   133     0
...

select cs.constructorstandingsid as csid
     , cs.constructorid          as cid
     , cs.position               as pos
     , cs.points                 as pnts
from   f1data.constructorstandings cs
where  rownum < 11
/
```

CSID	CID	POS	PNTS
6242	15	6	18
6241	1	5	32
6240	16	3	67
6239	3	4	41
6238	4	2	79
6237	6	1	174
6256	18	10	1
6255	17	9	5
6254	7	7	8
6253	19	8	7

...

Because these three tables all have constructor information (CONSTRUCTORS, CONSTRUCTORRESULTS, and CONSTRUCTORSTANDINGS) and you want to use the same policy for all three tables, add three shared static policies.

```
begin
  sys.dbms_rls.add_policy
              ( object_schema    => 'F1DATA'
              , object_name      => 'CONSTRUCTORS'
              , policy_name      => 'THISCONSTRUCTOR'
              , function_schema  => 'BOOK'
              , policy_function  => 'THISCONSTRUCTORONLY'
              , policy_type      => sys.dbms_rls.shared_static
              );
  sys.dbms_rls.add_policy
              ( object_schema    => 'F1DATA'
              , object_name      => 'CONSTRUCTORRESULTS'
              , policy_name      => 'THISCONSTRUCTORRESULT'
              , function_schema  => 'BOOK'
              , policy_function  => 'THISCONSTRUCTORONLY'
              , policy_type      => sys.dbms_rls.shared_static
              );
```

```
sys.dbms_rls.add_policy
            ( object_schema    => 'F1DATA'
            , object_name      => 'CONSTRUCTORSTANDINGS'
            , policy_name      => 'THISCONSTRUCTORSTANDING'
            , function_schema  => 'BOOK'
            , policy_function  => 'THISCONSTRUCTORONLY'
            , policy_type      => sys.dbms_rls.shared_static
            );
end;
/
```

Even though the policy function returns a predicate referencing the context, it doesn't rely on it. If the context changes, the predicate text is still the same. It *evaluates* differently with a different value in the context. You set the context by calling our set_ constructor procedure.

```
begin
  context_pkg.set_constructor( constructorid_in => 9 );
end;
/
```

When selecting data from the tables, the predicate is automatically added to the query, therefore only showing the data for Red Bull.

```
select c.constructorid as cid
     , c.name          as name
     , c.nationality    as nationality
from   f1data.constructors c
/

CID NAME             NATIONALITY
----- --------------- ---------------
    9 Red Bull        Austrian

select cr.constructorresultsid as crid
     , cr.constructorid        as cid
     , cr.raceid               as rid
     , cr.points               as points
```

489

```
from    f1data.constructorresults cr
/

CRID    CID   RID POINT
-----   ----- ----- -----
     9      9    18     0
    16      9    19     2
    27      9    20     2
    37      9    21     4
    49      9    22     2
    58      9    23     5
    66      9    24     6
    79      9    25     3
    92      9    26     0
   102      9    27     0
...

select cs.constructorstandingsid as csid
     , cs.constructorid          as cid
     , cs.position               as pos
     , cs.points                 as pnts
from    f1data.constructorstandings cs
/

CSID    CID   POS  PNTS
-----   ----- ----- -----
    14      9    7     2
    25      9    7     4
    36      9    6     8
    47      9    5    10
    58      9    5    15
    69      9    4    21
    80      9    4    24
    91      9    5    24
   102      9    5    24
   113      9    6    24
...
```

The queries return no data if the context has not been set or unset.

```
begin
  context_pkg.unset_constructor;
end;
/

select c.constructorid as cid
     , c.name          as name
     , c.nationality   as nationality
from   f1data.constructors c
/

  CID NAME              NATIONALITY
----- --------------- ---------------

select cr.constructorresultsid as crid
     , cr.constructorid        as cid
     , cr.raceid               as rid
     , cr.points               as points
from   f1data.constructorresults cr
/

 CRID   CID   RID POINT
----- ----- ----- -----

select cs.constructorstandingsid as csid
     , cs.constructorid          as cid
     , cs.position               as pos
     , cs.points                 as pnts
from   f1data.constructorstandings cs
/

 CSID   CID   POS  PNTS
----- ----- ----- -----
```

enable_policy

To enable or disable the policy, you use the dbms_rls.enable_policy procedure.

The enable_policy procedure can take the parameters described in Table 18-4.

Table 18-4. *Parameters for the Enable Policy Procedure*

Parameter	Mandatory	Description
object_schema		The schema in which the object that is protected resides If null, the current schema is assumed
object_name	Y	The name of the object that is protected
policy_name	Y	The name of the policy you want to enable or disable
Enable		Use TRUE to enable the policy, FALSE to disable the policy

drop_policy

Use the dbms_rls.drop_policy to drop the policy when it is no longer needed or when you need to re-create it with different options.

The drop_policy procedure can take the parameters described in Table 18-5.

Table 18-5. *Parameters for the Drop Policy Procedure*

Parameter	Mandatory	Description
object_schema		The schema in which the object that is protected resides If null, then the current schema is assumed
object_name	Y	The name of the object that is protected
policy_name	Y	The name of the policy you want to enable or disable

alter_policy

You can use the dbms_rls.alter_policy to associate or disassociate certain attributes with an existing policy.

The alter_policy procedure can take the parameters described in Table 18-6.

Table 18-6. *Parameters for the Enable Policy Procedure*

Parameter	Mandatory	Description
object_ schema		The schema in which the object that is protected resides If null, then the current schema is assumed
object_name	Y	The name of the object that is protected
policy_name	Y	The name of the policy you want to enable or disable
alter_option		Addition or removal of the associationdbms_rls.add_attribute_ associationdbms_rls.remove_attribute_association
namespace	Y	The namespace of the context
attribute	Y	The attribute within the namespace

Complex Policies

You build any predicate you want, using all your SQL skills. But be aware that this predicate is added to the statement and is executed for every row in the table, not just the ones in the result set. So, if you build something that takes up a lot of time, it takes up a lot of time multiplied by the number of rows in the table. Try to keep your policies in pure SQL.

If you want the constructor to see only the lap times of its own drivers, you can use the code displayed in Listing 18-4.

Listing 18-4. Constructor can only see information about its own drivers

```
create or replace context constructor_ctx using context_pkg
/
create or replace package context_pkg as
  procedure set_constructor( constructorid_in in number );
  procedure unset_constructor;
end context_pkg;
/
```

```
create or replace package body context_pkg as
  procedure set_constructor(constructorid_in in number) is
  begin
    dbms_session.set_context( namespace => 'CONSTRUCTOR_CTX'
                            , attribute => 'CONSTRUCTORID'
                            , value     => constructorid_in
                            );
  End set_constructor;

  procedure unset_constructor is
  begin
    dbms_session.clear_context( namespace => 'CONSTRUCTOR_CTX' );
  end unset_constructor;
end context_pkg;
/

begin
  context_pkg.set_constructor( constructorid_in => 9 );
end;
/

create or replace function lapsforthisconstructoronly
( schemaname_in in varchar2
, tablename_in  in varchar2
) return varchar2
is
begin
  return q'[(raceid, driverid) in
  (select r.raceid, rs.driverid
   from   f1data.races r
   join   f1data.results rs
   on     (r.raceid = rs.raceid)
   where  rs.constructorid =
          sys_context( 'CONSTRUCTOR_CTX'
                     , 'CONSTRUCTORID' ) )]';
end lapsforthisconstructoronly;
/
```

```
select lapsforthisconstructoronly( null, null ) from dual
/
THISCONSTRUCTORONLY(NULL,NULL)
--------------------------------------------
(raceid, driverid) in
  (select r.raceid, rs.driverid
   from   f1data.races r
   join   f1data.results rs
   on     (r.raceid = rs.raceid)
   where  rs.constructorid =
          sys_context( 'CONSTRUCTOR_CTX'
                     , 'CONSTRUCTORID' ) )
begin
  sys.dbms_rls.add_policy
                ( object_schema   => 'F1DATA'
                , object_name     => 'LAPTIMES'
                , policy_name      => 'THISCONSTRUCTORSLAPTIMES'
                , function_schema => 'BOOK'
                , policy_function => 'LAPSFORTHISCONSTRUCTORONLY'
                , policy_type      => sys.dbms_rls.STATIC
                );
end;
/
```

Redaction

Redacting data in the database ensures that data is only seen by those entitled to it, making compliance with privacy rules and regulations consistent. Redaction is done by masking (part of) the data when the results are sent back to the calling process. There are no changes made to the persisted data.

Let's assume you have a web application that displays the position of the drivers in a certain race. A driver must be logged in to see the lap times. By logging in, a context with driverid is set. Based on this context value being set, the time and milliseconds columns are displayed; otherwise, they are obscured from view.

First, create a context including the necessary package, as shown in Listing 18-5.

Listing 18-5. Driver context

```
create or replace context driver_ctx using driver_pkg
/
create or replace package driver_pkg as
  procedure set_driver( driverid_in in number );
  procedure unset_driver;
end driver_pkg;
/
create or replace package body driver_pkg as
  procedure set_driver(driverid_in in number) is
  begin
    sys.dbms_session.set_context
    ( namespace => 'driver_ctx'
    , attribute => 'driverid'
    , value     => driverid_in
    );
  end set_driver;

  procedure unset_driver is
  begin
    sys.dbms_session.clear_context
    ( namespace => 'driver_ctx' );
  end unset_driver;
end driver_pkg;
/
```

add_policy

To add a redaction policy to a table, you need to call the dbms_redact.add_policy
procedure. This procedure takes the parameters as described in Table 18-7.

Table 18-7. *dbms_redact.add_policy Parameters*

Parameter	Mandatory	Description
object_schema		The schema in which the object to be protected resides If null, then the current schema is assumed
object_name	Y	The name of the object that is to be protected
policy_name	Y	An arbitrarily chosen name Use to enable/disable, alter, and drop the policy
column_name		Name of one column to which the redaction policy applies If redacting more than one column, use ALTER_POLICY procedure to add the additional columns
function_type	Y	Type of redaction function to use Possible values are - DBMS_REDACT.NONE - DBMS_REDACT.FULL (default) - DBMS_REDACT.PARTIAL - DBMS_REDACT.RANDOM - DBMS_REDACT.REGEXP If function_type is DBMS_REDACT.REGEXP, function_ parameters must be omitted completely, and regexp_* parameters must define the data redaction policy

(continued)

Table 18-7. (*continued*)

Parameter	Mandatory	Description
function_parameters		Parameters to the redaction function
		Values depend on the value of the function_type provided
		– DBMS_REDACT.NONE: Can be omitted entirely and defaults to NULL
		– DBMS_REDACT.FULL: Can be omitted entirely and defaults to NULL
		– Masking parameters for partial character masking
		A comma-separated list with different contents for different field types
		Character Data Types
		– Input format: Enter V for each character that can be redacted. Enter F for each character you want to format using a formatting character. Ensure that each character has a corresponding V or F value.

(*continued*)

Table 18-7. (*continued*)

Parameter	Mandatory	Description
		— Output format: Enter V for each character to be potentially redacted. Replace each F character in the input format with the character you want to use for the displayed output.
		— Mask character: Specify the character to be used for the redaction.
		— Starting digit position: Specify the starting V digit position for the redaction.
		— Ending digit position: Specify the ending V digit position for the redaction. The F positions don't count.
		Settings for Number Data Types
		— Mask character: Specifies the character to display. Enter a number from 0 to 9.
		— Starting digit position: Specifies the starting digit position for the redaction, such as 1 for the first digit.
		— Ending digit position: Specifies the ending digit position for the redaction.
		Settings for Date-Time Data Types
		m: Redacts the month. To omit redaction, enter an uppercase M.
		d: Redacts the day of the month. To omit redaction, enter an uppercase D.
		y: Redacts the year. To omit redaction, enter an uppercase Y.
		h: Redacts the hour. To omit redaction, enter an uppercase H.
		m: Redacts the minute. To omit redaction, enter an uppercase M.
		s: Redacts the second. To omit redaction, enter an uppercase S.
		For more information on the different parameters, refer to the Oracle Database Advanced Security Guide documentation.

(*continued*)

Table 18-7. (*continued*)

Parameter	Mandatory	Description
expression		Boolean expression using sys_context
		If evaluates to TRUE, redaction takes place
enable		Is the data redaction policy enabled on creation?
		Default value is TRUE
regexp_pattern		Regular expression pattern up to 512 bytes
regexp_replace_ string		Replacement string for regular expression
regexp_position		Integer counting from 1, specifies the position where the search must begin
regexp_occurrence		0 - replace all occurrences of the match
		n - replace the n-th occurrence of the match
regexp_match_ parameter		Changes the default matching behavior Possible values are a combination of 'i', 'c', 'n', 'm', 'x'
policy_description		Description of redaction policy
column_description		Description of the column being redacted

```
begin
  sys.dbms_redact.add_policy
  ( object_schema       => 'f1data'
  , object_name         => 'laptimes'
  , policy_name         => 'maskedlaptime'
  , column_name         => 'time'
  , function_type       => dbms_redact.partial
  , function_parameters => 'VFVVFVVVVV,V:VV.VVVVV,X,1,3'
  , expression          => q'[sys_context( 'driver_ctx'
                            , 'driverid' ) is null]'
  );
end;
/
```

alter_policy

Since the table also holds a column with the time in milliseconds, you want to add another column to be redacted to the policy. Use the dbms_redact.alter_policy procedure for this.

The alter_policy procedure can take the same parameters as the add_policy procedure but has an action extra parameter, which can have one of the values described in Table 18-8.

Table 18-8. *Possible Values for the Action Parameter*

Constant	Description
ADD_COLUMN	Add a column to the redaction policy.
DROP_COLUMN	Drop a column from the redaction policy.
MODIFY_EXPRESSION	Modify the expression of a redaction policy (the expression evaluates to a boolean value: if TRUE, then redaction is applied, otherwise, not).
MODIFY_COLUMN	Modify a column in the redaction policy to change the redaction function_type or the function_parameters.
SET_POLICY_DESCRIPTION	Set a description for the redaction policy.
SET_COLUMN_DESCRIPTION	Set a description for the redaction performed on the column.

```
begin
  sys.dbms_redact.alter_policy
  ( object_schema        => 'f1data'
  , object_name          => 'laptimes'
  , policy_name          => 'maskedlaptime'
  , action               => dbms_redact.add_column
  , column_name          => 'milliseconds'
  , function_type        => dbms_redact.partial
  , function_parameters  => '9,1,4'
  );
end;
/
```

You can test the policy by setting the context. This provides clearer data.

```
begin
  driver_pkg.set_driver( driverid_in => 830 );
end;
/

select *
from    f1data.laptimes
where   driverid = sys_context( 'driver_ctx'
                             , 'driverid' )
/

RACEID DRIVERID LAP POS TIME        MILLISECO
------ -------- --- --- ----------- ----------
   942      830   1   8 2:04.666       124666
   942      830   2   8 1:59.138       119138
   942      830   3   8 1:59.055       119055
   942      830   4   8 1:59.800       119800
   942      830   5   7 2:07.565       127565
   942      830   6   7 2:17.508       137508
   942      830   7   7 2:17.854       137854
   942      830   8   7 2:01.301       121301
   942      830   9   7 1:57.250       117250
...<rest of result removed>
```

You get the redacted data if you query the lap times table without setting a context or clearing the context.

```
begin
  driver_pkg.unset_driver;
end;
/

select *
from    f1data.laptimes
where   1=1
and     driverid = 830
/
```

```
RACEID DRIVERID LAP POS TIME        MILLISECO
------ -------- --- --- ----------  ----------
   942      830   1   8 X:XX.666        999966
   942      830   2   8 X:XX.138        999938
   942      830   3   8 X:XX.055        999955
   942      830   4   8 X:XX.800        999900
   942      830   5   7 X:XX.565        999965
   942      830   6   7 X:XX.508        999908
   942      830   7   7 X:XX.854        999954
   942      830   8   7 X:XX.301        999901
   942      830   9   7 X:XX.250        999950
...<rest of result removed>
```

enable_policy

Use the enable_policy procedure to enable the policy.

The enable_policy function can take the parameters described in Table 18-9.

Table 18-9. *Parameters for the Enable Policy Procedure*

Parameter	Mandatory	Description
object_schema		The schema in which the object that is protected resides If null, then the current schema is assumed
object_name	Y	The name of the object that is protected
policy_name	Y	The name of the policy you want to enable or disable

disable_policy

To disable the policy, use the disable_policy procedure.

The disable_policy function can take the parameters described in Table 18-10.

Table 18-10. *Parameters for the Disable Policy Procedure*

Parameter	Mandatory	Description
object_schema		The schema in which the object that is protected resides If null, then the current schema is assumed
object_name	Y	The name of the object that is protected
policy_name	Y	The name of the policy you want to enable or disable

drop_policy

If you don't need the policy anymore, you can drop it using the `dbms_redact.drop_policy` procedure.

```
begin
  sys.dbms_redact.drop_policy
  ( object_schema        => 'f1data'
   ,object_name          => 'laptimes'
   ,policy_name          => 'maskedlaptime');
end;
/
```

Summary

Oracle Database provides a whole set of functionalities to either show or hide the data based on rules. Temporal validity allows you to see only valid data at a certain point in time. VPD allows you to have a single schema visible to different users as if they were using their own schema with their own data. The Redaction policies allow you to hide certain parts of your (sensitive) data from certain groups of users. Redaction is useful when users need to see part (but not all) of the data. Typical in call centers where they ask for the last digits of your credit card, phone number, SSN, and so forth to verify you.

CHAPTER 19

Upgrade Your Application with Zero Downtime

Upgrading a database application would always require downtime. It was simply not possible to replace PL/SQL objects that were in use. Throughout the years, numerous technologies were developed to reduce Oracle Database downtime, like standby databases, RAC, Streams, online index rebuilds, or online table redefinition. The one thing that could keep users from working uninterrupted is the actual database application that they are using. To overcome this "last piece of the puzzle", being able to replace PL/SQL objects while in use, Edition-based redefinition was developed.

Downtime

In essence, there are two types of downtime: planned and unplanned. Unplanned downtime occurs unexpectedly, and preparing for this scenario is very hard. Some measures can be taken to reduce unplanned downtime but eliminating it is almost impossible.

Planned downtime is known ahead of time, and Oracle has implemented features to reduce the amount of planned downtime. Hardware failures can be protected by physical and/or logical standby databases and RAC. The database doesn't need to be taken down to upgrade the database software itself. When you have logical standby and streams, it is possible to keep the database up and running while being upgraded simultaneously. Indexes can be rebuilt online. Tables can be redefined online, which allows the database to stay available.

© Alex Nuijten, Patrick Barel 2023
A. Nuijten and P. Barel, *Modern Oracle Database Programming*, https://doi.org/10.1007/978-1-4842-9166-5_19

The one thing that would require downtime was *your* custom application. Replacing PL/SQL at runtime was simply not possible. There can only be one version of a certain PL/SQL object, and replacing that would require a lock on the object. This object can no longer be executed and disrupts regular business processes. When a PL/SQL object is replaced, objects that depend on it might become invalid and require recompilation.

Edition-Based Redefinition (EBR) solves this problem and allows your custom application to be upgraded while it is in use. With EBR, you can create PL/SQL changes in the privacy of an edition. When the custom application is completely updated, it can be released to the users. End users using the application during the upgrade can continue to work as if nothing happened, while users that create a new connection immediately use the new application objects.

After the last user disconnects from the pre-upgraded application, the pre-upgraded application can be retired, and only the post-upgraded application is available.

Definitions

EBR uses certain terminology that is used throughout this chapter. Table 19-1 is an overview of the most commonly used definitions.

Table 19-1. *EBR Terminology*

Term	Description
Edition	Name identifying a non-schema object type to extend the standard naming resolution. Editionable objects are identified by edition, schema, and object name.
Editioning view	A special kind of view that acts as an abstraction layer for the underlying table. Because the editioning view exists in a certain edition, it reflects the current implementation of the underlying table. There are certain restrictions for the editioning view.

(continued)

Table 19-1. (*continued*)

Term	Description
Editionable object	Schema objects that are editionable. These include synonyms, views, and all PL/SQL object types.
Non-editionable object	These are all schema objects that are not editionable. These include tables or materialized views. An edition cannot have its own copy of a non-editionable object. A non-editionable object is shared by all editions.
Crossedition trigger	This is a special kind of trigger that can cross the boundaries of editions.
NE on E prohibition	Non-editionable objects cannot depend on editionable objects because the editioned object is invisible during name resolution. However, materialized views and virtual columns can specify an evaluation edition during name resolution.

Concept

The purpose of EBR is very straightforward: zero-downtime patching or upgrades. When you have the luxury of taking downtime, by all means, do so. It is a lot easier for all parties involved.

The distinction between a patch and an upgrade is the following. In the ideal situation, all the requirements for a program are implemented in the actual program. The program implements exactly the written specification. When the program doesn't implement what the requirement specifies, a patch must be applied to correct the situation and bring the implementation and the specification together. The patch should bring the program up to par with the functionality requirement.

The definition of an upgrade is when the requirement changes after the program are created. From this moment on, this distinction is not made any more in the text. A patch is also implied when it says upgrade and vice versa.

Of course, the database is not the only part of the application involved when you want zero-downtime upgrades. The method used to set up the connection to the database determines to which version of the application the connection needs to be set up. This can be done by a load balancer or traffic director. Sessions that are in flight, connected to the pre-upgrade application, connect through one application server. In contrast, sessions that set up a new connection use another application server and connect to the post-upgrade application.

Zero downtime must be designed deliberately in Oracle Database, the application server, and the client application.

Obtaining zero downtime means the application should always be available to the users. This is a big challenge: users of the pre-upgrade application don't want to stop what they are doing to allow a new application to be deployed. Users wanting to use the post-upgrade application don't want to wait until the users of the pre-upgrade application are done with their work, so they can finally connect to the application. Both applications—the pre- and post-upgrade versions—need to be active at the same time so they can accommodate the users using the pre-upgrade application and establish new connections to the post-upgrade application. This is called a *hot rollover*.

To be able to deploy a new application while there is an old application in use can be easy for certain types of applications. Deploying new source files might be sufficient.

When a database is involved, it proves to be a lot harder. Some elementary questions need to be answered.

The Challenges of Zero-Downtime Upgrades

How can you make changes to an application when someone is using the application?

Making changes to an application usually involves many modified objects, but you can't modify them one after the other. That would leave the application in an invalid state. On top of that, it is simply *not* possible to compile database code when someone is using it. All objects need to be changed at the same time, but that might interrupt the pre-upgrade application.

One possibility is to take a *complete copy* of the database with the pre-upgrade database application and make the changes needed to get to the post-upgrade state. This solves the first issue of being able to work in privacy for the upgrade.

Another option is to copy the database schema and make changes to this new schema.

Both options allow you to change objects in privacy and ready them for the post-upgrade situation, but they do not solve the next two challenges and might even make them harder.

How can you keep data in sync between two applications, the pre- and post-upgrade application?

As you can imagine, this is not an easy task to do. The original database objects are still in use, and data can be entered and altered. There must be a mechanism to allow data changes to propagate between the pre- and post-upgrade applications.

When the data is shared between the pre-upgraded and the post-upgraded application, the issue of synchronization is not trivial. The pre-upgraded application has access to the data that is created or changed by the post-upgraded application, and vice versa. The same is true for all objects that contain data, such as materialized views and indexes.

What if the data structures changes?

Upgrading an application might change data structures, so how do you define different data representations for each application when the data is common to both the pre-upgrade and post-upgrade applications?

Transactions performed in the pre-upgrade application must be reflected in the post-upgrade application. The reverse is also true during the hot rollover period. Changes in the post-upgrade application must also be reflected in the pre-upgrade application.

All three challenges with a zero-downtime requirement are met by EBR.

Solution

The mechanism to solve the three challenges are as follows.

- Changes are made in the privacy of a new edition.

- Different projections of the common tables are achieved by using an editioning view.

- The crossedition trigger keeps data changes in sync between different editions during the hot rollover period.

Besides these structures, introduced with EBR, two supporting features of Oracle Database make the picture complete.

The first supporting feature is non-blocking DDL. When you make changes to a table, like adding a column, this is done in a non-blocking fashion. Current transactions on the table do not prohibit this change.

The other feature is fine-grained dependency tracking. When you have a package that refers to a certain table, there is a dependency between the two. Changing the table, like adding a column, would invalidate the package in the past. This is no longer the case. The dependency nowadays is more fine-grained. Because there is no reference to the new column, the package does not become invalid. The same holds for adding new subprograms to a package specification. Dependents do not become invalid.

Implementing EBR is not as trivial as flipping a switch. The preparation phase of EBR is very important and might require changing the existing database design and source code.

Dependencies

Within an Oracle database, there are objects that hold data, like tables, materialized views, and indexes, and there are code objects, all PL/SQL objects.

As a rule of thumb: data objects *cannot* be editionable, and code objects *can* be editionable.

It is possible to have a table where one of the columns is based upon a user-defined type (like an object type). Because the user-defined type is editionable and the table is not editionable you can get into a situation that is not easily solved. Which user-defined type should be used when there are multiple versions across editions for the table definition? This predicament is called *NE-on-E prohibition*. A non-editionable object cannot depend on an editionable object. There has been a work-around for NE-on-E prohibition since Oracle Database 12.1. Instead of having the complete schema being edition-enabled, you can exempt objects from *ever becoming* editionable. In the example of the user-defined type in the table, you would want to define the user-defined type as non-editionable in the create type statement. Thus, you do not encounter NE-on-E prohibition .

Also, starting with Oracle Database 12.1, materialized views and virtual columns can have extra metadata, which provides information about the evaluation edition. Having this extra metadata is only relevant when the materialized view or virtual column uses a PL/SQL function call that is editionable. This metadata needs to be explicitly set by issuing CREATE and ALTER statements.

In versions before 12.1, public synonyms could not be edition-enabled, because that would violate NE-on-E prohibition. From version 12.1 onwards, the Oracle-maintained user called PUBLIC is edition-enabled, but all existing public synonyms are marked as non-editioned. Creating new public synonyms can be editioned.

During the hot rollover period, you can also test the post-upgrade application in the privacy of the new edition. When you must test DML in the post-upgrade application, make sure you use "fake data," which should be easily recognizable and not play a role in the business. With fake data, the actual data is not affected by the edition-based redefinition exercise and can be easily identified and removed once the tests are completed. The alternative is to test only in a read-only modus to prevent the removal of the edition from leading to remnant data.

If something goes wrong, or the functionality is not up to the specifications, you can keep going forward in the privacy of the post-upgrade edition. The objective is to create a post-upgrade application, which can only be achieved when mistakes are corrected.

When the hot rollover period is completed and testing has been done, no existing connections are using the pre-upgrade application, and the pre-upgrade edition can be retired. Preventing users from connecting to the pre-upgrade application might be the first step. The *crossedition triggers*, used to keep the data in sync between the pre- and post-upgrade application, are no longer needed. Objects in the pre-upgrade edition can be dropped, and eventually, the unused columns can be removed from the table.

If the EBR exercise fails and the latest edition must be removed, the edition can be dropped by a single statement. Remember that changes to the table are not reversed when an edition is dropped from the database. Also, changes to the data are not reversed and should be removed to return to the pre-upgraded version.

Preparation

Some steps must be taken to take advantage of EBR. Every Oracle Database version since 11gR2 has a default edition called ORA$BASE. This edition is there even if there is no intention to use EBR.

The first step is to enable EBR at the schema level. This one-time action is irreversible. Even though it is irreversible, it doesn't mean you must use EBR.

The schema is edition-enabled using the following statement.

```
alter user book enable editions
/
```

In versions before Oracle Database 12.1, the complete schema would be edition-enabled. Since then, it has been possible to mark certain objects as non-editionable, which normally would be editionable.

The following statement can be used to determine the current session.

```
select sys_context('userenv'
                  ,'current_edition_name'
                  ) "Current_Edition"
from    dual
/

Current_Edition
----------------
ORA$BASE
```

Tip When using SQLcl, the `show edition` command can be used to reveal the current edition, which is a lot more convenient than inspecting the current edition name in the `userenv` application context.

Privileges

In the previous section, the user "book" was edition-enabled, allowing additional editions to be created. There is a hierarchical relation between editions where an edition always has *one* parent. The only exception is ORA$BASE, or when this edition is eventually removed, the next edition in the hierarchy. This top-level edition is called the *root edition*.

Enabling the schema to use editions doesn't mean the user can create additional editions. To do this, the `create any edition` system privilege is needed. Besides this privilege, the user also needs `use` privileges on the root edition.

```
grant create any edition to book
/
```

When the user book creates an edition, the `use` privilege is automatically granted. This privilege can also be explicitly granted to other users.

```
grant use on edition <edition name> to <user>
/
```

Removing a root or leaf edition can only be done when the `drop any edition` system privilege is granted.

```
grant drop any edition to book
/
```

While connected to the database, it is also possible to change the edition by using an `alter session` statement.

```
alter session set edition = <edition name>
/
```

There cannot be an open transaction to change from one edition to another. Attempting to change the edition when the transaction isn't closed by a commit or rollback raises an error.

```
alter session set edition = r2
/
ERROR:
ORA-38814: ALTER SESSION SET EDITION must be first statement of transaction
```

Several Levels of Complexity

There are several levels of complexity when using EBR. The simplest EBR is where *only* PL/SQL objects are changed between editions.

The next level is where table structures are also changed between editions, but there is *no need* to keep multiple editions available at the same time. The users all move to the post-upgraded edition at a specified time in the future.

The most complex level is where there are table structure changes, and the users need access to multiple editions simultaneously. This involves keeping data in sync between multiple editions.

Each step involved is discussed in the next few sections, beginning with the simplest form: changing only PL/SQL objects between editions.

Only Changing PL/SQL Objects

The simplest form of EBR is to only change PL/SQL objects. The data model stays the same. In the following example, a procedure is created in the ORA$BASE edition to display the full name of a driver by supplying the first and last name as arguments.

```
create or replace
procedure format_fullname (p_firstname in varchar2
                          ,p_lastname in varchar2)
is
begin
   dbms_output.put_line (p_firstname
                         ||' '||
                         p_lastname
   );
end format_fullname;
/
```

When server output is enabled, this simple procedure shows the first and last names concatenated together, separated by a space.

With the introduction of EBR, the data dictionary was extended with a number of views that also reflect edition information. These dictionary views have _ae, short for *all editions*. One of these views is user_objects_ae. This data dictionary view shows that the create procedure format_fullname exists in edition ORA$BASE.

```
select object_name
     , object_type
     , edition_name
from   user_objects_ae
where  object_name = 'FORMAT_FULLNAME'
/
OBJECT_NAME      OBJECT_TYPE      EDITION_NAME
---------------  ---------------  ---------------
FORMAT_FULLNAME  PROCEDURE        ORA$BASE
```

> **Note**   When the preceding query reveals the `edition_name` column to be empty, the user has not been edition-enabled.

The next step is to create an additional edition called R1.

```
create edition r1 as child of ora$base
/
```

Although not strictly necessary to specify which edition is the parent edition, being explicit never hurts.

Creating the edition does not imply that the current session has switched over to it. To change the current edition to the newly created one, an `alter session` command needs to be issued.

```
alter session set edition = r1
/

select sys_context('userenv'
                   ,'current_edition_name'
                   ) "Current_Edition"
from    dual
/

Current_Edition
---------------
R1
```

Besides switching the edition with an `alter session` statement, it's also possible to specify the edition at connect time.

```
conn <user>/<password>@<database> edition = r1
```

Executing the `format_fullname` procedure in the R1 edition shows the following results.

```
begin
  format_fullname (p_firstname => 'Mick'
```

```
                    ,p_lastname  => 'Schumacher'
                    );
end;
/
Mick Schumacher
```

How is this possible? The procedure `format_fullname` was inherited from the parent edition ORA$BASE. All editionable objects are inherited from the child edition and can be used the same way as before.

The reason for introducing the new edition was to improve the functionality of the `format_fullname` procedure. This can be done by the very familiar method of `create or replace`. The replacement of the procedure happens in the *privacy* of edition R1 while leaving the original procedure intact and valid. Users connected to the ORA$BASE edition are unaffected by the new version of the `format_fullname` procedure.

```
create or replace
procedure format_fullname (p_firstname in varchar2
                          ,p_lastname  in varchar2)
is
begin
   dbms_output.put_line (initcap (p_lastname)
                         ||', '||
                         initcap (p_firstname)
   );
end format_fullname;
/
```

The procedure `format_fullname` is replaced in the current edition, and the `user_objects_ae` data dictionary view shows two procedures with the same name but in different editions.

```
select object_name
     , object_type
     , edition_name
from   user_objects_ae
where  object_name = 'FORMAT_FULLNAME'
/
```

```
OBJECT_NAME      OBJECT_TYPE      EDITION_NAME
---------------  ---------------  ----------------
FORMAT_FULLNAME  PROCEDURE        ORA$BASE
FORMAT_FULLNAME  PROCEDURE        R1
```

Users of the new edition get the following results when calling the procedure.

```
begin
    format_fullname (p_firstname => 'Mick'
                    ,p_lastname  => 'Schumacher'
                    );
end;
/
Schumacher, Mick
```

There is also the possibility that a PL/SQL object is no longer needed in the post-upgraded edition. The PL/SQL object can be removed by issuing a **drop** statement. Keep in mind that dropping the PL/SQL object removes it only from the current edition. The procedure with the same name still exists in ORA$BASE.

```
drop procedure format_fullname
/
```

Inspecting the user_objects_ae data dictionary view after dropping the procedure shows the following results.

```
select object_name
     , object_type
     , edition_name
from   user_objects_ae
where  object_name = 'FORMAT_FULLNAME'
/
OBJECT_NAME      OBJECT_TYPE      EDITION_NAME
---------------  ---------------  ----------------
FORMAT_FULLNAME  PROCEDURE        ORA$BASE
FORMAT_FULLNAME  NON-EXISTENT     R1
```

The preceding results reveal that there are still two references to an object named format_fullname; one in ORA$BASE and one in R1. Note that the object in ORA$BASE is a procedure, while the other object in R1 is non-existent.

Once an object is removed from a certain edition, it is no longer inherited by the next child edition, and therefore it can no longer be called.

Changing the procedure to a function (it makes more sense to have a function to format the driver's full name) is done by a combination of drop (to remove the procedure already done) followed by a create for the function implementation.

```
create or replace
function format_fullname (p_firstname in varchar2
                         ,p_lastname  in varchar2)
  return varchar2
is
begin
  return initcap (p_lastname)
         ||', '||
         initcap (p_firstname);
end format_fullname;
/
```

These actions yield the following results in the data dictionary.

```
select object_name
     , object_type
     , edition_name
from   user_objects_ae
where  object_name = 'FORMAT_FULLNAME'
/
OBJECT_NAME     OBJECT_TYPE      EDITION_NAME
--------------- ---------------- ----------------
FORMAT_FULLNAME PROCEDURE        ORA$BASE
FORMAT_FULLNAME FUNCTION         R1
```

These are the only steps needed to upgrade when only PL/SQL objects are involved. What is left to do is make the new edition available to the users and make the old edition unavailable (i.e., retire the old edition). These topics are covered in the next sections.

Table Changes: Don't Sync Between Editions

Sometimes it is necessary to change the structure of a table as progression to the new version is made. As stated before: tables cannot be editionable. It is not possible to have multiple versions of the same table. Two mechanisms help keep the application online while changes to the table are made: fine-grained dependency tracking and non-blocking DDL.

Fine-grained dependency tracking prevents objects from getting invalidated when changes to a table are made. Adding a column does not invalidate any PL/SQL object because there is no dependency on that column in the PL/SQL objects.

Because of non-blocking DDL, no sessions are hindered by adding columns.

In each edition, there needs to be a different representation of the data to expose the newly added columns.

EBR introduces the concept of an *editioning view*. As the name already implies, it is a view, but a special type of view. The editioning view act as an abstraction layer for the underlying table. Because the editioning view is editionable, it likely has a different structure in each edition. Because of the abstraction layer, the data is still stored in a single place, the underlying table. The table holds the data and is a single point of truth. Indexes and constraints remain on the table.

Introducing editioning views requires some downtime when it is the first edition-based redefinition exercise when tables are to be involved. This is a one-time operation needed to take an existing non-edition-based database application and prepare it for edition-based in the future. Once this exercise is completed, it is prepared for zero-downtime upgrades.

Note   Some features used on the tables might need to be rerouted to the editioning views, like privileges, triggers, and virtual private database (VPD). Gathering the scripts for these features beforehand makes switching to editioning views a lot simpler.

There are six steps to follow when introducing editioning views during the first EBR exercise.

1. Rename the tables.

2. Create editioning views.

3. Reroute privileges to the editioning views.

4. Re-create triggers on the editioning views.

5. Recompile PL/SQL objects.

6. Reapply VPD policies.

The editioning view is the abstraction layer between the actual table and the application. The application most likely references the actual table throughout the source code. Changing the name of the actual table in the source code to the editioning view can be quite a daunting task and might be error-prone. Naming the editioning view the same as the original table would have the least impact on the application and the source code. Unfortunately, this is not possible. There cannot be two objects with the same name. You can solve this predicament by first renaming the actual table and creating an editioning view with the same name as the original table.

Going forward, the table shouldn't be accessed directly in the application anymore, and creating a table name that is distinguishable from the regular table names should help prevent that. The following naming convention introduces a special character (usually an underscore) and makes the table case-sensitive.

```
alter table drivers rename to "_drivers"
/
```

The _drivers table can *only* be used when the name is in quotes because it is case-sensitive. This is not a common naming convention for the table name. Having special characters and being case-sensitive signals to developers that this table is special.

With this action, step one is completed. The next step is to introduce editioning views with the same name as the original table.

```
create editioning view drivers
as
select driverid
     , driverref
     , driver_number
     , code
     , forename
     , surname
     , dob
```

```
    , nationality
    , url
from    "_drivers"
/
```

An editioning view can only be based on a single table and can't contain aggregates or expressions.

Next, reroute privileges originally on the actual table to the editioning view. Think of privileges like select or insert granted to other schemas.

Having the privileges-scripts handy that were created for the original table simplifies this process tremendously. The editioning view has taken the name of the original table. The privileges are granted on the editioning view instead by re-executing the original grant script.

The next step is to re-create the table-level triggers from the original table to the editioning view. Having the original scripts created for the original table make this a trivial step. As there can't be two objects with the same name, the triggers currently associated with the table need to be dropped.

As the tables have been renamed, the source code has become invalidated, and the PL/SQL objects need to be recompiled. After this recompilation step, the compiled code references the editioning views.

The final step to complete the transition to EBR is to reapply the VPD policy functions. This step can be skipped when the VPD is not used.

When all these steps are followed, it is no longer necessary to have planned downtime when the application needs to be upgraded. Creating new functionality can be done in the privacy of an edition without affecting the existing application.

Adding columns to the tables can be done without the need to keep data in sync between different editions. As the column is missing in the parent edition, there is no representation to show the data.

A phone number is added to the _drivers table to demonstrate adding an additional column.

```
alter table "_drivers"
add (
    phone varchar2(10)
)
/
```

Changing the table does not invalidate any PL/SQL objects referenced by the object because of fine-grained dependency tracking. There is currently no code in the database that references this newly added column.

Exposing this column can be done in the privacy of an editioning by creating an editioning view.

```
create edition r2 as child of r1
/

Edition R2 created.

alter session set edition = r2
/

Session altered.

create or replace
editioning view drivers
as
select driverid
     , driverref
     , driver_number
     , code
     , forename
     , surname
     , dob
     , nationality
     , url
     , phone
from   "_drivers"
/
View created.

select forename
     , surname
     , phone
from   drivers
fetch  first 5 rows only
/
```

FORENAME	SURNAME	PHONE
Bernd	Schneider	
Paolo	Barilla	
Gregor	Foitek	
Claudio	Langes	
Gary	Brabham	

As seen in the results, the phone is shown, although without data. An application can be created or modified to expose the phone number, and this information can be maintained.

Because the phone is completely new, there is no need to keep the data in sync between multiple editions. The old editions do not know the column and are not using it.

Table Changes with Data Sync

The most difficult edition-based definition exercise is when data needs to be kept in sync between multiple editions.

The previous exercise, the six steps to implementing editioning views, should have already been taken before the steps outlined in this section can be done.

For the example, the _drivers table has the following changes: the columns "forename" and "surname" are going to be renamed to "first_name" and "last_name" respectively, and their length is increased from 25 bytes to 35 bytes.

It is very tempting to alter the existing columns, which is trivially easy to do, but this impact the existing application. Source code that references these columns become invalid and would cause (some) downtime. This goes against the objective of zero-downtime upgrades, so changing the existing columns is not acceptable.

```
create edition r3 as child of r2
/

Edition R3 created.

alter session set edition = r3
/

Session altered.
```

```
alter table "_drivers"
add (
      first_name varchar2 (35)
    , last_name  varchar2 (35)
    )
/
Table altered.

create or replace
editioning view drivers
as
select driverid
      , driverref
      , driver_number
      , code
      , first_name
      , last_name
      , dob
      , nationality
      , url
      , phone
from    "_drivers"
/
```

Adding the columns to the table is the easy part, as well as modifying the editioning view to expose the new columns. Because the underlying table is a non-editionable object, it doesn't matter in which edition the changes are made. But common sense dictates that performing DDL shouldn't be done in older editions.

The new columns, "first_name" and "last_name" don't contain any data. For the new situation, these columns should get the same values as the forename and surname in the original table. A straightforward update can accomplish this. A massive update like that might disrupt normal business because of the locking.

When the application users only use the latest version, edition R3 in this example, doing a massive update might be good enough. From that point forward, the users only have to deal with "first_name" and "last_name", and the old columns no longer have to be maintained.

A better method than a straightforward update statement is to utilize dbms_ parallel_execute to minimize the time required to complete the task. When a lot of data is involved, this is especially useful.

If there is a need to have both editions available to the users at the same time, called the *hot rollover period*, there needs to be an additional mechanism to keep the "forename" in sync with "first_name" and "surname" in sync with "last_name". Users of the older application that uses edition R2 see and manipulate "forename" and "surname", while users of the new application that uses edition R3 use "first_name" and "last_name".

The mechanism that does that—keeping data in sync across editions—is implemented using *crossedition triggers*. They are like ordinary table triggers, are editionable, and must be created in the new edition (R3).

```
create or replace trigger driver_R2_R3_Fwd_Xed
before insert or update on "_drivers"
for each row
forward crossedition
disable
begin
  :new.first_name := :new.forename;
  :new.last_name  := :new.surname;
end driver_R2_R3_Fwd_Xed;
/
```

The trigger is created on the underlying table, not the editioning view. The trigger needs to fire for each row and the "forward cross edition" instructs to fire whenever DML is executed in a parent edition, regardless of which one.

Tip   Create crossedition triggers in disabled mode. Only when the trigger is valid should it be enabled. Invalid triggers prevent DML from being completed.

The logic of the trigger is straightforward. The newly added columns are populated with the older representation of the drivers' names.

When the trigger is valid, it can be enabled so that data can be kept in sync when users from the old application are making changes.

```
alter trigger driver_R2_R3_Fwd_Xed enable
/
Trigger DRIVER_R2_R3_FWD_XED altered.
```

The following update shows how to validate the workings of the crossedition trigger.

```
alter session set edition = r1
/

update drivers
    set surname = surname
 where driverid = 102
/
commit
/
alter session set edition = r3
/
select first_name
      ,last_name
  from drivers
 where driverid = 102
/
FIRST_NAME       LAST_NAME
---------------  ----------------
Ayrton           Senna
```

Records touched by a DML statement in an older edition cause the crossedition trigger to fire, updating the newly added columns. Switching to an older edition and performing a mass update sync the data, but the downside is that this can be confusing and error-prone during the software installation.

A better alternative is to stay in the new edition and trigger the forward crossedition trigger by updating the underlying table in a special way.

> **Note**   Crossedition triggers don't fire when the underlying table is updated. They only fire when an editioning view is updated.

With dbms_sql you can trigger the crossedition trigger when updating the underlying table. In the parse procedure, pass in the name of the crossedition trigger that needs firing for the apply_crossedition_trigger argument. The following code sample fires the crossedition trigger to change all the newly added columns. The update statement used is bogus.

```
declare
    c number := dbms_sql.open_cursor();
    x number;
begin
    dbms_sql.parse
        ( c                           => c
        , language_flag               => dbms_sql.native
        , statement                   => 'update "_drivers"
                                          set   driverid = driverid'
        , apply_crossedition_trigger  => 'DRIVER_R2_R3_FWD_XED'
        );
    x := dbms_sql.execute(c);
    dbms_sql.close_cursor(c);
    commit;
end;
/
```

Now that the synchronization from the old edition to the new one is in place, the opposite also needs to be added. Users can add or alter data in the new application, which needs to be reflected in the old application.

The reverse crossedition trigger is also created on the underlying table, just like the forward crossedition trigger. In this case, the reverse crossedition phrase signals that the trigger should fire when changes are made in the latest edition. For the same reasons, the same tactic is applied to create the trigger in a disabled state.

There is a length discrepancy in the columns. The ones in the old edition are shorter than the new ones. Truncating the name to make it fit is unacceptable. A person's name shouldn't be truncated, hence the changes that this edition introduces. During the hot rollover period, the pre- and post-upgraded applications must contain valid data that the users enter.

The reverse crossedition trigger looks like the following.

```
create or replace trigger driver_R3_R2_Rve_Xed
before insert or update of first_name, last_name on "_drivers"
for each row
reverse crossedition
disable
begin
   if length (:new.first_name) > 25
   or length (:new.last_name) > 25
   then
      raise_application_error (-20000
       ,'During the hot rollover it is not possible to enter more'||
        ' than twenty-five (25) characters for the First or Last Name'
             );
   else
      :new.forename := :new.first_name;
      :new.surname := :new.last_name;
   end if;
end driver_R3_R2_Rve_Xed;
/
Trigger DRIVER_R3_R2_RVE_XED compiled
```

When the trigger is valid, it can be enabled.

```
alter trigger driver_R3_R2_Rve_Xed enable
/

Trigger DRIVER_R3_R2_RVE_XED altered.
```

Retiring Older Editions

When the EBR exercise has been completed, it is no longer necessary to maintain the old version of the application. When the old application is still accessible to the users, there is a chance that it might still be used. This is undesirable. The old version of the application should be retired so that the old application is no longer available to the users.

Although very uncommon, it is possible to have multiple editions running side by side for an extended period. The transition between the upgrade to the new application and the retiring of the old application should be as short as possible.

Revoking the use privileges on the old edition from every user and role in the database prevents anyone from setting up a new connection. A privileged user should execute the following statement.

```
revoke use on edition r1 from book
/
```

Editions can also be removed completely, but only when it concerns a root or leaf edition. Editions that have both parent and child editions can't be dropped.

Dropping editions, especially leaf editions, can leave behind non-editionable changes, such as changes to the underlying table. This also applies to changes in the data that have already taken place.

Dropping a child edition can be done by issuing the following statement by a user that has the drop any edition privilege.

```
drop edition r3 cascade
/
```

```
Edition R3 dropped.
```

Remember that the table changes cannot be reverted. The edition can't be in use by a session. This would result in an exception.

Similarly, the parent edition can be dropped, although not strictly necessary. Having multiple retired editions doesn't interfere with performance, as references are resolved at compile time. Removing all the objects from the pre-upgrade edition is advisable because they are no longer needed, and the crossedition triggers from the post-upgrade edition. This is just a matter of good housekeeping.

Change Default Edition

The default Oracle Database edition is ORA$BASE. When connecting to the database, and no edition is specified, it uses the default edition. Instead of changing the edition by issuing `alter session` commands, there is also the possibility of changing the default edition. Typically, the DBA takes care of the following.

```
alter database default edition = r1
/
```

This changes the default edition for the entire database immediately. The `use` privilege is revoked from all users in the former default edition, except SYS. At the same time, the `use` privilege is granted to PUBLIC.

Normal users can't connect to ORA$BASE anymore; SYS still can. This allows changing the default edition back to ORA$BASE if needed.

Summary

This chapter outlines the solution to reduce, or maybe even eliminate, planned downtime. Until Oracle Database release 11gR2, the application incurs planned downtime to upgrade your custom application. EBR is solving this planned downtime issue. Deploying an upgraded application in the privacy of an edition is key. Users are switched to the post-upgraded application when the upgrade is completed without experiencing downtime.

There are several levels of complexity that you can use, depending on your needs. From simply replacing PL/SQL objects in different editions to creating multiple editioning views with crossedition triggers to keep data synchronized across editions. The method to retire old editions was discussed as well.

Choosing the Right Table Type

The purpose of any database is to store data. To do this, you create tables in your database. Oracle Database provides many different table types, each with its own strengths and weaknesses.

How the data is stored directly affects how efficiently the data is retrieved. It is not difficult to imagine that when data that is queried together is also stored together, it is faster than when data is stored all over the place. An efficient application starts with an efficient design.

This chapter discusses the different table types. There is more choice than just the old-fashioned heap tables.

Heap Table

The heap table acts as you would expect from its name; all the records are in a giant heap with no order whatsoever. If you select rows from this table, there is no guarantee in which order the rows are returned to the calling process unless you include an `order by` clause in your `select` statement. If you execute the same statement repeatedly, it probably returns the rows in the same order every time. But as soon as the table changes, for example, because of any DML statement or a database restart, this order might be very different. Never rely on the order in which the records are returned unless you explicitly include the `order by` clause in your `select` statement.

531

© Alex Nuijten, Patrick Barel 2023
A. Nuijten and P. Barel, *Modern Oracle Database Programming*, https://doi.org/10.1007/978-1-4842-9166-5_20

Index

To speed up returning records, you can define one or more indexes on the table's columns. This is a separate data structure with only the data of the column(s) of interest and a pointer to the original record.

Suppose you have a table with the Formula 1 drivers of the last 70 years. If you want to find all the drivers with the surname Verstappen, then Oracle has no other option than to visit every row in the table, do a full table scan, and inspect the contents to satisfy this condition and eliminate the ones that don't. This can be seen when you inspect the explain plan for the select statement. With the following statement, you can create an explain plan.

```
explain plan for
select drv.forename
     , drv.surname
from   drivers drv
where  drv.surname = 'Verstappen'
/
```

After the explain plan is created, it can be inspected by executing the following.

```
select *
 From dbms_xplan.display( 'plan_table' )
/
```

Let's see how the search for a driver with the surname Verstappen is found in the drivers table.

```
select drv.forename
     , drv.surname
from   drivers drv
where  drv.surname = 'Verstappen'
/
```

```
-------------------------------------------------
| Id  | Operation                  | Name    |
-------------------------------------------------
|   0 | SELECT STATEMENT           |         |
| * 1 |    TABLE ACCESS STORAGE FULL | DRIVERS |
-------------------------------------------------
```

Predicate Information (identified by operation id):
```
-----------------------------------------------------

    1 - storage("DRV"."SURNAME"='Verstappen')
        filter("DRV"."SURNAME"='Verstappen')
```

When you add a B-tree index on this column.

```
create index ix_driversurname on drivers (surname, forename)
/
```

The explain plan changes.

```
-------------------------------------------------
| Id | Operation          | Name               |
-------------------------------------------------
|  0 | SELECT STATEMENT |                      |
|  1 |   INDEX RANGE SCAN| IX_DRIVERSURNAME |
-------------------------------------------------
```

Predicate Information (identified by operation id):
```
-----------------------------------------------------

    1 - access("DRV"."SURNAME"='Verstappen')
```

The SQL engine now uses the index created to satisfy this query. Even though the index is built on two columns, surname and forename, it can still be used because you query the leading column of the index. On this small table (less than 1000 rows), you probably see almost no difference in execution time, but if you have bigger tables, you can see considerable improvement.

Using indexes can speed up your select queries dramatically, but be aware that there is a price to pay. Indexes must be maintained. This is done at the same time the DML is executed, so instead of just an insert in the table, there is also an insert into the index, which might result in a reshuffling of its contents. This takes up time; not much, but some. If you have more than one index defined on a table, then all these indexes must be changed according to the change in the table.

B-tree

By default, indexes in Oracle Database are created as B-tree (or balanced tree) indexes. A balanced tree means that it always takes the same number of steps to go from the root, the starting point of the index, to the leaf, where the information is. They can either be normal- or unique indexes. With a unique index, each value is allowed at most once per index. This is also how Oracle Database enforces the primary key by creating a unique index on the table.

Bitmap Index

In a bitmap index, a bitmap is stored for each index key. Each index key points to multiple rows. The following describes when bitmap indexes are typically used.

- When there are not many distinct values in the indexed columns, compared to the number of rows in the table, for example, a gender column

- When the table is not often modified with DML statements or is read-only.

Bitmap indexes are mainly used in data warehouse applications and are not very often used in OLTP applications. For OLTP environments, it is not recommended to use bitmap indexes. DML on the base table has a dramatic impact on bitmap maintenance and, thus, a direct impact on the application.

Index-Organized Table (IOT)

The index-organized table was introduced in Oracle Database version 8. This is a combination of an index and a table. Where a normal heap table has no implicit ordering, this kind of table is an ordered set of records. Where a B-tree index has just the information for the indexed column or columns in it, together with a pointer to the full record, the index-organized table has the full record in the index, with no need for an additional table to store the rest of the record. This kind of table is best used for tables that are used as a lookup and with a limited number of simple columns, like VARCHAR2, NUMBER, and DATE.

To create an index-organized table for the drivers, it would look like the following.

```
create table drivers_iot
(
  driverid      number(11)    not null
, driverref     varchar2(255)
, drivernumber  number(11)
, code          varchar2(3)
, forename      varchar2(255)
, surname       varchar2(255)
, dob           date
, nationality   varchar2(255)
, url           varchar2(255)
, primary key (surname, forename)
)
organization index
/
```

For a heap table, you can define the primary key after the table has been created. But for an index-organized table, you must provide the primary key directly with the table definition.

The following statement is executed to fill the index-organized table with the same data as the `drivers` heap table.

```
insert into drivers_iot (select * from drivers)
/
```

Running the same `select` statement as before, but now on the index-organized table.

```
select drv.forename
     , drv.surname
from   drivers_iot drv
where  drv.surname = 'Verstappen'
/
```

Then you can see from the explain plan that all the data needed is already in the index. There is no need for an extra lookup in a table.

```
-------------------------------------------------
| Id  | Operation              | Name            |
-------------------------------------------------
|   0 | SELECT STATEMENT |                       |
|*  1 |   INDEX RANGE SCAN| PK_DRIVERS_IOT |
-------------------------------------------------

Predicate Information (identified by operation id):
-------------------------------------------------

   1 - access("DRV"."SURNAME"='Verstappen')
```

Clusters

A cluster is another method of storing data. A group of tables that share the same data blocks is a cluster. Because the tables share common columns and their data is often referenced together, it is a good argument to store their data close to each other. When you cluster tables based on a common field, Oracle Database physically stores all rows from all the tables with the same value in the common field in the same data blocks.

Because the related rows of different tables are stored in the same data block, you'll get two primary benefits.

- Disk I/O is reduced, and the access time is improved when joining clustered tables.

- The cluster key, which is the column or group of columns all tables in the cluster have in common, is stored only once, no matter how many rows in different tables contain the value.

- Therefore, less storage might be required to store the related table and index data in a cluster than in a non-clustered table format.

All the data is available in the F1DATA schema, but let's create the cluster in the schema (BOOK) and then copy the rows to compare the storage usage.

```
create cluster cl_f1laps
( raceid      number ( 11 )
, driverid    number ( 11 )
)
/
```

After creating the cluster, create the cluster index.

```
create index idx_cl_f1laps
   on cluster cl_f1laps
/
```

For creating a cluster index, the columns specified in the cluster are used. You cannot specify a different set of columns. Using clusters does not affect the creation of additional indexes on the clustered tables; they can be created and dropped as usual.

To create tables in the cluster, you have to specify in which cluster they should be created. When creating a table in a cluster, at least one of the columns should be specified in the cluster.

Let's create the RACES, DRIVERS and LAPTIMES table in the same cluster.

```
create table races (
  raceid                   number  (  11 ) not null
, year                     number  (  11 ) not null
, round                    number  (  11 ) not null
, circuitid                number  (  11 ) not null
, name                     varchar2(  255 )
, race_date                date               not null
, time                     date
, url                      varchar2(  255 )
, fp1_date                 date
, fp1_time                 date
, fp2_date                 date
, fp2_time                 date
, fp3_date                 date
, fp3_time                 date
, quali_date               date
, quali_time               date
, sprint_date              date
, sprint_time              date
, constraint pk_races
            primary key (raceid)
```

```
, constraint uk_races_url
              unique      (url)
)
cluster cl_f1laps( raceid )
/

create table drivers
(
  driverid                number  (  11 ) not null
, driverref               varchar2( 255 )
, driver_number           number  (  11 )
, code                    varchar2(   3 )
, forename                varchar2( 255 )
, surname                 varchar2( 255 )
, dob                     date
, nationality             varchar2( 255 )
, url                     varchar2( 255 )
, constraint pk_drivers
              primary key ( driverid )
)
cluster cl_f1laps ( driverid )
/

create table laptimes (
  raceid                  number  (  11 ) not null
, driverid                number  (  11 ) not null
, lap                     number  (  11 ) not null
, position                number  (  11 ) default null
, time                    varchar2(  255 ) default null
, milliseconds            number  (  11 ) default null
, constraint pk_laptimes
              primary key (raceid,driverid,lap)
, constraint fk_laptimes_races
              foreign key (raceid)
              references races (raceid)
```

```
, constraint fk_laptimes_drivers
            foreign key (driverid)
            references drivers (driverid)
)
cluster cl_f1laps ( raceid, driverid )
/
```

Now copy the data from the F1DATA schema into our tables to compare the query plans.

```
insert into races
select raceid
    , year
    , round
    , circuitid
    , name
    , race_date
    , time
    , url
    , fp1_date
    , fp1_time
    , fp2_date
    , fp2_time
    , fp3_date
    , fp3_time
    , quali_date
    , quali_time
    , sprint_date
    , sprint_time
from   f1data.races
/

insert into drivers
select driverid
    , driverref
    , driver_number
    , code
```

```
        , forename
        , surname
        , dob
        , nationality
        , url
  from f1data.drivers
/
insert into laptimes
select raceid
        , driverid
        , lap
        , position
        , time
        , milliseconds
from    f1data.laptimes
/
```

When comparing the size of the disk between the two schemas, you can see that the clustered tables take up less space for the same amount of information.

The following is in the BOOK schema.

```
select sum(bytes) bytes
from    user_segments
where   segment_type = 'TABLE'
and     segment_name in ( 'DRIVERS'
                        , 'LAPTIMES'
                        , 'RACES'
                        )
/

     BYTES
----------
  20250624
```

The following is in the F1DATA schema.

```
select  sum(bytes) bytes
from    user_segments
where   segment_type = 'TABLE'
and     segment_name in ( 'DRIVERS'
                        , 'LAPTIMES'
                        , 'RACES'
                        )
/

      BYTES
----------
   21299200
```

When querying these tables, the optimizer can save on the number of blocks accessed because the data for the tables in the cluster are in the same block on disk.

You should not use clusters for tables that are frequently accessed individually. That would defeat its purpose.

Temporary Table

Oracle Database 8i introduced the *temporary table*, which holds data for the length of a transaction *or* a session, and its data is invisible to other sessions concurrently running in the database. It is called global, but that is because the definition of the table is global. Oracle Database version 18c introduces the private temporary table where the definition of the table is limited to the session that created it.

Global Temporary Table

A *global temporary table* is "globally available." You must grant access to this table to other schemas like you do for any table. The data in this table is only available to the session that created the data. When you connect to the same schema using two different sessions, one session cannot see any data put into this table by the other session. So, the data is private to the session, but the definition of the table is globally available.

When defining a global temporary table, you must decide if the rows are available for the transaction only or the duration of the session. To have the rows available for the transaction only, you tell the table to delete the rows on commit. The following statement creates a global temporary table with a transaction-level duration.

```
create global temporary table gtt_drivers
( driverid     number  (  11 ) not null
, driverref    varchar2( 255 )
, drivernumber number  (  11 )
, code         varchar2(   3 )
, forename     varchar2( 255 )
, surname      varchar2( 255 )
, dob          date
, nationality  varchar2( 255 )
, url          varchar2( 255 )
) on commit delete rows
/
```

After populating the table with some data, it is available to query and manipulate as usual.

```
insert into gtt_drivers
  select *
  from   f1data.drivers drv
  where  drv.nationality = 'Dutch'
/

select code
     , forename
     , surname
     , dob
     , nationality
from   gtt_drivers
/
```

```
CODE FORENAME          SURNAME                 DOB        NATIONALITY
---- ----------------- ----------------------- ---------- -----------
     Huub              Rothengatter            08/10/1954 Dutch
     Michael           Bleekemolen             02/10/1949 Dutch
     Boy               Lunger                  03/05/1949 Dutch
     Roelof            Wunderink               12/12/1948 Dutch
     Gijs              van Lennep              16/03/1942 Dutch
ALB  Christijan        Albers                  16/04/1979 Dutch
DOO  Robert            Doornbos                23/09/1981 Dutch
     Jos               Verstappen              04/03/1972 Dutch
     Jan               Lammers                 02/06/1956 Dutch
     Dries             van der Lof             23/08/1919 Dutch
     Jan               Flinterman              02/10/1919 Dutch
VDG  Giedo             van der Garde           25/04/1985 Dutch
VER  Max               Verstappen              30/09/1997 Dutch
     Carel Godin       de Beaufort             10/04/1934 Dutch
     Ernie             de Vos                  01/07/1941 Dutch
     Ben               Pon                     09/12/1936 Dutch
     Rob               Slotemaker              13/06/1929 Dutch

17 rows selected
```

However, when the transaction has ended (with a commit or rollback), the data in the table is removed.

```
commit
/

select code
     , forename
     , surname
     , dob
     , nationality
from   gtt_drivers
/

CODE FORENAME          SURNAME                 DOB        NATIONALITY
---- ---------------   --------------------    ---------- -----------
```

The other option is to preserve the rows, which means the rows are available during the session. The following statement re-creates the global temporary table with session duration.

```
create global temporary table gtt_drivers
( driverid     number ( 11 ) not null
, driverref    varchar2( 255 )
, drivernumber number ( 11 )
, code         varchar2(   3 )
, forename     varchar2( 255 )
, surname      varchar2( 255 )
, dob          date
, nationality  varchar2( 255 )
, url          varchar2( 255 )
) on commit preserve rows
/
```

Populate the table with sample data, which is available for querying and manipulation as usual.

```
insert into gtt_drivers
  select *
  from   f1data.drivers drv
  where  drv.nationality = 'Dutch'
/

select code
     , forename
     , surname
     , dob
     , nationality
from   gtt_drivers
/
```

CODE	FORENAME	SURNAME	DOB	NATIONALITY
	Huub	Rothengatter	08/10/1954	Dutch
	Michael	Bleekemolen	02/10/1949	Dutch
	Boy	Lunger	03/05/1949	Dutch
	Roelof	Wunderink	12/12/1948	Dutch
	Gijs	van Lennep	16/03/1942	Dutch
ALB	Christijan	Albers	16/04/1979	Dutch
DOO	Robert	Doornbos	23/09/1981	Dutch
	Jos	Verstappen	04/03/1972	Dutch
	Jan	Lammers	02/06/1956	Dutch
	Dries	van der Lof	23/08/1919	Dutch
	Jan	Flinterman	02/10/1919	Dutch
VDG	Giedo	van der Garde	25/04/1985	Dutch
VER	Max	Verstappen	30/09/1997	Dutch
	Carel Godin	de Beaufort	10/04/1934	Dutch
	Ernie	de Vos	01/07/1941	Dutch
	Ben	Pon	09/12/1936	Dutch
	Rob	Slotemaker	13/06/1929	Dutch

17 rows selected

After issuing a commit statement, the rows are preserved.

```
commit
/

select code
     , forename
     , surname
     , dob
     , nationality
from   gtt_drivers
/
```

CODE	FORENAME	SURNAME	DOB	NATIONALITY
	Huub	Rothengatter	08/10/1954	Dutch
	Michael	Bleekemolen	02/10/1949	Dutch
	Boy	Lunger	03/05/1949	Dutch
	Roelof	Wunderink	12/12/1948	Dutch
	Gijs	van Lennep	16/03/1942	Dutch
ALB	Christijan	Albers	16/04/1979	Dutch
DOO	Robert	Doornbos	23/09/1981	Dutch
	Jos	Verstappen	04/03/1972	Dutch
	Jan	Lammers	02/06/1956	Dutch
	Dries	van der Lof	23/08/1919	Dutch
	Jan	Flinterman	02/10/1919	Dutch
VDG	Giedo	van der Garde	25/04/1985	Dutch
VER	Max	Verstappen	30/09/1997	Dutch
	Carel Godin	de Beaufort	10/04/1934	Dutch
	Ernie	de Vos	01/07/1941	Dutch
	Ben	Pon	09/12/1936	Dutch
	Rob	Slotemaker	13/06/1929	Dutch

```
17 rows selected
```

The data is preserved in this global temporary table until the session is ended.

You can add indexes to global temporary tables, but only when empty. If you try to add an index to a global temporary table that has on commit preserve rows set, you may encounter this error.

```
ORA-14452: attempt to create, alter or drop an index on temporary table
already in use
```

If this happens, and your session is the only session using the table, you can solve this by disconnecting and reconnecting or issuing a truncate table statement.

You can also create the global temporary table using a create table as select construction.

```
create global temporary table gtt_drivers
as
select *
```

```
from    f1data.drivers drv
where   drv.nationality = 'Dutch'
/
```

Since the default option is on `commit delete rows`, and any DDL performs in the implicit commit, the table definition is created, but the rows are removed immediately. To preserve the rows, you must create the table with the on `commit preserve rows` option.

```
create global temporary table gtt_drivers
on commit preserve rows
as
select *
from    f1data.drivers drv
where   drv.nationality = 'Dutch'
/
```

Private Temporary Table

Oracle Database 18c introduced the *private temporary table*. It is a temporary table that is private to the current session. Private temporary tables must use the prefix: ora$ptt_. The following statement creates a private temporary table.

```
create private temporary table ora$ptt_drivers
( driverid      number ( 11 )
, driverref     varchar2( 255 )
, drivernumber  number ( 11 )
, code          varchar2(   3 )
, forename      varchar2( 255 )
, surname       varchar2( 255 )
, dob           date
, nationality   varchar2( 255 )
, url           varchar2( 255 )
) on commit drop definition
/
```

Populate the private temporary table.

```
insert into ora$ptt_drivers
select *
from   f1data.drivers drv
where  drv.nationality = 'Dutch'
/

select code
     , forename
     , surname
     , dob
     , nationality
from   ora$ptt_drivers
/
```

```
CODE FORENAME         SURNAME               DOB        NATIONALITY
---- ---------------- --------------------- ---------- -----------
     Huub             Rothengatter          08/10/1954 Dutch
     Michael          Bleekemolen           02/10/1949 Dutch
     Boy              Lunger                03/05/1949 Dutch
     Roelof           Wunderink             12/12/1948 Dutch
     Gijs             van Lennep            16/03/1942 Dutch
ALB  Christijan       Albers                16/04/1979 Dutch
DOO  Robert           Doornbos              23/09/1981 Dutch
     Jos              Verstappen            04/03/1972 Dutch
     Jan              Lammers               02/06/1956 Dutch
     Dries            van der Lof           23/08/1919 Dutch
     Jan              Flinterman            02/10/1919 Dutch
VDG  Giedo            van der Garde         25/04/1985 Dutch
VER  Max              Verstappen            30/09/1997 Dutch
     Carel Godin      de Beaufort           10/04/1934 Dutch
     Ernie            de Vos                01/07/1941 Dutch
     Ben              Pon                   09/12/1936 Dutch
     Rob              Slotemaker            13/06/1929 Dutch

17 rows selected
```

Ending the transaction removes the private temporary table from the database.

```
commit
/

select code
     , forename
     , surname
     , dob
     , nationality
from   ora$ptt_drivers
/

ORA-00942: table or view does not exist
```

It is also possible that the private temporary table needs to exist longer.

```
create private temporary table ora$ptt_drivers
( driverid     number   (  11 )
, driverref    varchar2( 255 )
, drivernumber number   (  11 )
, code         varchar2(   3 )
, forename     varchar2( 255 )
, surname      varchar2( 255 )
, dob          date
, nationality  varchar2( 255 )
, url          varchar2( 255 )
) on commit preserve definition
/

insert into ora$ptt_drivers
select *
from   f1data.drivers drv
where  drv.nationality = 'Dutch'
/

select code
     , forename
     , surname
```

```
        , dob
        , nationality
from    ora$ptt_drivers
/
CODE FORENAME          SURNAME              DOB        NATIONALITY
---- ---------------   -------------------- ---------- -----------
     Huub              Rothengatter         08/10/1954 Dutch
     Michael           Bleekemolen          02/10/1949 Dutch
     Boy               Lunger               03/05/1949 Dutch
     Roelof            Wunderink            12/12/1948 Dutch
     Gijs              van Lennep           16/03/1942 Dutch
ALB  Christijan        Albers               16/04/1979 Dutch
DOO  Robert            Doornbos             23/09/1981 Dutch
     Jos               Verstappen           04/03/1972 Dutch
     Jan               Lammers              02/06/1956 Dutch
     Dries             van der Lof          23/08/1919 Dutch
     Jan               Flinterman           02/10/1919 Dutch
VDG  Giedo             van der Garde        25/04/1985 Dutch
VER  Max               Verstappen           30/09/1997 Dutch
     Carel Godin       de Beaufort          10/04/1934 Dutch
     Ernie             de Vos               01/07/1941 Dutch
     Ben               Pon                  09/12/1936 Dutch
     Rob               Slotemaker           13/06/1929 Dutch

17 rows selected
```

Ending the transaction no longer removes the private temporary table or the contents.

```
commit
/

select code
       , forename
       , surname
       , dob
       , nationality
```

```
from    ora$ptt_drivers
/
```

CODE	FORENAME	SURNAME	DOB	NATIONALITY
	Huub	Rothengatter	08/10/1954	Dutch
	Michael	Bleekemolen	02/10/1949	Dutch
	Boy	Lunger	03/05/1949	Dutch
	Roelof	Wunderink	12/12/1948	Dutch
	Gijs	van Lennep	16/03/1942	Dutch
ALB	Christijan	Albers	16/04/1979	Dutch
DOO	Robert	Doornbos	23/09/1981	Dutch
	Jos	Verstappen	04/03/1972	Dutch
	Jan	Lammers	02/06/1956	Dutch
	Dries	van der Lof	23/08/1919	Dutch
	Jan	Flinterman	02/10/1919	Dutch
VDG	Giedo	van der Garde	25/04/1985	Dutch
VER	Max	Verstappen	30/09/1997	Dutch
	Carel Godin	de Beaufort	10/04/1934	Dutch
	Ernie	de Vos	01/07/1941	Dutch
	Ben	Pon	09/12/1936	Dutch
	Rob	Slotemaker	13/06/1929	Dutch

```
17 rows selected
```

You can also create a private temporary table using a `create table as select` construction.

```
create private temporary table ora$ptt_drivers
as
select *
from    f1data.drivers drv
where   drv.nationality = 'Dutch'
/
```

The default for creating temporary tables is `on commit drop definition`. But since this is a memory-only construction, there is no implicit commit, so the rows are available in the table. You can add the option to preserve the definition after a commit.

```
create private temporary table ora$ptt_drivers
on commit preserve definition
as
select *
from    f1data.drivers drv
where   drv.nationality = 'Dutch'
/
```

The definition of a private temporary table is private to the current session; therefore on `commit preserve definition` means the definition stays until the end of the session and then goes away. You cannot create indexes on private temporary tables.

A private temporary table must be prefixed with a standard prefix. By default, this prefix is `ORA$PTT_` as it is set in the parameters.

```
select *
from    v$parameter
where   name = 'private_temp_table_prefix'
/
```

Restrictions on Temporary Tables

Although the temporary table looks and behaves like regular tables, there are some restrictions.

- Temporary tables cannot be partitioned, clustered, or index-organized.

- You cannot specify any foreign key constraints on temporary tables.

- Temporary tables cannot contain columns of nested tables.

- You cannot specify the following clauses of LOB_storage_clause: TABLESPACE, `storage_clause`, or `logging_clause`.

- Parallel UPDATE, DELETE and MERGE are not supported for temporary tables.

- The only part of the `segment_attributes_clause` that you can specify for a temporary table is TABLESPACE, which allows you to specify a single temporary tablespace.

- Distributed transactions are not supported for temporary tables.

- A temporary table cannot contain INVISIBLE columns.

All these restrictions apply to both global temporary tables and private temporary tables. Private temporary tables have some more restrictions on top of the preceding list.

- The name of private temporary tables must always be prefixed with whatever is defined with the init.ora parameter PRIVATE_TEMP_ TABLE_PREFIX. The default is ORA$PTT_.

- You cannot create indexes, materialized views, or zone maps on private temporary tables.

- Primary keys, or any constraint that requires an index, are not allowed on private temporary tables.

- You cannot define columns with default values.

- You cannot reference private temporary tables in any permanent object (e.g., views or triggers).

- Private temporary tables are not visible through database links.

Even though it looks like there are lots of restrictions on temporary tables, they can be very useful. You probably not be hindered by the restrictions

External Table

External tables allow you to read data from flat files like regular tables. The files must be placed in a location the Oracle database can access. If you are using files on a filesystem, you need to create a directory object and tell the Oracle database where to look.

```
create or replace directory f1db_csv
  as '/media/sf_Ergast_F1/f1db_csv'
/
```

Make sure you have read access to this location. You also need write access if using the logfile/badfile/discardfile.

Now you can start defining the external table using the `create table` … `organization external` syntax.

The first part of the definition is a lot like a regular table, except you tell it to be external with the `organization external` keywords.

```
create table drivers_ext
( driverid     number  ( 11 )
, driverref    varchar2( 255 )
, drivernumber varchar2( 255 )
, code         varchar2(  3 )
, forename     varchar2( 255 )
, surname      varchar2( 255 )
, dob          date
, nationality  varchar2( 255 )
, url          varchar2( 255 )
) organization external
/
```

Now you specify the attributes of the external table.

- `type` specifies the type of the external table. Each type is supported by its own access driver.

  - `oracle_loader` is the default access driver. It loads data from external tables to internal tables. It can only read text data files and cannot write to text files, i.e., it cannot be used to unload internal tables into external tables.

  - `oracle_datapump` can perform both loads and unloads. The data must be in binary dump files. You can use this driver to write a dump file only as part of creating the external table using a `create table as select` statement. It is a write-once-read-many operation. You cannot perform any DML on the external table.

  - `oracle_hdfs` extracts data stored in a Hadoop Distributed File System (HDFS).

  - `oracle_hive` extracts data that is stored in Apache HIVE.

- `default directory` specifies the default directory to use for all input and output files if you don't explicitly specify a directory object. It is a directory object, not a directory path.

- `access parameters` describe the external data source and implement the type of external table. Each type of external table has its own access driver and needs its own access parameters. Access parameters are optional. Some of the access parameters include the following.

  - `records delimited by newline` indicates the character that identifies the end of a record. On Unix or Linux operating systems, NEWLINE is assumed to be '\n'. On Microsoft Windows operating systems, NEWLINE is assumed to be '\r\n'. The newline is incorrectly parsed if you use a file created on a Windows system in a Unix environment. To overcome this issue, you can use `records delimited by detected newline`.

Note   Detected newline has been an option since Oracle Database 19c.

  - `skip <n>` specifies the number of records to skip before loading. Used primarily if the file contains header information.

  - `badfile <filename>` specifies the filename to which records are written when they cannot be loaded because of errors.

  - `logfile <filename>` specifies the filename to which all the messages are written while accessing the data.

  - `discardfile <filename>` specifies the filename to which all the records are written that fail the condition of the `load when` clause.

  - `fields terminated by` specifies the field separation character.

  - `optionally enclosed by` specifies field enclosure characters.

In the access parameters, you can also specify the columns found in the file. It must be a superset of the columns defined in the table definition. When specifying the columns, you can perform a limited set of operations on the columns, for instance, casting a date string to a `date` data type.

```
dob char( 10 ) date_format date mask "YYYY-MM-DD"
```

For all the other access parameters, check the Oracle documentation.

- location specifies the data file or data files for the external table. For
  oracle_loader and oracle_datapump, use directory:file format.
  The directory part is optional. The default directory is used if it is
  missing. When using the oracle_loader driver, you can use wildcards
  in the filename. An asterisk (*) signifies 0 or more characters, and a
  question mark (?) signifies a single character.
  For oracle_hdfs, it is a list of URIs (Uniform Resource Identifiers) for
  directories or files. Directory objects are not associated with a URI.
  For oracle_hive, the clause is not used. Instead, the Hadoop HCatalog table
  is used.

- reject limit <n> specifies how many records can be rejected
  before loading is stopped completely.

Instead of specifying filenames for the log file, the bad file, and the discard file, you
can specify the nologfile, nobadfile, and nodiscardfile options. No files are created.

The log files can be very useful and contain valuable information, but they can grow
very big. You probably want to use the nologfile option when promoting to a production
environment. If you want to use the logfile/badfile/discardfile, it is best to put them
in a different location, so the directory object with the files can be granted read-only
privileges.

Listing 20-1 is the complete script to create the external table.

Listing 20-1. Script to create the drivers_ext external table

```
create table drivers_ext
( driverid       number ( 11 )
, driverref      varchar2( 256 )
, driver_number varchar2( 256 )
, code           varchar2(   4 )
, forename       varchar2( 256 )
, surname        varchar2( 256 )
, dob            date
, nationality    varchar2( 256 )
, url            varchar2( 256 )
```

```
) organization external
(
  type oracle_loader
  default directory f1db_csv
  access parameters
  ( -- you can use comments,
    -- but only at the beginning the parameters
    records delimited by newline
    skip 1
    badfile 'drivers.bad'
    logfile 'drivers.log'
    fields terminated by ','
    optionally enclosed by '"'
    ( driverid
    , driverref
    , driver_number
    , code
    , forename
    , surname
    , dob             char( 10 ) date_format date mask "YYYY-MM-DD"
    , nationality
    , url
    )
  )
  location ( 'drivers.csv' )
)
reject limit 0
/
```

You can modify the settings after you create the external table, like pointing it to another file.

```
alter table drivers_ext location ( 'drivers100.csv' )
```

If you change the access parameters, be aware that every parameter you don't supply reverts to its default. It doesn't retain the setting you gave it earlier.

Oracle Database 12.2 introduced the option to modify some settings at runtime.

- You can change the filenames for the badfile, logfile, and discardfile in the access parameters. The other access parameters retain their values.

- Change the default directory; it must be a literal value.

- Change the location; it can be a literal value or a bind variable.

- Change the reject limit; it can be a literal value or a bind variable.

```
select count(*)
from   drivers_ext external modify (location ('drivers100.csv'))
/

  COUNT(*)
----------
       100

select count(*)
from   drivers_ext
/

  COUNT(*)
----------
       854
```

Since Oracle Database 18c, you can access external tables without creating an external table. All the code normally in the DDL for an external table can now be put inside the SQL statement.

```
select * from external (
  ( constructorId   number(11)
  , constructorRef  varchar2(256)
  , name            varchar2(256)
  , nationality     varchar2(256)
  , url             varchar2(256)
  )
```

```
type oracle_loader
default directory f1db_csv
access parameters
( records delimited by newline
  skip 1
  badfile 'constructors.bad'
  logfile 'constructors.log'
  fields terminated by ','
  optionally enclosed by '"'
  ( constructorId
  , constructorRef
  , name
  , nationality
  , url
  )
)
location ( 'constructors.csv' )
reject limit 0
)
```

If you previously loaded data into Oracle Database using the SQL*loader utility, you can generate the needed external table definition using the EXTERNAL_TABLE=GENERATE_ONLY option.

Immutable Table

Oracle Database 21c introduced the concept of immutable tables. Immutable tables are insert-only tables in which existing data cannot be changed. Deleting rows from the immutable table is prohibited unless the insert occurred more than the specified number of days ago. After creation, no DDL can be performed to alter the table's layout. It is possible to add and remove constraints and indexes, however.

The following statement is executed to create an immutable table.

```
create immutable table dutchdrivers
( driverid     number  (  11 ) not null
, driverref    varchar2( 255 )
, drivernumber number  (  11 )
, code         varchar2(   3 )
, forename     varchar2( 255 )
, surname      varchar2( 255 )
, dob          date
, nationality  varchar2( 255 )
, url          varchar2( 255 )
)
```

You have to specify the retention periods for dropping the table as a whole and deleting rows.

First, you specify the drop table condition.

```
no drop [ until <n> days idle ]
```

The minimum number of days you can specify for the idle option is 0.

Next, specify the records' retention time before being able to delete rows.

```
no delete ( [ locked ] | ( until <m> days after insert [ locked ] ) )
```

The minimum number of days you can specify for the delete option is 16 days.

You can choose to keep the data forever; then, you don't specify the number of days in these two clauses.

Tip   When experimenting with these options, make sure you set the number of days idle in the drop clause to a low value, preferably 0; otherwise, you may end up with a schema full of tables you cannot get rid of. There is no option to remove tables still in their retention period other than dropping your database completely.

The complete script to create the table can be found in Listing 20-2.

Listing 20-2. Create immutable table dutchdrivers

```
create immutable table dutchdrivers
( driverid       number  (  11 ) not null
, driverref      varchar2( 255 )
, driver_number number  (  11 )
, code           varchar2(   3 )
, forename       varchar2( 255 )
, surname        varchar2( 255 )
, dob            date
, nationality    varchar2( 255 )
, url            varchar2( 255 )
)
no drop    until 0  days idle
no delete until 16 days after insert
/
```

Now that you have created you can put data in it.

```
insert into dutchdrivers
select *
from    f1data.drivers drv
where   drv.nationality = 'Dutch'
/
```

So far, it is all the same as a normal table. This is not possible when you add a record that you want to change or remove later.

```
insert into dutchdrivers
select *
from    f1data.drivers drv
where   drv.drivernumber = 44
/
```

If you try to update the record, you'll hit an error.

```
update dutchdrivers ddv
set     ddv.nationality = 'Dutch'
```

```
where  ddv.drivernumber = 44
/
```

```
ORA-05715: operation not allowed on the blockchain or immutable table
```

If you try to delete the record, you'll hit the same error.

```
delete from dutchdrivers ddv
where  ddv.drivernumber = '44'
/
```

```
ORA-05715: operation not allowed on the blockchain or immutable table
```

When you want to remove the record, you have to wait for the number of days specified in the no delete until if you specified this.

This feature was introduced in Oracle Database 21c but backported to Oracle Database 19.11

This feature can be very useful when storing data that should not be tampered with, like contract data. If you want even more security than just making sure the records cannot be changed, you can use the blockchain table, where the records are chained together using a hashing algorithm.

Blockchain Table

Blockchain tables are append-only tables in which only insert operations are allowed. Deleting rows is either prohibited or restricted based on time. Special sequencing and chaining algorithms make rows in a blockchain table tamper-resistant. Users can verify that rows have not been tampered with. A hash value part of the row metadata is used to chain and validate rows.

The syntax for the blockchain table is almost identical to the immutable table. A blockchain table must contain one more clause to the table definition.

```
hashing using sha2_512 version v1
```

The hashing algorithm is calculated based on the existing data when records are added to the table, which increases the load time compared to an immutable table.

Listing 20-3 is a blockchain table created, similar to the immutable table created before.

Listing 20-3. Create blockchain table dutchdrivers

```
create blockchain table dutchdrivers
( driverid       number  (  11 ) not null
, driverref      varchar2( 255 )
, driver_number number  (  11 )
, code           varchar2(   3 )
, forename       varchar2( 255 )
, surname        varchar2( 255 )
, dob            date
, nationality    varchar2( 255 )
, url            varchar2( 255 )
)
no drop    until 0  days idle
no delete until 16 days after insert
hashing using sha2_512 version v1
/
```

This table has the same restrictions as an immutable table, so you cannot modify or remove the rows after inserting and committing data. The delete can be done if the retention time has passed, however.

This feature was introduced in Oracle Database 21c but backported to Oracle Database 19.10.

Summary

As you can see, Oracle Database is much more than just a "bag of tables." Some tables, like heap tables, are useful in an OLTP environment. In contrast, others, like index-organized tables, are very useful as lookup tables in OLTP and data warehouse environments. The B-tree index is more useful in an OLTP environment, but a bitmap index is more useful in a data warehouse environment. Sometimes you may want to unload data from memory to the database to use the full power of SQL but go easy on the available memory, where temporary tables can come in handy. If you want tables that cannot be tampered with, you can use immutable or blockchain tables.

Oracle Database provides you with all the options, and now you can understand why one type would be a better fit.

ORA-00000: Normal, Successful Completion

© Alex Nuijten, Patrick Barel 2023
A. Nuijten and P. Barel, *Modern Oracle Database Programming*, https://doi.org/10.1007/978-1-4842-9166-5

Index

A

Analytic functions
  accessing values, 42–45
  avg function, 36
  CASE expression, 45
  consecutive ranking, 47
  deduplication, 48–51
  fastest and slowest lap, 45–47
  first_value and last_value
    functions, 40, 41
  hood clause, 117
  lag and lead functions, 43, 44
  logical groups, 88–90
  meaning, 35, 36
  partitions, 36
  pattern matching
    pit stops/hazards, 101
  ranking functions, 47–49
  running totals, 37–41
  single driver, 38
  sum function, 37
  window, 36, 37
  windowing clause, 51–53
ANSI-style joins, *see* Joins
Application Express (APEX), 395
  advantages/availability, 395, 396
  calling web services
    dbms_output, 398
    environment_pkg, 400
    Ergast Developer, 397
    GET request, 397
    request headers, 399

    requirement, 396
    variable declaration, 400
    web service, 398
  JSON document, 401–404
  parsing data
    business case, 410, 411
    DESTINATION_TBL, 414
    file headers, 412
    get_columns function, 413
    predefined file
      patterns, 414
    requirements, 411–415
    TEMP_FILES table, 410
  spatial functions, 404–406
  utilities/text manipulations
    advantage, 406
    error message, 408
    get_initials, 409, 410
    join method, 407
    message format, 408, 409
    multiline message, 409
    string.split, 407
  Zandvoort circuit, 405
  ZIP files
    add_file procedure, 417
    data types, 417, 418
    get_file_content function, 416
    unzipping files, 416, 417
    working process, 415

B

Blockchain tables, 562–563

567

A. Nuijten and P. Barel, *Modern Oracle Database Programming*, https://doi.org/10.1007/978-1-4842-9166-5

E, F, G

Printed in the United States
by Baker & Taylor Publisher Services